SPEECH AND DEBATE AS CIVIC EDUCATION

RDD
RHETORIC AND DEMOCRATIC DELIBERATION
VOLUME 15

Edited by Cheryl Glenn and Stephen Browne
The Pennsylvania State University

Co-founding Editor: J. Michael Hogan

EDITORIAL BOARD:

Robert Asen (University of Wisconsin–Madison)
Debra Hawhee (The Pennsylvania State University)
J. Michael Hogan (The Pennsylvania State University)
Peter Levine (Tufts University)
Steven J. Mailloux (University of California–Irvine)
Krista Ratcliffe (Marquette University)
Karen Tracy (University of Colorado–Boulder)
Kirt Wilson (The Pennsylvania State University)
David Zarefsky (Northwestern University)

Rhetoric and Democratic Deliberation focuses on the interplay of public discourse, politics, and democratic action. Engaging with diverse theoretical, cultural, and critical perspectives, books published in this series offer fresh perspectives on rhetoric as it relates to education, social movements, and governments throughout the world.

A complete list of books in this series is located at the back of this volume.

SPEECH AND DEBATE
AS CIVIC EDUCATION

EDITED BY
J. MICHAEL HOGAN
JESSICA A. KURR
MICHAEL J. BERGMAIER
JEREMY D. JOHNSON

WITH A FOREWORD BY DAVID ZAREFSKY

The Pennsylvania State University Press   University Park, Pennsylvania

This volume was made possible, in part, by a Challenge Grant to the Center for Democratic Deliberation from the National Endowment for the Humanities. Any views, findings, conclusions, or recommendations expressed in the book do not necessarily represent those of the National Endowment for the Humanities.

A portion of chapter 1 first appeared in Angela G. Ray, "'A Green Oasis in the History of My Life': Race and the Culture of Debating in Antebellum Charleston, South Carolina," 2014 B. Aubrey Fisher Memorial Lecture (Salt Lake City: University of Utah, Department of Communication, 2014) and is reprinted here by courtesy.

Library of Congress Cataloging-in-Publication Data
Names: Hogan, J. Michael, 1953– , editor. | Kurr, Jessica A. (Jessica Anne), 1989– , editor. | Bergmaier, Michael J., 1979– , editor. | Johnson, Jeremy D. (Jeremy David), editor.
Title: Speech and debate as civic education / edited by J. Michael Hogan, Jessica A. Kurr, Michael J. Bergmaier, Jeremy D. Johnson ; with a foreword by David Zarefsky.
Other titles: Rhetoric and democratic deliberation.
Description: University Park, Pennsylvania : The Pennsylvania State University Press, [2017] | Series: Rhetoric and democratic deliberation | Includes bibliographical references and index.
Summary: "A collection of essays bringing together the leading scholars, teachers, coaches, and program administrators in the field of speech and debate, reflecting on the role of curricular and co-curricular speech and debate programs in civic education"—Provided by publisher.
Identifiers: LCCN 2017028320 | ISBN 9780271079059 (cloth : alk. paper) | ISBN 9780271079066 (pbk. : alk. paper)
Subjects: LCSH: Debates and debating—Study and teaching. | Public speaking. | Civics—Study and teaching.
Classification: LCC PN4181 .S686 2017 | DDC 808.53—dc23
LC record available at https://lccn.loc.gov/2017028320

Copyright © 2017 The Pennsylvania State University
All rights reserved
Printed in the United States of America
Published by The Pennsylvania State University Press,
University Park, PA 16802–1003

The Pennsylvania State University Press is a member of the Association of American University Presses.

It is the policy of The Pennsylvania State University Press to use acid-free paper. Publications on uncoated stock satisfy the minimum requirements of American National Standard for Information Sciences—Permanence of Paper for Printed Library Material, ANSI Z39.48–1992.

CONTENTS

Acknowledgments | ix

Foreword: Speech and Debate as Civic Education: Challenges and Opportunities | xi
DAVID ZAREFSKY

Introduction: Speech and Debate as Civic Education | 1
J. MICHAEL HOGAN AND JESSICA A. KURR

Part 1: History of Speech and Debate as Civic Education

1. Warriors and Statesmen: Debate Education Among Free African American Men in Antebellum Charleston | 25
ANGELA G. RAY

2. Renewing a "Very Old Means of Education": Civic Engagement and the Birth of Intercollegiate Debate in the United States | 36
JAMIE MCKOWN

3. Taking Women Seriously: Debaters, Faculty Allies, and the Feminist Work of Debating in the 1930s and 1940s | 53
CARLY S. WOODS

4. The Intersection of Debate and Democracy: The Shifting Role of Forensics in the History of American Civic Education | 64
MICHAEL D. BARTANEN AND ROBERT S. LITTLEFIELD

Part 2: Debate Education and Public Deliberation

5. Public Debate and American Democracy: Guidelines for Pedagogy | 81
ROBERT C. ROWLAND

6. When Argumentation Backfires: The Motivated Reasoning Predicament in Speech and Debate Pedagogy | 94
GORDON R. MITCHELL

7   Teaching Religion Through Argument, Speech, and Debate:
    Critiquing Logos and Mythos | 108
    DAVID A. FRANK

Part 3: Rethinking Competitive Speech and Debate

8   The CEDA–Miller Center War Powers Debates: A Case
    for Intercollegiate Debate's Civic Roles | 125
    PAUL E. MABREY III

9   Beyond Peitho: The Women's Debate Institute as Civic Education | 136
    CATHERINE H. PALCZEWSKI

10 Debating Conviction: From Sincere Belief
    to Affective Atmosphere | 149
    RONALD WALTER GREENE AND DARRIN HICKS

11 Debaters as Citizens: Rethinking Debate Frameworks to Address
    the Policy/Performance Divide | 163
    SARAH STONE WATT

Part 4: Cultivating Civic Skills and Literacy

12 Debate Activities and the Promise of Citizenship | 177
    EDWARD A. HINCK

13 Deliberation as Civic Education: Incorporating Public Deliberation
    into the Communication Studies Curriculum | 191
    SARA A. MEHLTRETTER DRURY, REBECCA A. KUEHL,
    AND JENN ANDERSON

14 Youth, Networks, and Civic Engagement: Communities of Belonging
    and Communities of Practice | 205
    G. THOMAS GOODNIGHT, MINHEE SON, JIN HUANG, AND ANN CRIGLER

15 Pathways to Civic Education: Urban Debate Leagues
    as Communities of Practice | 221
    MELISSA MAXCY WADE

Part 5: International Collaboration and Interconnections in Debate

16 Comparing Argument and Debate Modes to Invoke Student
    Civic Engagement: Learning from "The Ben" | 237
    ALLAN D. LOUDEN AND TAYLOR W. HAHN

17 The Worlds-Style Debate Format: Performing Global Citizenship | 250
    UNA KIMOKEO-GOES

18 *Suzhi Jiaoyu*, Debate, and Civic Education in China | 265
    LORAND LASKAI, DAVID WEEKS, AND TIM LEWIS

Notes | 277
Selected Bibliography | 315
List of Contributors | 323
Index | 331

ACKNOWLEDGMENTS

The editors gratefully acknowledge the support of a number of individuals and institutions that made this volume possible. Major funding for the volume and for the conference that preceded it was provided by a Challenge Grant awarded to the Center for Democratic Deliberation at Penn State by the National Endowment for the Humanities. Additional funding for the conference came from the National Communication Association and from the College of the Liberal Arts (CLA), Conferences and Institutes (CI), and the Department of Communication Arts and Sciences (CAS) at Penn State. We are especially grateful to Avis Kunz, CLA's assistant dean for online education and outreach, and Lindsay J. Miller, the program manager for CI, who handled most of the conference planning. In addition, we acknowledge a number of Penn State faculty and graduate students who assisted with the conference: Tom Benson, John Jasso, Kaitlyn Patia, Bryan Blankfield, and Brad Serber. Rosemary Petrunyak, staff assistant for the McCourtney Institute for Democracy at Penn State, handled many of the financial details, while Robin Haynes, faculty and facilities coordinator for CAS, assisted with travel and other conference logistics. Finally, we wish to say a special thanks to Kendra Boileau, editor in chief of the Penn State University Press, who provided support and encouragement for the volume throughout the process.

In recognition of the long history of speech and debate education at Penn State, we dedicate this volume to the memory of John Henry Frizzell, who came to Penn State in 1902 and pioneered the teaching of speech and debate as education for engaged citizenship in a democracy.

FOREWORD: SPEECH AND DEBATE AS CIVIC EDUCATION: CHALLENGES AND OPPORTUNITIES

DAVID ZAREFSKY

Like many others, I began my experience with speech and debate as a participant in competitive activities in high school and college. I initially was urged to become involved by high school teachers who had worked with me and thought I might do well. The experience was transformative. To begin with, it was fun to match wits with others who were interested in current events. I discovered that I was good at it, and since I was lacking in athletic and musical talent, this was an important source of self-esteem. Fellow students became my close friends, and we formed a sense of community within large and somewhat anonymous schools. My coaches remain my lifelong friends. Participants at other schools became a network in which I was pleased to be involved. I learned valuable life skills, ranging from time management and sophisticated library research to dealing in a mature fashion with victory and defeat and recognizing that neither is final. I learned that winning was not unethical per se but that there should be educational benefit in wins and losses alike.

Valuable benefits, all. I learned more from speech and debate than from any high school or college class—and I was fortunate, especially as an undergraduate, to have had many stimulating classes. But in retrospect, something was missing. I had no sense that what I was doing was contributing powerfully to my civic education, although in fact it was. I don't think I even knew what civic education was, and if I did, I took it for granted. Since I want to discuss it now, let me define the term. By *civic education*, I mean, broadly, the acquisition of knowledge and skills to enable understanding of and participation in public life. The emphasis is on that part of our lives that we live together with (often anonymous) others, as opposed to our lives alone or with our families and close friends. There are many ways to equip oneself for a rich and rewarding private life. But if there is a better preparation for public life—a better means of civic education—than speech and debate, I have yet to find it.

Looking back, I can recognize several ways in which I was receiving a good civic education without realizing it. First, I was learning about timely and important public policy topics. While the Kennedy administration and Congress were locked in conflict over federal aid to education, I debated the resolution that the federal government should equalize educational opportunity by means of grants to the states for public elementary and secondary education. Right before the landslide 1964 election made it possible, I debated the resolution that Social Security benefits should be extended to include complete medical care. And at the height of the Vietnam War, the debate topic was that the United States should substantially reduce its foreign policy commitments. Meanwhile, in extemporaneous speaking I spoke about current events, and in original oratory I addressed the mood of the country in the aftermath of the Kennedy assassination.

Second, I learned that all these matters are uncertain and contingent; that is a characteristic of public life. Debating both sides of the question, making opposing arguments in successive hours, was a powerful teacher. It did not induce vicious relativism—even my emerging convictions were stronger than that—but it did induce some sense of humility rooted in the recognition that we might be wrong. It helped teach me that there is very little we know *for sure*. When it works well, public life is the province of restrained partisans, people who are committed to their viewpoint yet respectful of and willing to engage alternative views. When it malfunctions, public life is under the sway of those who apply the certainty of their unshakeable convictions to matters about which certainty is not given to us.

Third, I was learning about what I call the *topoi* of public life—the common values and premises, the ways of thinking and talking by which we manage our differences and through which we confront public life's core predicament: needing to make a decision but lacking all the information about which it ideally would be based. Especially in American culture, these *topoi* are often tensions, because American public life was born in argument and was marked by the embrace of contradictory positions. We never finally resolve, but continually contest, liberty versus equality, freedom from versus freedom to, the role of the state versus the role of the individual, centralized versus localized control, commitments to the present versus commitments to the future, and similar *topoi* too numerous to list. Speech and debate teach how we carry on in the face of critical yet unresolvable conflicts and, thus, how we manage uncertainty. This may be the essence of democratic deliberation, working out our differences case by case and recognizing that the outcomes are always subject to reexamination.

Fourth, speech and debate provided some exposure—too little, but some—to cultural difference. Competing against students of differing social class, ethnicity, gender, and occasionally race helped me to see that my own perspectives, which I was tempted to universalize, were only partial. Having attended an elite, racially segregated public high school and an elite private university, this recognition was particularly valuable. In today's increasingly segmented society, activities like speech and debate may be among the first occasions that students of diverse backgrounds encounter one another. The resulting tensions have raised issues for public discussion about the role and importance of civility in discourse.

Finally, without realizing it, I was experiencing the kind of deliberation with which a democracy addresses problems and makes decisions. There are real differences of interest and opinion, not mere misunderstandings. Yet that condition must be the beginning, not the end, of democratic deliberation. It is easy to resolve differences when the parties share the same worldview and one can convince the other through conversation. But far more often, neither party will convince the other nor be convinced. Both will appeal for the decision of a third party, acting as arbiter, and will agree to abide by that person's judgment. The third party models the citizenry at large: people who are not personally involved in a controversy but who will be affected by the decision. The speech judge—and especially the debate judge—models a citizen audience, and the contestant models the policy advocate. Repeated hundreds of times over the course of one's speech and debate career, a participant gains experience and insight into how a democracy deliberates and decides.

So it turns out that I gained quite a bit of civic education without fully realizing it at the time. My argument is that speech and debate would be better off if we made this realization explicit and deployed it far more prominently in our justifications of our competitive activities. Doing so would put a nobler face on our enterprise than that of a self-satisfying activity for intelligent people without athletic prowess, or a rewarding intellectual game, or a contribution to school spirit or alumni generosity alone. It would give us more confidence and less trepidation when a school or university administrator, learning that there is a speech or debate tournament on campus, asks to stop by and watch a round.

And more important, it would give us a normative standard against which to evaluate our practices in the hope of narrowing the gap between standard and practice. To be sure, a healthy dose of civic education will take place even if we ignore the concept of civic education altogether. But the public understanding and stature of speech and debate could be far greater if we led with this justification and connected it more explicitly to our actual practices.

What's stopping us? Some simple things, such as inertia or the tendency for day-to-day needs to drive out long-term thinking. To some degree, it is the tendency to view things from the perspective of the individual competitor rather than from the perspective of the activity as a whole. And to some degree, it is the fact that too few of our programs are directed by professionals with a long-standing commitment to the activity and an academic orientation that will incline them to think in these terms.

But it is also the case that our professed commitments may be undercut by some of our practices. These tensions represent challenges if we are to live out our commitment to speech and debate as civic education. For example, dealing with ongoing disputes on a case-by-case basis, utilizing the *topoi* of public life, is strengthened by perspective taking and deliberation. But it is weakened by advancing nondebatable claims to identity that are said to justify rejecting competing arguments out of hand. The question is not whether identity claims should be advanced as arguments; of course, they should. Encountering them is part of what is involved in coming to terms with diversity. The question, rather, is whether they will function as arguments or whether they will function to prevent arguments, whether they will promote candor in discussing difference or whether they will shut the discussion down.

For another example, competition is an amazingly good motivator of strong performance, making the testing of ideas and claims more rigorous and reliable. The knowledge that one will be confronted by a worthy opponent stimulates advocates to formulate the strongest claims they can, thereby promoting the cause of democratic deliberation. But one must not confuse the means with the end. If competitive success is regarded as the ultimate reward, then why should one hold out for rigorous and sound argument? Competitive success becomes its own virtue, whether or not it serves the cause of civic education, and the *techne* of speech and debate can become separated from the larger purpose.

A third example: becoming familiar with the *topoi* of public life is enhanced by engaging them, framing and refuting arguments that employ them and set them into competition with one another. This is promoted by smart selection of topics that correspond to issues actually being discussed in the public forum, especially those issues on which attitudes are divided, and by a wide range of experience on different types of topics, such as those concerning military policy, diplomacy, economics, and social welfare. But this benefit is offset if one concocts bizarre arguments in order to evade any reasonable understanding of the topic, or if one designs all-purpose arguments that can be advanced regardless of what the opponent says, in order to divert the discussion away from the topic and toward something else that an advocate might prefer to talk about. This is not to suggest that all claims one advances must be predictable. Surprise has a place; it enables one to practice thinking on one's feet when one is not fully prepared with a developed argument. But the relationship between means and ends once again should be kept in mind. The goal, after all, is to employ the *topoi* of public life, not to escape them.

Yet a fourth example: participation in speech and debate allows those involved to constitute themselves as a community, sharing at least some common experiences and values as well as a sense of friendship and solidarity. It is not unusual for participants and coaches to self-identify as a community. Yet there also are strong centrifugal forces in speech and debate. Organizations proliferate, usually championing one or another format or pedagogical practice. Too often, however, these differences are seen not as reflecting matters of taste but as embodying righteous indignation. It is not necessary to castigate proponents of a different approach to speech and debate in order to champion one's own. The speech and debate community is not so large that it can afford civil wars without losing sight of the larger goal of preparing students to understand and experience public life. Against that goal, the quarrels of the community can seem incredibly petty, if not altogether quaint.

A final example: public life presupposes agency—the belief that people can make a difference. The field of action is understood to be open; change is thought to be possible. This is not a Pollyannaish belief that anyone can do whatever he or she puts the mind to; constraints on action are real. But they are far from total. Indeed, the challenge of public life often is to find maneuvering room in the face of constraints. The ability to do this is strengthened by focusing on the real-world applications of speech and debate arguments. But it is weakened if, caricaturing critical theory, participants ground claims in overly deterministic assumptions about seemingly oppressive hegemonic social systems. Trying out these critical-theory positions in speech and debate competition often does not work very well. If things really were so hopeless and agency altogether lacking, there would be no reason to participate in speech and debate or to seek to engage public life at all.

I have described these five concerns in general terms, because it is not my desire to point fingers or to indict particular programs or individuals. If nothing else, I myself am too far removed from participation in speech and debate activities to do so with any credibility. I want instead to make the more gentle suggestion that if we were more conscious of our contribution to civic education, we could advocate more effectively for our programs and could be more aware when our practices in speech and debate unintentionally undercut our goals.

Let me instead close with a more positive challenge. The world of speech and debate is highly pluralistic, and that is to the good. Programs make choices about the participation base, the speaking formats they will use, the places where they will compete, and a host of similar matters. But there is a place, especially in our leading academic institutions, for a more comprehensive speech and debate program. I am thinking of places like Penn State, where there was a historic commitment to speech and debate but where the program lay fallow for many years. Recently, a commitment to revive and strengthen debate at Penn State has created the possibility of doing so much more, with an abundance of goodwill and resources dedicated to the effort. Let such institutions model the comprehensive speech and debate program: one with both curricular and cocurricular components, featuring both competitive and noncompetitive activities, involving both speech and debate, on the local and national circuits, oriented both to the campus as a protopublic space and to public life generally. Such a program should have both a disciplinary foundation in argumentation and rhetoric, and also a multidisciplinary aspect. It should involve tenure-track faculty as well as graduate student instructors, and it should include a curriculum in argumentation at both the graduate and undergraduate levels, utilizing both face-to-face and online instruction. A program like this would achieve national leadership by precept and example, exerting the agenda-setting power illustrated by the revived program at Penn State.

This is a tall order and may not be fully achievable. Only a small number of institutions are able to offer this comprehensive a program, though if they succeed at it they will strengthen us all. But let us adopt ambitious goals in the service of civic education. The health of our public life makes it necessary, and what we have to contribute makes it possible.

INTRODUCTION:
SPEECH AND DEBATE AS CIVIC EDUCATION

J. MICHAEL HOGAN AND JESSICA A. KURR

Perhaps it goes without saying that our political discourse has become shallow, polarized, contentious, and degraded. The grand eloquence of the nineteenth century has given way to a "vernacular style" that makes "intimacy, narrative, and self-reference" the "unchallenged norms of political discourse."[1] The most strident voices attract the most media attention, and what used to be denounced as demagoguery has been normalized within the political mainstream. Meanwhile, our elected politicians duck the really tough issues, appealing to the lowest common denominator and pandering to the masses with "quantifiably safe" speeches.[2] No wonder so many young people have dropped out of politics, convinced that the "political process is both morally bankrupt and completely insulated from public pressure."[3]

In his final State of Union address, President Barack Obama called upon Congress to "fix our politics," emphasizing the need for more "rational, constructive debates."[4] Yet the demise of substantive and productive debate in American politics is not just the fault of the politicians or a news industry that rewards rhetorical extremism. It also reflects weaknesses in how we educate for citizenship. Indeed, it is an indictment of our entire educational system, which in recent years has neglected its most fundamental mission: educating for citizenship.

To fix our politics, we need an educational renaissance emphasizing not just workforce training but also the habits and skills of engaged citizenship. We need a renewed commitment to what David Mathews, president of the Kettering

Foundation, calls a "deliberative public democracy"—a democracy in which ordinary citizens are taught to "choose and act, not instead of government, but along with it."[5] This volume contributes to that effort by reminding educators of the importance of speech and debate to civic education. Taking inspiration from the ancient art of rhetoric, it offers studies in how speech and debate can equip young people with the knowledge and skills they need for civic life.

Speech and debate education benefits students in many ways. It teaches them not only to be better speakers and critical listeners but also more informed, engaged, and responsible citizens. By studying speech and debate, students develop a keen appreciation for credible research, well-constructed arguments, and sound evidence and reasoning. They develop a better understanding of the rights and responsibilities of free speech, and they become more attuned to the threats posed by propaganda and demagoguery in a free society. They learn how to solve problems collaboratively, and they come to better appreciate the diversity of voices in our increasingly complex and global society. All this has long been recognized, of course, as speech and debate programs have been central to civic education in the United States for more than a century. Yet, in recent years, that civic mission has been neglected, not only in speech and debate programs but in our educational system in general.

The contributors to this volume include many of the leading scholars, teachers, coaches, and program administrators in speech and debate from across the nation. With support from the National Endowment for the Humanities, the Center for Democratic Deliberation at Penn State invited them to reflect on some of the challenges, trends, and innovations in speech and debate education. Gathering first for a three-day conference, they revised their conference presentations for publication in this volume. The collection includes historical case studies, theoretical reflections, and reports on curricular and cocurricular programs that utilize speech and debate pedagogies to educate for citizenship. It represents a first-of-its-kind collection of the best ideas for reinventing and revitalizing the civic mission of speech and debate for a new generation of students.

We begin this brief introduction by reflecting a bit more on the ongoing debate over the health and vitality of America's civic institutions and traditions. We then discuss the relationship between America's civic health and how we teach speech and debate in American colleges and universities. Finally, we preview some of the specific contributions of this volume to ongoing conversations about speech and debate pedagogies. As Hogan has argued elsewhere,[6] some of the most promising solutions to declining civic health in America lie not in legal or political reforms, but in a revival of the *rhetorical* tradition of civic education. For such a revival to take place, however, we must restore the study of speech and debate to the core of the liberal arts, and we need to develop new pedagogical strategies for engaging our increasingly diverse and technologically savvy students. We also need to revive cocurricular programs in speech and debate, giving students more opportunities to *practice* the skills of democratic deliberation outside of the classroom. Finally, we need to reach out beyond the schools and cultivate a better appreciation for the "critical role" of speech and debate in the "discourse and decision-making" of American civic life.[7] If we hope to "fix" our politics, as President Obama has suggested, we must recommit ourselves to educating for citizenship.

America's Civic Malaise

The publication of Robert Putnam's *Bowling Alone* in 2000 ignited a remarkable national debate over the health and vitality of America's civic culture.[8] Synthesizing an enormous body of data, Putnam documented declines in virtually every measure of civic engagement, from voter turnout, to attendance at community meetings, to the number of people working for political parties, signing petitions, and writing letters to their elected representatives. As Putnam summarized the bad news, fewer Americans were taking part "in the everyday deliberations that constitute grassroots democracy. In effect, more than a third of America's civic infrastructure simply evaporated between the mid-1970s and the mid-1990s."[9]

Since the terrorist attacks of September 11, 2001, there have been encouraging signs of civic renewal. As Putnam himself observed, 9/11 at least "interrupted" the long downward trend in "political consciousness and engagement" among Americans, as the public's interest in political affairs rose to levels "not seen in at least three decades."[10] This spike in political awareness seemed clearly evident in the 2004 and 2008 elections, when Americans voted at the highest rates since the 1960s.[11] Yet voter turnout in 2012 dropped back to less than 60 percent of eligible voters,[12] and only about a third of eligible voters turn out in off-year national elections.[13] When all is said and done, the sad fact remains that the United States trails all but a handful of the world's democracies in the proportion of its citizens who turn out to vote.[14]

Even more troubling, the signs of political apathy and civic decay in recent years have been most pronounced among young people. By the turn of the last century, as political scientist Michael X. Delli Carpini reported in 2000, young

Americans had become not only "less knowledgeable about the substance or processes of politics" but also less trusting of their fellow citizens and less likely to participate in any sort of political activity. Not only did young people vote in lower numbers, but they also were less likely to join with others in their community to "address public problems through collective action or the formal policy process."[15] A more recent report on the "civic health" of millennials confirmed that many of these trends continue. According to that report, virtually all measures of civic engagement among young people have trended downward since the 1970s, with "group membership, attendance at meetings, working with neighbors, trusting other people, reading the news, union membership, and religious participation" all down over the past fifty years.[16]

As with older Americans, there have been *some* signs of a civic revival among young people. Young people today are much more likely to volunteer or engage in community service than previous generations of young people. Many are also politically active online, engaging in political conversations or even activism online, mostly on social networking sites.[17] In a 2007 report, the Center for Information and Research on Civic Learning and Engagement (CIRCLE) reported that the millennial generation of college students was "more engaged" than the so-called Generation X, concluding that today's young people were "neither cynical nor highly individualistic" but rather are just exploring new ways "to engage politically." According to CIRCLE, millennials are understandably turned off by the "spin" and "polarized debates" of today's mass-mediated politics, and they are looking for more "open conversations" and more "authentic opportunities for discussing public issues."[18]

For some, all this means is that youth engagement is not really declining but is simply being channeled in new directions. Some have even celebrated these trends as evidence of a new "lifestyle politics," as young people reject "old forms" of politics in favor of "new forms of political interest and engagement."[19] According to political scientist Russell Dalton, for example, young people today may not vote or join political parties as often as their elders, but they also are less polarized, less rigid in their thinking, and more tolerant and open-minded. More likely to engage in protests, boycotts, and other forms of direct political engagement, many young people today embrace new norms of "engaged citizenship" that emphasize "direct, policy-focused, and individualized forms of action" over traditional forms of politics.[20]

However one interprets the data, one thing seems clear: the modes and methods of civic engagement have changed dramatically. For many Americans—and especially young people—getting involved now means participating in politics virtually by posting their opinions on social media or supporting a cause or candidate online. Social media in particular have expanded "opportunities for youth to engage civically and politically," as CIRCLE notes, but they also create "echo chambers" of like-minded young people and fail to expose them to the "healthy give-and-take of democratic debate."[21] Meanwhile, our election campaigns and public policy debates have been hijacked by paid professionals—the "hired guns" of modern politics—who raise and spend hundreds of millions of dollars promoting special interests. Ordinary citizens might support those interests by donating money or pledging their loyalty online, but that is a poor substitute for real deliberative engagement. Perhaps W. Lance Bennett is right: we have entered a new era of "lifestyle politics," with "new patterns of communication and civic engagement" that are "closer to home, less conventionally organized, and more likely to be defined in terms of struggles over evolving notions of rights, morals, and lifestyle values."[22] But so too is Harvard political scientist Theda Skocpol right when she warns of a "diminished democracy," governed not by the people but by "professionally managed advocacy groups and institutions."[23]

How can we, as educators, help revitalize our nation's civic health? How can speech and debate educators in particular help young people reclaim their democracy from the political professionals and special interests? In an age of "lifestyle" politics, is it even possible to change the tone of our politics, as President Obama has advocated, and engage in "vigorous debate" without "demonizing" those with "strongly held convictions on the other side"?[24] These are the questions that inspired this volume, and they are questions that speech and debate educators can help answer. Although reforms in our political system are no doubt needed, we believe that the best hope for reviving the civic health of our nation lies in better educating our young people for citizenship. Simply put, we need to teach young people *how* to be citizens, equipping them with the knowledge and skills they need both to speak out and to demand better from all who speak, debate, and deliberate in public.

Speech and Debate as Civic Education

In a report commissioned by the U.S. Department of Education in 2012, the National Task Force on Civic Learning and Democratic Engagement called for a "more comprehensive vision" of civic education, one that goes beyond a narrow focus on U.S. history and government.[25] Titled *A Crucible Moment:*

College Learning and Democracy's Future, the report called for making civic learning an "integral component" of American education at every level, "from grade school through graduate school, across all fields of study." Challenging us to "expand education for democracy so it reaches all students in ever more challenging ways,"[26] *A Crucible Moment* advocates "investing on a massive scale in higher education's capacity to renew this nation's social, intellectual, and civic capital."[27] In our culturally diverse "ecosystem" of "civic alliances, social norms, and deliberative practices,"[28] the report emphasized the need for historical, civic, and information literacy, communication and critical thinking skills, and an ethical perspective on the responsibilities of democratic citizenship. The report also stressed the need to give students more hands-on practice actually "doing" democracy.

A Crucible Moment's vision of civic education is, in some ways, a throwback to the classical rhetorical tradition. Emphasizing communicative competencies within a strong *ethical* framework, it echoes the pedagogical philosophies of ancient rhetoricians from the Sophists to Isocrates, emphasizing the skills and ethical commitments needed for self-governing citizens to deliberate among themselves.[29] At the same time, *A Crucible Moment* reflects the fact that we live in a very different world from the ancients, a world in which increasingly diverse populations are segmented not only by racial and ethnic differences but also by ideology, economic class, and life experiences. Educators today face challenges never imagined by the ancients, including the proliferation of new technologies with the potential to both educate and distract.

How, in this brave new world, do we teach "the necessary skills of a democratic public: how to listen, how to argue, and how to deliberate?"[30] How do we close what Meira Levinson calls the "civic empowerment gap" among poor and minority youth,[31] encouraging civic engagement among *all* citizens in our diverse society? How do we deploy new technologies in ways that engage rather than alienate, polarize, or pacify citizens? We believe that at least part of the answer lies in reviving and reforming the distinctively American tradition of speech and debate education dating back at least to the Progressive Era.

Americans in the Progressive Era faced many of the same challenges we face today: rapid technological change, economic inequality, environmental degradation, racial tensions, loss of community, and political disaffection. As Hogan has argued, Progressive reformers did not address these problems simply by passing new laws or implementing governmental programs.[32] Rather, they sought ways to promote more public deliberation and looked for solutions to their problems in the collective wisdom of the people. For many Progressives, the essential challenge of the era was what John Dewey called "the problem of the public": the need to educate the masses in "the methods and conditions of debate, discussion, and persuasion."[33] In an increasingly complex world, Progressives feared that powerful special interests had supplanted the "voice of the people," and they sought ways to revitalize or even reinvent the public sphere.

This concern with public deliberation was at the heart of many of the reform initiatives of the Progressive Era, from the "social centers" movement that opened school buildings to town meetings and public debates, to the founding of many of the civic and voluntary associations that still exist today. Progressives staged community forums in settlement houses, revived the Chautauqua movement, and appointed "civic secretaries" in local communities to organize public meetings and debates. They also invented school newspapers and student governments to teach young people about politics and civic affairs. The University of Wisconsin even established a Department of Debating and Public Discussion to promote off-campus public debates on the income tax, woman suffrage, and other issues.[34]

Not surprisingly, speech and debate programs thrived during the Progressive Era,[35] and their pedagogical mission was clear: to teach the research, critical thinking, and communication skills needed for "the wise disposition of important matters in a democratic society."[36] Trained in the ancient art of rhetoric, the first professors of speech broke from the National Council of Teachers of English in 1914 to form their own professional association, the National Association of Academic Teachers of Public Speaking (NAATPS), for the express purpose of distinguishing the study of civic discourse from literary studies. Soon the NAATPS had its own journal, the *Quarterly Journal of Public Speaking*, and by 1921 the Universities of Iowa and Wisconsin were offering doctoral degrees in the field. From the start, these programs emphasized "the teaching of speech as a means of providing students with the tools of democracy."[37] Later, through two world wars and into the Cold War, that emphasis became even stronger, as speech teachers celebrated free speech as the distinguishing mark of a democratic society and declared it essential that all Americans learn not only how to talk "effectively, intelligently, and responsibly" but also how to "listen and judge."[38]

Today, many public speaking textbooks still invoke the classical or neoclassical rhetorical tradition. Treating the *mechanics* of public speaking much as the ancients did, most textbooks still divide the subject into the five classical "canons" and distinguish among Aristotle's three "modes of proof." Like the ancient rhetoricians, speech teachers today also emphasize adapting to one's audience, making reasoned arguments, and avoiding emotional or stylistic excesses that might alienate or offend listeners. Yet, with few exceptions, today's public speaking textbooks say little about the role of speech and debate in democratic life. Nor do they say much about the personal *character* of the speaker or the *ethics* of speech. Most pay lip service to mundane ethical issues, such as plagiarism or citing one's sources, but they say little about the rights and responsibilities of citizenship, the limits of free speech, the threat posed by propaganda and demagoguery, or the ethics of political advocacy. They have nothing even remotely resembling Quintilian's portrait of the ideal speaker—the "good man skilled in speaking"[39]—with its emphasis on ethics, citizenship, and devotion to the common good.

If speech and debate education is to prepare students for citizenship, we need to revive the classical emphasis on the role of speech in a free society. We need to teach about the responsibilities as well as the rights of citizenship,[40] and we need to place more emphasis on the ethics of speech. We need to teach our students what it means to deliberate in good faith, and we need to reflect more on the limits of free speech, including the threats to our democracy posed by propaganda and demagoguery. At the same time, we must take better account of technological and cultural changes, equipping our students for civic life in a technologically advanced and culturally diverse global society. We also need to engage, educate, and empower those who, because of race or socioeconomic conditions, have been left behind in our educational system. Finally, we need to reach out beyond the classroom and fight for what President Obama called more "rational, constructive debates" in the public sphere.[41]

Historically, of course, cocurricular debate programs served as a "laboratory for the democratic process and an important training ground for future policy makers."[42] Debate and forensics programs were also good public relations, attracting the best and brightest students to the study of rhetoric and speech communication. In recent years, however, policy debate in particular has come under intense scrutiny, with critics denouncing the activity as elitist and hypercompetitive, while others complain about its lack of gender and racial diversity. In 2008, the criticism peaked when a debate at the Cross Examination Debate Association (CEDA) national tournament culminated in an obscenity-laden shouting match and the "mooning" of a judge by a faculty debate coach.[43] The incident attracted national media attention and focused attention on larger questions of race, gender, ethics, and the educational mission of debate.

The competitive debate community has long been struggling with questions of inclusion and diversity. Numerous studies have documented the lack of participation and competitive success in debate and forensics among students of color.⁴⁴ The Urban Debate Leagues and similar programs have begun to increase the racial and ethnic diversity of debate,⁴⁵ but progress has been slow. Similarly, critiques of the lack of participation and success among women in speech and debate programs have been common in the literature,⁴⁶ and initiatives such as the Women's Debate Institute (see chapter 9 of this volume) have begun to address that gender imbalance.⁴⁷ Efforts to diversify debate and forensics have extended to disabled students as well.⁴⁸ But, again, progress has been slow, perhaps because all these efforts have forced the debate community to rethink the basic rules and norms of competitive speech and debate. Do those traditional rules and norms of debate—rules grounded in the classical rhetorical tradition's emphasis on civil and rational argumentation—inherently disadvantage women or students of color? How might we make debate and forensics more welcoming for students who historically have been excluded from the activity, and what sorts of debate styles or strategies work best for those students? Debate scholars and coaches have begun to address these questions,⁴⁹ but much work remains to be done.

The racial divide in speech and debate has proven to be the most difficult challenge. Students of color often feel "invisible" in debate, as Sarah Stone Watt suggests later in this volume, or they feel targeted by criticisms of new, nontraditional styles of debate that better reflect their own lived experiences. In 2014, for example, Towson University's Ameena Ruffin and Korey Johnson attracted widespread criticism after they won the CEDA national championship with a debate style incorporating rap lyrics and poetry, along with scholarship from African American studies.⁵⁰ During the round, the affirmative team shifted the debate from the resolution's focus on presidential war powers to the U.S. government's "war" against poor black communities. In a debate that included profanity, hip-hop, and poetry, they challenged not only the rules of debate but broader norms of civility and decorum. Critics of this turn toward "performative" debate included right-wing groups such as the Council of Conservative Citizens, which cited Ruffin and Johnson's victory as more evidence of the far left's subversion of American education. Yet criticism also came from prominent figures within the debate community itself, such as Aaron Hardy, who coaches debate at Northwestern University. According to Hardy, the turn toward performative debate diminishes the pedagogical value of the activity by shifting the focus from in-depth research and substantive arguments about policy issues to the rules of debate itself. Hardy has also expressed disappointment over the lack of civility and decorum at recent tournaments featuring performance-style debates.⁵¹

Not surprisingly, these controversies have exacerbated the fracturing of the collegiate speech and debate community into a multitude of more specialized and often competing organizations. Policy debate is now housed in three different national organizations, which share the same annual resolution but hold separate end-of-year national tournaments. Meanwhile, Lincoln-Douglas debate is administered by the National Forensic Association, which sponsors tournaments that also include individual speech events. Parliamentary debate is governed by at least four separate organizations, and competitive speech events are sponsored by the American Forensic Association and Pi Kappa Delta. All of these organizations have their own constitutions, by-laws, committees, sanctioned tournaments, and competitive rules and norms. Obviously, this fragmentation only makes efforts to diversify speech and debate programs even more challenging.

If we hope to broaden and reinvigorate the educational mission of speech and debate—whether in the classroom or in cocurricular debate and forensics—we must return to some very basic questions: What sorts of knowledge and skills do we hope to inculcate in our students? How do those knowledge and skill sets relate to diverse groups of students and to the changing rhythms of civic life in the twenty-first century? In teaching speech and debate, what are the *ethics* of public advocacy we hope to instill in students, and how do classical notions of "reason" and "civic virtue" relate to today's more diverse student populations? How will new technologies—technologies that have radically changed how we communicate—affect how we teach speech and debate? How can we give students more practice "doing" democracy, as *A Crucible Moment* advocates, and how might we take advantage of new communicative technologies to invent new forums for productive speech and debate? Finally, how might we cultivate a renewed appreciation for the intellectually compelling argument or the well-crafted speech? In short, how can we encourage more "serious speech," in the words of political commentator E. J. Dionne Jr.? How can we encourage more speech "in search of truth"; speech designed not just to defeat political adversaries but to aid citizens in their "common search for understanding"; speech that *engages* citizens in "a continuous and ongoing effort to balance worthy but competing values, to mediate conflicts, to resolve disputes, to solve problems?"[52]

This volume has ideas for addressing all those questions and more. It contains reflections from leading speech and debate educators—many who have been involved in discussions over the educational mission of speech and debate for many years—on the history, current challenges, and future prospects of speech and debate as civic education. It also provides both theoretical and practical rationales for investing in the civic mission of speech and debate education. From studies of the historical involvement of women and minorities in debate to calls for new philosophies and pedagogies of speech and debate education, this volume has both time-tested ideas and innovative proposals for reinvigorating speech and debate programs by renewing their historic commitment to civic education.

Speech and Debate Education in the Twenty-First Century

This volume marks an important moment in the history of speech and debate education in America. At a time when some feel speech and debate programs have lost their way, it grapples with historical questions about whether there has been too much emphasis on competitive forms of speech and debate, and it acknowledges competitive debate's problems with inclusion and diversity. At the same time, it reminds us of speech and debate's historical role in civic education, and it introduces new ideas for speech and debate education in the twenty-first century. In short, this volume includes critiques of speech and debate's shortcomings, but it is mostly a celebration of its promise.

In the chapters that follow, several of our authors revisit past controversies over debate's logocentric norms of argumentation, its masculinist biases, and its perpetuation of ideologies of white supremacy and U.S. exceptionalism. Reflecting on debate's historical traditions and competitive structures, they acknowledge that there are still barriers to participation and success for many students, particularly women and students of color. Pivoting from those past controversies, however, most of our authors look to the future, reflecting on how speech and debate might become more relevant to civic education in our increasingly complex and diverse modern world. In addition to ideas for reforming traditional speech and debate programs, this volume explores exciting new initiatives that move beyond the conventional speech and debate curriculum to emphasize dialogue, deliberation, networking, and community building.

Part 1 consists of four studies in the history of speech and debate education. In chapter 1, Angela G. Ray tells the story of the Clionian Debating Society, a group of free black men in antebellum Charleston who diligently researched and debated the great issues of the day despite their lack of citizenship status. They did so, Ray argues, because they aspired to become leaders within the free black community—and, perhaps, because they dreamed of someday having a real political voice. For these young men in the Reconstruction South, Ray explains, debate served as a "collective, experiential affirmation of their humanity as intellectual beings: for themselves, for each other, and for Charleston's free black community."

In chapter 2, Jamie McKown takes us back to the birth of competitive academic debate in the Progressive Era. Reporting on a large-scale project to "identify, document, and map" the earliest years of intercollegiate debate, McKown shows how early debate educators rejected the "overly stylized oratorical practices" of nineteenth-century literary societies and instead emphasized the sorts of "rhetorical instruction most directly relevant to civic engagement"—rhetorical theory, argumentation, and the history of American public address. In the process, they illustrated both the promise and potential pitfalls of debate education. On the one hand, debaters at this time addressed "timely matters of public policy" and gained experience debating in large public spaces in front of public audiences. On the other hand, they struggled with issues still with us today, such as competitive pressures to cut ethical corners or deploy technical styles of speech divorced from real-world deliberations.

In our third chapter, Carly S. Woods inaugurates an important theme throughout this volume: the challenges and benefits of women's debate. Taking us back to the 1930s and 1940s, Woods uses archival sources to illustrate how early women debaters "accessed the benefits of civic education through debate, while simultaneously contending with forces that would limit their participation, devalue their contributions, and raise questions about their very presence in higher education." Focusing on women's debate at Penn State, Woods tells the story of Clayton H. Schug, a faculty debate advisor who "valued women debaters, insisted on including them in forums previously dominated by men, and battled to secure resources." She also tells the story of the debaters themselves: their reasons for participating, their experiences in a male-dominated activity, and the benefits they derived from their experience—most notably, the skills they needed to navigate their role as citizens in the postwar world. In the process, Woods illuminates how women's debate historically functioned as a "protofeminist activity" and raises questions about "how we might productively push the boundaries of debate still further" as we "reenvision civic education in the twenty-first century."

Michael D. Bartanen and Robert S. Littlefield conclude part 1 with their study of two distinct periods in debate history: the "public oratory era" and the "technical era." During the former, the emphasis was on educating for citizenship, and debate was viewed as more of a "public" than a "private" good. Reflecting the spirit of the Progressive Era, students spoke before judges of ordinary citizens and defended their convictions publicly. Then came the growth of tournament debating and, in the context of World War II and the Cold War, a more "technical" era of debate when the competitive "game" took precedence over civic education. Now the emphasis was on shaping "smart, articulate, and dedicated competitors" rather than "good citizens." Bartanen and Littlefield conclude with a call for striking a new balance between competition and civic education, offering students the chance to compete while finding new ways to enhance debate's educational value.

Part 2 of this volume picks up on that theme of how speech and debate might best educate for citizenship with three studies of the relationship between debate pedagogy and public deliberation. In chapter 5, Robert C. Rowland draws from the writings of James Madison to illuminate the relationship between the skills taught by debate and those needed for public deliberation. Showing how Madison envisioned a "politics of public opinion" as the "republican remedy" to the problems of a republican government, he suggests how academic debate might embody Madison's vision by fostering debate across the curriculum, focusing on a wider variety of practical questions, debating both sides of issues, and training debaters to "adapt to a broad general audience of reasonable people." If debate is to educate for citizenship, Rowland argues, it must train students to "translate complex arguments" into more broadly "understandable and persuasive" forms of speech.

In chapter 6, Gordon R. Mitchell complicates Rowland's Madisonian vision by reminding us "how rarely everyday arguers tend to engage in the sort of critical thinking valorized in argumentation textbooks." Citing recent research in social psychology, Mitchell argues that many Americans today have sorted themselves into "echo chambers," where they hear only "like-minded arguers" and become so politically indoctrinated that "classical argumentative techniques," such as direct rebuttals, only encourage them to "dig in and cling even more tightly" to their settled beliefs. How might debate and forensics educators respond to this new reality? According to Mitchell, the best answers lie in debate pedagogies that augment "debiasing strategies" developed by philosophers and psychologists with "cooperative" and "coalescent" theories of argument built upon the foundations of ancient Greek and Roman argumentation pedagogy. Mitchell thus envisions new approaches to speech and debate pedagogy that are "responsive to contemporary exigencies" yet "linked to ancient rhetorical traditions" and "strengthened by interdisciplinary integration."

David A. Frank concludes part 2 of the volume with an argument for more fully incorporating religious argument into the study of speech and debate. Reminding us of the importance of religious faith in public life, Frank suggests ways that speech and debate educators might better prepare students to understand and critique religious arguments from diverse faith traditions, drawing on the ancient rhetorical tradition's treatment of *logos* and *mythos*. Both the *mythos* of religion and the *logos* of science should be put to "the test of argument," Frank argues, and that means teaching secular students the "art of debating mythos" and religious students how they might "benefit from opening their mythos to the interrogation of logos." Illustrating how such pedagogies work at two religious schools and one secular university, Frank concludes that speech and debate educators can perform "a valuable public service" by teaching students to better manage those disagreements that arise when religion becomes implicated in public policy debates.

Part 3 shifts our focus from the public to the competitive arena of speech and debate, focusing on innovations and challenges in intercollegiate debate. In chapter 8, Paul E. Mabrey III reports on a successful collaboration between CEDA and the University of Virginia's Miller Center that involved student debaters in larger national conversations about presidential war powers. Responding to criticisms that policy debate has become too insular, CEDA framed its 2013–2014 national debate topic around an increasingly controversial public issue: presidential war powers. The topic fit neatly with the Miller Center's interest in national security issues, and the result was a series of public debates involving both CEDA debaters and leading experts on U.S. foreign policy. Participants in those debates gained "two important dimensions of civic learning," according to Mabrey: knowledge of an important issue and the experience of debating in a public forum. At the same time, student debaters had an impact on subsequent conversations within the national security community and among policymakers. Mabrey concludes that this successful collaboration can serve as a model of how we might better realize the promise of intercollegiate debate as civic education and engagement.

Chapter 9 turns to a perennial issue in competitive debate and forensics: how to make debate more welcoming and inclusive for women. In a chapter reflecting her own personal experiences, Catherine H. Palczewski both champions and critiques intercollegiate debate, calling it an "incredibly powerful form of civic education" with "liberatory potential" yet lamenting how it historically has been "premised on an exclusion and sexualization of women and feminine bodies." If speech and debate are to realize their full potential as "robust forms of civic education," Palczewski argues, we need to reflect more deeply on why women participate and succeed less in intercollegiate debate than men, and we need to challenge those norms and practices that "hinder diverse women's civic engagement." Palczewski concludes with a discussion of the Women's Debate Institute, an organization that embodies her "transformative understanding of debate and speech as civic education"—a vision that foregrounds the ideals of "respect, continuing the conversation, and community building."

The last two chapters in part 3 both touch on an issue that has provoked considerable controversy within the competitive debate community and beyond: the emergence of new "performative" styles of debate rooted in the lived experiences of African Americans and other students of color. In chapter 10, Ronald Walter Greene and Darrin Hicks offer a theoretical reflection on that controversy, illuminating how a Cold War–era controversy over "switch-side" debating foreshadowed today's controversy over performance debate. Recalling their own earlier work on that controversy, Greene and Hicks revisit their critique of debating both sides as a "reassignment of conviction" that aligned debate with "a variant of Cold War liberalism that promoted free speech as proof of American exceptionalism." Noting how that earlier controversy has now "interacted with new challenges to how the debate game embeds certain racial logics of white supremacy," they reflect on the implications of challenges to the norms and practices of debate for civic education. The authors conclude that by turning debate tournaments into "sites of social activism," performance debaters are once again challenging "the liberal framework of debate" by fostering a new, "affective atmosphere" that is more about community building than winning debates.

In chapter 11, Sarah Stone Watt also grapples theoretically with the performance/policy divide, drawing from the work of Danielle Allen. Lamenting that arguments over the substance and style of policy debate have become increasingly divisive, she insists that "identity-driven debate is here to stay" and urges the debate community to attend to the larger tensions in contemporary U.S. politics reflected in those new styles of debate. Rooted in alienation and distrust, particularly among African Americans, those tensions, if left unresolved, threaten not only debate but democracy itself, and we cannot simply ignore them. "Just as our nation needs reflection and reorientation to preserve its democratic experiment," she argues, so too must debate deal with the "growing distrust" among minority students. If we hope to teach "the skills necessary for democratic engagement in our increasingly diverse and polarized society," Watt concludes, we must place more emphasis on "communication skills not always emphasized in the competitive model of debate": empathy for the "political sacrifice" of marginalized citizens and techniques for building trust across racial divides.

Part 4 includes four chapters that reflect on the *kinds* of civic knowledge and skills students learn from speech and debate. In chapter 12, Edward A. Hinck synthesizes work from across a range of argumentation and communication theory to develop a vision of debate education that goes beyond critical thinking and persuasive speaking to help students develop "a sense of humane citizenship." Responding to *A Crucible Moment*'s call for civic education that promotes a concern for others, Hinck outlines a typology of advocacy skills that encourage productive dialogue and personal development. Finally, he looks to a well-known school of communication research, the Coordinated Management of Meaning project, for ideas on how to teach students to manage disagreement and develop a humane sense of citizenship. When done right, Hinck concludes, speech and debate can provide the "kind of transformative learning that makes coordinating meanings more possible in a very complex world."

In chapter 13, Sara A. Mehltretter Drury, Rebecca A. Kuehl, and Jenn Anderson discuss their efforts to incorporate deliberation pedagogies into the communication curriculum at two different educational institutions in the Midwest. Staging deliberative events at both a midsize public university and a small liberal arts college, the authors involved students from several different courses in community forums on topics ranging from breastfeeding in public to ways to improve the quality of life in their local community. The authors then analyzed both instructor and student reactions, finding "positive outcomes across a variety of institutional settings" from these experiments in deliberative pedagogy. Elaborating on "the opportunities and challenges of deliberation as a pedagogical practice in civic education," they conclude that deliberation is "an effective pedagogical tool for promoting *rhetorical citizenship*," or the kind of "embodied practice of participating in deliberations and other civic activities" called for in *A Crucible Moment*.

Chapter 14, by G. Thomas Goodnight and three of his colleagues, reports on the results of another town-gown collaboration, this one engaging diverse, multicultural school populations in Los Angeles in deliberation and advocacy about community needs. Called Penny Harvest, the program is part of a nationwide child philanthropic program, the Common Cents Foundation, and it involves bringing local elementary and middle school students together to discuss community needs, design a public advocacy and fund-raising campaign, and build "communities of belonging and of practice." As our authors report, Penny Harvest has been under way in Los Angeles for four years, and it already has made a difference, both for students and for the communities they touch. Based on their success, our authors sketch "a preliminary model for youth training in public communication and democratic participation" to guide civic education in other multiethnic urban contexts. Based not on the traditional, "forensics" model of debate but on a "network pragmatics" approach to deliberation and civic engagement, our authors describe how students can build their "civic capacities" by participating in "acts of discovery, personal expression, critical thinking, and community discussion."

Melissa Maxcy Wade concludes part 4 of the volume with reflections on one of the best known programs using debate to motivate and empower students in socioeconomically disadvantaged schools, the Urban Debate League (UDL). As the founder of the Atlanta UDL, Wade helped create the model for some twenty-four UDLs in major cities across the United States—programs that, at last count, have served more than forty thousand teachers and students.[53] Reflecting on this success, Wade shows how UDLs have helped level the playing field of American education by empowering neglected school populations and building multigenerational communities of practice. Former U.S. Secretary of Education Arne Duncan praised UDLs for promoting the traditional "'Four C's' of 21st century skills—critical thinking, communication, collaboration, and creativity" and for adding a fifth: "civic awareness and engagement." Quoting from the memoir of one former participant, Ed Lee, and citing evidence of the impact of UDLs on standardized test scores, graduation rates, and other measures of educational success, Wade makes a powerful case for UDLs as a form of advocacy-based civic education that has immediate and tangible impacts on students and may even help revive our deliberative democracy.

In part 5 of this volume, our contributors reflect on how we might promote international collaboration and interconnection through debate, in the process defining citizenship in more global terms. In chapter 16, Allan D. Louden and Taylor W. Hahn report on a successful debate institute sponsored by the U.S. Department of State, the Benjamin Franklin Transatlantic Fellows Summer Institute (BFTF). Bringing together high school students from the post-Soviet states, Western Europe, and the United States, the BFTF is a monthlong program where participants develop skills in international collaboration, diplomacy, civic engagement, and political advocacy through a combination of classroom instruction and civic outreach to local communities. Experimenting with a variety of innovative methods, the program has demonstrated the benefits of approaching debate and civic engagement as mutually reinforcing activities. Despite the variations, the benefits for participants have remained constant: an increase in intellectual dexterity and critical thinking, a greater appreciation of the synergy between the theory and practice of argumentation and debate, and a renewed faith that critical thought and vigorous debate does not hamper but rather promotes social and political progress.

Chapter 17 focuses on another international program of debate education: Worlds-Style debate. Reflecting on her experience as a teacher and coach, Una Kimokeo-Goes argues that this style of debate, based on the British parliamentary model, encourages students to adopt a global perspective on citizenship, become more aware of international issues, and develop a better appreciation of cultural diversity. By participating in Worlds debate, she argues, students come to "understand citizenship not as a fixed concept but as something that is *performed* every day." Conceding that Worlds-Style debate is "far from a perfect space for practicing citizenship," Kimokeo-Goes acknowledges some challenges, such as language barriers and the same biases of gender, race, and "elite domination" that historically have plagued competitive debate. But despite these challenges, Worlds-Style debate remains "a useful arena for students to practice and perform the habits and skills of citizenship" by engaging students from other countries on global issues.

Our final chapter takes a closer look at a debate program in China that has been highlighted by the *Chronicle of Higher Education* and other national media: the National High School Debate League of China (NHSDLC).[54] As the largest sponsor of English-language debate in China, the NHSDLC stages some eighty tournaments per year in forty cities across mainland China. According to our authors, the program's explosive growth and its enormous popularity in China reflects widespread dissatisfaction with a traditional educational system based upon rote memorization and standardized testing. It also reflects an educational reform movement that, in many respects, mirrors discourse in the West about "21st century skills" and the need to educate students to participate in an "interconnected, globalized marketplace." Our authors downplay any potential democratizing effects from the program, but they do show how English-language debate in China reflects some of the dramatic cultural changes in that nation in recent years, particularly a new openness to Western ideas about education and civic engagement. Although student debaters in China still may not aspire to Western-style democracy, the authors conclude that debate can still educate for citizenship in China by counteracting apathy, promoting a collective moral conscience, and shaping a shared identity.

In the foreword to this volume, David Zarefsky, one of the most prominent scholars of argumentation and debate in America, reflects on the challenges and opportunities involved in approaching speech and debate as civic education. Like many contributors to this volume, Zarefsky's early interests and personality were shaped by his experiences as a high school and college debater, and in looking back on those days he now recognizes "several ways in which [he] was receiving a good civic education without realizing it." Reflecting on the challenges of making debate's commitment to civic education more explicit and prominent, Zarefsky introduces many of the issues and controversies discussed throughout the volume: the danger of overemphasizing competition, the lack of support for professional debate educators, the fragmentation of the debate community into competing organizations, and the denial of human agency implicit in some of the newer theoretical perspectives on speech and debate. In imagining solutions to those challenges, Zarefsky calls upon educators to push for more comprehensive speech and debate programs—programs with both curricular and cocurricular components, both competitive and noncompetitive activities—involving speech and debate in larger conversations about important issues on campus and in "public life generally."

Yet there are other challenges to speech and debate that cannot be met solely by devoting more resources to the activity or by building more comprehensive programs. As a number of the chapters in this volume emphasize, we also need new theories of speech, argumentation, and debate, and we need a more welcoming, inclusive, and broadly cross-cultural or even global perspective on the subject. If we hope to atone for debate's history of marginalizing or excluding women and students of color, we need to think more broadly about how rhetorical theories grounded in the lived experiences of marginalized people might be incorporated into speech and debate, and we need to redesign speech and debate programs to educate *all* students for citizenship. That, then, is the challenge of the future—a challenge that this volume only begins to address. Our hope is that this volume will at least get that conversation started in the right direction.

Conclusion

Not everybody agrees that civic education ought to be a top priority—in speech and debate, or in our educational system more generally. Over the past decade, educational reformers have emphasized the need to improve math and science training, and the whole idea of civic education has been criticized by both leftist academics and right-wing cultural warriors.⁵⁵ This antipathy toward civic education has in turn contributed to an erosion of support for the humanities, and it has undermined the best rationale for a well-rounded liberal education. With more colleges and universities embracing a workforce training model of higher education, we risk further declines in the historical and civic literacy necessary to sustain our democratic republic. With so many Americans ill-prepared for their civic responsibilities, we risk becoming what David Mathews of the Kettering Foundation has called "a citizenless democracy."⁵⁶

The first professors of speech and debate—the founders of the discipline in the Progressive Era—showed us the way to revive both humanistic education and our deliberative traditions. Dedicated to educating for citizenship, they pioneered speech and debate pedagogies that better prepared young people for citizenship, and they shared their expertise with the broader public, holding all who spoke in public to a higher standard. In that same spirit, we need to pioneer new ways to teach speech and debate that reflect the changing civic landscape of the twenty-first century. We need to take account of new technologies of communication, changing social norms and values, increased cultural diversity, and the effects of globalization. We need to find new ways to engage today's young people in conversations about civic life, and we need to speak out against those who degrade our public discourse with the techniques of the propagandist or demagogue.

In this volume, we have begun a journey toward the new frontiers of speech and debate education. We have explored new theories of argumentation and debate, and we have explored ways to make speech and debate more inclusive and welcoming for women and students of color. We also have introduced a variety of ideas for programmatic innovations. But much more needs to be done. Looking to the future, we see countless other possibilities for alternatives to the traditional speech and debate curriculum, ranging from pedagogies grounded in theories of affect and empathy to initiatives informed by critical race theory, feminist thought, cross-cultural communication research, or studies in mediation, dialogue, and coalition-building. The possibilities are truly endless, and the conversation has just begun.

The need for new approaches to civic education is pressing, and speech and debate have important contributions to make. As a special task force of the American Political Science Association (APSA) concluded, the United States is a "democracy at risk," and we need to act now if we hope to stop the further erosion of our public sphere. By showing our students and others how to be more discerning and engaged citizens, we can help improve the quality of our political discourse. We also can create "more opportunities for the exchange of reasons and arguments in deliberative settings," as the APSA task force recommends, and we can look for ways to reduce "elite polarization and with it rancor and unproductive conflict." Finally, we can find new ways to empower the voiceless and make our political communities more inclusive.[57] As the heirs to the traditions of the ancient rhetoricians, speech and debate educators are well positioned to contribute to efforts to improve the civic health of our nation. By combining the civic mission of the classical rhetorical tradition with innovative speech and debate pedagogies, we can make a difference.

PART I
HISTORY OF SPEECH AND DEBATE AS CIVIC EDUCATION

I

WARRIORS AND STATESMEN:
DEBATE EDUCATION AMONG FREE AFRICAN AMERICAN
MEN IN ANTEBELLUM CHARLESTON

ANGELA G. RAY

Two decades after the end of the Civil War, Simeon W. Beaird judged a public debate at the Schofield Normal and Industrial School in Aiken, South Carolina. The local African American community had strongly supported the school since its postwar founding by Martha Schofield, a Pennsylvania Quaker. Beaird, a fifty-nine-year-old African Methodist Episcopal (AME) minister, was one of three judges who rendered a verdict for the affirmative on the resolution: "That a warrior is of greater benefit to his country than a statesman." A visitor pronounced the debate "grand."[1] This quotidian anecdote, reported in the AME Church's *Christian Recorder*, signaled Beaird's long-standing commitment to education generally and to debate in particular. Further, the terms of the resolution highlighted images of male leadership—vigor in struggle, cooperation in negotiation—that nineteenth-century debate education promised to advance.

This chapter is about that promise: first its realization in the public life of an individual, and then, in greater detail, its contours as proffered in a debating society to which that individual belonged as a young man, in the late antebellum era. The utility of debate education for the individual is demonstrable, but historical eventualities—such as the profound sociopolitical changes wrought by the Civil War and Reconstruction—could not have been predicted from a prewar vantage point. The dynamics of history encourage questioning the value of debate in conditions of oppression, and the specifics of the case demonstrate that debate can prove meaningful not only as preparation for citizenship but also as a consequential intellectual and social endeavor in its own right.

The Individual Debater

Simeon Beaird knew both struggle and negotiation. Born in 1826 and reared in Charleston's free black community, he studied in this community's clandestine schools, which educated boys and girls despite state laws that prohibited teaching either slaves or free persons of color to read. By the 1850s, Beaird was running his own school, and he would later recall having "taught against the laws of the land" while encouraging "every black child to believe he was as good as Queen Victoria's son."[2] At the same time, Beaird sought ways to continue his own education. Between 1847 and 1858, he participated actively in the Clionian Debating Society, one of at least three debating societies in antebellum Charleston run by and for young, free men of color. Clionian members and honorary members were exclusively male, although women of the community attended special meetings and sometimes donated books or money.[3] In 1850, the Clionians considered the warrior-statesman question: "Who has the greatest chance to show forth his patriotism in time of war," they asked, "the statesman in the hall of power, or the soldier on the field of battle?" After an energetic debate, the Clionian president endorsed the soldier.[4]

A founder of the Clionian Debating Society, Beaird served as its first president and was often an officer. Twice an elected orator, he gave speeches on "Industry, Perseverance and Patience" and "The Influence of *Principle* and *Action* on the Future Destiny of Man." Beaird frequently participated in debates, arguing issues ranging from the condemnation of Socrates to the justice of the U.S.-Mexican War.[5] Then in 1858 he was a member of the dissolution committee, formed because "present *political* disadvantages" made continuance impossible. The term *political disadvantages* in the society's manuscript minute books pointed obliquely to aggressive restrictions with which powerful white elites terrorized free persons of color in South Carolina. In the second half of the 1850s, repeated legislative efforts at widespread enslavement joined long-standing prohibitions on travel outside the state, prohibitions on learning, discrimination in churches, and threats of violence.[6]

Within the debating society, Beaird and his fellows created a place for learning, camaraderie, and the performance of a commitment to public life, enacting self-respect and community involvement even as external threats mounted. The Clionian Debating Society thus exemplifies the organizational form that Catherine R. Squires labels an enclave public, a "discursive institution" separate from dominant publics—often "deployed in response to conditions of intense oppression"—that can serve as "a source of history, pride, or community connections" and can generate "ideologies of self-determination."[7]

The Civil War and Reconstruction brought opportunities for some former Clionians to deploy their knowledge and skills in public service for their country's benefit, even literally as soldiers and statesmen. Some, such as Isadore A. Hyames and Conrad D. Ludeke, were light-skinned enough to be perceived as white, and both joined the Union Army in 1861. Ludeke had achieved the rank of captain by the time he mustered out in 1866.[8] Others, including Henry Cardozo and William O. Weston, were among those whom historian Eric Foner has labeled "freedom's lawmakers," serving in postwar state legislatures and local governments.[9] For his part, Simeon Beaird brought his learning and leadership to bear in education, politics, and religion. Shortly after the war's end, he was in Augusta, Georgia, working as a teacher, minister, and Republican political leader. In 1867–1868, he served as an elected member of Georgia's state constitutional convention, and in 1870 he chaired a delegation to Washington to express the grievances of the African American population of Georgia to President Ulysses S. Grant. In the 1870s, Beaird moved back to South Carolina, where he worked as an educator and as county treasurer of Aiken County. Following the renewed suppression of African Americans in U.S. public life at the end of Reconstruction, Beaird ceased to hold a government post, but he persevered as a community leader in his ministerial role until his death in 1894. As the *Christian Reporter* attests, he also fostered the educational advancement of others.[10]

The unique political situation of Reconstruction and the comparative privileges of Beaird's own situation—especially his gender and his lifelong free status—created conditions under which he was able to use his rhetorical abilities in a variety of settings, from schoolrooms to legislative assembly rooms, from church sanctuaries to the White House. Working within enclaves and also, at times, speaking in the forums of dominant power on behalf of other African Americans—as Squires puts it, "to argue against dominant conceptions of the group and to describe group interests"—Beaird enacted the participatory politics that he and his fellow Clionians had practiced before the war, engaging in verbal struggle and in policymaking negotiation.[11]

Yet other factors—white supremacy and the curse of slavery, the capricious constraints on people of color—meant that Beaird and other Clionians lived in dangerous conditions both before and after the war. Recalling the crushing oppressions of the antebellum era at a postwar political meeting, Beaird highlighted their effects on intellectual ambition, linking his commitments as a teacher positively with the promises of U.S. founding documents and negatively with race-based limitations on learning: "I say to-day, as I have felt from my boyhood, . . . that all men were created equal. From my school-boy days, when I ran barefooted to school, I have looked at the white man going to college, and I felt that I wanted to go there too."[12] Here Beaird, always careful with language, does not conflate a desire for access to educational opportunity with mimicry of the other: he wants to "go there too," not "be like him." It is plausible that self-respect, anger at prohibitions and hypocrisy, and a longing to learn motivated Beaird and his fellows to create an association for themselves in 1847.

The story of Simeon Beaird provides vivid confirmation of the power of rhetorical education as a foundation for civic leadership, even as it narrates the intersections of learning with race-based oppression, gender-based privilege, and the vagaries of historical circumstance. If we shift focus from personal experience over a lifetime to shared experience over a decade, how might we understand the value that debate participation had for young, free men of color in Charleston during the late antebellum era?

Debating in Society

The Clionians shared in a national culture that had long recognized the popular debating society as a familiar social form. College literary societies had held debates since the 1720s, but individuals without access to institutions of learning also sought skills in debate and public speaking as well as the fun of interaction. By the 1830s, the noncollegiate debating society was ubiquitous across the nation, in urban and rural areas alike. Participants in these civic associations—often though not always men, often though not always white—typically practiced debate, public speaking, and parliamentary procedure in a context of homosocial camaraderie, learning and rehearsing the forms of political, social, and cultural leadership.[13] Free African American men and women, especially in urban centers such as Philadelphia and New York, established associations that promoted education and racial uplift, as scholars such as Emma Jones Lapsansky, Elizabeth McHenry, and Shirley Wilson Logan have shown.[14] When in 1847 the young men of the Clionian Debating Society stated their goals as "the promotion of their connection [to each other] and the improvement of their intellect," they rhetorically linked themselves with other intellectual aspirants across the nation.[15]

Their social and political circumstances, however, were profoundly different from those of young white debaters in the nation's cities or rural settlements. They also differed from the situations of young, free black men and women in the urban North. Historians of Charleston, such as Edmund Drago, Bernard E. Powers Jr., and Amrita Chakrabarti Myers, have provided invaluable foundations for the study of Charleston's free black community, from its heightened color consciousness to its religious, occupational, and wealth-holding characteristics.[16] Protestant Christianity was an important basis for moral action among this tight-knit community, and many free persons of color were involved in religious, economic, and benevolence societies. Skilled occupations were typical, with women working as seamstresses and mantua makers, and men as carpenters and tailors, shoemakers and barbers, butchers and masons. Some among Charleston's most prosperous free persons of color owned considerable property in homes, shops, and even slaves. Larry Koger and Loren Schweninger have shown that both altruism and commercial advantage motivated slaveholding among this population.[17] Yet comparative prosperity and participation in slaveholding did not insulate free persons of color from increasing threats as the sectional crisis intensified.

Within the enclave of the debating society, chaos was held at bay. Members subsumed their activities under a framework of intense orderliness, an investment in the rule of law, and a commitment to language—written and read—as the foundation for ethical action. Indeed, the group spent many meetings discussing their own governance procedures, such as the time and frequency of meetings; the restriction on members joining other, similar societies; and the appropriate level of involvement in debates by the society's president, the officer empowered to render a verdict.[18] Such deliberations enacted procedures similar to those found in government assemblies, potentially creating adherence to a deliberative ideal through the recurrent experience of creating rules for self-governance and altering those rules when they became cumbersome or irrelevant.[19] For these young men, of course, such adherence likely illuminated the many ways in which realities in the United States fell far short of espoused ideals. Their records, however, do not discuss democratic hypocrisy.

The formal debates of the society were situated within a broad program of rhetorical practices, making debate one among several means through which the young men could participate in the oral, scribal, and print cultures of their time. The debating society provided regular opportunities for public speaking, not only in speeches given before members but also in prepared orations delivered to members and community guests at annual anniversary celebrations. Further, the society promoted careful record-keeping by society officers, who created collaborative, scribal accounts that performatively asserted the value of the group and its activities and that today continue to affirm the society's existence, aspirations, and actions. Finally, the Clionians not only emphasized speaking and writing but also the reading and study necessary for competent oral performance and intellectual growth. Between 1849 and 1855, they gathered materials for a society library, through purchases and donations.[20] The Clionians and their patrons sought standard printed works, such as Thomas Babington Macaulay's *The History of England* and Noah Webster's unabridged dictionary, as well as locally significant public statements. These included a speech, in pamphlet form, on the value of education by Professor Francis W. Capers of the Citadel and another on geology delivered to the South Carolina legislature by Professor Richard T. Brumby of South Carolina College.[21] Military and political history dominated the holdings, but in 1850 the group purchased Elizabeth Starling's *Noble Deeds of Woman*, shortly after supporter Emma Farbeaux gave the society three books by "distinguished Authoresses."[22]

The society's debates were embedded within complex practices of learning, and they occurred within an intricate, rule-bound organizational structure. A Committee of Queries proposed several questions for debate at a future meeting and the society chose among them. Two members were then appointed, often in an alphabetical rotation, to prepare the affirmative and negative cases. On the evening of the debate, the two men presented their cases, other members of the society joined in, and the debate concluded at a time stipulated in advance. The society's president rendered a decision, although reports of meetings do not specify whether it was based on the so-called merits of the question or the strength of the arguments. Antebellum societies rendered decisions in different ways, and there was not a common standard.[23] The Clionian records supply the verdicts, although without sure knowledge of the basis for decision making, extrapolating meaning from them is risky. Many judgments were consonant with what we would expect this group to support, such as an affirmative decision on the question "Is education beneficial to society?"[24] Yet the president ruled for the negative in a debate asking "whether the United States was right in declaring her Independence," and the terms of that debate and the rationale for the decision remain a tantalizing mystery.[25]

The inspiration for the specific queries is likewise uncertain. Whereas historians of Charleston have correctly observed that the questions debated by the Clionians were similar to those debated by young white men at the College of Charleston, that does not mean that the Clionians followed the lead of the collegians. More often than not, the Clionians debated questions before they were argued at the college.[26] Furthermore, debating questions were similar around the country—and had been for decades—in college societies and popular groups alike. Although organizational records typically remained private, questions regularly appeared in newspapers and in published books. For example, in 1833 the son of former Yale president Theodore Dwight published a book of his father's decisions and commentaries on forty-one questions debated at Yale in 1813–1814, from "Ought Capital Punishments ever to be inflicted?" to "Can the Immortality of the Soul be proved from the Light of Nature?"[27] From the early 1840s, Charles Morley's pocket-sized handbook, *A Guide to Forming and Conducting Lyceums, Debating Societies, &c.* listed topics and questions that were already conventional, from "Are fictitious writings beneficial?" to "Did Napoleon do more hurt than good to the world?"[28] Later texts, such as Frederic Rowton's *The Debater* (1846) and James N. McElligott's *The American Debater* (1855), listed hundreds of debating questions along with advice about arguments, evidence, and resources.[29] There is no evidence to show whether members of the Clionian Debating Society owned texts like these, but the crucial point is this: the details of what counted as a good debating question and hence an appropriate focus of intellectual energy were circulated widely throughout antebellum U.S. culture. The same questions recurred time and again and became standards, whether they were transferred through print, handwritten letters, or conversation.

Although we cannot say for sure where the Clionians got their debating questions, the specific questions chosen for debate offer insight into the dynamics of the group. The Clionians debated ninety-three questions over the society's life span. Like other debaters throughout the country, they argued issues of policy and value, both specific and abstract. Sometimes they drew attention to current events. For instance, in 1848 they asked whether "the acquisition of California [would] be of any great use to the U.S." In 1851, they considered whether the Great Exhibition at London's Crystal Palace would "bring about the contemplated union of intercourse among the nations of the earth." And in 1854, they asked of the ongoing Crimean War, "[Are] France & England right in interfering in the present struggle between Russia & Turkey?"[30] Such questions situated the debaters as individuals competent to assess contemporary geopolitics, enacting the roles of national and world leaders. Like young white male debaters across the nation, the Clionians debated many questions, including the soldier/statesman query, that configured U.S. national interest as a central concern.[31] At the same time, these young men, who lacked full citizenship in their state and nation, may have approached foreign policy questions with a more cosmopolitan imagination, as Ronald J. Zboray and Mary Saracino Zboray have observed among disenfranchised women lecturegoers in antebellum New England.[32]

As followers of Clio, the Greek muse of history, the Clionians spent considerable time on questions of historical interpretation.[33] Like debaters elsewhere, they often emphasized Western classical antiquity, asking, for example, whether Demosthenes or Cicero "accomplished the greatest good for his country" and whether "Caesar [was] right in crossing the Rubicon or not."[34] Military careers were a favored topic. The Clionians not only debated the comparative value of the soldier and the statesman in general terms, but they also debated the conduct of Roman general Marcus Atilius Regulus, the virtues of George Washington and Alexander the Great, and the characteristics of Napoleon. They compared Napoleon's military prowess to that of Hannibal, debated whether "ambition ... led Napoleon to battle," argued about the meaning of Wellington's victory at Waterloo, and twice debated whether the exile to St. Helena had been right.[35]

As a society with explicit commitments to intellectual development, the Clionians debated questions about learning, asking whether "Ancient or Modern history" was "more interesting" and "whether success in difficult Sciences [is] the results of Genius, or Industry and Perseverance."[36] The final query that the society adopted for debate—a question never debated—turned out to be a poignant one. It was "Which is more conducive to Individual improvement—Solitude or Society?" At the group's next minuted meeting, eight months later, the members discussed the possibility of changing the society "from a *debating* to a *reading* association." Although a majority that evening chose only to reduce the required quorum, the group would soon dissolve.[37] As the sectional crisis pressed closer to bloodshed, improvement gleaned through social interaction would have to wait.

Some questions that were common elsewhere were not taken up by the Clionians, so we must elicit meaning through absence. Direct questions about local and state-level politics, slavery, emancipation, and laws related to sectionalism were frequent in debating societies throughout the nation.[38] Although it is probable that discussions of slavery arose during debates among the Clionians on questions about the U.S.-Mexican War or the expansion of U.S. territory, such details were not recorded in the minutes.[39] The society's records did not mention controversial topics such as the Fugitive Slave Act of 1850 or the *Dred Scott* decision of 1857, and the terms *slavery*, *emancipation*, and even *the South* were absent.[40] Why? Did the Clionians fear that their records might fall under the surveilling eyes of enemies? Did they envision retaliation by local whites? Did they wish to avoid fostering ill will among themselves, since their families were both slaveholding and nonslaveholding? Or did they wish to use the comparatively safe enclave to practice their argumentative skills on questions that did not hit so close to home, to perform freedom *from* the ever-present culture of slavery?

Silence is suggestive but not conclusive. In addition to questions of slavery and sectionalism, the Clionians did not debate common topics such as dueling, the political rights of women, or the value of theatrical entertainments, although they did debate Indian removal and capital punishment, two of the most common issues for debaters nationally.[41] If, as Drago observes, the Clionians did not discuss dueling because Charleston's "free black elite could ill afford to indulge in dueling or pander to its code of honor," then it is also true that political participation was elusive for the men as well as the women of this community, and religious activity was of more overt significance than entertainment to many of these young men.[42] Yet personal salience was clearly not a primary rationale for choosing debating questions.

One can imagine, however, the possible import of a question such as "Emigration: does it tend, or has it ever tended[,] to the advancement of civilization?" The Clionians debated this topic in 1852, concluding with a negative verdict. *Emigration* was a term frequently used to describe not only the colonization of African American people in other parts of the world but also the exodus of free persons of color from the slaveholding South. Two years before, a Clionian member had introduced the subject of "having Diplomas to present to members that may in time leave the State." Later in 1852, a member wrote from Philadelphia to resign, saying that he "had left the State 'probably for life.'" Departures of free black Charlestonians would become common through the late 1850s and early 1860s. Yet the 1852 debating question was framed in such general terms that it might have invited a discussion of foreign immigration to the United States, an ordinary topic among antebellum debaters.[43]

Although the Clionians' extant records are reticent about rationales for the choice of questions and the development of arguments, they do provide frequent hints of the emotional dimensions of debating activities. The questions are earnest, but society secretaries inscribe a sense of youthful zeal, not deadly solemnity. Records refer to the "spirited," "animated," or "heated" nature of the debates, or they claim that only the onslaught of time prompted debates to end. For example, in 1851 Henry Cardozo, then the society secretary, reported a debate continued from the previous meeting: "In a short time," he noted, "the heat of the former debates [was] rekindled and fresh fuel being now added thereto, created a flame, which would have continued to spread, were it not that that powerful Engine—Time arrived and quenched its glowing ardor."[44] Whereas local curfews imposed on Charleston's black population made clock-watching vital for these young men, society secretaries tended to reframe the fact of legal restrictions into a commentary on the members' passion for debating. Society records portray the members as devoted and enthusiastic, and they depict debate as a cooperative enterprise directed toward collective improvement, not violent competition. They only rarely use competitive terms such as *winner* or *triumph* to describe success in debate, and the term *victory* appears once, to refer to newly installed society officers who were described as "doubly nerved to fight the battles of Clio and lead her sons on to glorious victory"—a collective, not an individual, goal.[45] Debates are "heated," but "harmony," "union," and "brotherly" camaraderie are posited as common features of meetings. Society records use metaphors of soldiery and of statesmanship, but like the militant metaphors of scripture, they recur to a collective mission, to fight "the good fight of usefulness to ourselves and to others."[46]

Warriors and Statesmen

The value of speech and debate as education for citizenship is frequently heralded as a rationale for rhetorical pedagogy. The story of Simeon W. Beaird supplies support for this posited linkage, as it highlights the power of civic education as preparation for participation and leadership in religious, educational, and political forums. At the same time, Beaird's exceptional historical circumstances place into high relief the conditions of opportunity that are necessary if speech and debate are to contribute to civic involvement. As an individual privileged by his gender, his free status, and the temporary political circumstances of Reconstruction, Beaird had access to settings in which he could develop and utilize his rhetorical abilities productively.

Conversely, the history of the Clionian Debating Society calls attention to the uncertain value of speech and debate education in oppressive environments where full citizenship is granted only to some and opportunities for civic participation are limited. Beaird and his fellows in the 1840s and 1850s likely imagined themselves becoming leaders within Charleston's free black community, but they were decisively not included in discourses of national democracy like that trumpeted in 1856 by San Francisco's *Daily Evening Bulletin*, which urged young (white) men to participate in a debating society because "in a country like ours, . . . every man may be called upon to take part in the great national assemblies."[47] As the Clionians debated questions involving national legislation or the prospects of war, it is unlikely that they perceived their activities as direct preparation for future military or legislative vocations. What, then, were they doing?

Their records emphasized the value of individual learning and communal service, and they demonstrated a commitment to reading, writing, study, and the generation of argument within clear procedural frameworks. The records did not imply, however, that the Clionians deployed Western educational forms, such as an emphasis on classicism, in an attempt to build an alliance with white power. In an era when standard scholarly works—such as French historian Charles Rollin's *Ancient History*, which the Clionians purchased in 1850—made uncontroversial arguments about the influence of Egyptian learning on ancient Greek culture, and when Greek and Roman classics were taught broadly across lines of class, gender, and race, a fascination with antiquity could lay claim to the heritage of world culture generally, not circumscribed by individual circumstance but owing to curiosity and imagination.[48] In 1903, W. E. B. Du Bois would write in *Souls of Black Folk*: "From out the caves of the evening that swing between the strong-limbed earth and the tracery of the stars, I summon Aristotle and Aurelius and what soul I will, and they come all graciously with no scorn nor condescension. . . . Is this the life you grudge us, O knightly America?"[49] Read beside the poetic genius of Du Bois, the everyday records of the Clionian Debating Society from fifty years earlier resonate with a similar impulse. The group's activities illustrate what Darlene Clark Hine and Earnestine Jenkins call some of "the myriad ways in which slaves and free people in the Americas, against all odds, kept alive the will to survive, for themselves and their descendants, with their humanity intact."[50]

The Clionians' records imply that they practiced speech and debate as a collective, experiential affirmation of their humanity as intellectual beings: for themselves, for each other, and for Charleston's free black community. In the Clionian Debating Society, these young men could learn and practice the skills of verbal combat and cooperative deliberation. They also could experience the delight of intellection within a supportive context. People from any historical moment who love learning can recognize that the thrill of shared discovery does not require an orientation to the future. The practical benefits for individuals like Simeon Beaird are clear, but we can also imagine that, for the youthful Beaird and his fellows, pursuing knowledge in society, not solitude, was not just practice for an unimagined future but also an experience of joy.

2

RENEWING A "VERY OLD MEANS OF EDUCATION":
CIVIC ENGAGEMENT AND THE BIRTH OF INTERCOLLEGIATE
DEBATE IN THE UNITED STATES

JAMIE MCKOWN

Intercollegiate debaters are known for their research acumen. Many will not hesitate to spend thousands of hours delving into one particular topic, only to repeat the same process the next year. Yet one subject seems to elude their gaze: the history of their own activity. Aside from a few well-known stories passed down over the years or an occasional discovery in a college archive, we actually know very little about how intercollegiate debate got started. What historical accounts do exist have often focused on case studies of convenience: those anecdotal or disconnected examples which provide the most visible and accessible materials. However, reliance on such a small number of examples makes it difficult to get a wider view of the curricular and cocurricular contexts in which intercollegiate debate first emerged.

Some assume that intercollegiate debate simply developed in the United States alongside other similar activities, such as literary societies and oratorical contests. After all, a substantial body of work already exists that documents the development of oratorical instruction, broadly defined, at educational institutions throughout the United States. Perhaps we can assume that the development of intercollegiate debate was part of these larger trends. Yet these accounts fail to explain why debaters "went on the road" to face teams from rival schools. More importantly, these broader accounts cannot speak to how the emergence of this particular form of debate left a distinctive mark on the educational landscape around it. To do that, we need to develop a richer understanding of intercollegiate debate on its own terms, independent of other activities that were taking place at the time.

In the spring of 2014, we began a systematic project to identify, document, and map the earliest years of intercollegiate debate in the United States.[1] While this remains an ongoing project, several themes have already emerged in the initial stages of our work. There is little doubt that intercollegiate debate, when it first emerged in the last decade of the nineteenth century, had an immediate and significant impact on the educational environment of those institutions where it initially took hold. This impact was distinctive and directly correlated to the features of intercollegiate debate that differentiated it from earlier forms of speech and debate on college campuses.

Most significantly, the birth of intercollegiate debate brought with it a renewed student interest in the study of public discourse and its relation to the broader political world. At the same time, the specific demands of this new form lent themselves well to—perhaps even necessitated—a particular pedagogical approach that stressed the critical faculties that could be developed through the study of rhetoric, argumentation, and public address. Intercollegiate debate became popular precisely because it pivoted away from the instructional focus on elocution, style, and oratory that had fallen into disfavor in the previous decades. Instead, the emergence of intercollegiate debate would signal a return to what Columbia University professor of rhetoric Charles Sears Baldwin once called a "very old means of education,"[2] one that renewed the idea that effective civic education was predicated on critical engagement with public discourse.

What follows is a preliminary overview of some of the dominant themes that emerged from our study. I first review the existing accounts of debate that laid the foundation for our work. I then briefly describe our project and some of the initial results of our cataloging efforts. I close with some conclusions that have begun to emerge from our qualitative survey of student and faculty accounts of the period.

Debate in the Early Years

Only a handful of accounts document intercollegiate debate as it emerged as a distinct practice in the United States. While they serve as good starting points, these existing accounts leave a great deal of the earliest days of the activity unexamined. One of the most notable attempts to systematically catalog the breadth of these activities can be found in Egbert Ray Nichols's 1914 edition of *Intercollege Debates*.[3] This "yearbook" includes an extensive appendix that lists early forerunners to more modern intercollegiate debate "leagues." Unfortunately,

Nichols's work tells us little about the context that gave rise to these debate arrangements. These organized debating relationships did not emerge overnight, but Nichols provides very little historical background prior to 1910.

To get some idea of how intercollegiate debate emerged prior to 1910, one must turn to David Potter's 1944 work *Debating in the Colonial Chartered Colleges: An Historical Survey, 1642 to 1900*.[4] Many contemporary accounts of oratory and debate as educational practices have relied on Potter's work for their understanding of the development of intercollegiate debate.[5] The bulk of Potter's study charts the rise and subsequent decline of both syllogistic and forensic debate within the classroom, as well as extracurricular literary and debating societies. In the final pages of the work, Potter briefly summarizes the growth of intercollegiate debate beginning in the 1890s.

According to Potter's account, the traditional literary and debating societies that had been active during the early and mid-nineteenth century fell out of favor and gradually withered in the two decades following the Civil War.[6] However, a renewed interest at the close of the century breathed new life into the practice of debate. This new interest resulted from a series of well-publicized debates between Harvard and Yale in the winter of 1892. While Potter concedes that at least two debates between Rutgers and New York University had previously taken place, these high-profile debates produced a rapid explosion of interest by other schools wanting to emulate the Harvard-Yale (and later, Princeton) model.[7] Other schools quickly moved to set up similar debate exchanges. By the turn of the century, Potter notes, intercollegiate debating would be ready for its "coming of age."[8]

Potter's work serves as an instructive starting point, but it is limited in what it can tell us about intercollegiate debate throughout the United States. It was, by Potter's own admission, far from a systematic accounting of the period. Potter restricted his initial survey to the original chartered schools of William and Mary, Yale, Princeton, Columbia, the University of Pennsylvania, Rutgers, Dartmouth, Brown, and Harvard. Beyond these institutions, we have little to go on. Furthermore, while Potter's work situates the rapid growth of intercollegiate debate after 1892 in the context of broader forensic activities, he doesn't consider how this newly emergent form of debate brought with it a set of distinctive features that potentially set it apart from those activities.

Documenting the Early Debates

In order to fill these gaps, we began a project in early 2014 to pick up where Potter's work left off. Our primary goal was to systematically document and catalog the full range of intercollegiate debate activities that began in the late nineteenth century and continued into the first decade of the twentieth century (at which point Nichols picks up the story). In doing so, we hoped to more thoroughly document Potter's claim that intercollegiate debate did not become popular in the United States until after 1892. A second related goal of the project was to ask what, if any, impact this new form of debate had on broader institutional and educational practices at colleges and universities. Was there something qualitatively distinctive about the practice and form of intercollegiate debate that set it apart from its predecessors and potentially transformed its relationship to the broader curriculum?

The obvious first step in this process was to build a dataset of individual instances of documented intercollegiate debate prior to 1910. For the initial stage of this data collection, we relied primarily on digitally archived newspapers as our main source of information. From there, we began to incorporate material from digitized institutional databases at various colleges and universities as well as other relevant archives. In the process we quickly discovered that student-produced newspapers, bulletins, yearbooks, and magazines were excellent resources not only for cataloging debates but also for providing a more detailed perspective on how the debates were organized. Our current efforts have documented 986 intercollegiate debates involving more than 256 institutions that took place prior to 1910.

While the collection and systematic analysis of this dataset is ongoing, there are several identifiable trends that stand out and provide productive avenues for future research. Most notably, our work has tended to confirm Potter's original accounting of the first years of the activity. The Harvard-Yale debates of 1892 clearly mark the beginning of a rapid growth in intercollegiate debate in the United States. This does not mean that intercollegiate debates did not take place before 1892. However, our findings suggest that they were sporadic and scattered. Of the 986 debates we have documented, only 13 took place prior to 1892. Furthermore, these 13 are stretched over a twenty-year period.[9] None of these activities seems to have generated the same type of rapid and expansive interest in intercollegiate debate that emerged after 1892. There is also little doubt that the visibility of the Harvard-Yale debates contributed to its rapid emulation by other institutions. These annual debates were covered extensively by the national media, as well as by various student-produced campus publications across the country. While further data collection and network modeling may one day give us a clearer picture of the pathways through which debate emerged and spread from institution to institution between 1892 and 1910, the more qualitative contours of the practice as it diffused through individual institutions tell us something about the impact it had on the educational practices of the time.

The institutions we examined for this project vary greatly in terms of mission, philosophy, size, location, prestige, student base, financial resources, and previous traditions of debate and oratory. As such there are many outliers that do not fit easily into broader characterizations of intercollegiate debate during this period. However, our work suggests that it is possible to generalize about how intercollegiate debate after 1892 differed from the debate activities that came before it. Indeed, the popularity of intercollegiate debate after 1892 was predicated precisely on how it differed from the older traditions.

A Renewal of Debate

The single most obvious impact that the rapid rise of intercollegiate debate had on the broader educational world was a dramatically renewed interest in all things related to debate. Intercollegiate debate's rapid growth in the short span of a few years was not the culmination of some long-simmering interest in the activity before 1892. In fact, it was just the opposite. The well-documented decline of literary societies in the late nineteenth century had brought with it a decline in society debates. College and university publications from the period consistently worried that interest in literary society participation, as well as the quality of the debates they produced, were waning. Campus debates generally were not well attended, and they were criticized for their excesses of oratory and elocution. This led to a concurrent deemphasis on "oral expression" within the curriculum.[10] As one Columbia professor remarked, the older oratorical traditions of past decades were now "wholly out of sympathy with the new ideals of the modern college world."[11] Interest in debate and other forensic activities hit a low point.

The resurgence of intercollegiate debate after 1892 reversed this trend. Debate now became one of the most venerated extracurricular activities. What made such a dramatic turnaround possible? Part of the answer lies in the nature of intercollegiate debate itself. Like intercollegiate athletics, the competitive nature of the activity sparked broad student interest rooted in pride for one's home institution. Local and regional media quickly borrowed the rhetoric of "rivalry" that was already commonplace in reporting on intercollegiate athletic events. Similarly, many reports suggest that alumni actively attended debates and "rooted" for their teams, some even agreeing to sponsor or host debaters. While intersociety rivalry had generated interest in past debates, this paled in comparison to the enthusiasm generated when colleges competed against each other.

The high-profile visibility of post-1892 debates also dwarfed the earlier literary society activities on campus. In years past, members of the literary societies would stage periodic intrasociety debates within larger programs of oratorical exhibition. They would also, on occasion, host a competition between the best debaters from the rival societies. These intersociety debates were often associated with ceremonial events such as graduation. However, the new intercollegiate debates were of an entirely different magnitude of visibility. They nearly always took place in much larger venues, including public venues off campus. The audiences for these debates were much larger and more diverse. Local community members, visitors from the rival school, alumni, and dignitaries often attended. The debates often included high-profile guests and judges. During the two decades we surveyed, it was not uncommon to have a sitting governor, senator, state chief justice, or even a former president act as the presiding officer for the debate. Media coverage—both regional and, at times, national—was equally common. Just two years removed from their first debate, the president of the Harvard Debating Union speculated that "college papers now give double the space, and the University at large now pays twice the attention to public speaking."[12] Campus publications at the time suggest that the excitement generated by this new activity far exceeded that produced by traditional literary society activities.

Given both its visibility and the added elements of "rivalry," it is no wonder that this new activity quickly caught fire. Intercollegiate debating became the pinnacle of nonathletic extracurricular activity on campus. Student editorials suggested that intercollegiate debates had become a barometer of the intellectual health of the institution and the quality of education. Likewise, being selected to the intercollegiate team became one of the highest honors to which a student could aspire. It was not long before students began to clamor for more institutional resources to help them compete against their debate rivals. This included not only calls to hire the first real debate coaches but also a growing interest in debate instruction within the curriculum.

Shifting the Locus of Debate

While the excitement surrounding these early intercollegiate debate events did translate into a renewed student interest in all forms of debate activities, this did not necessarily benefit those institutions and practices that traditionally had been associated with debate. For instance, there is evidence that the growth of intercollegiate debate in the 1890s actually had a negative impact on other forensic activities. Intercollegiate oratorical leagues had been hosting regional tournaments long before intercollegiate debate became widespread. While there were some early attempts to integrate intercollegiate debate into these existing oratorical leagues, none appear to have been successful.[13] Unlike today, the model of intercollegiate debate that was becoming popular in these early years did not lend itself to the tournament structure that oratory had developed. The oratorical associations simply were not able to allocate the requisite time for the lengthier format of six-person intercollegiate debate. As such, these new intercollegiate debates developed independent of the existing structures of oratorical competitions.

Furthermore, while they remained popular in certain regions of the country, many students and educators had already begun to see these oratorical contests as remnants of a dated and excessively grandiloquent mode of rhetorical training. For these critics, intercollegiate debate was a more relevant and salient mode of speech, one that was suitable for a new era of civic engagement and professional life. A Minnesota student, reflecting on why so many orators were leaving the activity for debate, noted: "They feel that the benefits derived from entering oratorical contests are too insufficient to pay for the trouble. They get almost no practice in public speaking. Most of the time is taken up memorizing and in giving the oration an artificial polish, much more ornamental than useful."[14] As a practical matter, intercollegiate debates also offered the chance to perform in front of a much larger audience. With their centralized tournament systems, the oratorical contests typically took place before much smaller audiences. Furthermore, the on- and off-campus media coverage of intercollegiate debates quickly eclipsed reporting on these oratorical tournaments. As students flocked to participate in debate, participation in oratory declined, as did the quality of the product. As one student noted, the intercollegiate debate contest had "superseded everything else. Oratorical contests have been relegated to the past."[15]

Similarly, this new renewed interest in debate did little to reinvigorate the literary societies that had once served as the primary vehicle for oratorical and debate activities. While they may have benefited initially from this interest, the distinctive features of intercollegiate debate worked to systematically undercut the status of these societies. In part, this had to do with how debaters were selected. If a college or university was going to send their best debaters to compete against a rival, it would need a process for selecting those debaters.

Elaborate systems of preliminary debate rounds were established in order to select students to represent the institution. In many instances (especially early on), the literary societies would play a role in this process. Intrasociety debates were used to determine which members would enter the preliminaries for the intercollegiate contest. While this generated some renewed interest in the society events, over the long term this preliminary system began to erode the primacy of the literary societies. As students expressed concerns that everyone should have a chance to compete in the preliminary debates, the gatekeeping function of the society events declined.

Perhaps more importantly, the intricate planning required to stage an intercollegiate event necessitated the creation of a new governing body. These early debates often involved a series of lengthy negotiations over rules, topics, judges, and financing. The debate over these debates could become quite heated and would often play out publicly in the local media. As such, there arose a need for governing entities that could represent the best interests of the whole campus, not just one literary society. Furthermore, college administrators were cautious about trusting this responsibility entirely to students. Faculty members (typically ones associated with debate and rhetoric) were thus asked to lead or advise the new debate committees. While there was a great deal of diversity across institutions, most schools engaged in intercollegiate debate had, by the turn of the twentieth century, created some type of governing entity tasked with both negotiating the terms of debate and selecting their teams. Over time, these new entities expanded their reach over other forms of debate on campus. The next step in this process would be the creation of a unified debate union, club, or society that would be connected in some way to the governing entity. These new clubs or societies would focus primarily, if not exclusively, on intercollegiate debate without having to worry about the other social obligations often associated with traditional literary societies.

Perhaps most notable within these shifting dynamics is the increasingly important role of debate faculty. The growing interest in intercollegiate debate led to student calls for additional curricular support, which led to the hiring of faculty who could serve as both teachers and coaches. It also encouraged institutions to assign faculty new responsibilities for overseeing preparation and planning for debates. The relationship between curricular and extracurricular debate thus became more intertwined.[16] In some cases, institutions hired recent graduates to serve as nonfaculty coaches. However, the growth of interest in intercollegiate debate also promoted new faculty hiring in the areas of argumentation and rhetoric. It also resulted in calls for additional courses in debate and argumentation by existing faculty. Rather than return to the oratorical techniques of the past, these new courses emphasized a new type of debate instruction tailored to the activity as it was currently practiced—a pedagogy that arguably signaled a return to a much older past.

A New Kind of Debate Activity

One of the clearest trends that distinguished this new practice from the past involved the nature of the topics being debated. Presumably in an effort to garner significant interest from both the students and the broader community, debate organizers privileged topics that involved timely issues that were familiar to the public at large. A "successful" intercollegiate debate was predicated, as one organizer noted, on having a "live issue."[17] Nearly all of the topics involved matters of public policy—foreign and domestic—that were in the news at the time. This development is especially striking when one considers the broad range of topics that were debated in the past. While past debates periodically addressed contemporary policy controversies, they more often focused on "value" topics involving abstract ideas or statements of fact. In some instances, debaters were called upon to draw from their own philosophies and opinions. For instance, a debate topic in the 1850s might have been: "Resolved, that ambition is a stronger incentive to action than fear."[18]

This difference in topic was directly relevant to practices of preparation. The abstract nature of literary society topics would be better suited to the often limited or extemporaneous style of preparation. Students could draw from material covered in their regular coursework or from personal experience as "evidence" for their claims. In contrast, an intercollegiate debate topic on a timely policy issue required students to go beyond the information they had acquired from their coursework. It often necessitated extensive outside research. In this sense, it was not simply the topic but the time and energy spent preparing for the debate that differentiated the new intercollegiate debate from its previous incarnations. An overwhelming number of the accounts we surveyed, from both students and educators, pointed to this as perhaps the most significant change ushered in by intercollegiate debate.

In earlier decades, a debate might be only one of a series of ongoing literary exercises that students would be expected to participate in as members of a literary society. Debate then evolved to the event that everything else led up to. The topics for these new debates—themselves often the product of protracted negotiations—would be decided months in advance. Once settled, this topic would become the sole focus for everyone associated with the activity. Preliminary debates would be scheduled, often using the same topic for their rounds. Once the final team (along with alternates) had been selected, they would spend months researching the topic, writing briefs on the various issues, honing their arguments, and engaging in practice debates with "scrub" teams from their campus. This process became so intensive that many students began to request course credit for their efforts. The result was that debate-related activities became not only a vehicle to hone one's speaking skills but a way to explore a single topic in more depth than the traditional curriculum permitted. Indeed, some debate topics led to the development of expertise in an area barely touched upon in regular classes. As one Vassar student put it:

> The question chosen is always a comprehensive one and for ten weeks debaters and committee set themselves to a thorough and independent investigation of all its phases. Because they consider one question alone, they are able to study it more exhaustively and co-ordinate their material more completely than they are usually able in a course of undergraduate study. They apply the methods which it has been the aim of the college to teach and they apply them to a subject with which they are not familiar, the result being that powers of independent and original work are developed and that a new field of interest is opened to them.[19]

These were not debates during which students were expected merely to deploy information that they had acquired from their coursework. Instead, they demanded that students employ the habits of research and critical analysis they had learned in their classes to digest the complexities of an issue that was timely and relevant to the broader political world.

Thus, debate came to serve as a bridge between educational institutions and public deliberation. The confluence of larger venues, more diverse audiences, high media visibility, and timely policy topics meant that those involved in the activity also began to consider the impact of intercollegiate debate beyond the confines of the campus. In the past, even the most prominent debates between competing literary societies served primarily to showcase the talents of young orators and highlight the quality of their education at a particular institution. While the new intercollegiate debaters still were aware of how their performances reflected on the quality of instruction at their institution, the public nature of the event raised the stakes even higher.

Many of these debates drew audiences of five hundred or more, including residents of the local community, notable alums, and invited dignitaries. Furthermore, the transcripts of these debates (or, at least, a summary of arguments) were made public in newspapers and collected anthologies. In reading the accounts by the students and faculty who were involved, one is left with the distinct impression that they viewed these debates as contributing to broader public debates and to the civic health of the nation. No longer were debates viewed merely as performances demonstrating the educational accomplishments of students. Debate was now serving society by providing in-depth analysis of important issues for a broader public audience. Debate had become its own form of direct civic engagement. In lamenting a recent loss to rival Wisconsin, Minnesota professor of rhetoric O. W. Firkins gave expression to this view of debate's larger significance: "It remains only to express our acknowledgement to the young men who are performing a work of almost equal benefit to education and politics—a work by which the state and the college are made contributors to each other's welfare—the sign and foreshadowing of that happy time when all problems shall be rendered easy by the infusion of purpose into scholarship, and of culture into patriotism."[20] This idea that intercollegiate debate might contribute to broader political debates over important national issues in turn shaped how some educators choose to approach teaching debate.

Intercollegiate Debate as Civic Education

Given its rapid growth over such a short period of time, it is no surprise that intercollegiate debate had some ripple effects on the broader curriculum. From our survey of student and faculty accounts, a distinctive (though far from homogenous) pattern appeared, one enmeshed within a larger conversation about the nature of education in a "modern" democratic society. Among both its proponents and its detractors, there was wide agreement that intercollegiate debate had, at the very least, reignited interest in the broader study of what we might term *public discourse*. Future research might more directly tie this renewed interest to the broader movement toward public speaking instruction that led to the founding of the National Association of Academic Teachers of Public Speaking (NAATPS) in 1914. It is worth noting, however, that many of the founding members of NAATPS came from institutions that we found to be very active in debate during this period, including Northwestern, Iowa, Minnesota, Harvard, Wisconsin, and Illinois.

Our preliminary survey found at least some indications that the excitement and interest generated in the wake of the 1892 debates gave rise to new forms of debate instruction—forms that were shaped by the contours of this new type of activity. Debate instruction would evolve to include a much greater emphasis on argumentation, topic analysis, critical thinking, strategy, and the much-venerated rebuttal. However, while many advocates for this new form of debate were quick to criticize the stylistic excesses of the past, they also recognized that speech instruction had to retain some emphasis on the core principles of oratorical delivery. Students and educators alike worried about the dangers of overemphasizing logic and the bare accumulation of statistics.

Effective debate, at least in this new intercollegiate model, involved the synthesis of argument and audience adaptation in a way that balanced reason with the demands of persuasion. Students, it was argued, needed to focus less on the technical skills associated with style, memory, and delivery, and instead focus on those topics more directly relevant to invention: the analysis of a controversy, the articulation of arguments, and the crafting of an appeal that "fits" an audience. This meant forms of instruction that would not be "diverted from their main purpose by over-regard for abstract theories or oversensitiveness [sic] to literary effects."[21] Although there remained a great deal of variance from institution to institution, the arrival of intercollegiate debate would often spark calls for a new approach to rhetorical training, one that was perhaps most akin to Aristotle's "faculty of observing in any given case the available means of persuasion."[22] Perhaps this is what Professor Baldwin was referring to when he suggested that intercollegiate debate had led to the rediscovery of "a very old means of education which at present is once more new."[23]

The case of Harvard professor George P. Baker is particularly illustrative of how faculty responded to intercollegiate debate. Baker was instrumental in teaching debate and argumentation at Harvard during this initial boom period. As such, he was witness to how this new activity shaped curricular offerings. Eight years after the first Harvard-Yale debates, Baker reflected on how those debates had impacted curriculum. In "Oratory and Debating: Intercollegiate Debating," he wrote: "I am quite sure that the recent rapid development at Harvard of interest in the study of forms of public discourse would have been impossible in anything like the same amount of time without this swift and popular growth of intercollegiate debating."[24] Although Baker supported this development, he also expressed concern that students might conflate debate with all forms of public discourse and, as such, "misemphasize" the importance of debate at the expense of other forums of public speaking (105). Intercollegiate debate may have renewed interest in speech, but it was only one of many forms of public discourse. Baker also predicted, perhaps accurately, that this new form of debate competition might evolve into a "highly developed special form"—an "intellectual sport"— that would become increasingly disconnected from public discourse (105). He concluded that "constant vigilance" would be necessary "if some of the past evils of athletics are not to creep into this intellectual sport" (111).[25]

For Baker, productively channeling the excitement around debate meant constructing a curriculum that focused more on rhetoric and argumentation and less on the specific techniques one might employ to win a debate. Baker originally had been responsible for two advanced courses taught within the English department at Harvard. The first, English 18: Expository and Argumentative Composition, focused on principles of composition in written essays and was open only to upperclassmen. In addition, Baker taught English 30: Forensics and Debating. This class, apparently open to all students, also focused on argumentation, although the emphasis was on oral forms of delivery. It is notable that students were not allowed to take both courses for credit; they had to choose one or the other.

In 1900, Baker revised English 18, apparently in response to the rising interest in debate. Now called The Forms of Public Address, the course was opened to more students and covered the basic principles of argumentation. Once a solid base in argumentation had been built, the focus shifted to "a consideration of the various forms of public discourse," including "what, in the past has made those kinds of work successful" (116). In the process, students were asked to reflect on how one might adapt various arguments to different audiences. English 30 also changed, dropping "Forensics" from its title in favor of "Debate." The class was also now limited only to juniors and seniors who had previously taken English 18. This two-course sequence was meant to provide a broader grounding for the growing number of students interested in debate. They could participate in the debate seminar only after they had built a foundation in argumentation and the history of public address. When considered in the context of Baker's thoughts about the nature of intercollegiate debate, it becomes apparent that this shift in pedagogy was, at its core, as much about civic education as it was about debate preparation.

For Baker, the value of intercollegiate debate had little to do with winning competitions. From his perspective, courses that emphasized winning debates provided no benefit to those aspiring "to be leaders in public thought" (107). Instead, courses in debate and argument should "train youths to think seriously on questions of the day, striving to get at the heart of them, and to present the results of their thinking clearly and persuasively" (107). Effective persuasion in this broader context resulted not simply from the technical proficiencies of oratory but, more importantly, from the reflective development of skills in critical analysis and argumentative explication. Once students had briefed an argument, they would then be challenged to consider how it might be adapted to a variety of audiences. This "problem" of audience, Baker believed, would force debaters to think beyond their own limited viewpoints and, in doing so, "the whole broad field of persuasion" would open before them (106).

Baker's approach stood in stark contrast to debate instruction in the past. The danger of a curriculum that overemphasized eloquence was that it never confronted this "problem" of audience. Instead, it left students with "a fine hopefulness that constant assertion, combined with persistent ignoring of the other side, ... will carry them through to victory" (108). A better pedagogical approach would start from the assumption that "knowledge of the other man's case must be a prerequisite for any helpful discussion of topics of the day" (108). It was therefore not surprising to find Baker advocating the instructional practice of asking students to debate both sides of a question. He explained, "I put them on either side of a question because I am almost ready to say that the best thing which can happen to an undergraduate debater is to be put on the side of the question in which at the outset he thinks he disbelieves, for either he wakes up to know that, for good reasons, he believes it the stronger, or he is amazed to see how much basis the other man has for his opinion. In either case he has gone through a broadening process" (110). It is significant that Baker's point was not that such instruction would help students "win" debates. Rather, the goal was to better prepare students for the democratic world around them. The "broadening process" involved developing a healthy suspicion of one's own position, along with respect for opposing views. More so than previous incarnations, this new approach to intercollegiate debate, with its emphasis on the thorough explication of what Baker called the "topics of the day," prepared students for engaged citizenship.

Baker's approach to teaching argumentation and debate was premised on the realization that a majority of students taking his courses would never take part in intercollegiate debate. Instead, as Baker explained, he aspired to "produce in the public mind that ability to think clearly and fairly on important questions"—an ability essential to the civic health of a democratic system of government. Baker continued, "Surely, then, in working, even if slightly, for this clearer thinking on the part of the public, we are working for that larger and better citizenship which our increasing and very important duties so seriously demand" (117). For Baker, debate was not about honing the skills of oratorical performance, as in the past, but about cultivating habits of critical engagement with important public controversies among all students, not just debaters.

Not all institutions involved with debate adopted Baker's specific pedagogical approach. Nor was the appreciation for the activity universally positive across campuses. Nonetheless, even skeptics such as Oregon professor Henry Sheldon were optimistic that these new forms of debate instruction signaled something bigger, a new approach to public speaking that would improve the quality of public discourse. Elaborating on that connection between debate and civic discourse, Sheldon wrote:

> Intercollegiate debating, with its careful training and statement of facts, forms a valuable antidote to the tendencies of American stump speaking. A distinguished critic has referred to our national style as turgid and inflated, as marked by rhetoric which is Rhodian rather than Attic, overloaded with tropes and figures, and aiming to conceal poverty or triteness in the thought by profusion of ornament, and appeals to sentiment too lofty for the subject or occasion. It is when contrasted with such a style that we are able fully to appreciate the training which the college course in forensics and intercollegiate debate are offering to the youth of today. The careful preparation, the absence of display, the analysis of argument, lay the foundations for a new style of speaking.[26]

Sheldon's distaste for "display" was a common sentiment at the time. Among students, faculty, alumni, and even outside observers, there was a hope—perhaps naive—that the revival of intercollegiate debate after 1892 marked a new era in educating young people for more constructive engagement in the political affairs of "modern" society.

A Closing Window

Our initial survey suggests that the period following the Harvard-Yale debates of 1892 marked a watershed moment in the history of debate education in the United States. The previous half century had witnessed the gradual erosion of debate activities associated with literary societies. Students, educators, and the general public increasingly viewed the overly stylized oratorical practices of the literary societies as irrelevant to contemporary affairs. The wave of interest in debate that swept colleges and universities in the two decades after the Harvard-Yale debates reversed this trend, but only by completely reinventing the practices and models of debate instruction. Over time, the literary societies and oratorical associations previously associated with debate would be eclipsed by new debate organizations (called unions, clubs, or societies) whose sole purpose was to prepare students for intercollegiate debate competitions.

The new style of debate would (for a time, at least) be conducted in larger public spaces in front of diverse audiences. The topics discussed would be timely matters of public policy, issues ostensibly on the minds of the public audiences in attendance. The debaters would spend months gathering evidence, drafting briefs, sparring in practice debates, and thoroughly testing every avenue of argumentation on the topic. They increasingly did so under the guidance of faculty, some of whom were hired in response to growing student interest in argumentation, rhetoric, and public discourse. While the resulting curricular reforms varied from institution to institution, the distinctive features of this new type of debate lent themselves to a renewed emphasis on those elements of rhetorical instruction most directly relevant to civic engagement.

Yet even in the heyday of this movement toward debate as civic education, there were those who warned that the hypercompetitive nature of intercollegiate debate was pushing it toward an increasingly technical style, one that risked alienating broader audiences. It is striking how many of the concerns expressed then remain with us today. The hiring of full-time debate coaches was already provoking concerns about inequality between institutions, and some continued to raise questions about the pedagogical value of the activity. Ethical questions about what constituted "cheating" also emerged. Commentators noted that there was, at times, a tendency by some debaters to try to cram as much evidence into a speech as possible. Concerns about debaters talking too fast, with little regard for their audience, are hardly new.

Perhaps the biggest concern was the amount of time and energy required to participate in this form of debate. In their appeals for credit-bearing debate classes, students complained that participation in intercollegiate debate threatened to negatively impact their grades. Furthermore, some astute commentators noted that the general excitement surrounding intercollegiate debate on campus was not translating into more individuals wanting to participate in the activity. Indeed, the number of students actually "doing debate" was—at least at some institutions—declining. While this new type of debate placed greater emphasis on democratic deliberation and civic engagement, it would have little impact if fewer participated. While it would still be several decades before the emergence of tournaments and specialized judging, Baker's warning that the intense fervor surrounding debate could lead to a singular focus on winning at the expense of all other pedagogical considerations seems prescient.

The early formative years of intercollegiate debate provide a rich case study in the relationship between debate, civic education, and public discourse. Our ongoing project to document these early debates has just begun to illuminate those connections. This chapter highlights some of our initial impressions, and as such it is more of a starting point than a final statement on the topic. Nonetheless, it is clear that intercollegiate debate, as a specific practice that emerged at a particular moment in the United States, deserves closer examination for what it can teach us about the possibilities of debate instruction. Doing so will help us better understand both where debate is today and, more importantly, where we might want it to go in the future.

3

TAKING WOMEN SERIOUSLY:
DEBATERS, FACULTY ALLIES, AND THE FEMINIST
WORK OF DEBATING IN THE 1930S AND 1940S

CARLY S. WOODS

Debate is a vital practice in the history of speech education. As many scholars have noted, debate pedagogy also played a central role in the formation of the communication discipline in the twentieth-century United States.[1] At colleges and universities across the country, speech communication faculty often served as advisors to debating teams, working closely with students as they prepared for and participated in debating competitions. The process of teaching and learning about intercollegiate debate offered opportunities to research important public issues, craft argument strategies, and finesse oratorical skills. Accordingly, the journals of the early discipline were steeped in scholarly exchanges about debate instruction and practice. As William M. Keith explains, "the proper organization and judging of debate provoked fierce quarrels, in which the civic implications of pedagogical choices became clear."[2] For example, one such topic aired in the very first issue of the *Quarterly Journal of Public Speaking* was whether faculty advisors should focus on educating debaters or guiding their teams to victory.[3] This chapter spotlights another underappreciated dimension of faculty advising in twentieth-century debate history: the rise of intercollegiate women's debate teams and the importance of the faculty members who advocated for them.

What might we learn from women students and faculty coaches who took part in debate during a period predating second-wave feminism in the

The author is grateful for the Helen F. Faust Women Writers Research Award, which enabled her to travel to the Penn State Archives & Special Collections for this research.

United States, when women's presence in the activity and in higher education was greeted with suspicion? I argue that by coaching women debaters when resources were limited and stereotypical gendered attitudes prevailed, faculty advisors had a unique opportunity to push the boundaries of civic participation. Drawing from the archived testimony from debaters at the Pennsylvania State College (later the Pennsylvania State University) in the 1930s and 1940s, I develop broader insights about the historical experience of women in the activity and the role of faculty allies as coalition-builders who can use their positions of power and privilege to promote diversity in higher education.[4]

The Rise of Women's Participation in Intercollegiate Debate

The twentieth century ushered in unprecedented opportunities for U.S. college students to participate in intercollegiate debating. However, because debate was "created by men and for men," it was also characterized by a dominant paradigm of "white male hegemony."[5] Some women had participated in literary and debating society activities at coeducational institutions of higher learning since at least the 1830s, but institutional support for women debaters ebbed and flowed in the early twentieth century.[6] The experience of women students at the University of Nebraska–Lincoln offers a stark illustration of this oscillating relationship. They were active debaters in literary societies and even represented the university in interstate debates in the last two decades of the nineteenth century. In 1901, however, the debating association reorganized and voted to bar women from membership, thus enacting a prohibition that stayed in place on campus for forty years. Not until 1941 were women again permitted to try out for the debate team. They did, and two years later the University of Nebraska–Lincoln had an all-women's debate squad, as many men students were called to serve in World War II.[7]

In general, though, there was "rising interest in debate on the part of women students" across the country in the 1920s, which was coupled with increased institutional support through the creation of separate women's teams.[8] According to one survey of fifty-six institutions in the Midwest Debate Conference, forty-four had separate women's teams, and eleven had a separate women's debate coach or advisor in 1928.[9] These debate teams and their newly appointed faculty coaches encountered gendered assumptions about the activity, even as the number of women enrolled in higher education rose steadily.[10] The 1930s and 1940s thus represent a period of growth for U.S. women debaters, but one in which ideas about proper feminine behavior had to be carefully navigated. They accessed the benefits of civic education through debate while simultaneously contending with forces that would limit their participation, devalue their contributions, and raise questions about their very presence in higher education.

Remembering Penn State Debate

The Pennsylvania State College (Penn State) provides an ideal case study for probing the tension between the liberal civic ideal of inclusion and the lived experience of women students in debate during this period. As women students enrolled at Penn State in growing numbers during the interwar period, the debate team served an important role on campus.[11] Many students encountered the debate activity for the first time at the university, though a select few had experience with high school debate squads. The women who participated in Penn State debate during this period were predominantly white, middle class, and hailed from Pennsylvania or nearby states. As a large coeducational institution, Penn State fielded teams of men and women debaters for intercollegiate competitions, extension events for schools and community groups, and radio debates. Men and women debaters interacted socially and were united under the umbrella organization of the Penn State Forensics Council, but they largely kept their competitive endeavors separate. Clayton H. Schug was hired to coach the women's debate team in 1931. He remembered the 1930s as a time when the debaters donned "long velvet evening gowns" and "'fans' would pack the auditoriums" for debate events.[12] Eager audience members would even ask the debaters for their autographs. Under Schug's guidance, the women's team flourished. Only eight debaters participated in 1931; four years later, the team had seventy students on the women's debate squad.[13]

Schug was a persistent and perennial advocate for women's debate, struggling over the years to build the reputation of the women's program among students, faculty, and administrators. Though Depression-era budgeting and World War II rationing limited their intercollegiate travel, he fought vigorously for continued funding and promoted the team in the local and regional press. Media coverage, however, often fixated on how the debaters were bucking gender conventions. For example, consider the title of the feature in an alumni publication, "Varsity Debaters (Did They Ever Look Like This, Boys?)." The article juxtaposed a discussion of Penn State women's debate triumphs with photographs of three team members in traditionally feminine poses: their lips are painted, their hair is curled, and they look dreamy and demure. The suggestion is that *their* visages do not come to mind when one is asked to picture a varsity debater. The *Centre Daily Times*, the local newspaper in State College, framed a 1952 article on the Penn State women's debate team similarly: "[w]omen are notorious for talking much and saying little. But a junior at the College has found the perfect excuse for speaking out to her heart's content."[14] Outrageously, a news story purportedly aimed at lauding the accomplishments of the women's debate team begins by hurling a sexist insult to all women. The second line of the story is no improvement, as it belittles a star debater's participation in the activity as little more than an outlet for her idle chatter. Rather than providing a straightforward account of their achievements, reporters routinely used gender difference as a hook when writing about women's debate. They played on the idea that women were not typical debaters, and then used this frame to underline just how extraordinary it was that women were not only present but also competing quite successfully in the activity. Whenever he was interviewed, Schug used his platform to insist that women debaters were equal to their male counterparts in their ability to speak eloquently, reason logically, and argue persuasively. Nevertheless, the real news seemed to be that women were debating at all.

Schug remained in the position for forty years, coaching a total of 1,072 debaters over his tenure. As such, this man—perhaps ironically—was also the face of women's debate at Penn State, a constant and unwavering figure as generations of students moved through the institution in four-year increments. When he retired in 1971, many alumnae were inspired to write letters to commemorate his career. These letters were compiled in a scrapbook, now housed in the Clayton H. Schug Papers at the Penn State University Archives. As I surveyed these materials, I was struck by the powerful difference that faculty educators can make in creating environments that support and sustain women students.

It is important to note at the outset that Schug was no radical critic of gender norms—in fact, some of his views were quite traditional. Yet alumnae letters consistently lauded Schug for his actions in the face of overt (or covert) sexism. He made students feel like the gendered expectations of the period were not at odds with debating and, by extension, with other ventures into civic life. Schug's role in their education was multifaceted. As one class of 1939 debater summarized, he was not simply their professor, but also a "chauffeur, confidant, counselor, and always [their] friend."[15] These documents provide insight into the richness of students' debate participation in the 1930s and 1940s, and the ways in which that participation shaped their lives later on. Memories of the topics and specific competitions grew fuzzy with the passing years, but they repeatedly commented on how participating in debate under Schug's guidance helped them learn argumentation skills, build confidence, and develop their own feminist beliefs.

The first major theme in the alumnae letters was the enduring value of the debate experience. This sentiment was inflected with a range of anecdotes. Former debaters commented that the "self-confidence, self-command, and self-assurance" learned through the activity was more valuable than any other experience during their college education.[16] Other benefits of debate mentioned in the letters included practice in controlled and methodical thinking, experience in public speaking, an awareness of social problems, the ability to articulate a specific perspective, and the importance of conviction.[17] One alumna noted that she learned the life lesson that an appointment made was an appointment honored when road conditions prevented the debaters from getting to a public debate competition in a nearby town. Instead of giving up, they held their debate at Schug's residence, with Mrs. Schug serving as a sole audience member.[18]

Schug required the debaters to do extensive research, rewrite and rework their speeches, and practice repeatedly if they wanted a coveted space on the team.[19] Some debaters could recall the details of the knowledge learned on specific debate topics or in the course of competition, but the majority remembered the broader social elements of their participation, such as traveling to new cities, meeting like-minded friends, and encountering new ideas. For some, like Harriet Morgan Knauff, class of 1948, debate was a thread interwoven into a broader memoryscape of college life. As her rather poetic letter to Schug recalled, "Penn State to me was the roar of the Nittany lion, the giggles of girls in my sorority, the beauty of the campus in the surrounding mountains, [and] the challenge and satisfaction of women's debating."[20]

The alumnae also translated their debating skills into a vast array of careers and endeavors. While such skills were commonly conceived of as precursors to male-dominated careers in law, the ministry, or public affairs, women students in the 1930s and 1940s faced more limited career opportunities. When Schug was interviewed in 1945, he suggested that in addition to law and politics, debate served as important preparation for a career dominated by women—teaching—because it taught participants to keep their cool under pressure. Acknowledging that not all women of the period would go on to pursue careers outside of the home, he added that debate "will certainly make them better and more enlightened citizens . . . and more interesting and intelligent companions and wives."[21] These comments were prescient for some debaters. For example, Sara Bailey Wagner, who served as debate team manager during her time at Penn State in the early 1940s, confessed that her experience "has been used only in defense of self against two teen-aged children." She then added that "perhaps it will prove more useful as I defend my doctoral dissertation [in the Department of Education at Wayne State University] next quarter."[22] Rosalind Schnitzer Miller wrote that, in 1943, she anxiously made her way to the front of the classroom in Penn State's home economics building, "knees trembling, hands tightly gripping a few three by five cards, silently hoping that I still had a voice somewhere within me." Twenty-eight years later, she put the skills she learned that day to work as she commanded the classroom as an associate professor in the Columbia University School of Social Work.[23]

Beyond the home and the classroom, Penn State women's debaters reported that their involvement in the activity had helped them in a number of other arenas as well. They testified that they called upon their debate skills when they moderated televised political debates,[24] negotiated labor contracts,[25] and did social work with community organizations and clients.[26] Elsie Douhett Withey, class of 1935, sounded this theme in more detail than most, organizing her letter around the ways that Schug's teachings had benefited her postgraduation life. Her letter artfully repeats the phrase "you were there" in successive anecdotes: Schug's voice guided her when she later coached high school boys in debate, when she served as a health educator during World War II, as she advocated on behalf of food co-ops after the war, when she made waves in parent-teacher associations, and when she spoke to adult education conventions about individualized learning. Withey maintained that learning how to speak with conviction was the most important and enduring skill she took from debate. She joked about Schug's constant attempts to get her to stay within her time limits during her speeches, noting that the only reason she was able to win debates despite the penalties she accrued for going over time was the strength of her convictions.[27] Intriguingly, Withey alluded to the way that her participation in debate gave her the tools to pursue radical change, stating that it was Schug's "encouragement to 'speak out' [that] caused all the furor!"

Similarly, G. G. Rosen Michelson, class of 1945, said that there were probably many in the business world—and many husbands—who were secretly happy to hear that Schug would no longer influence generations of confident debating women, as "the ability to marshal one's facts, organize ideas, analyze logically, and to discuss clearly and concisely are things they could live without."[28] Although Schug may not have envisioned his coaching leading to dramatic social change for women in these diverse contexts, the comments of both Withey and Michelson suggest that the skills he taught often manifested themselves in actions subversive of prevailing gender roles.

In a related vein, the alumnae remembered debate in light of burgeoning social movements. After all, they had participated in the 1930s and 1940s but were writing their letters amid widely publicized feminist activism in 1971. As a result, several alumnae credited the activity with sparking a feminist awakening in them, framing their debate experience as an expression of liberal feminism and the gender politics that emerged later. Debate provided a forum in which women recognized power differentials and gender discrimination yet simultaneously felt empowered. Because their time at the university preceded the second wave of the U.S. women's liberation movement, they used these letters to make the connection. For example, Joan Huber, class of 1945, reported that Schug's retirement was a great loss in many ways, not the least of which was that it came "at a time when equality for women has surfaced as a public issue." Huber lamented that young women entering Penn State in the future would not be able to "work with a man who believed in equality for women when the idea was quite unpopular." She concluded, "I shall always appreciate the fact that Professor Schug demonstrated with his lifework the belief that women were worth teaching."[29]

Huber punctuated this point with an anecdote about how the women's team had been unfairly treated by the men's team during the war. Their travel budgets were distributed based on the sex distribution of the total student body, and because women outnumbered men in 1944, the women's debate team had a larger budget that year. The men tried to convince the women to share with them, and the women agreed, on the condition that the men would give them an equitable share of the budget once the war was over. The women's proposal was declined. For Huber, this incident was representative of the gender politics of debate at the time: women were permitted to participate, but no one would go so far as to give up some of their unearned privilege in order to treat them as equals. She still remembers "the sense of shock that the men who wanted fair treatment in 1944 didn't feel obliged to apply the same definition of fairness after the war." She felt sorry not just for herself and the other women debaters but for Schug as well: "I do remember that Professor Schug was clearly paying a heavy price for coaching women." She contended that he had suffered because although his teams were competitively successful, they had not been given the chance to debate in England, as the men's teams had.[30] The controversy over wartime debate budgets made Huber acutely aware of the struggles that Schug faced in advocating for women's debate over his forty-year career at Penn State.

Other debate alumnae were even more explicit in connecting the budding women's liberation movement with the themes they encountered as debaters in the 1940s. Ina Rosen Friedman, class of 1947, described how she pushed boundaries by performing a tap dance at the beginning of her speech "Actions Speak Louder than Words." The judges of the debate were none too pleased at her unorthodox performance, but Schug assured her that she was ahead of her time and that the judges just failed to see the brilliance of her innovation. In her memory, a word of praise or reassurance from her debate coach was worth more than a victory. Summarizing her feelings about the incident and her coach, she wrote: "Dr. Schug bullied us, irritated us, overworked us, but always, he taught us to give our best. He was the original Women's Lib guy."[31]

Jean Hootman Eisenhower, class of 1949, similarly remembered "the frown of the conservative disciplinarian," yet she too sensed something more beneath that frown: "We knew it always masked the pride and subtle humor of a man whose patience equaled that of Job." She remembered how Schug had "developed character in a group of embryonic 'Women Libbers' with ease."[32] In this sense, Schug's contribution to women's rights was not overt. It involved taking women debaters seriously in a university environment and a broader culture that did not treat them as equals. What these "embryonic 'Women Libbers'" did as a result of being taken seriously at this time is the truly intriguing part of this historical investigation.

The occasion of Clayton Schug's retirement in 1971 prompted cohorts of debaters to stop and reflect on what this college experience really meant to them. Collectively, these letters detail how even seemingly small acts of educational empowerment can make a large impact in the life trajectories of participants. Debating in the 1930s and 1940s enabled women students to develop a range of skills important for participation in civic life. These skills translated well to their future endeavors in many contexts—the home, the classroom, the business world, and so on. But more than that, their membership on the women's debate team in the 1930s and 1940s contributed to an emerging feminist consciousness among many of the debaters. While Schug was characterized as a "conservative disciplinarian" who certainly did not envision himself as an activist aiming to subvert gender norms, the women looked back at his advocacy for the team as a courageous act. Moreover, the rhetoric of women's liberation in 1971 yielded vibrant testimonies about the value of debate. The unfolding women's movement of the 1960s and 1970s provided these debaters with a vocabulary to articulate how debate had empowered them in an earlier period. In retrospect, they came to see how their liberation was ignited by an activity that inspired confidence and facilitated by a faculty advisor who thought that they were worth the time. In the next section, I argue that this history is also suggestive of what the pedagogical choices of contemporary educators might accomplish.

Women Debaters and the Promise of Civic Education

The period examined here represents something of a golden age for the expansion of women's debating. By the late 1940s, many programs across the United States noted a decline in women's debate as men's debate experienced a postwar boom.[33] Penn State maintained its sex-segregated teams, even as intercollegiate tournament debating increasingly allowed for mixed-sex competition. Women's debate advocates continued to use the argument that debate offered training in citizenship. In 1952, Emogene Emery wrote in the pages of the *Southern Speech Journal* that women's debate must not be left to languish. She maintained that colleges and universities should continue to recruit women students for the activity because they needed to learn how to navigate their roles as citizens in the postwar world: "Since she has the opportunity to voice her convictions concerning the political course of her country, state, and nation by exercising the right to vote, she needs to develop her powers of reflective and critical thinking if she is to meet the problems confronting her as a responsible American citizen. The debate situation creates the atmosphere in which such qualities can be developed."[34] In sum, Emery promoted women's debate with the idea that the activity would help them realize their potential as good citizens. If women were to exercise their franchise, they needed to do so wisely, and experience in debate could help develop the necessary wisdom.

Moreover, the argument for a more inclusive civic education is evident in the testimony of women debaters who used debate to navigate identity-based difference during this period. When I interviewed Mimi Barash Coppersmith, a Penn State debate alumna who graduated in 1954, she echoed the messages of her predecessors about debate as a protofeminist activity for women. She also underlined the social role that debate played in helping her as a Jewish woman, stating that "debate allowed me to feel equal. When I was young and Jewish, there were places I couldn't go to. But as a debater, I wasn't Jewish, I was a person."[35] Though it hardly solved all her problems, participation in the activity created a sense of civic belonging that could hedge against other forms of discrimination.

One of the ongoing issues in civic education is how to approach social diversity: Should it be embraced? Accommodated? Rejected in favor of the common good?[36] Discourses of citizenship served to justify women's presence in twentieth-century higher education as they enrolled in greater numbers.[37] This historical case study demonstrates how debate provided one means for women to embrace that rationale, as it had long been an activity lauded for its civic value. For students in the 1930s and 1940s, it offered the promise of inclusion, even as women experienced exclusion in many other arenas of public life. Participation in debate was significant because it equipped women with the tools to resist marginalization based on gender, and the letters of Penn State alumnae attest to the varied ways that they were able to put these tools to work in their postgraduate lives.

Citizenship, Sasha Roseneil argues, is a "troubling proposition for feminism." Although intensely "luring in its expansive, inclusionary promise," it is "inherently rejecting in its restrictive, exclusionary reality," and therefore it represents "an ambivalent object for those of us committed to radical social transformation."[38] So what can be done to make good on the inclusionary promise of citizenship? To be clear, my focus on Schug in this chapter is not meant to romanticize the past or create a "great male coach" narrative of debate history. Women debaters are clearly the central figures in counternarratives to the male-dominated paradigm of twentieth-century debate. However, there are lessons to be learned about the significance of faculty advisors in this history. Schug may not have been an exemplary "social justice ally" by today's standards, yet whether by choice or by default, he was ahead of his time when it came to advocating for women students.[39] The commentary about Schug's impact on the women debaters of the 1930s and 1940s should remind contemporary faculty educators of their potential as advocates for marginalized participants.

Today, sex- and gender-based diversity remains an issue of significant and ongoing importance in understanding speech and debate as civic education.[40] While historical parallels are never perfect, recurrent themes in testimony from past women debaters suggest *some* ways that we might make civic education more inclusive across multiple and overlapping differences. Speech and debate educators can send influential messages about who belongs in higher education. In the course of recruiting, mentoring, coaching, and teaching, educators can reach out to students who have been traditionally excluded from educational opportunities due to gender, race, ethnicity, class, sexuality, or ability. These messages may come in the form of micro-level acts of support, like the words of encouragement that Schug offered the women debaters, and in more coordinated and systematic efforts to encourage diverse participation in debate, such as the Women's Debate Institute, Urban Debate Leagues, and debate programs at historically black colleges and universities.[41]

This chapter details a powerful example of a faculty advocate who valued women debaters, insisted on including them in forums previously dominated by men, and battled to secure resources. This history of women's debate demonstrates how a simple act like taking women debaters seriously can reverberate through the decades in a number of unexpected ways. It is a strong argument for asking anew how we might continue to push the boundaries of debate as part of the larger effort to reenvision civic education in the twenty-first century.

4

THE INTERSECTION OF DEBATE AND DEMOCRACY:
THE SHIFTING ROLE OF FORENSICS IN THE HISTORY
OF AMERICAN CIVIC EDUCATION

MICHAEL D. BARTANEN AND ROBERT S. LITTLEFIELD

For nearly 125 years, competition in speech and debate has been justified by its role in preparing students for the demands of active citizenship. In recent years, that connection between forensics and citizenship has frayed, as the demands of competition seem to have overwhelmed the values of civility, rigorous argumentation, and balance among the rhetorical canons in Western theories of civic rhetoric. Thomas Merton observed that, "happiness is not a matter of intensity, but of balance, order, rhythm and harmony."[1] This chapter, grounded in our research into the history of American forensics, calls for striking a new balance between two styles of debate that have characterized different periods in the practice of competitive speech and debate in the twentieth century.[2]

The first period, the public oratory era, was a time when forensics emphasized the rhetorical canons of style and delivery.[3] This period was distinguished by a clear focus on forensics as a public good. During this time, the activity aimed at teaching debaters how to address what Chaïm Perelman and Lucie Olbrechts-Tyteca have described as the "universal audience."[4] The second period, the technical era, emphasized the canons of invention and arrangement, with the focus shifting to forensics as a private good and to the needs of the particular audience. Both eras had obvious strengths and weaknesses, but the complexities of modern society dictate that we find a new balance between the rhetorical emphases of these divergent views. In today's world, we need to reimagine debate and forensics in ways that can truly engage future generations of students, teachers, and audiences. We believe that this is possible only by heeding Merton's wisdom and identifying ways to mitigate the excesses of current practices by restoring balance, order, rhythm, and harmony to debate.

Our discussion proceeds in three sections. First, we analyze a framework for citizenship training within higher education, joining in the ongoing conversation about whether higher education ought to focus merely on career preparation or be an integral part of education for citizenship in a democracy. Second, we reflect on the history of competitive forensics and the two distinct eras in debate education, beginning with an earlier era when forensics was firmly grounded in citizenship education, then discussing how it later evolved to become a more technical and personal activity. Finally, we speculate on how striking a new balance between the public and technical dimensions of debate might reestablish a critical role for forensics in broader efforts to reform citizenship training in the twenty-first century.

The Role of Education in Citizenship Training

The relationship between education and citizenship training is ancient in origin and has roots in a wide variety of intellectual traditions. As Shirley Mullen, president of Houghton College, has written, "the link between civic responsibility and education has been taken for granted throughout much of history. Civic responsibility has been understood to be one of the appropriate ends of education, and education has been assumed to be necessary for civic responsibility to be well stewarded."[5] Historically, this relationship between education and citizenship has had two important limitations. First, it focused rather narrowly on the education of elites. Second, it assumed a set of commonly accepted societal values. As Mullen notes, these historical assumptions have been challenged over time as the diversity of those being educated has dramatically expanded and the consensus about shared values has dissipated. This is hardly news, of course. We live in a time when conflict about the very purpose of education threatens to overwhelm society's ability to balance educational opportunity with the broader social functions of learning. Should education focus merely on career preparation? Does the rising cost of higher education portend a return to the education of only the elite? Whose voices should be listened to and valued in the academy? Is higher education even worth the time and expense? These are critical questions, but they are questions with no easy answers.

There seems to be wide consensus that equal opportunity must be a core value of higher education, particularly in the United States. But the matter of higher education's social functions is much more difficult. Carol Geary Schneider, president of the Association of American Colleges and Universities (AACU), has identified the difficult balance that must be struck between opportunity and function:

> Policy and philanthropic leaders have clearly signaled a new determination to provide postsecondary education to many more Americans than ever before. Today, about one in three Americans have completed a two- or four-year college degree; the new goal is to increase that number to six out of ten Americans. This priority reflects a widespread understanding that the global economy places a premium on higher-level skills and offers dramatically lessened opportunities for those who lack them.
>
> Yet the new policy emphasis on "access and completion" has been strikingly devoid of any discussion about what today's students actually need to accomplish in college. To date, the discussion has focused on jobs and training; even the call for "higher-level skills" has been vague and underdeveloped.[6]

Schneider has identified two competing visions of the future of higher education: "civic mission discarded" (CMD) and "civic mission reclaimed" (CMR). The CMD model rests on the assumption that higher education should perform a strictly economic function, serving as a form of advanced technical training. The CMR view, in contrast, envisions universities that engage with their communities to address significant issues in a collaborative manner.[7] As the old saying goes, the devil is in the details, as it is hard to imagine, even in a for-profit world of higher education delivery, opposing the idea of education devoted, at least in part, to civic engagement.

How can higher education promote civic engagement? The solutions are varied and reflect many of the inherent issues in education, particularly those involving assessment, academic freedom, and cost. The first issue is how civic engagement can be assessed—an issue complicated by the fact that there is no single definition of civic engagement. Corey Keyes, Winship Distinguished Research Professor at Emory University, for example, argues that civic engagement involves both social commitment and personal growth:

> The purpose of civic engagement is not just to fix social problems. We're a nation that says you actually can be involved in helping engage the civic fabric of life, which awakens all sorts of good things in people: their sense

of contribution, their acceptance of others, the belief that they can make sense of what's going on in the world around them. Engaging in the civic fabric of life increases people's confidence to express their own ideas and opinions; it gives them a purpose in life. All these good things also happen to be the same things we look for to determine whether someone is functioning well and flourishing in life.[8]

The challenge of measuring that sort of outcome, of course, is formidable, especially in elementary and secondary education. In an age when quantitative assessment has almost become a form of tyranny, it may well be impossible to satisfy demands for measurable success. Nevertheless, the AACU, as part of an effort called the Core Commitments initiative, has identified five characteristics of personal and social responsibility that provide a useful starting point. Designed to facilitate efforts to promote civic education in schools, the AACU's assessment rubric focuses on personal and social outcomes that might be difficult to measure but are nevertheless essential:

1. Striving for excellence: developing a strong work ethic and consciously doing one's very best in all aspects of college
2. Cultivating personal and academic integrity: recognizing and acting on a sense of honor, ranging from honesty in relationships to principled engagement with a formal academic honor code
3. Contributing to a larger community: recognizing and acting on one's responsibility to the educational community and the wider society, locally, nationally, and globally
4. Taking seriously the perspectives of others: recognizing and acting on the obligation to inform one's own judgment; engaging diverse and competing perspectives as a resource for learning, citizenship, and work
5. Developing competence in ethical and moral reasoning and action: developing ethical and moral reasoning in ways that incorporate the other four responsibilities; using such reasoning in learning and in life[9]

These dimensions of learning allow concrete assessment but also are flexible enough to provide great latitude to local institutions in shaping curricula. No single pedagogical choice is appropriate for every institution—or, for that matter, every student. Colleges and universities can make choices that are consistent with their own traditions, values, and mission statements. Of course, there is one last consideration: cost. In an era when the rising cost of higher education is becoming a growing concern, institutions are under intense scrutiny and growing pressures to justify their curriculum in terms of return on investment. Presumably, the CMD model is a response to those economic pressures, but the case can be made that the CMR vision is a better long-term investment for higher education generally, and competitive forensics in particular.

Competitive Forensics as a Reflection of Competing Educational Visions

The debate regarding the proper role of education is hardly new, tracing back in Western philosophy at least to Plato and Aristotle. Disagreements over the role of debate and speech in education for citizenship are more recent, but they mirror that larger controversy. The history of forensics must be understood within the context of social change and the evolution of educational systems. In this section, we outline our argument, developed more fully elsewhere,[10] that the history of forensics is like a pendulum that has swung back and forth between an emphasis on private versus public goods. We posit that the future of forensics lies in finding a practical balance between the forces underlying the conflict between the CMD and the CMR visions of education. To invoke Merton again, we believe that balance, order, and harmony can be restored to higher education with curricula that emphasize both personal growth *and* the public good.

Competitive speech and debate competitions date back at least until the 1870s, and possibly earlier. The gradual decline in the appeal of literary societies, coupled with the emergence of residential colleges, created a critical mass of students seeking more robust academic opportunities. This helps to account for the relatively sudden emergence of interest in competitive debate, which first drew widespread public attention when Harvard debated Yale in 1892. By the turn of the century, debates were common at secondary and postsecondary educational institutions, reflecting the more vibrant public sphere of the Progressive Era. The draw of listening to people giving speeches and participating in debates was well established, dating back to the New England town meetings of colonial times. The study of rhetoric and argumentation also had a long history, as courses in classical rhetoric were common in colonial colleges and most of the nation's leaders in both the eighteenth and nineteenth centuries were well schooled in the classical tradition of argumentation and debate.

The significant change that occurred in the early twentieth century was the embrace of competition as both a means and an end. Educators immediately were drawn to competition as a motivator for students to critically examine public issues and delve deeply into their complexity. Writing in the *Quarterly Journal of Public Speaking* in 1916, for example, forensic educator W. H. Davis characterized competitive debate as training for "the wise disposition of important matters in a democratic society."[11] This educational justification has endured for generations and spawned many of the intellectual controversies over such matters as debating both sides of a resolution, the role of trained versus untrained judges, and the appropriateness of debating particular subjects.

These various controversies all arose out of concerns with how competitive speech might best foster responsible civic engagement. Those who advocated debating both sides of a topic, for example, touted "the educational value of doing more research and learning more" about important issues of the day.[12] Those on the other side, like Theodore Roosevelt, worried that learning to debate both sides might encourage *sophistic* rhetoric and lead to a morally "flawed democracy."[13] Both sides in this debate exerted considerable effort to influence competitive debate practices. In the end, so-called switch-side debating survived because prominent speech scholars, such as A. Craig Baird, argued that it allowed students to learn more about a topic without compromising their intellectual integrity or their political views: "The debating game properly played should not necessarily produce Sophists, archaic militants, or unscientific investigators."[14]

The tension between competition and civic preparation has also been at the bottom of controversies over who should determine the winner of debates. Advocates for the trained judge or expert critic identified competitive debate as an extension of the classroom, where mastery of specific skills should be the basis for the decision. This sort of judging could be done only by someone trained in argumentation and debate practices.[15] In contrast, if debate were, in fact, preparation for civic life, it only made sense to have ordinary citizens judge debates. In the public arena, we assume that untrained listeners should be able to discern which arguments were most relevant and make a decision about who won a debate. We presume some level of basic education and knowledge about civic affairs among general audiences in a democracy, but we do not presume they have specialized knowledge of the tests of good evidence or logical reasoning.

The choice of subjects to be debated also has been a source of controversy between those who consider forensics as a contest and those who believe that the activity should promote civic mindedness. Should students be required to take a side of a resolution that goes against the national interest of their own country? Or should they debate resolutions that go against the national interest (e.g., the 1954–1955 topic was "Resolved: The United States should extend diplomatic recognition to the Communist government of China")? As we have observed elsewhere: "The decision to debate a controversial resolution with no possible chance of being enacted by the Federal Government was a sign to many in the country that academic debate was more an elitist exercise than a method of exploring controversial issues in the context of creating good citizens."[16]

It would be remiss, however, to ignore one other part of the equation: that forensics was almost immediately valued by some for its competitive element. This element made many educators and participants uneasy for at least the first half of the twentieth century. Schools embraced the short-term benefits of competition, such as the publicity value of having success by defeating a rival school, while framing the competition as only a secondary concern. The nascent honorary societies (Delta Sigma Rho, Tau Kappa Alpha, and Pi Kappa Delta, later joined by Phi Ro Pi) each defined their activity and membership as a combination of competition, academic success, school prestige, and ethical behavior.

This disinclination to emphasize competition for its own sake staked out forensics as a public good which was best understood as an important means of citizenship training. The fact that students found it both challenging and "fun" was an added bonus.[17] As a result of this emphasis on citizenship, competitive forensics almost immediately became a force for social change. Women began to compete almost immediately, and historically black colleges and universities were early adopters as well. The idea that any debate team from any school—no matter how lacking in resources or prestige—had a chance to defeat the mighty Harvard Crimson was enticing in a nation obsessed with upward mobility. Such aspirations seemed natural in a nation beginning to assume a leadership role in the world with its successful war against Spain, the digging of the Panama Canal, and the defeat of the Axis powers in World War I.

We do not mean to paint an overly rosy picture of the early years of competitive debate and forensics. Squabbles over unexpected rule changes or the wording of resolutions were common. Concerns about the fairness of the judging pool, most frequently selected by the host institution, were also widespread. Racial segregation remained the norm for many years, and debates between white and black college and high school teams were rare. But the conditions for rapid growth and the public's embrace of forensics competition were right. Students clamored for trained coaches and college classes to improve their skills. The power of the elocutionary movement gave way to a more scholarly approach to public speaking, which in turn inspired speech teachers to break from English departments and create their own departments and professional organizations.

A new Pandora's box was opened with the introduction of the tournament format, most likely at Southwestern College in 1924. Prior to the advent of the tournament, debate competitions were rare and took much advance negotiation and planning. The few national competitions, such as the Interstate Oratory Contest and the Pi Kappa Delta Convention, were unique, with their own sets of rules and procedures. The tournament format created new fissures in the relatively stable forensics environment, where competition was only one of several values connected with the activity. The tournament began to dissipate the civic-centeredness of forensics and refocus the emphasis on the technical and personal benefits of competition.

After the introduction of the tournament, scholars began to tout the personal benefits of forensics in order to justify the need for more practice and a deeper commitment from participants. Efforts to standardize the activity with common rules and a single, annual debate resolution drove the activity at the national level. Significant cleavages in the activity quickly emerged. Voices decrying tournament competition became fewer and weaker in influence. The honorary societies became less influential in balancing competition with values such as academic performance, civic engagement, and ethical behavior. More students, representing more high schools and colleges, began speaking and debating in more tournaments in seasons that culminated in national events. This trend crowded out the emphasis on educating for citizenship, replacing it with more of a focus on winning competitions.

Of course, few openly admitted that the forensics landscape was evolving from an emphasis on personal rather than public values. Yet the trend continued as the speech communication discipline drifted further away from debate and forensics with its new emphases on rhetorical theory, persuasion, mass communication, and speech science. Another group of scholars and teachers was more explicit in condemning the growing emphasis on competition in debate, promoting a new subdiscipline of communication studies emphasizing dialogue and discussion. This emphasis resonated with academics and civic leaders who were becoming increasingly nervous about teaching confrontational approaches in the years leading up to World War II, the atomic age, and the Cold War era. Much of this evolution was so gradual, however, that it was largely invisible to a public that still thought of debate and forensics as citizenship training.

World War II was the key moment in the pendulum swing from public oratory to a more technical era in debate and forensics. Education, particularly at the postsecondary level, changed after the war. The Cold War brought a dramatic shift of emphasis toward scientific and technical training. As a glut of new students took advantage of the GI Bill, the number of graduate students and doctoral programs increased dramatically. In a time of the Cold War and a race to explore space, competition emerged as a core value. Television increased the pace of life and made the world seem smaller and more dangerous, while the Cold War became more than an abstraction, escalating into a frightful military and economic competition. The changing social and academic environment had an almost immediate impact on debate and forensics.

In the public oratory era, forensics activities typically occurred at a local or regional level. There was no national-level competition outside of the two events mentioned earlier, and the largest of those, the Pi Kappa Delta National Convention, was closed to nonmembers. In the technical era, national competitions dramatically increased, and along with that change came a rapid shift toward viewing forensics as a private good which benefited individuals and schools but only secondarily benefited society. Those involved with debate and forensics always assumed that the activities benefited the individual, but now the emphasis was on shaping smart, articulate, and dedicated competitors rather than good citizens equipped to participate in democratic deliberation.

The distinction between viewing forensics as a public versus a private good may be understood theoretically in terms of Perelman and Olbrechts-Tyteca's distinction between the "universal" and the "particular" audience.[18] As a public good, debate emphasized audience-centered advocacy appealing to the "universal audience," or an ideal, even imagined audience composed of all intelligent and competent people. Embracing this paradigm, judges were expected to represent a wide range of viewpoints, and they were to judge competitions in terms of the quality of arguments rather than the debaters' successes in winning a particular debate. As a private good, the focus is more on the "particular audience," and concerns about argumentation and speaking skills are subordinated to assessing, in particular debate rounds, which debaters marshaled the most effective claims, evidence, and rebuttals at that particular moment.

Put another way, the technical era in debate brought about a new emphasis on the strength of individual arguments by individual speakers in a particular debate or competitive round of public speaking. The primary emphasis shifted from "Who did the better job of debating?" to "Who won?" The idea that competition should take place in front of public audiences, or that it would be preferable to have a wide range of judges (including judges untrained in the intricate norms of contemporary speech and debate), became passé. On those occasions when debates were still held before public audiences, they became so highly scripted that they were more a form of entertainment than an exercise in civic engagement. In the increasingly technical world of competitive public speaking and debate, competitions became tests of intellectual dexterity rather than exercises in civic engagement.

Yet not all members of the debate and forensics community were happy with these changes. The technical era also witnessed a frenzy of organizational splintering, where teachers and programs chose "flight over fight" against norms and practices with which they disagreed. New organizations were formed in the hope that they might reestablish the historical link between forensics education and citizenship training. Eventually, many of these new organizations were either co-opted by their predecessors, or they succumbed to the pressures of competition that led to their creation in the first place. Thus, the splintering continued, with the dissenters breaking away again and again to form still more organizations devoted to reforming the activity. This cycle has led to the current state of affairs, where forensics as an organized activity consists of many small and fragmented groups pursuing their own visions and implicitly asserting their moral, intellectual, and educational superiority. Forensics has become a suburb of "gated neighborhoods," whose explicit and implicit actions discourage efforts to find common ground or promote a shared vision of the power of forensics as citizenship training.

Re-creating a Balance

We propose that forensics is not broken so much as its potentially transformative role in a robust CMR educational environment has not yet been realized. Thousands of high school and college students still compete, learn, have fun, make friends, and build their own self-esteem and confidence. Forensics is epistemic—a way of knowing and learning. Perhaps that is enough. Conversely, forensics holds a unique place as an educational form that has, for generations, successfully modeled experiential learning. It also has enjoyed consistent public support as a desirable student experience, and it has the potential to contribute to improved public discourse through the application of rhetorical skills that are not learned as effectively in any other context. The key is finding a balance between the public and private benefits of participation—a balance that might allow debate and forensics to become a key part of Schneider's CMR model.

There is an obvious fit between many of the AACU objectives for civic education and the benefits of debate and forensics pedagogy. Some of those objectives seem best served by the competitive model of debate, and others by a more civic-oriented model. Returning to those objectives, we might first reflect on how well the competitive model advances each of those goals:

1. *Striving for excellence: developing a strong work ethic and consciously doing one's very best in all aspects of college.* The competitive model of debate and forensics has excelled in this regard. The amazing success of the Urban Debate League experiment validates the relationship between academic success and competition.[19]
2. *Cultivating personal and academic integrity and acting on a sense of honor, ranging from honesty in relationships to principled engagement with a formal academic honor code.* Most competitive forms emphasize academic integrity through existing ethical codes and the checks and balances of competition.
3. *Contributing to a larger community: recognizing and acting on one's responsibility to the educational community and the wider society—locally, nationally, and globally.* This has been one of the possible weaknesses of the competitive model. The competitive model assumes that students learning the skills honed through competition will later use those skills to serve their communities. But encouraging a contribution to society outside of the competitive context is not part of the pedagogy of competitive forensics.
4. *Taking seriously the perspectives of others: recognizing and acting on the obligation to inform one's own judgment; engaging diverse and competing perspectives as a resource for learning, citizenship, and work.* Depending on one's perspective, the existing activity may or may not accomplish this end. While taking seriously the perspectives of others may be one of the ideals of academic debate, this may not be the reality of an activity sometimes dominated by arcane argument about unrealistic policy scenarios. Increasingly popular debate formats are also devoid of serious research obligations. Above all, the emphasis on winning may undermine the objective of truly understanding and empathizing with others.
5. *Developing competence in ethical and moral reasoning and action: developing ethical and moral reasoning in ways that incorporate the other four responsibilities and using such reasoning in learning and in life.* This is the

heart of the matter. To what extent does the existing competitive model encourage ethical or moral reasoning and action? Unfortunately, the perception—if not the reality—of the competitive model is that ethical and moral concerns have become secondary to the drive to "win."

Thus, we return to our original theme of seeking balance. Can there be balance between those elements of competition that attract and motivate students and those elements that prepare students for responsible, ethically driven civic engagement? We believe that there can, and we conclude with some suggestions for actions that might begin to restore that balance.

1. *Reintegrate competitive forensics into the university curriculum and reaffirm its centrality to a CMR vision for the future.* In the context of curriculum revision and general education reform, promoting critical thinking skills rises to the top of the list of desired outcomes. Debate and forensics provide endless opportunities for students to gather information, weigh evidence, formulate arguments, articulate positions, and respond to conflicting positions. If training citizens to be informed and think critically about arguments for or against particular policies and practices is a major goal of curriculum reform, then the case certainly can be made that forensics should be an important part of that conversation.

2. *Reconceptualize the reward system in debate and forensics to emphasize civic engagement.* The competitive environment of debate and forensics might be deemphasized by shortening the debate season, incorporating more diverse forms of activities, and making it more welcoming and accessible for underrepresented groups. The competitive model that rewards individuals for their mastery of particular skills has its place. However, the forensics community must reimagine the reward system to include civic engagement. At the high school level, the National Speech and Debate Association (formerly the National Forensic League) is leading the way with its emphasis on rewarding service and participation. In addition to modifying the reward system, the nature of the competitive environment should be changed. Shorter seasons do not necessarily make the activity less competitive, but they might encourage participants to try a wider variety of forensics activities. In addition, a shorter season might be attractive to those underrepresented students who feel they cannot focus on forensics at the expense of their academics, other extracurricular activities, or jobs.

3. *Significantly revise competitive standards to reestablish a balance among the rhetorical canons in competitive events.* The rhetorical canons of style and delivery provided the main bases for judging forensics during the public oratory period. While we would not advocate a return to those days, we do believe that a better balance between those canons and the canons of invention and arrangement that dominate today would provide a better, more holistic experience for participants in debate and forensics. An innovation being implemented in graduate programs across the country is the three-minute dissertation. Doctoral candidates in some programs are now being required to present a summary of their dissertation research in the form of a three-minute presentation designed for a nonacademic audience. Perhaps forensics could examine ways to add such an element to competitive debate: a final summary for a general audience. At the very least, judging standards should be revised to reward speakers and debaters who can effectively translate complex, multilayered arguments for the benefit of a general audience that may be unfamiliar with the topic. If we rewarded participants for clear, well-delivered speeches, it would provide better training for civic-minded students who hoped to someday communicate with real-world constituents.

4. *Reestablish a dialogue between the widely divergent members of the debate and forensics community to identify common interests and goals.* Debate and forensics could become a role model for the kind of organizational change that is needed throughout our society—change driven by passionate commitment but effected through collegial and respectful dialogue among participants with diverse perspectives. This is perhaps the most important thing the debate and forensics community could do to restore that necessary balance between competition and civic education. As American society has become more polarized, our public dialogue has become increasingly dominated by extremists unwilling to consider any point of view other than their own. The far left and the far right have drawn further apart, while the vast majority of the American people are left in the middle, feeling that they are without a voice or opportunities for meaningful communication. Similarly, the American forensics community has spent far too much time and effort separating themselves instead of identifying common interests and goals. Some promote competition for its own sake; others emphasize civic education and the public good. Both might modify their practices to realize

the benefits of both approaches to debate and forensics. Then we might begin a dialogue about finding the right balance for debate and forensics in the twenty-first century.

Conclusion

The challenge of finding balance between the private and public benefits of debate and forensics—and between competition and civic education—has been a part of conversations among forensics educators in the United States since the activity began more than a century ago. What makes this conversation even more pressing today is the growing concern about how to justify forensics at a time of growing competition for limited resources. Moreover, we live in an era of polarized public debate, where incivility and arguing at the opponent has replaced thoughtful and responsive interaction about critical issues of the day, pointing to the need to do a better job of educating young people about productive and ethically responsible democratic deliberation.

There is great promise in embracing Schneider's CMR perspective as the guiding principle for the forensics activity. This provides a framework for both practicing and justifying forensics at all levels and helping to rebuild trust in the ability of educational institutions to do more than simply train people for jobs, but to contribute to the public good.

We believe that restoring balance between the competitive and civic impulses in debate and forensics offers the best hope for the future—for both the activity itself and our political culture. Driven by economic pressures, colleges and universities have been cutting back on civics education, and those economic pressures threaten debate and forensics programs, as well. Yet more and more educators now realize that investments in civic education are among the most important investments we can make in our nation's future. By reminding ourselves of our roots in educating for citizenship, the debate and forensics community can play an important role in the movement to revive civic education in America.

PART 2
DEBATE EDUCATION AND PUBLIC DELIBERATION

5

PUBLIC DEBATE AND AMERICAN DEMOCRACY:
GUIDELINES FOR PEDAGOGY

ROBERT C. ROWLAND

Academic debate is often justified as a laboratory of democracy and a means of training citizens to participate in the rough-and-tumble of the public square.[1] In a review of the development of debate and forensics education in the United States, Michael Bartanen and Robert Littlefield noted "the powerful role played by speech and debate pedagogy in the creation and sustenance of democratic institutions." They added, "The practice of engaging students in speaking and performing activities stemmed from the belief that these skills would prepare students to be more engaged as citizens."[2]

The important role of debate in training engaged citizens was recognized as early as 1912, when E. C. Robbins observed that the "part debate has played in world affairs is seen on every page of history and it is one of the great educational forces." Robbins claimed that students who participated in debate "are the ones who later on are chosen by their fellow men to carry on the more difficult and important tasks in State and national life."[3] Robbins's thinking has been echoed in argumentation and debate texts for more than a century.[4]

In this view, debate teaches skills that are widely applicable to public life and essential in a democracy. It is not only argumentation scholars who defend the centrality of debate to effective democracy. Writing in the *Bulletin of Science, Technology and Society*, Mitchell Thomashow observed: "If we were to build a stone wall comprising the features of strong, participatory democracy, certainly we would include large boulders representing the importance of public debate and discussion."[5] Advocates of deliberative democracy make similar claims.

For example, Thomas Christiano identified a host of benefits, including "better decisions," that will accrue to "a society that promotes public deliberation."[6]

At the same time, the norms of academic debate are quite different from those in the school board, the legislature, or even political campaigns. To take only one example, unlike academic debate there are many times in public life that the most persuasive way of responding to the argument of an opponent is to ignore that argument altogether—a strategy that is especially effective if the argument can be labeled as extreme or esoteric. In the run-up to the invasion of Iraq, for example, arguments made by experts in the State Department received precisely this treatment from the Secretary of Defense, Donald Rumsfeld, and others. The result, as it turned out, was disastrous. At this point, then, those justifying the value of academic debate must ask: To what degree is debate training really pedagogically useful for citizens hoping to develop the real-world skills they need in political debate?

I argue that the key to justifying the pedagogical function of debate is to consider the role of debate in American democracy itself. Debate can be justified as a pedagogical form of citizen education by demonstrating that the skills it teaches closely map the skills needed by citizens participating in the give-and-take of deliberations over issues of public controversy at all levels of American government. The place to ground this analysis is with the man who more than any other created the blueprint for the American democracy: James Madison. Madison was the primary author of the Constitution and the Bill of Rights, along with many of the most important essays in *The Federalist Papers*, which is "generally considered the most important work of political theory in American history."[7] One of those essays, *Federalist* 10, is so important that "a consensus has emerged that it is the most important theoretical statement to come out of this era."[8] Richard Matthews referenced "Madison's now universally acknowledged importance in the founding of the American republic" and added that he is often labeled the father of the "Constitution . . . the Bill of Rights . . . political parties . . . [and] democracy" itself.[9]

Much of Madison's writing now seems quite dated, referencing issues that no longer have relevance. In a more fundamental sense, however, his writings about the key role of public debate and the skills that citizens need to participate are anything but dated. Madison was committed to creating a democratic society that would endure, but he also was a realist about the strengths and weaknesses of representative democracy. He recognized that the most important means of protecting the new nation was to create a system in which the give-and-take of public debate could, in the words of *Federalist 10*, provide "a republican remedy for the diseases most incident to republican government."[10] Colleen Sheehan observed that in his role as the "chief philosophic architect" of "the politics of public opinion," Madison created a "conception of participatory politics . . . to avert the problem of the tyranny of the majority," a conception that also "encouraged the communication of the citizens' views." He did so because of his belief that the "the communication of ideas and the refinement of views throughout the land" could "result in the attainment of 'the reason of the public,'" which he viewed as "the republican way to achieve impartiality in government."[11] In other words, Madison believed that public debate was the most important safeguard ensuring good governance.

In the following, I discuss the threats to representative democracy that Madison identified in his writings, and then argue that those same threats remain today. Next, I develop Madison's analysis of what Sheehan calls the "politics of public opinion" to explain how Madison envisioned a representative democracy employing the give-and-take of public debate as the "republican remedy" to the problems of a republican form of government. Finally, I build on that analysis to develop guidelines for what a productive form of academic debate might look like as education for citizenship.

Threats to Representative Democracy

The key to understanding Madison's theory is to identify how he accounted for the forces he saw menacing democracy. In *The Federalist Papers*, Madison isolated three related threats to democracy: the danger of factions and majority tyranny, the potential for leaders who were not wise, and a risk that public emotion and irrationality would lead to disastrous action.

Madison defined faction as "a majority or minority of the whole, who are united and actuated by some common impulse of passion, or of interest, adverse to the rights of other citizens." Factions were dangerous because "the most powerful faction must be expected to prevail."[12] One danger that he described in *Federalist* 62 was that factions would govern for their own interest, creating a situation in which "laws are made for the *few*, not for the *many*."[13] The danger that factions will make self-interested or ideological arguments for their own ends is clearly an inherent and quite contemporary risk in representative democracy.

Madison also was fearful that political leaders themselves might threaten democracy. He did not believe that legal or even constitutional restrictions—what he called "a mere demarkation on parchment"—would be sufficient to "guard against those encroachments which lead to a tyrannical concentration of all the powers of government in the same hands."[14] Madison's doubt about protections written into "parchment" was driven by his very realistic assessment of the likely character of future elected leaders. In *Federalist* 10, he observed mildly that "[e]nlightened statesmen will not always be at the helm."[15] He certainly was right about that.

Finally, Madison did not place great faith in the people. Much of *Federalist* 10 is about the danger posed by the citizenry. Madison cited several factors that could lead to dangerous actions, including a "zeal for different opinions concerning religion," "an attachment to different leaders ambitiously contending for . . . power," economic self-interest, and divisions that produce "mutual animosity." He recognized that this problem is endemic to democracy, observing: "So strong is this propensity of mankind to fall into mutual animosities that where no substantial occasion presents itself, the most frivolous and fanciful distinctions have been sufficient to kindle their unfriendly passions, and excite their most violent conflicts."[16] Madison did not believe that these problems would necessarily be overcome simply because the new system was a democracy. In *Federalist* 37, he observed: "It is a misfortune, inseparable from human affairs, that public measures are rarely investigated with that spirit of moderation which is essential to a just estimate of their real tendency to advance or obstruct the public good."[17] Rather than relying on reasoned deliberation, Madison feared that many people would be driven by "the impulse of sudden and violent passions" and could "be seduced by factious leaders into intemperate and pernicious resolutions."[18] Madison's warning about groups motivated by "sudden and violent passions" has been a recurring theme in American history, with the excesses of the Tea Party during the Obama years only the latest manifestation.

Given these views and the many checks and balances built into the Constitution, a number of scholars have questioned Madison's "democratic credentials" or even argued that his writings sounded the "death knell for popular government."[19] This critique of the "father" of the Constitution and the Bill of Rights (and one of the co-founders of the Democratic Party) as antidemocratic is too strong. In fairness, Madison was a realist about the many forces that limit citizen deliberation and designed a system that safeguarded against those dangers.

Clearly, Madison would view many of today's advocates of participatory or deliberative democracy as naive. Madison would have agreed with the judgment of Amy Gutmann and Dennis Thompson that "deliberative democracy affirms the need to justify decisions made by citizens and their representatives."

He also would have agreed that the "first and most important characteristic" of deliberative democracy is "its *reason-giving* requirement."[20] He also would most certainly have endorsed the attitude of John Rawls: "Public reason is characteristic of a democratic people"[21]—although he probably would have said "ought to be" rather than "is." Put another way, Madison would have seen the ideal of a well-functioning deliberative democracy as aspirational rather than realistic. For a similar reason, he would have viewed modern proposals to increase public deliberation by mandating a national "deliberation day" prior to elections as utopian.[22]

It is not that Madison was against reasoned deliberation. To the contrary, as Matthews notes, he held it up as the highest ideal: "If Madison worshipped a deity, it would be reason . . . the instrumental reason of the modern age."[23] But Madison recognized that people are driven by many forces other than reason. Madison saw that, by itself, a commitment to reason would not be enough. He felt he needed to find a way to balance faction against faction to create a system that in the end might make reasoned decisions.

It is important to recognize that while Madison's conception of the public was not based in the sort of evidence demanded in contemporary scholarship, research in political science and brain science is remarkably consistent with his description of how the public processes issues. One line of research is summarized by Nobel Prize winner Daniel Kahneman in *Thinking, Fast and Slow*. Kahneman distinguishes between two ways that humans process information: intuitive thought, or thinking fast, and "deliberate and effortful forms of thinking," which demand more time.[24] Deliberation, of course, falls into the category of "effortful forms of thinking." The bad news is that humans overwhelmingly rely on intuitive rather than deliberative thinking, and there are many factors that bias intuitive decision making. The result is that intuitive thinking "operates as a machine for jumping to conclusions," creating a situation in which "people let their likes and dislikes determine their beliefs about the world."[25] Kahneman also identifies a number of cognitive biases—many tied to emotion—that limit the degree to which people make sensible judgments.

The obvious solution to this problem would be to increase reliance on thinking slow, which Kahneman calls "system 2" thinking. While Kahneman supports such efforts, he argues that achieving that goal would be difficult: "We would all like to have a warning bell that rings loudly whenever we are about to make a serious error, but no such bell is available."[26] A separate line of research focused on the emotional bases of moral reasoning yields similar conclusions about how people process information. From his experiments in human thinking,

Jonathan Haidt concluded that "people were making a moral judgment immediately and emotionally. Reasoning was merely the servant of the passions, and when the servant failed to find any good arguments, the master did not change his mind." Haidt adds that research demonstrates that "independently reasoned judgment is possible in theory, but rare in practice."[27] Overall, cognitive brain science thus provides a picture of human decision making quite consistent with the one developed by Madison.

Other research focuses on public knowledge about issues and the American democratic system. The Pew Research Center has conducted a number of surveys that demonstrate the abysmal status of public knowledge from the most basic principles of how the system is organized to the details of public policy.[28] The problem is so bad that "only about 50 percent of voters could correctly place the major candidates or parties to the right or left of each other—a relatively easy task." The result is a situation in which "the public is awash in ignorance about parties' and candidates' policy positions."[29]

Public Debate and the Republican Remedy

Given the threats to democracy that Madison recognized in his own time—threats that are still with us today—we might have expected him to be quite skeptical of democracy. How could he have been the architect of the American system? One explanation is that Madison was both a romantic and a realist. He was a romantic in his principled support for representative democracy, observing in *Federalist* 49 that "the people are the only legitimate fountain of power." But Madison was also a realist. Later in *Federalist* 49, he warned of the danger that factional leaders will appeal to "the prejudices of the community," and then spoke of that risk: "The *passions* therefore not the *reason*, of the public, would sit in judgment. But it is the reason of the public alone that ought to control and regulate the government."[30] The key, then, was to create a system that over time activated "the reason of the public." Madison saw robust debate as "the republican remedy"—as a means of erecting "over the whole one paramount Empire of reason, benevolence and brotherly affection."[31] The constitutional system was designed to "help stimulate public deliberations among the diverse electorate."[32] Such debate could uphold a "policy of supplying by opposite and rival interests the defects of better motives."[33] Madison had faith that, over time, even fractious, uninformed, and irrational debate would lead to good governance because a "bad cause seldom fails to betray itself."[34] Madison's complex system of checks and balances was designed to produce the "republican remedy" of rough-and-tumble debate in the public square as a means of achieving effective governance. One might summarize Madison's core argument as stating that strong and strident public debate—debate in which all parties are represented prior to making a decision—is the single most important element in a well-functioning democracy.[35]

As noted earlier, Kahneman argues that there is no "warning bell" telling us when we are about to make a bad decision—a judgment amply supported by recent political history. Madison's insight was that free and open debate could provide that "warning bell." However, citizens need training to develop the critical skills necessary to recognize unsound arguments. Madison's "republican remedy" provided a vision of democratic debate that assigned a crucial role to reason in public life, yet he was also realistic in recognizing that public debate could be anything but reasonable. One of the difficulties with some approaches to deliberative democracy is that they rest on an idealized vision of public debate that is obviously not achievable in the real world. In contrast, Madison presented a realistic model of how public debate actually functions.

Madison's faith in the power of reasoned debate reflected the Enlightenment view that practical reason was the best protection against the power of the church, the crown, and landed elites. This faith was so basic to his worldview that he saw little need to defend public reason as necessary for democratic governance. Madison did not outline a theory of public reason, probably because he could not imagine the need to do so. He would have been dumbfounded by those who attack Enlightenment reason as a cause of totalitarianism, war, environmental destruction, and a host of other ills. He would have derided those claims not as proof that reason failed but as proof of the dangers present when ideology, self-interest, and passion overwhelm reasoned debate. At the same time, Madison would have doubted that public debate could ever live up to the norms assumed by some of today's advocates of deliberative democracy. While viewing such norms as utopian, however, he would have supported efforts to encourage reasoned public debate and make it more focused on the common interest—as opposed to the interests of any given faction. Madison would have seen training citizens to base their arguments in practical wisdom rather than in the interests of faction as the best hope for his "republican remedy." In fact, his writings implicitly lay out the skillset needed by citizens to make the "republican remedy" work. This skillset in turn has important implications for speech and debate pedagogy.

First, given Madison's faith in reason, he would have seen it as crucial that citizens be taught basic principles of reasoned advocacy. Debate will be much more profitable if it is informed by principles of a pragmatic argumentation theory, such as those that were developed in response to Stephen Toulmin's critique of formal logic.[36] In Madison's view, it was the "reason" of the public, not preexisting ideology, religion, or economic interest, that should guide debate. This means that citizens need training in order to help them become more adept at reflective or dialectical argument—what Kahneman labels system 2 thinking. Even Kahneman agrees that there are basic principles that can be taught that could improve decision making. For example, he notes that "rationality is generally served by broader and more comprehensive frames."[37]

Madison's vision of the "republican remedy" also suggests the importance of a debate pedagogy emphasizing the best available evidence, including expert opinion. Madison undoubtedly would have found the postmodern critique of the expert and technical reason to be incoherent. One can imagine him asking, "You'd rather rely on someone who isn't an expert?" He made the point again and again that legislators and others in politics and governance needed expert guidance.[38]

Finally, I noted earlier Madison's view that "public opinion sets bounds to every government." But he also added that in cases where public opinion was not "fixed, it may be influenced by the government." In other words, he suggested that elected representatives had a right (and perhaps even a duty) to try to educate public opinion in order to shape legitimate action, a point he emphasized when he referenced the danger that public opinion could be "counterfeited."[39] Here Madison defended the ideal of open debate both as a freedom to be protected and a method of producing good governance, but he also implicitly was getting at a key skill needed by legislators and other leaders in the new republic: the ability to express ideas clearly, back them up with strong arguments, and present them in a way that was understandable and persuasive to the people.

Madison's speeches in the constitutional convention and his writings in *The Federalist Papers* and elsewhere can be understood as not only outlining and defending the new system of representative democracy but also envisioning the proper roles of both citizens and leaders within that system (in terms of both style and substance). The legislator in particular needed to be informed by the best expert opinion, but also be able to explain that opinion in a way that was accessible to ordinary citizens. Madison was so strongly an advocate for reason that Matthews claims that his "doctrinaire commitment to reason" can be traced "throughout his life."[40] But while Madison's rhetoric exhibited clarity in both language and argument, it also reflected adaptation to the audience of the time. It is a testament to his skill as a rhetorician that the arguments he made in his contribution to *The Federalist Papers* and other works in the 1780s and 1790s were both persuasive in their own day and continue to resonate today.

Madison never wrote specifically about debate as a pedagogical instrument for training citizens, but his writings clearly suggest the need for skills that we today associate with debate training. These include practical wisdom (as theorized in the pragmatic argument tradition), an understanding of the importance of seeking out the best available evidence, research to discover the strongest expert knowledge on any given topic, and an ability to express informed pragmatic arguments in a way that is both clear and also adapted to the knowledge and passions of the particular audience. It is striking that Madison's implicit arguments about the skills needed by citizen advocates remains applicable in a world dominated by ideological sources of news (e.g., Fox News and MSNBC), the information cornucopia provided by the Internet, the ability to communicate instantly to millions through social networking, and an increasingly diverse population with both wildly shared and great value conflicts. Matthews calls Madison the "constant liberal Prince," a phrase that is exactly on target and at the same time fails to ring true. Madison saw no need for princes, but he did believe in the principles of liberalism that undergirded his support for representative democracy. He believed that the best protector of both liberty and good government was the give-and-take of passionate and sometimes irrational public talk. In the end, he believed that the better ideas likely would win out.

Madison, Practical Knowledge, and Pedagogy

While the ideals of Madison and other framers provide strong support for the importance of a robust debate pedagogy, they do not speak to specifics of format, topic, strategy, or paradigm for teaching informed debate. One cannot read Madison to address the details of contemporary issues of pedagogy or tactics. With this said, some broad generalizations can be drawn based on the vices that Madison saw as threatening representative democracy and his recipe for addressing those vices through debate in the public square.

First, Madison focused on the value of debate for addressing policy issues, and he also addressed the need for practical wisdom among legislators and other representatives of the public. Thus, it seems clear that the most useful practice for debate as a tournament activity (as opposed to occasional in-class exercises) would likewise focus on practical questions that governments address through legislative, executive, or judicial action. Debates about questions of philosophy, art, history, or science would seem to have less value as pedagogical instruments. In the case of philosophy, such debates lack the practical import in addressing problems of the community. Issues of art are inherently personal and therefore not addressable in a principled way through debate. And issues of science or history may not be suitable for debate because in many instances the arguments overwhelmingly favor one position. A debate about the theory of evolution is unlikely to be pedagogically valuable, for example, because the scientific evidence for evolution is unassailable and the faith-based reasons that some have for rejecting the theory are not subject to counterargument.

Science and history (and perhaps philosophy as well) might be contested as subsidiary issues in larger debates about policy. It seems clear, however, that the most pedagogically valuable forms of tournament debate will focus on a call for change in some area of government policy. Issues of practical policy are also more fruitful subjects for debate than broad ideological controversies, both because real-world evidence is much more available on the practical questions and also because there is less risk of terministic rigidity, or the tendency to reject all contrary positions out of hand when discussing issues of ideological doctrine.

Second, debate will be most useful as a pedagogical instrument if advocates learn to debate both for and against a given policy proposal. One of the values of debate pedagogy is that it exposes students to multiple sides of an issue and presses them to find the best expert opinion for each position. This is valuable not only because it develops research, analysis, argument development, and audience-adaptation skills, but also because it educates the debater that their particular ideological view of the world is sometimes not supported by the best evidence. Star Muir made this point when he argued that "encouraging research skills, is fundamentally an attachment to the 'real world,' and is enhanced by requiring debaters to investigate both sides of an issue."[41] Debate pedagogy teaches the individual to check to see whether their predispositions about an issue are, in fact, supported by the best data. In that way, it reinforces a basic virtue found in the reflective argument defining system 2 thinking, a virtue that is a corrective to the dangers of intuitive thought. This form of debate "does teach values," especially the importance of "providing a hearing for alternative points of view."[42] Thus, a form of debate in which advocates must debate both for and against a set of policies will provide important training in a variety of skills and perhaps more importantly teach an attitude of epistemological uncertainty prior to thoroughly researching a topic. This attitude is a reflection of what Young refers to as the "epistemic function of democracy," a function that requires exposure to all sides of an issue. Young argues that "[i]f citizens participate in public discussion that includes all social perspectives in their partiality and gives them a hearing they are more likely to arrive at just and wise solutions to their shared problems."[43]

A format in which students only have to debate one side of a position, or in which they could apply the same ideological worldview regardless of the approach taken by their competitors, would dramatically reduce the benefits previously described. Such an approach to debate might instead teach students that ideological rigidity and a failure to account for counterevidence and competing positions was a virtue, rather than a vice. The most valuable form of debate does the opposite: it forces students to address the arguments for and against a given policy action.

Finally, the most useful form of debate will in some way provide students with the skills they need to adapt strong arguments to the variety of audiences. Here the goal should not be to train students to pander to the prejudices of a particular community but rather to give them the skill to make the best reasoned case they can for a given position. One way of thinking about the ideal audience for debate is through what Chaïm Perelman and Lucie Olbrechts-Tyteca call the "universal audience."[44] The universal audience is an imagined audience of reasonable people with general knowledge about government and the community, but lacking in specialized field-dependent knowledge. Training students to debate in a way that would be understandable for such an audience gives them the skills to make the best case possible for a position to any group, whether ordinary citizens at a school board meeting or highly educated academics at a conference. This also implies that the judges in pedagogical debate should be open to argument and counterargument and not so ideologically committed to one side that this acts as a blinder to limit the debaters' argumentative options. Of course, debate focused on an expert audience also has value in training students to account for the complexity of the arguments on any given topic. Thus, the key is that the format both provides training in argument skills and training in how to translate complex arguments into a form that is understandable and persuasive for the broader audience that actually participates in deliberations in the public sphere.

The foregoing analysis of three broad norms that should guide the pedagogy and format of academic debate revolves around what is needed to effectively train citizen advocates. It lays out a general blueprint for tournament debate practice that educates for citizenship. It does not suggest whether the topic of debate should relate to foreign, domestic, or local issues. It does not speak to many issues of tactics, strategy, details of format, or the organization of any competition. But it does suggest the importance of focusing debate on practical questions, using a format that forces students to address the issues both for and against a given position, and training students to adapt to a broad general audience of reasonable people.

Conclusion

At first glance, one might think that the speeches and writings of James Madison at the time of the drafting and ratification of the Constitution have little direct relevance to debate pedagogy. A closer look, however, reveals that Madison's system of governance—the system that continues to this day in the world's oldest democracy—was based around debating a given issue before making a decision. It was this reasoned debate that would protect the nation from bad government and allow the nation to muddle through the crisis of the moment.

Madison did not write a debate manual, but he did draft the blueprint and provide the justification for a form of representative democracy built around public debate. This was his republican remedy for whatever else might ail the republic. His work suggested the kinds of skills that citizens need in the public square to participate effectively. It also strongly implied basic principles of format and structure essential to fulfilling the pedagogical aims of debate.

Madison's work also suggests that controversies over the particulars of debate format, organizational structures, argument paradigms and practices, and similar issues, while perhaps important in the context of tournament debate, are less important than the power of debate to train citizens in many pedagogical settings. A primary lesson of Madison's writings is the need for debate across the curriculum and in many different forms. Madison's republican remedy worked because there is great power in the give-and-take of debate for revealing "a bad cause." Precisely the same point can be made about debate pedagogy. As long as there is free and open debate on important issues, debate will serve its pedagogical function of enhancing system 2 thinking and providing citizens with the other skills they need to participate at all levels in civil society. I have argued that the most useful approach to debate, especially in the context of tournament competition, focuses on public policy in a format that requires students to debate for and against a given policy proposal and also adapt to different audiences. Yet other forms of debate also would have utility.

Debating about questions of science, literature, or history can help students learn to think critically, even if the focus is not directly on public policy. While such topics might not be appropriate for tournament competition, they still have value as a classroom exercise. Perhaps the greatest need is for more debate throughout the curriculum. Debate exposes participants to competing ideas, demands the latest research, and teaches the most basic critical thinking and advocacy skills needed by citizens. I've highlighted what the writings of America's greatest political philosopher suggest about the optimal form of debate for training citizens to participate in their own governance, but any form in which "[a]mbition . . . counteract[s] ambition" is valuable.[45] Thus, debate is both the core process holding together a democracy built around Madisonian ideals and the most valuable means of teaching the critical thinking skills that are at the heart of being an informed citizen.

6

WHEN ARGUMENTATION BACKFIRES:
THE MOTIVATED REASONING PREDICAMENT
IN SPEECH AND DEBATE PEDAGOGY

GORDON R. MITCHELL

What do Malcolm X, Richard Nixon, and Hillary Clinton have in common? All former debaters, they cite early argumentation training as a formative influence that would come to shape their mature public voices later in life.[1] Their careers, following starkly different political trajectories, navigated what William Rehg calls the "transfer" challenge—taking argumentation skills learned in organized settings and applying them to practical contexts beyond the controlled learning environment.[2] Of course, this challenge is relevant not only for former debaters turned prominent political leaders but also for the myriad ordinary reasoners who study argumentation in speech and debate classrooms: "Methods of analysis and evaluation must be feasible to employ by ordinary reasoners who want to assess everyday arguments of the sort that appear in newspapers and magazines, and on the Internet. And the skills involved must be learned in such a way that students are continually transferring them to such contexts."[3]

The transfer challenge recasts argumentation pedagogy in a particular light. The objective of teaching students how to argue cogently with classroom peers has been a perennial priority, but the transfer question highlights additional concerns regarding how such skills actually may *play* in the world beyond the classroom. Since that world beyond is not a vacuum, argumentation patterns in prevailing social, cultural, and political milieus become especially salient for teachers and students to ponder.

Recent scholarship provides rich food for thought on this count. Demographic studies document that U.S. citizens increasingly tend to sort themselves into echo chambers where like-minded arguers make and hear arguments that resonate with their settled beliefs. Social psychology research highlights how rarely everyday arguers tend to engage in the sort of critical thinking valorized in argumentation textbooks. Other research findings suggest that classical argumentative techniques such as direct rebuttals can even result in "backfire effects," causing interlocutors to dig in and cling even more tightly to their views when challenged.

Philosopher Jeffrey Maynes engages the transfer challenge by theorizing that a pedagogical emphasis on "metacognitive skill" can help "inculcate debiasing habits" in students, helping them to avoid falling prey to some of these "cognitive biases" and errant reasoning patterns.[4] While promising, Maynes's proposal suffers from an important limitation that highlights the need for a more rhetorically oriented pedagogical approach, one that is sketched in the latter section of this chapter. The opening two sections review relevant literature on motivated reasoning and consider how so-called backfire effects may complicate Maynes's debiasing strategies. Drawing from "cooperative" and "coalescent" argumentation theory, section three explores how debiasing strategies proposed primarily by philosophers and psychologists might be socially thickened, with conceptual depth added by revisiting ancient Greek and Roman foundations of argumentation pedagogy.

The overall objective of this chapter is to contribute to the ongoing conversation about speech and debate as civic education by honing a perspective on argumentation pedagogy that is responsive to contemporary exigencies, linked to ancient rhetorical traditions, and strengthened by interdisciplinary integration.

Motivated Reasoning

Ideal models of argumentation, such as those found in Dutch pragma-dialectical theory, invite us to envision a world populated by arguers who gather evidence, test the strength of the evidence, and then carefully infer warranted conclusions based on that evidence.[5] Of course, no one is perfect, so mistakes can be expected and fallacies are bound to occur in practice. But social psychology research suggests that everyday patterns of argumentation do not just deviate from such ideal norms; they tend to *invert* them. This inversion occurs when arguers begin with anchored conclusions and then proceed to seek confirmatory evidence in support of those conclusions, often subconsciously ignoring or discounting contrary evidence along the way.

This pattern of "motivated reasoning," according to Daniel Kahan, is characterized by "the tendency of people to conform assessments of information to some goal or end extrinsic to accuracy."[6] One classic study of the phenomenon documents how Princeton students "saw" a Dartmouth football team make twice as many penalties as Dartmouth viewers "saw" when both audiences were shown the same videotaped game.[7] In another study, nearly identical scientific research reports that agreed with scientists' prior beliefs were judged to be of higher quality than those that ran counter to their prior beliefs.[8] Other research shows how men judged the risk of engaging in unprotected sex to be negatively correlated with the sex appeal of a hypothetical partner, even though such judgments lacked any factual basis.[9] Finally, an article titled "Motivated Reasoning and Yard-Sign-Stealing Partisans: Mine Is a Likable Rogue, Yours Is a Degenerate Criminal" reports that political partisans reacted to dirty campaign tricks in a motivated way, "expressing exceptional concern when the perpetrators are political opponents" while tending to rationalize such mischief when committed by political allies.[10] The empirical research base on the motivated reasoning phenomenon has solidified during the last half century, with many other controlled experiments producing similar findings.[11]

As understanding of motivated reasoning's dynamics on an individual level has developed, researchers have begun to deploy the theory to explain society-wide communication patterns regarding political issues such as wildlife disease risk,[12] regulation of emergent technologies,[13] and the Monica Lewinsky scandal.[14] A prominent theme in this literature concerns the way motivated reasoning patterns relate to what journalist Bill Bishop calls "the big sort"—how Americans have formed geographic, economic, and political clusters that tend to function as like-minded echo chambers.[15]

Is motivated reasoning a by-product of our current age of political polarization and homogenous demographic clustering? Or is it something that has been with us for a much longer time? Behavioral economist and Nobel Laureate Daniel Kahneman sheds light on this question with his "dual-process" theory of human cognition (see table 6.1).[16]

From an evolutionary perspective, Kahneman posits that a threatening environment prompted early humans to develop brain capacity for making snap, fight/flight, friend/foe judgment calls. This "system 1" thinking, by necessity, tends to operate more or less unconsciously, drawing heavily on intuition and emotion to process information quickly and generate nimble reactions under time pressure. Later, humans formed more complex communities and social structures, with brains evolving to add "system 2" thinking, a more deliberate

Table 6.1 The "dual process" model of human cognition.

System 1	System 2
Unconscious reasoning	Conscious reasoning
Judgments based on intuition	Judgments based on critical examination
Processes information quickly	Processes information slowly
Hypothetical reasoning	Logical reasoning
Large capacity	Small capacity
Prominent in animals and humans	Prominent only in humans
Unrelated to working memory	Related to working memory
Operates effortlessly and automatically	Operates with effort and control
Unintentional thinking	Intentional thinking
Influenced by experiences, emotions, and memories	Influenced by facts, logic, and evidence
Can be overridden by system 2	Used when system 1 fails to form a logical/acceptable conclusion
Prominent since human origins	Developed over time
Includes recognition, perception, orientation, etc.	Includes rule following, comparisons, weighing of options, etc.

Source: Kahneman, *Thinking, Fast and Slow.*

and reflective mode of cognition adapted to enable critical examination and logical reasoning based on facts and evidence.

Notably, many of the characteristics of system 2 thinking in Kahneman's dual-process theory match up with core principles of argumentation pedagogy. Could the instances of errant motivated reasoning reported in the scholarly literature involve cases where research subjects use system 1 thinking to solve problems calling out for argumentative analysis?

Human brains evolved, says Kahneman, to be capable of both system 1 and system 2 thinking. People toggle between these modes of thought, using quick, gut-level reactions to guide some decisions and more deliberate and logical judgments to handle others. There is simply not enough time to use slower system 2 thinking for every decision, yet system 1 thinking is not sufficiently robust to sort through complex, multifaceted, and high-stakes judgments requiring extended reflection. Some people finesse this dilemma by adeptly switching between modes of thought, depending on the situation. Others, such as many of the research subjects participating in the motivated reasoning studies cited earlier in this section, have more difficulty using system 2 thinking to "override," in Kahneman's terminology, system 1 thinking when appropriate.

The next section considers how this overriding function might be integrated as a component of critical thinking pedagogy designed to check some of motivated reasoning's troubling tendencies.

Debiasing: Backfires and Boomerangs

If motivated reasoning tends to produce cognitive errors, can the process be checked or reversed? This question has prompted scholars to explore possible "debiasing" strategies to enable people to better understand and orchestrate their modes of cognitive engagement. Jeffrey Maynes takes up this challenge in theorizing about critical thinking pedagogy designed to improve students' argumentative acumen. To better equip students for the task of avoiding cognitive traps associated with motivated reasoning, Maynes calls for classroom cultivation of "metacognitive" skill: "[t]he metacognitive skills involved in critical thinking are those skills involved in recognizing *when* these cognitive skills should be used, knowing *how* to use them, and *why* to use them."[17]

Drawing from the work of educational psychologist Gregory Schraw, Maynes suggests that students can develop metacognitive skill through the use of a "strategy evaluation matrix."[18] This exercise invites students to make an explicit inventory of the cognitive strategies they have available for accomplishing certain classroom assignments. According to Maynes, such strategies may include:

- The "consider-the-opposite" strategy, in which students try to put themselves in the position of someone who believes the opposing (or different) view, and to give the best case they can for it.
- The "values analysis" strategy, in which students write down, for themselves, what their values on a new issue are before engaging it.
- The "argument mapping" strategy, in which students diagram an argument to better understand how it works.[19]

Students in Maynes's classes are asked to conduct journaling exercises in which they report on cases where they applied one of the strategies in the matrix to an argument they made in the past week. Through this process, students "cultivate the habit of metacognitive reflection," enabling them to perform "motivational monitoring" that Maynes says can work to control some of the implicit biases associated with motivated reasoning.[20]

Maynes makes a strong case that the strategy evaluation matrix may be a useful tool for students to use in sharpening their metacognitive skills. His philosophical perspective is reflected in the fact that the pedagogical windfall associated with use of the matrix is located purely at the level of individual introspection. While a student supremely adept at metacognitive reflection may indeed be able to minimize *their own* motivated reasoning errors, the transfer challenge raised at the outset of this chapter still looms, asking how well this skill will play in the "human barnyard"[21] beyond the controlled classroom space.

Metacognitively adept thinkers may find their skills useful in negotiating the gauntlet of difficult life decisions they are likely to face in today's complex and fast-moving world. But what happens when these same thinkers find themselves thrown into situations where they are called on to make joint decisions about controversial issues with others, some of whom may be far more prone to make motivated reasoning errors? Pragma-dialectical argumentation theory would suggest that in these situations, interlocutors might turn to the process of critical discussion to sort out disagreements by exchanging fact-based standpoints. Students and teachers of argumentation may find this familiar remedy especially appealing. Yet in practice, studies have shown that classical argumentation strategies, such as pointed rebuttals, can drive interlocutors utilizing system 1 thinking to circle the wagons and hold even more firmly to their pre-argument beliefs. For example, in an experiment designed to test subjects' reactions to corrections regarding false or unsubstantiated beliefs such as whether Iraq had weapons of mass destruction immediately before the U.S. invasion in 2003, Brendan Nyhan and Jason Reifler found that "direct factual contradictions can actually *strengthen* ideologically grounded factual beliefs."[22] Sol Hart and Erik Nisbet observe similar "boomerang effects" following attempts to correct subjects' factual misperceptions regarding climate change science.[23]

Reviewing the literature in this area, Sahara Byrne and Philip Hart identify several psychological mechanisms that may account for backfire and boomerang effects, including *reactance* (perceived threats to behavioral freedoms motivate individuals to reestablish them), *selective attention and perception* (individuals attend to parts of arguments and ignore others), and *activation of social norms* (exposure to a strategic message leads the receiver to deduce that the undesirable behavior being targeted is a social norm, e.g., when "an adolescent female may observe a campaign intending to promote sexual abstinence and deduce that most of her peers must be having sex. Otherwise, no need would exist for such a campaign").[24]

The backfire effect prompts Stephan Lewandowsky and colleagues to theorize a social dimension to debiasing strategies. Moving beyond Maynes's focus on individual cognition, they hypothesize that certain ways of performing speech acts in social contexts can determine whether debiasing efforts will tend to backfire or not. Noting that "simple myths are more cognitively attractive than complicated refutations," for example, Lewandowsky and colleagues recommend simple, brief rebuttals to minimize the "overkill backfire effect" (see figure 6.1). And to dampen the "worldview backfire effect" (i.e., "evidence

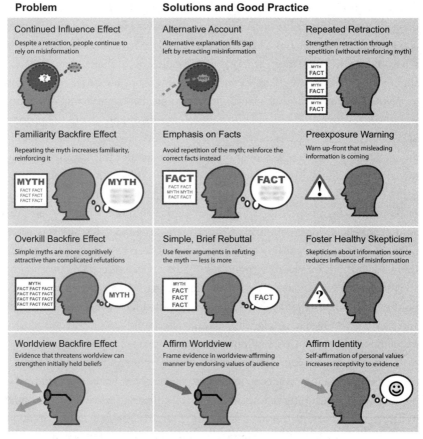

Fig 6.1 Graphical summary of findings from the misinformation literature relevant to communication practitioners. Source: Stephan Lewandowsky et al., "Misinformation and Its Correction: Continued Influence and Successful Debiasing," *Psychological Science in the Public Interest* 13, p. 122, copyright © 2012 by SAGE Publications. Reprinted by permission of by SAGE Publications, Inc.

that threatens worldview can strengthen initially held beliefs"), they counsel practitioners to affirm the worldview of interlocutors ("frame evidence in a worldview-affirming manner by endorsing values of the audience") and affirm the identity of interlocutors ("self-affirmation of personal values increases receptivity to evidence").[25]

The previous section explored how potentially errant motivated reasoning patterns might be checked, on an individual level, by introspective debiasing tools such as the strategy evaluation matrix. The potential utility of such tools beyond the classroom setting may be limited by backfire and boomerang effects, evident when anchored interlocutors using system 1 thinking react negatively to pointed argumentation challenges. However, such negative reactions are not inevitable. Argumentation theory tells us that audience reception can be shaped by how arguers frame and present their positions. Likewise, backfire and boomerang effects might be dampened by social debiasing strategies that focus on how speech act performance structures the quality of interactive sequels in argumentative exchanges, particularly with respect to the willingness of interlocutors to invest energy in cognitively taxing system 2 thinking.

Antilogic, Coalescent, and Cooperative Argumentation

Can the social debiasing strategies proposed by Lewandowsky and colleagues help arguers transfer skills honed in the classroom to politically polarized contexts? Detailed answers to this question may prove elusive until the strategies are fleshed out as theoretically grounded and thick normative principles suitable for guiding argumentative practice. Fortunately, interdisciplinary overlap between the psychology literature on social debiasing and several strands of argumentation theory reveals opportunities to sharpen, thicken, and ground the normative principles under consideration (see figure 6.2).

The following subsections dwell on the "pedagogical sweet spot" located at the intersection point between these two scholarly literatures in psychology and argumentation. Michael Mendelson's "antilogical" argumentation pedagogy, Michael Gilbert's theory of "coalescent argumentation," and Josina Makau and Debian Marty's "cooperative argumentation" are considered in turn, with an eye toward identifying key elements from each approach that have the potential to inform the conversation regarding how social debiasing strategies might address the motivated reasoning predicament.

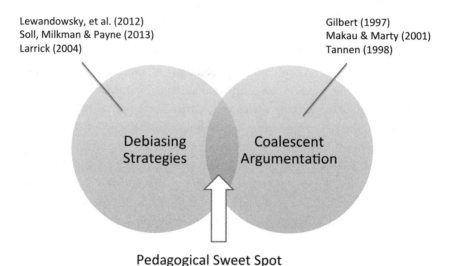

Fig 6.2 Overlap of psychological literature on social debiasing with selected strands of argumentation theory.

Antilogic

The name of Mendelson's pedagogically inflected program of "antilogic" gestures toward the "two-logoi" fragment left by the Greek sophist Protagoras ("there are two opposing logoi present concerning everything").[26] In Protagoras's "human-measure" doctrine,[27] Mendelson locates the taproot of a dynamic tradition that privileges oppositional argumentative multivocality. Tracing the evolution of this tradition from Protagoras through Carneades to Cicero and Quintilian, Mendelson articulates a pedagogical approach that emphasizes *aidos* (respect for communicative partners) and *epoche* (suspension of judgment) in argumentation.

Carneades emerges as an important transitional figure in the rich historical narrative underwriting Mendelson's project. Succeeding the skeptic Arcecilaus as the third head of Plato's Academy in the third century BCE, Carneades endorsed Arcecilaus's insistence that all dogmas, including the very idea of certain human knowledge itself, should be subjected to critique.[28] The wise person, on this view, should strive to achieve a mental state of *ataraxia* (mental interpurturbability or inner tranquility) by learning how to reserve judgment on any claim of fact or opinion. Carneades modified Arcecilaus's absolute skepticism by developing an account of plausibility (*to pithanon*) that moves beyond purely negative critique to incorporate positive criteria for making practical decisions.[29] Carneades carried the Hellenistic tradition of argumentation to the Roman world, making a famous visit to Rome in 155 BCE. On the first day of his visit, Carneades delivered a public speech praising the Roman system of justice. On the second day, he gave a different address that presented a dramatic refutation of what he said the day before.[30] The "coup de théâtre" spectacle sparked Roman interest in Greek antilogical techniques, indirectly influencing (through Philo of Larissa) Cicero to make *in utramque partem* (arguing on either side of the case) a central feature of his writings on oratorical eloquence.[31]

Imitating Plato's writing style exhibited in the Socratic dialogues, Cicero developed many of his pedagogical and philosophical positions in fictional dialogue form, with principles emerging from the interaction between characters. Mendelson points to one such dialogue in particular, the exchange between Antonius and Crassus in Book I of *De Oratore*, as paradigmatic of Cicero's views on argumentation: "Cicero's pedagogical stance, as represented by the dialogue's leading figures, is uniquely compatible with his rhetorical theory and particularly instructive for contemporary teachers of argument."[32] Antonius and Crassus model *aidos* (respect for communicative partners) and *epoche* (suspension of judgment), deploying rhetorical devices such as courteous contradiction (*peritrope*) as they iteratively adjust and update their positions in response to the ebb and flow of the dialogue.

The Lewandowsky group's "affirm worldview and identity" social debiasing strategies find correlates in the concept of *aidos*, while the "foster healthy skepticism" strategy mirrors the prominent role of *epoche* in antilogical pedagogy. These conceptual intersections reveal potential for contemporary students and teachers of argumentation to draw on exemplars, such as the exchange between Antonius and Crassus, as inventional resources for fashioning argumentative interventions designed to avert backfire effects. In the epilogue of *Many Sides*, Mendelson describes specific classroom exercises suitable for this purpose, such as disputatious analysis of model texts and simulated dialogical argumentation, modeled on Quintilian's *controversia* declamations.[33]

In the antilogical approach, students hone argumentation skills through *imitatio* (artful imitation of exemplars). A central premise underlying this pedagogical orientation is that the human imagination can be enlarged by exposure to model performances that enact virtuous qualities such as *aidos* and *epoche*. Future scholarship might usefully explore how the interactive elements of the Lewandowsky group's social debiasing strategies can be further understood and refined in light of the antilogical tradition's emphasis on the imitative dynamic of human speech.

Coalescent Argumentation

Recall the Lewandowsky group's insight that debiasing efforts can backfire if discussion unfolds purely on the surface level of argumentation (e.g., "repeating the myth increases familiarity, thereby reinforcing it"). This view resonates with Gilbert's observation that argumentation scholars too often take *claims* to be central artifacts in their analyses. This claim-based perspective can be prone to blind spots, since, as Gilbert points out in his book *Coalescent Argumentation*, "claims are best taken as icons for positions that are actually much richer and deeper," and a "position" is "a matrix of beliefs, attitudes, emotions, insights and values connected to a claim."[34]

Gilbert elaborates procedures for practitioners and analysts to understand their interlocutors' argumentative positions (not just their claims). This can be a challenging endeavor, as it requires "exploration of all the available modes of argumentation," including not only the logical dimensions of a surface claim but also the "emotional, visceral, and kisceral (or intuitive) aspects of a view."[35] With a firmer grasp on this multifaceted substructure undergirding an argumentative claim, interlocutors become better prepared, in the "coalescent stage" of argumentation, to locate points of contact and commonality between positions. In this way, Gilbert concludes, "the shared goals, values, and attitudes held by both participants form the starting point for further discussion."[36]

Gilbert's theory of coalescent argumentation provides another way to operationalize the Lewandowsky group's guideline regarding the importance of affirmation in debiasing dialogues. Options to "affirm the worldview or identity" of an interlocutor may seem elusive if arguments remain limited only to the exchange of conflicting claims (e.g., "global warming is a hoax" vs. "it's a fact that the ice sheets are melting"). However, if an interlocutor's position is understood to encompass a much broader web of emotions, beliefs, and commitments, selected affirmation of some of those emotions, beliefs, and commitments may enhance the likelihood that debiasing strategies will be received in a more deliberative and reflective posture grounded in system 2 thinking.

Cooperative Argumentation

The "overkill backfire effect," according to Lewandowsky and colleagues, occurs when arguers inundate their interlocutors with a phalanx of challenging facts and claims.[37] Since people generally prefer simple to complex explanations,[38] intricate critiques, even if logically cogent, may prompt interlocutors to cling more tightly to misinformed beliefs rooted in simpler explanations. This backfire effect may be pronounced in cases where the challenging argument is presented in a threatening way.[39]

Building from feminist critiques that view the "argument culture" as one in which arguers deploy violent metaphors to gain the upper hand in "winner-take-all" fights,[40] Makau and Marty advance a perspective on argumentation informed by an "ethic of interdependence." This ethic calls on us to "view those who disagree with us as resources rather than as rivals."[41] The principles and practices associated with their program of "cooperative argumentation" may be especially salient for arguers seeking to avoid the "overkill" and "worldview threatening" backfire effects posited by the Lewandowsky group.

Makau and Marty propose a number of classroom exercises designed to hone student skill in cooperative argumentation. One activity invites students to critique television talk shows or congressional debates to explore the impact of "competitive exchanges" on the participants and audience members. Following this, students are asked to "envision cooperative alternatives to these competitive exchanges."[42] To the extent that such exercises enable students to transcend the "overkill" and "worldview threatening" performance frames isolated by Lewandowsky and colleagues, potential for transfer of these skills beyond the classroom space may be promising.

Cooperative argumentation theory may also implicate social debiasing strategies on another level. In focusing their attention on a specific type of communicative interaction—"corrections of misinformation"—Lewandowsky and colleagues presuppose a cognitive asymmetry between their "correcting" arguer and their "misinformed" interlocutor. If one takes *epoche* seriously and buys into cooperative argumentation's insistence that both parties to a dispute view each other as allies in a joint search for understanding that transcends both of their individual frames of reference, it would seem incumbent on the "unbiased" interlocutor to admit the possibility that their "correct" information could be in error. However, as the "manufactured controversies" over issues such as tobacco addiction, missile defense, and Holocaust denial illustrate, this line of thought carries the danger of yielding not "backfire" but "stall" effects, as interlocutors become paralyzed, mired in endless rounds of argument about facts that should not really be in dispute.[43]

Conclusion

Psychological research on motivated reasoning presents wrinkles for argumentation scholars seeking to facilitate the transfer of argumentation skills beyond controlled learning environments. Philosopher Jeffrey Maynes posits that students can tame some of the tendencies of motivated reasoning to distort their own critical thinking by cultivating "metacognitive skill" through the use of tools such as the strategy evaluation matrix. Yet Maynes's advice provides only limited help to arguers who seek to avert the "backfire effects" that can result when their challenges prompt interlocutors to respond by entrenching their previously held views.

To address the social dynamics entailed in these boomerang scenarios, Lewandowsky and colleagues propose tailored "debiasing strategies" designed to increase the effectiveness of attempts to correct misinformed views held by others. By attending to the conceptual intersections between these debiasing strategies and a branch of argumentation theory focusing on "antilogic" and "coalescent/cooperative argumentation," this chapter generates insight regarding possible ways to thicken the Lewandowsky group's strategic recommendations while simultaneously informing efforts to achieve student transfer of argumentation skills in a highly polarized social milieu.

The preceding analysis has touched on some tangential issues that may warrant further treatment beyond the limited space available here. We saw how the distinction between system 1 and system 2 thinking in Kahneman's "dual-processing" theory of human cognition helps explain the backfire effect phenomenon. The evolutionary element of this account highlights how human brains have evolved to be capable of both system 1 and system 2 thinking, with people challenged to discern when the use of each cognitive mode is most appropriate. This finding may suggest that the generic notion of a "motivated reasoner" may be a category mistake. Rather, we are all hardwired to use motivated reasoning, for better or worse, in certain circumstances. Protagoras's ancient insight that humans require help from each other in order to make reliable measurements and judgments about the world suggests that the same may hold true when it comes to the challenge of rooting out "implicit bias" and adeptly toggling between system 1 and system 2 modes of thinking.

An important limitation of the current study stems from the fact that in focusing on Lewandowsky and colleagues' social debiasing strategies, the study's findings may not be generalizable beyond the specific argumentative situation involved in one party's attempts to "correct misinformation" held by another party. For example, although so-called competitive arguing strategies, such as withering critique, may prove suboptimal for correcting misinformation, such approaches may still be effective—indeed, perhaps essential—in other contexts.[44] Competitive and cooperative theories of argumentation, on this view, necessarily lack universal scope. Just as in the case of system 1 versus system 2 thinking, the challenge becomes figuring out when and how to deploy competitive and/or cooperative argumentation tools in particular situations. Rather than striving for some grand resolution of the perennial debate between "competitive" and "cooperative" camps of argumentation theory, perhaps a more promising pedagogical approach involves diversifying students' skill sets, enabling them to become proficient in a wide array of different argumentative tools, including Maynes's "metacognitive skill" (to help inform choices regarding when and how to deploy those skills).

The colloquy between Lewandowsky's group and the quartet of argumentation theorists featured in section three of this chapter prompted an occasion to revisit some of the premises undergirding the "correction of misinformation" project. After all, can't "debiasing" become "rebiasing" in the hands of someone whose seemingly "correct" views are the product of their own implicit bias? This possibility suggests that the accounts provided by the debiasing literature could be strengthened by shifting from a binary, fact-based ontology toward one informed by concepts such as *ataraxia*, or the mental tranquility sought by ancient Greek thinkers such as Carneades, who aimed to calibrate a delicate balance between *epoche* (suspension of belief) and *phronesis* (practical wisdom regarding the imperatives of action and decision).

7

TEACHING RELIGION THROUGH ARGUMENT, SPEECH, AND DEBATE: CRITIQUING LOGOS AND MYTHOS

DAVID A. FRANK

American academic speech and debate has its origins, as Michael Bartanen and Robert Littlefield detail in *Forensics in America*, in secular institutions of education that honored the wall of separation between church and state.[1] Most texts in argumentation and debate, beginning with George Baker's 1895 *Principles of Argument*, do not discuss debate in religious contexts or take on the task of teaching the religious how to speak, argue, and debate.[2] Indeed, the study of argument and debate in the American academy unfolds out of the Enlightenment tradition, which features the powers of rationality, placing religion in the realm of superstition and emotion. I claim here that scholars and teachers of speech and debate should incorporate religion and other topics related to "ultimate meaning" into a broad rhetorical curriculum, and that mythos and secular reasoning expressed through argumentation should both be curricular touchstones in a robust rhetorical education.

Karen Armstrong, the noted scholar of religion, has identified two forms of interlocking reasoning: logos and mythos. Logos stresses the rational, scientific, and pragmatic; mythos seeks ultimate meaning and the transcendent, often expressed through religion (although, as Phil Zuckerman has demonstrated, "ultimate meaning" can be set forth by a secular mythos as well).[3] The ancients saw logos and mythos as complementary; they need not be mutually exclusive. In contrast to the critique offered by the new atheists that declares religion irrational, significant contemporary Christian theological movements hold that modern science and faith can be mutually reinforcing. To illustrate:

Pope Francis's letter *Laudato si'* yokes Christian scripture requiring followers to save and repair God's creation to the science on climate change. Integrating Christian mythos and scientific logos, the pope calls for policy action to mitigate global warming.[4] Pope Francis makes arguments in the public sphere using mythos and logos, which are open to critique. Not surprisingly, he has been criticized for breaching the divide between science and religion.[5]

Both logos and mythos, I argue, should be put to the test of argument. If speech educators are to offer students "equipment for living," they need to provide students with the skills they need to critique both logos and mythos within speech and debate.[6] The essential core of speech and debate is argument. I draw from the work of Chaïm Perelman, Lucie Olbrechts-Tyteca, Henry Johnstone Jr., and Kenneth Burke to develop a view of argument as an expression of reason designed to test evidence offered in support of claims based in both mythos and logos.[7] Those who engage in genuine argument put at risk their beliefs and may find at the end of an argumentative encounter that their mythos is transformed and changed as a result. In the process, they may come to better appreciate both the power and limitations of logos.

Accordingly, I initially consider why secular students should learn the art of debating mythos and how students committed to religious traditions benefit from opening their mythos to the interrogation of logos. I then provide two illustrations of religious institutions using rhetorical education practices, Whitefield Academy and Liberty University, to prepare their students for the secular world. I follow these illustrations with a brief overview of efforts I have made to provide students with experience arguing about mythos and logos at the University of Oregon. To conclude, I consider the need for a rhetorical pedagogy for speech and debate designed to teach students how they should approach and engage in arguments about logos and mythos.

Debating Logos and Mythos

Students reared in secular homes and schools often do not understand religion and, as a result, cannot fully engage their friends and colleagues who are religious.[8] Students reared in religious households often cannot explain or defend their faith. Without a basic understanding of religion and things religious, students can turn dogmatic in their secular beliefs, with some toxic consequences. Similarly, those who move in the direction of religious fundamentalism do so without having an invitation to consider the role reason plays in their faith traditions. Michael Walzer, in his *Paradox of Liberation*, observes that secular leaders of the liberation movements in India, Israel, and Algeria did not understand the religious traditions of their compatriots.[9] The leader of the Indian independence movement, Jawaharlal Nehru, "was mostly tone deaf" to religion.[10] Theodor Herzl, who led the Zionist movement, "had not much of a Jewish education."[11] And the leaders of the Algerian liberation movement "did not spend much time learning about the principles of Islam."[12] As a result, they sought to purify their postliberation societies of religious thought and control. In response, the religious engaged in a fundamentalist backlash, resisting the attempt of the secular leaders to desacralize their societies. In the three societies Walzer studied, the secular logos rejected religious mythos as irrational. And in response, the religious fundamentalist movements rejected the secular logos of the revolutionaries. The consequence, Walzer observes, was that the secular revolutionaries and religious fundamentalists in these societies could not engage in civil argument because their fundamentalisms prevented the discovery of common ground. An argument pedagogy seeking to bring critical reason to bear on both logos and mythos is necessary for finding the common ground that allows for genuine engagement between the secular and religious.

Students from secular backgrounds should come to appreciate that the mythos held by their religious friends host humane values and sanction the use of reason. To be sure, religious figures have used interpretations of sacred texts to justify inhumane behavior and to deny intellectual freedom. These interpretations are often opposed by normative religious doctrine, however, and there are ongoing debates within religious communities about the use and misuse of scripture. To illustrate, at a recent conference in New Delhi on women's rights, numerous female participants sought to argue their case from within an Islamic paradigm, quoting verse after verse from the Qur'an and citing traditions attributed to the Prophet to argue their case for gender justice. Students from secular backgrounds should understand that the interpretation of scripture is open to argument and debate. They should be prepared to identify within the religious traditions of those with whom they argue principles (or what rhetoricians call loci) that can form common ground for rhetorical engagement.

Similarly, research clearly suggests that keeping students in a tight cocoon of religious doctrine, insulated from the critique of their faith traditions, does not prepare them for the arguments they will encounter in the secular world. Some 80 percent of the students taught in private religious elementary and secondary institutions leave the faith once in college.[13] These students report having significant intellectual questions that remain unanswered. Once they enter secular universities and colleges, they find that their faith cannot withstand the interrogations of their dormitory roommates and professors. They see and understand the power of secular logos—that it can clarify social issues and provide what they come to view as more realistic and humane outlooks on the world. Unfortunately, many are not exposed at all to the traditions of critical thinking, speech, and debate that are deeply embedded in most theistic and nontheistic religions.

Most major religions sanction debate, argumentation, and the use of rhetorical reasoning when religious communities face disagreement. The God of the monotheistic religions of Judaism, Christianity, and Islam gave humans the gift of reason. Debate and argument are prominent in these traditions. God and humans argued, in the Jewish tradition, with God conceding when defeated in argument: "My Children have defeated me, My Children have defeated me." Talmudic argument displays a way of reasoning meant to help Jews bridge sacred principle to secular problems. Jesus argued with his disciples, the Pharisees, and with God.[14] Based on the argumentative model offered by Jesus, Christians set forth the art of casuistry, which encouraged a reasoned approach to judging when and how theological principles should be adapted to particular problems and cases. Muslims debate and argue about Islamic scripture and how it should be used to frame the problems Muslims face. In the nontheistic tradition of Buddhism, argument and disagreement are essential characteristics of making decisions.[15]

We should acknowledge and fold into our argument pedagogy these traditions of argument that question mythos with logos. The types of argument we teach (e.g., deduction, induction, abduction, and analogy) and the various tests of reasoning stressed in our pedagogy are on display in debates and arguments within religious communities. As Michael Perry has written, religiously based argument needs to be interrogated in the public sphere. "Ideally, such arguments will sometimes be tested, in the to and fro of public political debate, by competing scripture or tradition-based religious arguments."[16] Students should learn that sacred scripture can yield plural and conflicting interpretations. Perry cites Johnson's admonition that liberal Christians must not let interpretations of Christian scripture that sanction intolerance of women and gays remain uncontested.[17] There are methods of understanding and interpreting scripture, Johnson and others argue, that can be used to challenge texts that are used to justify inhumane policy.

On close inspection, these debates and arguments suggest a normative humility and pluralism often overshadowed by religious zealots (a tiny minority within most religious communities) who make use of extreme and marginal interpretations of sacred scripture. In the normative religious traditions, practitioners are aware that their understanding of spiritual imperatives should be approached with tentativeness, and that there can be a variety of reasonable interpretations that can be fetched out of the same sacred text. We should remember that religious arguments were marshaled to confront (and defend) slavery and were foundational to the American civil rights movement (and those who opposed it).

There is a mythos undergirding logos, which is often not acknowledged. The Enlightenment thinkers privileged rationality and reason over revelation. The foundational mythos of logos seeks freedom from superstition and idols. Unfortunately, the Enlightenment was as prone as religion to succumb to prejudice, racism, and anti-Semitism. Enlightenment logos could not provide an immaculate view of the world, as it provided "evidence" that blacks were inferior to whites, that Jews could not be part of Western culture, and that scientific rationality should trump religious mythos.[18] Religious mythos can serve as a check on the presumptions of the Enlightenment rationality, when the sacred principles of equality and the sanctity of life are set against the prejudice of "scientific racism" and dehumanized rational thought.

In the next section, I consider in more concrete terms how three educational institutions have attempted to encourage students to use speech and debate to critique mythos and logos. The first two are religious institutions. Whitefield Academy is an elementary and secondary school that embraces a "classical" approach to education to "equip students for a life of learning and service to the glory of God."[19] The second, Liberty University, seeks to develop "Christ-centered men and women with the values, knowledge, and skills essential to impact the world."[20] The third, the University of Oregon (my home institution), is a secular state university that seeks to help "individuals question critically, think logically, reason effectively, communicate clearly, act creatively, and live ethically."[21] The first two institutions are guided by "mythos," with specific theological ends in mind, and the third is oriented more toward "logos" and does not predetermine the theological aspirations individuals should seek, nor what it means to "live ethically." By looking at how these three institutions approach the teaching of speech and debate, we can begin to develop a better understanding of how rhetorical pedagogy might be revised to better account for the role of both mythos and logos in contemporary public discourse.

The Classical Method: Mythos and Logos at Whitefield Academy

"Used to develop students for more than 2,000 years," states the mission statement of Whitefield Academy, "the Classical method involves rigorous focus on grammar, logic and rhetoric."[22] Those who study the rhetorical tradition recognize that Whitefield is anchoring its curriculum in the trivium and in the liberal arts curriculum invented by rhetoricians in the Middle Ages. The trivium is complemented at Whitefield with the quadrivium (arithmetic, geometry, music, and astronomy), thereby constituting the seven disciplines at the foundation of a traditional liberal arts education. Importantly, this liberal arts tradition encourages free thinking and creativity—impulses emphasized by the instructors at Whitefield. The explicit pedagogical principle in play at Whitefield is that the students should have a command of all the tools of logos that will in turn encourage them to freely choose and defend the academy's mythos. That mythos, of course, is "Christ-centered" and in service to God.

Whitefield's mission statement elaborates on its pedagogy of speech, debate, and critical thinking in this manner: "The classically trained mind is able to process facts and make inferences with limited information in order to make well-reasoned decisions and fully develop well-considered ideas. Knowing is not enough, however. Students are simultaneously trained how to articulate, orally and in writing, the logic underpinning the decision or idea. The Classical objective is to teach students how to think, not what to think."[23] This pedagogical statement is strikingly similar to the mission statements of many secular educational institutions, and at first glance it actually might seem inconsistent with the objective of creating students who will serve God. However, Whitefield's focus on teaching students "how to think" rather than "what to think" reflects both a pragmatic and a theological purpose.

Whitefield recognizes that a didactic approach—one in which students are told what to think and believe—is counterproductive. James Selby, Whitefield's dean, told me that he and his staff are fully aware of the research showing that many students who receive parochial educations do not remain committed to Christianity.[24] He noted that students need to make an informed (not a forced) choice to remain within the fold of the Whitefield mythos. At the same time, Dean Selby suggested that when students learn the classical method, they become better equipped to detect errors that might lead to sin. With the trivium at the core of its curriculum, Whitefield provides its students with a rhetorical education revolving around speech, debate, and critical thinking.

Whitefield's curriculum features "Great Books," exposing students to a host of competing philosophical and theological perspectives. In their classes, students are encouraged to engage in dialogue and debate about the different points of view they encounter, and they are assigned as part of progymnasmata to engage in switch-side argumentation. This might seem a tricky pedagogical exercise, as instructors—in presenting, say, the works of atheists—must do so fairly, while also remaining in service to Whitefield's mythos. Yet, committed to Aristotle's belief that stronger arguments ultimately prevail over weaker ones, Whitefield's instructors have faith that students will find God's words and the presence of Jesus to be persuasive. And, again, there is a pragmatic factor in play: if instructors gratuitously favor Whitefield's mythos over the strong arguments made by Enlightenment thinkers, the students may end up endorsing the Enlightenment logos over the mythos at the center of the academy's mission. Having read and engaged in argumentative exercises in support of Enlightenment thought, students trained in critical thinking would likely detect such a bias and might be more likely to reject Whitefield's mythos.

Secularists might look with suspicion at the Whitefield curriculum, seeing it as a pedagogy of inoculation rather than one of free thinking—the intent of a true liberal arts education. They might suspect that Whitefield teaches weakened versions of arguments against a Christ-centered, God-serving life, or that they teach secular ideas with the goal of building resistance against them, not treating them as reasonable alternatives to the mythos advocated by Whitefield. I am not in a position to assess this critique. Yet Whitefield does put its mythos at risk by subjecting it to the interrogation of argument and debate, and given the significant failure of Christian elementary and secondary schools to keep their students rooted in the faith, the academy's faculty has a strong motivation to give all points of view a fair hearing. If the academy does teach Enlightenment ideas and equip its students with the tools of debate and critical thinking (and the test scores of its students on the ACT and other secular tests suggest that it does), then its students leave well equipped to freely choose other mythos, including those associated with a secular worldview. Dean Selby, in my interview with him, stated that some of his students do, indeed, "wander" from the faith after leaving the academy. Yet many others go on to lives in service to the religious principles they studied at Whitefield and are, in all probability, better able to explain and justify those principles when challenged.

Mining for Truth in Switch-Side Debating: Mythos-Informed Intercollegiate Debate at Liberty University

Zev Chafets, in a *New York Times* profile of the Liberty University debate program and its then-coach Brett O'Donnell, attempted to explain its success in NDT (National Debate Tournament) style debate.[25] Chafets attributed the rise of the program to national prominence to O'Donnell and the founder of the university, Reverend Jerry Falwell. Unlike Whitefield Academy, Falwell and O'Donnell did not celebrate the classical method, the trivium, or the liberal arts as pedagogical inspirations for their debate program. Rather, Falwell talked about creating "champions for Christ" and forming an "army of people who know how to make our case."[26] Nevertheless, Liberty University, like Whitefield, is willing to expose students to positions at odds with its theology.

Because Liberty's debaters engage in switch-side debating (the NDT and other intercollegiate debate organizations require students to argue both sides of the resolution), they are, on occasion, expected to represent positions at direct odds with the theology promoted by their university. One year, the resolution required Liberty students to debate the abortion issue, and Falwell allowed his students to argue in favor of abortion rights. As a result, Liberty's debate rooms "became the only place on campus where students were free to argue in favor of Roe v. Wade."[27] According to Chafets, Falwell's reasoning was that the debate program needed to follow the rules of the debate game.

O'Donnell's successor, Michael Hall, highly values the perspective-taking required by switch-side debating and offered another reason why Liberty students should take positions different from those endorsed by their university.[28] To Hall, the admonition offered by Jesus Christ that one should love one's neighbor carries over into the realm of academic debate. According to Hall, if his students are to love other people, they must give their positions the best hearing and representation that is possible. He calls his students to immerse themselves in the worlds of their neighbors and to represent their points of view fully and fairly. Switch-side debating, Hall believes, allows students to mine for truths outside the boundaries of Liberty.

Hall, who debated for Liberty as an undergraduate, testifies that switch-side debating forced him to confront his very conservative, fundamentalist upbringing. His involvement in academic debate prompted a significant change in his understanding of race in America. He entered Liberty as a self-professed reactionary and left the university holding more progressive views on race. He does not remember a single transformative moment, but as he conducted research and his beliefs were confronted in the academic debate arena, his attitudes changed. He concluded that there were good reasons for affirmative action, given that African Americans had suffered under slavery and Jim Crow for centuries, and that the drug laws in the United States discriminated against blacks. He remembers feeling embarrassed by his lack of knowledge, which was followed by guilt when he was faced with the evidence on racial disparities in the United States.

Hall's program is nested within Liberty University's theological mythos, and the yearly schedule he creates and the values he teaches are designed to promote the gospel of Jesus Christ. With the blessing of the university, Hall's students are allowed to follow all the secular rules of the academic debate organizations, but they do not participate in some of the cultural practices on display at tournaments, including swearing, casual dress, drinking, or drug usage. To the credit of the debate community, their secular opponents in turn respect and tolerate Liberty's conservative values and ethos. Chafets writes, "Everyone on the college circuit is aware that Liberty is a conservative Christian university. This could be a problem—judging is highly subjective. 'Ninety-five percent of the debate community, including the judges, are more liberal than the most liberal members of Congress,' O'Donnell says. But he isn't complaining. Judges can be idiosyncratic, but most of them will be swayed by strong argument, O'Donnell says; some even bend over backward to correct for their liberal bias."[29] In context, the "strong argument" O'Donnell refers to is one based on evidence drawn from the secular world: logos, not mythos.

Hall, however, is not troubled by academic debate's emphasis on secular logos, for he sees all truths—secular and religious—as God's truths. His program roots students in a theology that allows them to explore these truths with the method of debate and argumentation. Given that all truths are God's truths, he tells students they should not fear honoring the positions different than their own. He and his program vest the research students conduct in preparation for policy debate with spiritual value, in that they are learning about the worlds inhabited by their neighbors and the variety of God's truths. Like Whitefield Academy, the logos taught through speech and debate is viewed by Liberty University as in service to its mythos, which is to share the gospel and bring people to Christ.

Secular critics who value logos for itself might find Liberty's subordination of logos to its Christ-centered mythos profoundly troubling. For all the affirmation Liberty might shower on academic debate, the institution sees it as a means to its evangelical end. Christian rhetoric, as George Kennedy and a host of scholars note, has always served an instrumental function.[30] Beginning with Augustine, Christian theologians have valued rhetoric because it can be used to bring converts to the tradition and reinforce, through ritual and inoculation, the commitments made by adherents to the faith. Liberty's program quite consciously wraps religious ritual around its students, tethering them to its theological mission. Students begin the year in a retreat, where they reflect on what it means to be a Christian in a secular debate community. During the academic debate season, Liberty staff and students meet to worship, pray, and reinforce the values of their community.

Both Whitefield Academy and Liberty University use debate as means to an end. Yet they place these ends in jeopardy when they teach their students how to use logos. There is no guarantee that students will remain within their faith traditions once they subject them to the scrutiny of rational argument. From another angle, Whitefield sees its use of the classical method as a conservative revival of an ancient Christian educational program that was based on the trivium, quadrivium, and progymnasmata; Liberty does not seem to fear logos, as Hall and his students appear to believe that their religious mythos can withstand critique. Whitefield and Liberty are both placing bets that students equipped with a command of logos will not only find arguments against their faith traditions weak but that their commitments to God and Christ will be strengthened and inoculated after they are confronted with secular logos.

The Value of Logos: Critiquing Mythos at a Secular Public Institution

As a public, governmentally supported institution, the University of Oregon must honor the church-state divide. Religion can be a subject of study, but no one religion must be given preference, which marks the major difference between Whitefield Academy, Liberty University, and my university. I have offered students and the public many opportunities to critique the mythos of religion through speech and debate, but I identify two that stand out: *classroom simulations* and *public forums*.

Classroom Simulations

In courses on the Israeli-Palestinian and Northern Ireland conflicts, as well as a course I taught on the prevention of mass atrocities, I feature the use of simulations in which I assign students to portray key characters in each of the respective conflicts. The Israeli-Palestinian conflict, which is a civil war of recent vintage, is marked by a dispute between Judaism and Islam. I assign students to roles they will play in a negotiation simulation. One student, for example, will play the role of the leader of Hamas (the Palestinian Islamic Resistance Movement), Khaled Meshal. Another student is assigned the role of Aryeh Deri, who is the leader of the Shas Party (the Guardians of the Torah). In preparing students to assume these roles, I encourage them to conduct deep research on their characters. Once prepared, the students can portray their characters in their complexity.

Although both Hamas and Shas are fundamentalist religious movements, both have made ideological adjustments to the realities they face. Meshal and Hamas have proposed a "hudna," or a truce with Israel justified by the Quran, while Shas has declared, based on a reading of the Torah, that lives are more important than territories. Based on these historical developments, the students can engage their counterparts in negotiation, developing positions that are nuanced. The hudna proposed by Hamas and the lives-over-land hierarchy endorsed by Shas are the results of argument and debate carried out in both communities. Students learn that religion and religious beliefs are significantly influenced by context and that both are to a large degree products of culture.

The course I taught with a colleague on the conflict between Catholics and Protestants in Northern Ireland also emphasized religion. Students learned that the two Christian denominations offer the resources to justify both violence and peace. During the negotiation simulations, students drew from their research to engage in robust negotiations and argument about possible agreements that might address the concerns of both parties. Through structured negotiations, the students in both courses came to understand that religious doctrine is contested, permeable, and open to interpretation through argument.

Public Forums

Pacifica Forum, a "discussion group" at my university, was listed by the Southern Poverty Law Center (SPLC) in 2009 as a White Nationalist Hate Group.[31] It supported and defended an anti-Semitic mythos, with its members making horrifically derogatory comments about Jews. As Kenneth Burke and others have demonstrated, anti-Semitism is a mythos that mimics the structure and form of religion.[32] The group invited Mark Weber, David Irving, and other Holocaust deniers to campus. At that time, I was dean of one of our colleges, and I engaged upper administration and my colleagues on what the university should do in response to Pacifica Forum's discourse. The First Amendment guaranteed their right to speak, although I argued—unsuccessfully—that their language constituted hate speech. We decided that the best approach was to fight bad speech with good speech.

Toward this end, I worked with student groups and faculty to organize a forum designed to subject the claims made by Pacifica Forum to critical scrutiny by scholars in history and religious studies. Four of my colleagues engaged and critiqued the anti-Semitic mythos of Pacifica Forum and the arguments made by Mark Weber, whom Pacifica Forum had invited to campus a week before our forum. Our professors calmly and insightfully punctured the anti-Semitic mythos of Pacifica Forum with the best available scholarship. More than eighty students and community members attended. The forum was cited by the SPLC as an illustration of our community speaking "strongly against the spate of anti-Jewish and racist speakers."[33]

The University of Oregon, as a secular institution, cannot endorse one religion over another. However, the university can rightly critique racism, anti-Semitism, and other ideologies that make for a climate of fear that prevents learning. Speech and debate serves an important function during these moments, as faculty, students, and staff speak out against and debate the claims made by those who seek to spread their toxic mythos. Those who confront mythos designed to intimidate and dehumanize must have a strong command of the research and advocacy skills needed to debunk them.

Conclusion: Arguing with Logos and Mythos

Teachers of speech and debate can provide students with the equipment they need to critique and defend mythos. An exclusive focus on logos will not prepare them for the rhetorical situations they will encounter. Secular students need to understand why religious principles are foundational to some members of their audience and the role mythos plays in their lives. They can adapt to those listeners by identifying those values within their faith traditions that might be shared with others. In turn, students from religious backgrounds should appreciate the gift of reason offered to them through their faith traditions. Whitefield Academy and the Liberty University debate program recognize this gift and offer good models, I suggest, of a healthy relationship between logos and mythos in religious educational institutions.

The wall between church and state in the United States should be revered and protected. However, "because of the role that religiously based moral arguments inevitably play in the political process," as Perry writes, "it is important that such arguments, *no less than secular moral arguments*, be presented in, *so that they can be tested in*, public political debate."[34] Religiously based arguments should be open to the light of reason, questioning, and the powers of logos. David Tracy, echoing Dean Selby's observation that logos can reveal errors leading to sin, calls religious believers to learn from feminists about the patriarchal nature of many religions. He also argues that a willingness to consider the challenges and insights offered by Feuerbach, Darwin, Marx, Freud, and Nietzsche can help to explain how truth may be distorted by the sins of ignorance and belief in illusions. This is precisely the reason Dean Selby at Whitefield assigns Hegel and other critics of religion to his students.[35]

Speech and debate can perform a valuable public service when there is disagreement about the religious interpretations informing public policy. As Perry argues, because "religious illiteracy—and, alas, even prejudice"—is "rampant among many nonreligious intellectuals," we need to be reminded that "at its best religious discourse in public culture is not less dialogic—not less open-minded, not less deliberative—than is, at its best, secular discourse in public culture."[36] Deliberative discourse on religiously inflected arguments—no less than debates over secular issues—should be informed by reason. A form of logos is invariably at work when there is disagreement over the interpretation and use of scripture in public policy debates. Mythos in turn might constrain the pretensions of logos in those same debates.

Logos must be nested within a moral system. Absent any moral restraint, the power of Enlightenment reasoning, which rejects religion because it sees it as based solely on emotion, superstition, and irrationality, can lead to great destruction. Scholars have documented the "ice-cold" deductive logic used to justify the Holocaust and other episodes of mass genocide.[37] When a group of people is defined as an "out-group" or made to be a scapegoat, then a logic unfolds that, if left unchecked, can result in demonization and ultimately in efforts to eliminate that group. Religious convictions that sanctify life can serve as a check on Enlightenment reasoning, and those who are religious can honor a secular morality that Zuckerman suggests "hinges upon little else than not harming others, and helping those in need, both of which flow easily and directly from the golden rule's basic, simple logic of reciprocity."[38]

Our argument pedagogy must bring logos and mythos into alignment. Students from secular backgrounds who go on to leadership positions will benefit from an understanding of religion and how to engage the religious. This will allow them to learn from the mistakes of Ben-Gurion, Nehru, and the leaders of the Algerian revolution, all of whom were (by all accounts) both ignorant and dismissive of religion. Students from religious backgrounds can come to honor logos as a means to better understand their scripture and the wonders of God's creation. Whitefield Academy's classical curriculum and the debate program at Liberty University come close to achieving a rapprochement between logos and mythos. My university, with its logos-centered mission, provides a good model as well when it confronts issues such as anti-Semitism and religious justifications for sexism.

The "new rhetorics" of Perelman/Olbrechts-Tyteca and Kenneth Burke provide anchors for this integration, as they both offer the theoretical insights necessary for argument about logos and mythos. These new rhetorics have been used to provide critical analysis of religious discourse with secular logic, and they offer as a rhetorical mythos concepts such as "communion" and the "universal audience." The next step in developing an argument theory that honors both mythos and logos might be to draw from these new rhetorics a pedagogy that equips our students to engage in speech and debate using logos to critique mythos and mythos to help define the boundaries for argument. Students from secular backgrounds should command the ability to use and interrogate sacred scripture as they attempt to persuade audiences who adhere to religious truths. And those from religious backgrounds should understand and use the tools of science and critical reason to persuade audiences who do not adhere to religious truths. As this new pedagogy emerges and spreads across more institutions of higher learning, we can hope for more constructive, less polarizing public debate over the many public policy issues that touch on both religious and secular concerns.

PART 3

RETHINKING COMPETITIVE SPEECH AND DEBATE

8

THE CEDA—MILLER CENTER WAR POWERS DEBATES:
A CASE FOR INTERCOLLEGIATE DEBATE'S CIVIC ROLES

PAUL E. MABREY III

If we're going to have arguments, let's have arguments, but let's make them debates worthy of this body and worthy of this country.

—President Barack Obama

Hence the interscholastic debate is a viable instrument for democracy to have, for with it a full stream of light may be turned on from a source which the opposition to good government cannot touch nor control.

—James Leonard Highsaw

On May 13, 2013, the Cross Examination Debate Association (CEDA) announced the topic for the 2013–2014 college policy debate season: presidential war powers.[1] With this announcement, thousands of United States college students and debate coaches dedicated an entire year to researching, arguing, advocating, analyzing, and debating the role of the president in taking the country to war—specifically, his authority under the Constitution and later war powers legislation. As Kelly Young and his coauthors noted in their winning topic proposal, "debates about reducing presidential power would provide

The epigraphs to this chapter are derived from Barack Obama, "Remarks by the President in State of Union Address," *The White House*, January 20, 2015, https://obamawhitehouse.archives.gov/the-press-office/2015/01/20/remarks-president-state-union-address-january-20-2015, and James Leonard Highsaw, "Interscholastic Debates in Relation to Political Opinion," *Quarterly Journal of Public Speaking* 2 (1916): 382.

a critical examination of one of the most fundamental controversies in government policymaking and constitutional checks and balances."[2] The college policy debate community shined a "full stream of light" on a crucial issue by selecting the topic, and it could not have come at a better time for democracy and the people of the United States.

In the summer of 2013, the United States was facing a new controversy at home and continuing controversies abroad related to presidential war powers. The United States was continuing its counterterrorism efforts in response to the 9/11 attacks, including intelligence gathering, detentions, targeted strikes, and even boots on the ground in Afghanistan. But magnifying concerns about these efforts was Edward Snowden's leak of National Security Agency documents revealing that the U.S. government had been monitoring the actions and conversations of citizens at home as well as both allies and enemies abroad.[3] This was one of the top concerns cited in the paper announcing the CEDA topic, along with military uses of unmanned aerial vehicles, the president's authority to detain enemy combatants, and the continued detention of alleged terrorists at Guantanamo Bay. Underlying concern over all these issues was the feeling among some that the U.S. government, and the president in particular, was making crucial decisions about national security without public debate. These concerns over unchecked executive authority demanded further deliberation and debate.

What role, if any, does intercollegiate debate play in broader discussions of important issues such as the president's war powers? Is college policy debate really part of the national civic dialogue, or is it even an effective mode of civic education for young people? Finally, what might debate organizations do to enhance the educational value of intercollegiate debate within the larger context of public policy controversies? This chapter looks at one successful attempt to connect intercollegiate debate to larger conversations and thereby enhance its value as a form of civic education and engagement: the CEDA–Miller Center War Powers Debates. This national public debate series took place throughout the academic year of 2013–2014, and it engaged CEDA debaters in conversations and debates with leading experts on U.S. foreign policy.

I begin by briefly reviewing the landscape of civic education, reflecting on its role in higher education and its connections to intercollegiate debate. Next, I describe the origins and the idea behind the CEDA–Miller Center War Powers Debates, recalling the collaborative effort behind the debate and some of the deliberations over the debate's format and participants. Finally, I suggest how the War Powers Debates functioned as civic education, informing later political discussion of presidential war powers and creating a model for future partnerships between intercollegiate debate organizations and other academic or scholarly associations.

Civic Education and Debate

The importance of civic education to the health and vitality of our democratic system has been noted since its founding. James Madison, one of the architects of the U.S. Constitution, put it succinctly: "Knowledge will forever govern ignorance, and a people who mean to be their own Governors, must arm themselves with the power knowledge gives."[4] As Madison and many others since have recognized, an informed and well-educated public is foundational to a well-functioning democracy. In fact, many institutions of higher learning emphasize how their curriculum prepares students for civic life after graduation, not just for jobs but for participation in civic life. How one acquires, uses, and is motivated to achieve the knowledge and skills necessary for engaged citizenship has been debated and discussed widely in recent years.

The role of American higher education in civic education has been the subject of a number of recent reports, books, and articles. Most notably, the Association of American Colleges and Universities, in 2012, published *A Crucible Moment: College Learning and Democracy's Future*.[5] Written by the National Task Force on Civic Learning and Democratic Engagement, *A Crucible Moment* sounded a clarion call for colleges and universities to provide more meaningful preparation and pathways for students to learn, live, and love civic education and engagement. Calling for a new vision of civic learning for the twenty-first century, the report argued that "higher education must in this next generation of civic learning investments build a broader theory of knowledge about democracy and democratic principles for an age marked as it is by multiplicity and division."[6] Civic education, in this view, is more than learning about governmental structures and voting. One also must learn to work with individuals different from oneself on important public issues and problems. To do this, the task force encouraged postsecondary educational institutions to build partnerships between faculty, students, organizations, and communities, providing more opportunities for students to work on solving contemporary public problems.

Encouraging students to get involved in their communities has even been touted as a means of promoting economic mobility. Opportunity Nation, which describes itself as "a bipartisan, national campaign compromised of more than 300 businesses, educational intuitions, nonprofits and civic organizations,"[7] published a 2014 report arguing that "[c]ivic engagement can help low-income youth build social capital and find meaningful education and career pathways."[8] Here civic education and engagement is cast not in opposition to workforce training (as it has often been) but rather as a complement to preparing students for meaningful work and economic advancement. Again, this suggests a new kind of civic education, focusing not just on voting or participating in political campaigns but on building stronger communities. According to Opportunity Nation, civic education is not only good for our democracy but for the health and economic vitality of students and the communities in which they live.

Given the resurgence of interest in civic education, it should come as no surprise that there is also renewed interest in the connections between intercollegiate debate and forensics and civic learning. After all, debate traditionally has been viewed as a training ground for political and civic leaders, and debate scholars and practitioners have long claimed that debate is an effective way of promoting civic learning and engagement.[9] As William Keith argued in his keynote address at a major debate conference in 2010, however, the recent resurgence of interest in civic education and engagement, while providing "an incredible opportunity for debate, given its history of different modes of training for discursive civic participation," also requires that we rethink *how* we teach debate and the *kinds* of debate we teach. Urging debate to "return to its history," Keith called on his colleagues to recover debate's traditional emphasis on the civic, "yet with the tools and concepts more recently developed."[10] Specifically, Keith urged his colleagues to embrace less competitive, more *public* forms of debate based on the rise of scholarly interest in deliberation and dialogue.

Many within the debate community have already begun to heed Keith's call for more collaborative, more public, and more "real-world" forms of debate and forensics.[11] Within the policy debate community, as Anjali Vats has argued, "civic engagement through policy debate is becoming a community norm as opposed to an isolated practice that characterizes particular teams."[12] There also have been increases in the number of public debates, high school outreach programs, Urban Debate Leagues, prison debate leagues, and other noncompetitive forms of debate and forensics. At the programmatic level, debate scholars such as Sarah Partlow-Lefevre and Timothy O'Donnell have suggested that civic education and engagement be treated as central learning outcomes for students participating in debate.[13] On a curricular level, the interest in civic engagement has taken the form of writing assignments based on attendance at public debates, as suggested by Michael Davis and Pete Bsumek, or instruction on how to create digital debate archives, as suggested by Carly Woods and colleagues.[14]

Public debates in particular represent "sites of social learning where the spirit of civic engagement can flourish, ideas can be shared, and the momentum of social movements can be stoked," as Gordon Mitchell has argued.[15] Even the process of choosing debate topics itself might be better geared toward civic education and engagement, as Gordon Stables has suggested in urging those proposing topics to consider their "potential public benefits."[16] In short, the debate community is already moving toward reenvisioning debate's role in civic education in the twenty-first century. Reclaiming its historical roots in civic education and public deliberation, the debate community has become part of the growing movement to better prepare young people for citizenship.

The CEDA–Miller Center War Powers Debates

On August 22, 2013, CEDA and the Miller Center, an affiliate of the University of Virginia promoting research and public outreach on issues relating to the presidency, public policy, and political history, announced a new public debate series, the War Powers Debates.[17] The War Powers Debates consisted of a series of three public debates on various aspects of presidential war powers, coinciding with the 2013–2014 debate season focusing on the same topic. The debates featured undergraduate student debaters from across the country debating specific war powers in front of public audiences, moderated by a scholar or other expert on U.S. foreign policy or national security issues. CEDA hoped that the War Powers Debates would "serve as a model for future CEDA endeavors to establish collaborative partnerships" that would "showcase" and "provide exceptional opportunities" for student debaters while also contributing to "important public conversations."[18]

The Miller Center proved to be an ideal partner for the War Powers Debates for two reasons. First, the Miller Center organized the National War Powers Commission, a group whose 2008 report has grounded much of the recent national debate about presidential war powers. The commission was led by two former U.S. Secretaries of State and included experts from around the country. Its recommendations included repealing the War Powers Resolution of 1973 and passing a new War Powers Consultation Act, which would strengthen the consultative process between Congress and the president on military actions. Second, the mission of the Miller Center aligned well with CEDA's mission and its ambitions to extend the civic influence of debate beyond the classroom. According to the Miller Center's website, the center specializes in "presidential scholarship, public policy, and political history and strives to apply the lessons of history to the nation's most pressing contemporary governance challenges." The Center is committed to work "grounded in rigorous scholarship and advanced through civil discourse."[19] Their focus on presidential scholarship and public policy aligned well with CEDA's interest in advancing academic debate's emphasis on civic engagement and its impact on broader public debates.

The collaborative partnership between CEDA and the Miller Center was essential to the success of the War Powers Debates. Each organization was able to leverage its expertise and relationships to make the debates happen. For example, CEDA was able to attract the attention of thousands of college debaters who were focusing on the topic of presidential war powers because of the college debate topic. Meanwhile, the Miller Center was able to call on its network of leading scholars and experts on the presidency and public policy to provide both venues and participants for the program. They were able to help schedule one of the public debates at the Ronald Reagan Presidential Library and Museum, for example, while CEDA identified college debaters from the local area interested in participating. Similarly, the Miller Center drew on its network to identify special guests and debate moderators for each debate, while CEDA identified speakers and moderators for the debates. Dr. G. Thomas Goodnight, a former debater and debate coach who is now a leading scholar in argumentation theory, moderated the public debate at Reagan Library, while Senator Tim Kaine, a leading advocate of reform and accountability in war powers legislation, spoke at the opening public debate hosted by George Washington University in Washington, D.C.

The collaborative partnership also maximized publicity and promoted the organizational goals of both CEDA and the Miller Center. For the Miller Center, a national public debate series proved to be a great way to keep the issue of war powers and the recommendations of the National War Powers Commission on the agenda of the public and the media. Moreover, involving student debaters helped the Miller Center reach an audience that its traditional programs typically did not reach: college students. For CEDA, the War Powers Debates was a great way to attract positive publicity for intercollegiate debate, CEDA, and individual programs and debaters. The debates attracted media coverage and a national audience to the activity of intercollegiate debate, showcasing the insight, creativity, and skills of today's generation of college students. Members of both organizations also benefited from coming together to brainstorm ideas, write public relations releases, contact media outlets, design materials, and more. Working together through the War Powers Debates, the Miller Center and CEDA were able to advance their respective organizational missions.

The actual organizing of the War Powers Debates raised a number of questions and posed several challenges. Programming the events began with some obvious questions. Who should debate? Where should the debates happen? When should the debates be scheduled? And what format should be used? After considerable discussion, the organizers decided on a long table format, in which three teams of two debaters on each side of the question—affirmative and negative—are seated behind a table facing a public audience. The long table format has been used for more than a decade at the James Madison University's Madison Cup, a public debate tournament held at the end of the competitive policy debate season.[20] The format encourages both the competitive and cooperative aspects of intercollegiate debate while also fostering audience-centered public debate. Debaters are still required to speak in favor or against the resolution, but they must do so while cooperating with their colleagues on other teams. Meanwhile, the presence of a public or lay audience encourages the debaters to focus on the most important issues, simplify complex concepts, and speak in a conversational voice that can be heard and understood by nondebaters. Debaters are also able to ask and answer questions from their opponents during the debate. Following the debate, the moderator invites questions and discussion from the audience and may also make some closing remarks.

The two organizations collaborated on a number of details to assure that the debates went smoothly and attracted significant audiences. For example, CEDA maximized student interest and participation by making sure the debates were not scheduled in conflict with academic demands or tournament travel. Similarly, the Miller Center worked with potential host sites to avoid scheduling conflicts or competing events. After extensive conversations, the three sites were chosen: George Washington University, the Ronald Reagan Presidential Library and Museum, and the Franklin D. Roosevelt Presidential Library and Museum. These hosts were selected because they best met a list of criteria that included relevance to the topic, available dates and facilities, and interest from collegiate debate programs in the area.

Once the sites and format were selected, CEDA and the Miller Center had further conversations about the particular topics to be debated at each site. It was important that all involved, including the sites selected for each debate, have a say in this decision. From the original CEDA announcement of the 2013–2014 controversy, a number of possible topics arose, including the War Powers Commission recommendations, targeted killing, and the indefinite detention of alleged enemy combatants. The last War Powers Debate at the Roosevelt Presidential Library provided an excellent example of how the topics were ultimately chosen based on the interests of the participating organizations. Given President Roosevelt's executive order indefinitely detaining more than 100,000 Japanese Americans during World War II, it was only natural that the topic chosen for debate at that venue was the president's authority to detain individuals deemed a national security threat.

Participant selection was the last programming issue that needed to be decided. Here CEDA took the lead because of the organization's network of collegiate debate programs and debaters. Individual debate programs were invited for the debates based on prior public debate experience and support for other modes of public debate. CEDA also attempted to invite programs that reflected the diversity of membership. Also important was the host institution's interest in inviting particular local programs that already had connections to the site. None of these organizational details, of course, were easily resolved. But with good collaboration among the cosponsors and host institutions, this valuable experiment in debate as civic education and engagement was a major success.

The Civic Value of the War Powers Debates

The War Powers Debates provide a model for how debate organizations can design and implement programming that promotes civic ends, contributing both to civic education and to public deliberations on important issues. Obviously, the War Powers Debates provided a good opportunity for civic learning. By participating in the debate, the students gained two important dimensions of civic learning emphasized in *A Crucible Moment*: knowledge and the experience of actually engaging in democratic deliberation. Preparing for the public debates also provided the students with different kinds of civic education than they normally would get by participating in competitive tournament debate. Because they spoke before public audiences, the debaters had to do more work translating the technical concepts of debate and the war powers issue for a lay audience. In the process, they themselves became civic educators, helping to educate and inform the public. Public debate participation also models the *actual engagement* called for in *A Crucible Moment* and other recent calls for reforming civic education. In the debates, the students were not just reading about an important issue but arguing, advocating, and participating in the democratic exchange and contestation of ideas. After the debate, the learning continued, as students were asked to explore the issue more deeply and argue for their own views outside of the debate context.

An excellent example of the "real-world" experience students gained from participating in the War Powers Debates occurred after the debate at the Reagan Library. After one of the debaters spoke about the impact of using drones to attack enemy targets, one audience member disputed her argument by pointing out that none of the debaters had ever been in harm's way. The audience member said he had friends who were actual pilots and that the arguments in the debate failed to take sufficient account of the dangers faced by pilots in manned air strikes. The debater listened carefully and first thanked the audience member for the comments. Then the debater responded by agreeing that pilots sent into combat faced grave dangers and that, having never served herself, she could not speak from the perspective of pilots. The debater finished by affirming that the audience member had raised an important point. This exchange demonstrated not only how such exchanges might serve to broaden the perspective of student debaters but also how they might learn about engaging even hostile audience members with civility and respect.

Curriculum development is another example of how the War Powers Debates might provide opportunities for civic learning. One of the benefits of partnering with different presidential libraries was the possibility of educational programming. Libraries have an interest in getting students wanting to learn more about important issues and archival resources. So they were happy to collaborate with others involved in the War Powers Debates on a curriculum packet on the topic. These packets were never completed, but the plan was to publish and distribute them to high school students throughout the country. Librarians and archivists were to provide the historical documents, such as an old executive order, and debate scholars would write accompanying interpretative texts highlighting their contemporary relevance. While this plan for curriculum development was never realized due to budget cuts, it does provide a good example of the kind of material that could come from future organization partnerships.

The War Powers Debates also showcased ways in which debate organizations can collaborate both within and beyond the debate community to have an impact on deliberations beyond the classroom. A significant example of this is the effect the first War Powers Debate had on Senator Tim Kaine (D-VA). Senator Kaine, writing for a publication of the National Defense University's Center for Complex Operations, recalled attending the War Powers Debate at George Washington University and concluded:

> One student startled me by saying: "I know nothing about war, but I know nothing but war." We have been at war for nearly 13 years and many of our young do not know an America at peace. But, with an all-volunteer force where only 1% of Americans serve in the military, many lack any meaningful connection with the realities and sacrifices that war entails.

> We can restore the original constitutional vision of executive and legislative branches working together to make these tough decisions. If we do so, our deliberation and debate will educate our citizens and produce, when necessary, the strongest consensus behind any military mission and the men and women we rely on to carry it out.[21]

Here Senator Kaine cites, as evidence of the need to reform war powers authority, the speech of a student from George Washington University at the opening War Powers Debate. And he is doing so within a publication that circulates widely within the defense and security decision-making communities. One could not have imagined this kind of impact when we first began organizing these debates.

Another example of the kind of impact these kinds of debates might have is the inclusion of the War Powers Debates on the Miller Center's National War Powers Commission webpage. On that webpage, which also includes the commission's final report, is a section labeled "Partnership with Cross Examination Debate Association."[22] In that section, one finds the dates, locations, and press releases announcing the debates, along with videos and pictures from two of the debates. To the side is a picture from the opening debate of Senator Kaine speaking at the first CEDA debate. The text, which describes CEDA as "the nation's largest intercollegiate debating organization," also notes that students from twenty-four colleges and universities were expected to participate in the debates. Thus, the CEDA–Miller Center partnership has become an important part of the institutional public memory of the War Powers Commission, and the videos and other materials on the site might be used to inspire or even train debaters who take on similar projects.

Finally, the War Powers Debates suggest how reforms in the debate topic selection process might encourage similar partnerships promoting civic learning and engagement. Since Gordon Stables proposed including the criterion of public benefit into the topic selection process, several of the winning topic proposals have emphasized how the topic area might lend itself to public debates and deliberation.[23] But the discussion of this in topic proposal papers might go deeper, including more detail into how these sorts of partnerships and public debate projects might be staged. For example, future topic area papers might suggest academic or other organizations, like the Miller Center, that might make good partners for a series of public debates. Or they might identify university organizations or particular debate programs equipped to take the lead in organizing such projects.

The major national debate organizations, such as CEDA, the National Debate Tournament, and the American Debate Association, have the institutional capital and other resources to make events like the War Powers Debates a success. Additionally, they can leverage the interests and capacity of the entire debate community rather than just one or two local debate programs. In the case of the War Powers Debates, CEDA was able to ensure that many different programs were able to participate and access the civic programming. With one large organization managing the programming, they were also able to build sustainable relationships that may lead to similar partnerships in the future. To facilitate this, national debate organizations should have program directors or teams to manage such events. These sorts of events benefit more than just the participating programs. Civic debate events like the War Powers Debates benefit the entire debate community, as they bring positive attention to the various forms of debate and our community members.

Individual debate programs stand to benefit most from civic programming like the War Powers Debates. Student debaters benefit by meeting and collaborating with other members of the debate community, audience members, host organizations, and other participants at the event itself. In the language of Opportunity Nation, this helps build their social capital. Participation in public debates also helps students think more about how to adapt or translate their ideas to diverse audiences. Debate team organizations can build institutional capital by meeting their own institutional goals for civic learning, education, and engagement. These events also provide great opportunities for programs to engage in alumni outreach.

The War Powers Debates represent just one model of how the debate community might better realize the promise of intercollegiate debate as civic education. With the announcement of a new debate topic each year, an opportunity is created for thousands of the brightest college students to engage in serious research on an important public issue. Student debaters think creatively about public policy problems, engage controversial issues that many citizens never seriously ponder, and deliberate and problem solve with other members of the community. Collaborating with one another and their coaches, intercollegiate policy debaters are capable of making significant contributions to democratic deliberation in America. More events like the War Powers Debates would help the intercollegiate debate community realize its potential for contributing to efforts to reform and reinvigorate civic education. Such events epitomize the movement to invent new modes of civic education grounded in community engagement and action.

9

BEYOND PEITHO:
THE WOMEN'S DEBATE INSTITUTE AS CIVIC EDUCATION

CATHERINE H. PALCZEWSKI

This chapter was one of the most difficult I have ever had to write. I struggled with it, until I figured out what was befuddling me. Two quandaries emerged.

First, I struggled because this chapter is full of contradictions, inconsistencies, and incoherencies. To wit: I am an unapologetic debate and speech booster. I believe debate and speech are civic education, and an incredibly powerful form of civic education at that. I would not be the person, the advocate, the scholar, or the teacher I am without the education that debate and speech has given me. However, I am also an unapologetic critic of debate and speech. I believe competitive debate and speech, like all practices and institutions in the United States, are sexed/gendered.[1] I also believe citizenship and civic education are sexed/gendered. How can I both boost and condemn debate and civic education? The answer leads to the second struggle.

In fifth grade, my otherwise singularly unblemished report card sent a strong disciplinary message to my young girl self. I received the highest marks in every subject regarding "Scholastic Progress." I also received the highest marks regarding "Social Characteristics—Work Habits," such as "Uses time wisely," "Follows directions," "Respects authority," "Completes assignments," "Accepts responsibility," and "Exercises self-control." All perfect scores, *except*

My thanks to the UNI writing group for feedback, especially Kyle Rudick, Ryan McGeough, and Philip Hopper, and to my fellow WDIers, whose hard work and embrace of argument sustain me.

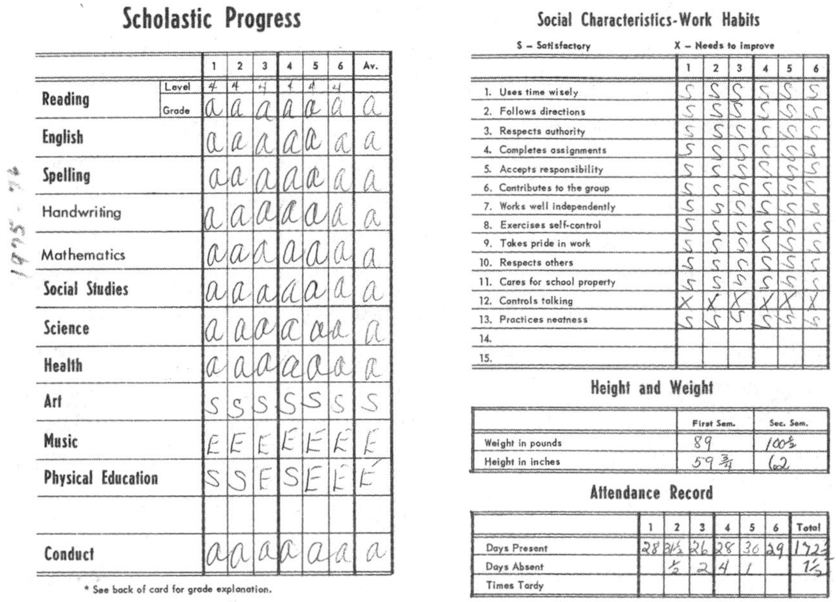

1975–76

Scholastic Progress

		1	2	3	4	5	6	Av.
Reading	Level	4	4	4	4	4	4	
	Grade	a	a	a	a	a	a	a
English		a	a	a	a	a	a	a
Spelling		a	a	a	a	a	a	a
Handwriting		a	a	a	a	a	a	a
Mathematics		a	a	a	a	a	a	a
Social Studies		a	a	a	a	a	a	a
Science		a	a	a	a	a	a	a
Health		a	a	a	a	a	a	a
Art		S	S	S	S	S	S	S
Music		E	E	E	E	E	E	E
Physical Education		S	S	E	S	E	E	E
Conduct		a	a	a	a	a	a	a

* See back of card for grade explanation.

Social Characteristics-Work Habits

S – Satisfactory X – Needs to improve

	1	2	3	4	5	6
1. Uses time wisely	S	S	S	S	S	S
2. Follows directions	S	S	S	S	S	S
3. Respects authority	S	S	S	S	S	S
4. Completes assignments	S	S	S	S	S	S
5. Accepts responsibility	S	S	S	S	S	S
6. Contributes to the group	S	S	S	S	S	S
7. Works well independently	S	S	S	S	S	S
8. Exercises self-control	S	S	S	S	S	S
9. Takes pride in work	S	S	S	S	S	S
10. Respects others	S	S	S	S	S	S
11. Cares for school property	S	S	S	S	S	S
12. Controls talking	X	X	X	X	X	X
13. Practices neatness	S	S	S	S	S	S
14.						
15.						

Height and Weight

	First Sem.	Sec. Sem.
Weight in pounds	89	100½
Height in inches	59¾	62

Attendance Record

	1	2	3	4	5	6	Total
Days Present	28	31½	26	28	36	29	172½
Days Absent		½	2	4	1		1½
Times Tardy							

Fig 9.1 Fifth-grade report card of Catherine H. (née Cathy) Palczewski, 1975–76, Ridgeview Elementary School, San Antonio, Texas.

for one category: "Controls talking." There, my report card contained an unrelenting row of six X marks, denoting "Needs to improve."

The message was loud and clear. I talked too much and that, alone, was a problem. It did not interfere with my ability to complete work, nor did it seem to interfere with others' work given that I received good marks on "Contributes to group" and "Respects others." It may have had something to do with the lively debates I had with my fifth-grade teacher, Mr. Stark (who also happened to be my first male teacher), over whether the biblical story of creationism was metaphorical or literal, but I think not. Instead, I think I was a girl who talked, and that was not to be encouraged . . . until high school, when I was recruited to join the debate and speech team. On the Robert E. Lee High School team, I competed in extemporaneous speaking, original oratory, prose, impromptu, student congress, Lincoln-Douglas debate, and policy debate. The debate and speech team was a place where I was encouraged to talk. For me, debate and speech taught me how to be a complete citizen, not just one who respected authority and others but also one who respected myself enough to advocate, forcefully, for my beliefs.

To be clear: my story should not be read as representative of all women. Even as I focus on sex/gender, I must note that identity is intersectional. One is never only sexed/gendered. We also are composed of races, sexualities, classes, religions, ethnicities, and citizenship statuses.[2] Many of the challenges faced by white women in debate and speech are magnified for women of color, where racial pressures for silence exist alongside, and supercharge, sexed/gendered pressures for silence.[3] Similarly, the challenges faced by ciswomen are not identical to the challenges faced by transwomen. I realize my ability to gain what I did from debate and speech was enabled by my white race, my cisgender body, and my U.S. citizen status, even as my sex and class may have created challenges.

Despite these reservations, I advocate for debate and speech as robust forms of civic education, *as long as* educators attend to the way in which debate and speech are sexed/gendered and to how women in debate and speech can challenge forms of sex/gender that hinder diverse women's civic engagement. Debate and speech can be transformative for women's civic education because they (provisionally) free women from the social constraints of performing womanhood in the form of a pure, pious, domestic, and submissive (often manifested as silent) femininity.[4] The term *women debaters* need not be an oxymoron.[5] I also advocate for the profound way in which women are transformative for debate and speech. Should we ever achieve parity in participation along sex/gender (and race) lines, then we will also have profoundly affected the forms and functions of debate and speech. Women's social location allows us to see—and critique—the elements of debate that hinder its liberatory and educational potential.

To demonstrate how I came to these conclusions, I work through four arguments. First, debate and speech are premised on an exclusion and sexualization of women and feminine bodies. Second, civic engagement and citizenship are premised on an exclusion and sexualization of women and feminine bodies. Third, civic education, with its focus on civility as politeness, disciplines disagreement and hinders engagement. Fourth, the Women's Debate Institute (WDI) offers a vision of what a transformative understanding of debate and speech as civic education would look like. Throughout this chapter, I move between the micro and macro, historical and contemporary, ideal and actually existing, and descriptive and proscriptive. But it all has to make sense, or else someone like me would not exist.

The Exclusion and Sexualization of Women in Debate

Debate and speech, given their foundations in rhetoric, are premised on an exclusion and sexualization of women and feminine bodies. Charles Morris and I worked through the history of sex/gender and sexuality in a chapter for the National Communication Association's centennial volume.[6] Here are a few of the highlights.

In classical times, mythic figures tied sexual violence to persuasion. The Greek goddess Peitho personified persuasion *and* seduction; the two were inseparable. Peitho was "utterly essential in democratic states, where persuasion, rather than violence, was the ideal," yet in "vase painting she has overwhelmingly erotic implications."[7] In a casual aside, the Theoi Greek Mythology website explains: "Peitho was usually depicted as a woman with her hand lifted in persuasion or fleeing from the scene of a rape," as though these two are parallel.[8] The sexualizing of rhetoric would go even further with the designation of rhetoric and eloquence as the "harlot of the arts," a phrase that appears to find its origin in the writings of first-century historian Tacitus.[9] In the Middle Ages, Peitho would transform from a goddess to Rhetorica, Dame Rhetoric, who would then revert to the harlot.[10] C. Jan Swearingen has summarized perceptions of that transformation during the Renaissance in explicitly sexualized terms: "The noble and beautiful Lady Rhetoric of the twelfth and thirteenth centuries has become a whore, a mother of harlots and lies."[11]

These characterizations are not relics of a time long gone. In a 1989 issue of *Communication Education*, Michael Burgoon called for the discipline of communication to divorce "Dame Speech."[12] Referencing "recently published indices of productivity," he proclaimed: "It is clear that *most* Speech teachers do not do scholarship and would have to be relegated to the role of spectators in their field."[13] Arguing against a model in which communication departments offer a general education course in speech "for the masses," Burgoon declared: "Speech departments are campus whores who truly live in fear of not being loved enough by others."[14] We need to grapple with the implicit assumptions about debate and speech that have crept into our disciplinary history.

Contemporary debate and speech are sexed insofar as girls/women do not participate in anywhere near equal numbers to boys/men. During the 1990s, women's participation at the National Debate Tournament (NDT) was consistently below 20 percent, and at the National Parliamentary Debate Association national tournament it was below 30 percent.[15] The statistics have not changed much during the 2000s. Data from 2005–2013 for the NDT and Tournament of Champions place women's participation at around 22 percent.[16] Statistics from Individual Events competition also show a success gap.[17] Analysis of the 2009, 2010, and 2011 National Individual Events Tournament results demonstrates that even though women compete at levels comparable to men, they earn awards at far lower rates, and the awards decrease even more if the event is one that issues a call to action (e.g., persuasive speaking as compared to informative speaking). Debate and speech are also gendered insofar as traditionally masculine styles of communication that focus on instrumentality, assertiveness, and competitiveness are privileged.[18]

Citizenship as Exclusionary

Just as debate and forensics are sexualized to the detriment of women, so too are the concepts of civic engagement and citizenship premised on an exclusion and sexualization of women and feminine bodies in the public sphere. Until the 1900s, to be a "public woman" meant, socially, that one was a prostitute.[19] Legally, women were not allowed to vote in the United States until 1920, and culturally women were not consistently trained or rewarded for the practices of citizenship in the public sphere (e.g., advocacy and debate) even long after they won the franchise. Although women's actual public participation is far more rich and complex than the narrative of separate spheres would indicate,[20] women faced discipline for venturing into public spaces well into the twentieth century. Carolyn Eastman's oratorical history of the United States, *A Nation of Speechifiers*, makes clear that during "the early decades of the new United States . . . many Americans embraced the idea that the new nation would be inhabited by well-spoken, publicly engaged women."[21] However, "this environment that cultivated vocal, publicly engaged women did not last long; by the 1810s the discourse about women's public roles had begun to change toward advocating exaggerated verbal modesty and decidedly away from earlier visions of female oratorical excellence."[22] Public women were problem (and problematic) women.

As much as civic engagement on the part of white women sexualized them, white men feared woman suffrage would strip them, and the nation, of their sexual virility. As I have argued elsewhere, popular cultural images of the emasculated man were prevalent during the woman suffrage debate, including images of Uncle Sam, bereft of whiskers, in a dress.[23] This fear was actually articulated once during congressional debates over the suffrage amendment during World War I. In 1918, Representative Edward W. Gray of New Jersey worried: "A nation will endure just so long as its men are virile. History, physiology, and psychology all show that giving woman equal political rights with man makes ultimately for the deterioration of manhood. . . . Because I want our Nation to possess the male virility necessary to guarantee its future existence

... I am opposed to the pending amendment."[24] Representative Gray wanted to make sure civic decisions were made only by "the real, manly men of America," men who could "watch their life-blood flow without whimpering."[25] I leave unspoken what most every woman reading this thinks of the ability to watch lifeblood flow.

Men opposed to woman suffrage particularly feared the specter of the debating woman. Representative Frank Clark, a Democrat from Florida, offered this dystopian vision of a world in which women could vote and debate:

> [W]e would find the husband and wife constantly engaged in political disputation, which would grow warmer, more heated, and more acrimonious as the campaign advanced, until finally a veritable conflagration of domestic infelicity would be kindled, consuming the marital tie, destroying the home, and sending the children, to all intents and purposes, orphans out on the cold charity of the world to become charges of the State. It may be said that this picture is overdrawn, but, sir, it is not. Man and wife to live happily together must be in harmony.... Disagreement will supplant concord; discord will take the place of harmony; home will be neglected for the political rostrum; household duties will be left unperformed while political rallies are attended; children will be left without the guiding hand of mother while she goes valiantly forth to save the Nation; respect of wife for husband will give way for contempt, and love will vanish while hate ascends the throne.[26]

Debate and speech, as well as the vote, seemed to operate on a zero-sum field. Any gain for white women was a loss for white men.

A few contemporary examples demonstrate the continued demonization of the debating woman. Googling the phrase *disagreeable woman* reveals an interesting terministic cluster; it generates about 644,000 results, almost all of which define her as a woman who is an unpleasant person. *Disagreeable person* shows up in definition searches, but a search for *disagreeable man* takes you to *disagreeable person*. If one searches for stock images of *disagreeable woman* (on a site like Shutterstock), the images that appear are of women disagreeing with men (not with women), of women saying no (consent, anyone?), of women correcting men, or of women standing firm.

The vernacular examples raise the question "Can a woman disagree without being disagreeable?" Psychological definitions of *agreeableness* include kind, sympathetic, cooperative, warm and considerate, empathetic, friendly, generous, helpful, and generally likable, pleasant, and accommodating in social situations.[27] If one is familiar with the literature on feminine styles of communication,[28] the similarities between agreeableness and femininity are stark. Thus, to be a good woman, one needs to be an agreeable woman. Where, then, is the space for a woman to advocate, to debate, to disagree? If educators seek to use debate and speech as civic education, we need to address the embedded legacy that the civically engaged, debating woman is a threat.

Disciplining Disagreement

The cultural bias against "disagreeable" women leads naturally to my third argument: that civic education, with its focus on civility as politeness, disciplines disagreement, particularly for women but in ways that also discipline men and limit the possibilities of productive civic engagement. An approach to civility that foregrounds attitudes (e.g., respect) rather than actions (e.g., continuing conversations even when they are difficult) is doomed to fail. Debate is one place where the habit of continuing conversations even in the face of disagreement is operationalized.

A (necessarily short) summary of the literature demonstrates how civic education consistently centers respect, civility, and community.[29] In terms of respect, the ideal may be respect for others, their opinions, or their differences. Unfortunately, respect often seems to devolve into refusal to disagree. Or, in some contexts, disagreement itself may be perceived as disrespectful. Don Waisanen offers a way to work through the role of respect during disagreement when he argues:

> With respect comes a recognition that there are others whose lives, needs, and well-being are implicated with one's own, and that in public settings, diverse messages and standards deserve spaces for expression. Without such respect, communicators run the risk of assuming their messages about politics can speak for everyone's demands, a task they surely cannot. Between respect and civic demands, I contend, we thus find civility: not simply respect for respect's sake, but expressions that others are valued amid disagreements over pressing social issues.[30]

Respect must be manifested in the midst of disagreement, meaning disagreement must be allowed. For this to happen, a sense of community needs to exist. For me, *community* does not mean that a group shares some ascriptive or locational characteristic but rather that each member sees an obligation—a civic obligation—to others.

Civic education's emphasis on civility may be short-circuiting this robust form of respect, because it may divert people away from disagreement in the first place. Civility is one place where gender/sex may point out civic education's differential impact on women, and where women's experiences as debaters may induce us to rethink what we mean by civility. Waisanen provides a robust and critical literature review in "Toward Robust Public Engagement: The Value of Deliberative Discourse for Civil Communication," making it clear that civility norms often privilege those with power.[31] One way this happens is through the conflation of civility with politeness.

Dr. Kyle Rudick, a colleague of mine, has been researching how white students understand civility. They tend to talk about it as politeness, specifically hyperpoliteness. They are so worried about giving offense that they avoid even engaging, which, I argue, is an even greater offense, because a refusal to engage is a refusal to recognize and witness another as part of the community. To borrow Waisanen's words, it is a refusal to see how others' lives are always already implicated in our own. This, indeed, is where the *civic* comes in, where people see a responsibility to others, not just themselves.

Politeness is an even greater interactional burden for women. Dreama Moon's research identifies how "hyperpoliteness" guides much of women's interactions.[32] Moon relies on Kate Davy's description of how, particularly for white women, being middle (rather than low) class is not defined by economic position but instead denotes a "kind of hard-earned . . . 'gentility' in the form of civility (a bedrock concept of imperialism) that encompasses a plethora of values, morals, and mores that determine . . . the tenets of respectability in general."[33] Being a good white girl means abiding by what bell hooks calls "bourgeois decorum": "suppressing critical comments or making them in private one-on-one settings where there are no witnesses."[34] So, to be a good woman means to be polite, to not disagree, or at least to not disagree *publicly*.

But when women debate and speak publicly, they disagree, they are disagreeable women. Given this, how might we think about the possibility of civic education, the training of members of a community to engage in civic discourse, given its impossibility for women? Women, in a way, have the answer. Women, when they disagree, are disagreeable, giving offense by the simple act of disagreement, and so we have had some time to figure out how to keep the conversation going even when others are offended. Women in debate have figured out a way to argue and induce (at least a few) people to listen.

My understanding of civility is informed by my experiences as the fifth grader who did not control her talking, the high school and college debate and speech competitor who was encouraged to talk all she wanted, the debate and speech coach who has tried to work with students to make them open to hearing others' disagreement as valid, and the teacher who has sought to create classrooms that are safe, though never too comfortable. In all these roles, I did not think of civility as the avoidance of giving offense. Instead, I thought about how debate can train us to react when offended and how to respond to being called out (or called in) when we have offended others. To be clear, continued argument is not an end in itself (although it is often a necessary condition, and so generating it may be a goal). It is, however, a necessary means for figuring out what we should do, even if only contingently, momentarily, and with some degree of uncertainty.

We need to stop describing civility in classroom policies as avoiding offense and instead start thinking of it as norms for dealing with the offense that will inevitably happen. This requires recognition of the civic right of others to correct you when they think you are wrong and your willingness to continue conversations even when offended (or offending). When offended, how does one advocate for one's self and, in the comic frame, educate rather than slay? And when one offends, how should one react to this being pointed out? For me, the mark of civility is not the refusal to offend (for offense is inevitable) but an openness to being corrected and to correct as one keeps the conversation going even in the face of offense.

Some civility literature leaves space for this approach. For example, Ronald C. Arnett and Pat Arneson, in *Dialogic Civility in a Cynical Age*, argue for an approach to civility that departs from the therapeutic/relational interpersonal perspective.[35] They define *dialogic civility* as "a minimal set of background ethical commitments designed to keep a conversation going in an era of postmodern disagreement about virtues."[36] The important move here is that the emphasis is not placed on some abstract form of respect but instead on a commitment to "keep a conversation going." Even as they write about "respect for the other [a]s a basic building block for a public narrative of dialogic civility," they also emphasize the "need to keep the other in the conversation."[37] Ultimately, "dialogic civility suggests a minimal commitment to a public reciprocal respect for the other out of a pragmatic communicative need to keep the conversation going."[38] An attitude of respect alone is not sufficient; a commitment to action—to keeping conversations going—is necessary.

This leaves open the question "How do we train people to keep the conversation going even in the face of disagreement or offense?" Here is where I find debate and speech training invaluable. My time participating in and coaching debate and speech informed my conception of civility and civic engagement, remembering that *engagement* is a necessary condition of civility. Debate and speech teach how to keep conversations going, even in the face of offense, whether given or received. Debate and speech do this by teaching (and living) the following lessons:

1. Disagreement is not a sign of disrespect. Debate teaches that disagreement is normal. I will tell you that you are wrong. You will tell me that I am wrong. And then, we keep talking.
2. Disagreement—an argument saying this is what I believe and here is why—is not the end of the conversation; it is the beginning.
3. Disagreement is welcome; it is a form of witness. One's arguments are deemed worthy because they are worthy of a response.
4. Debate and discussion *can* continue even when offense occurs because it *must* continue. Not debating is not an option. The default is talk and engagement, not avoidance.
5. Criticism should be expected and welcomed. The worst critique from a judge is being told "good job," period. This means there is so much to correct that the judge does not know where to start. In contrast, thirty minutes on how you could have done a better rebuttal is the epitome of praise; it means the judge thinks you are worthy of a significant time investment.
6. Women's disagreement can be normalized, at least a bit. This is not to say that women do not face double standards in debate and speech. Expectations for dresses, skirts, and heels persist in speech, and the threat of being called bitchy (rather than praised for being aggressive) persists in debate. But, at least to an extent, women who disagree are not reduced to being disagreeable women.

I come to these conclusions not because women debaters are different or unique but because the perspective of an outsider within allows distinct pathways to these conclusions. I come to these conclusions because, so many times, I have had to articulate them in order for people to hear past me being just a disagreeable woman.

What might this vision of feminist debate—and feminist civic education—look like? Where might we witness the ideal of keeping the conversation going as the end goal of civility? I conclude with some reflections on how the WDI has begun to put some of the ideas I have discussed into practice.

The Women's Debate Institute

The WDI offers a vision of what a transformative understanding of debate as civic education might look like. It foregrounds the key elements of civic education: respect, continuing the conversation, and building community. The WDI is the one educational forum in debate and speech where debating women are the norm and where norms, structures, and messages foreground keeping the conversation going and building community.

Founded in 1999 by Leah Castella and her college debate partner, the WDI's current organizational mission is "to close the gender gap in competitive debate by advocating for and facilitating a more gender-inclusive environment that advances educational and professional opportunities for marginalized gender identities." Its primary mechanism to achieve this is hosting an intentionally and strategically separatist debate workshop: a five-day-long summer camp for high school and college women debaters, staffed entirely by women.[39] After intensive (and continuous) fund-raising efforts, the camp is now free. The curriculum includes traditional debate skills, topic lectures, feminist theory lectures, information on applying to college, and—equally important—roundtable discussions about sex/gender in debate and intensive community-building exercises.

The WDI seeks to train women and those with other marginalized gender identities to be advocates *for themselves* in—and to challenge their very exclusions from—the debate community. It is distinct from other cocurricular activities because "WDI empowers participants . . . to learn advocacy skills through the transformative power of debate."[40] Even with its short length, the institute achieves remarkable things: community building (across schools and generations), consciousness raising (the stories shared by the people at the institute make clear much more work needs to be done to achieve sex and gender equity in the activity), mentorship (the ability of young people to teach each other, and for more senior folk to assist them, is made manifest), and, finally, allyship (the WDI demonstrates a model of civic engagement and connection built not on the horse-trading typical of contemporary coalition politics but on a complex interweaving of personal and political alliances). The WDI provides a lesson for the larger community. Debate and speech, even in its competitive form, should be about much more than wins and losses. Yet it appears many coaches have forgotten this, training debaters only to win and not educating them in the important work of community formation.

The WDI represents a place where women are encouraged to disagree, even at the risk of offense. It is a place where women and other marginalized gender identities learn to advocate, sometimes for ourselves and sometimes for others. It is a place where disengagement is not an option, or at least it is a much more difficult option. The community-building work encourages people to keep talking even in the face of offense. It is a place where every person is being mentored and is mentoring someone else. Comments from the women who staff the institute make this clear. Beth Mendenhall, a former Kansas State debater and CEDA champion, summarized what the WDI meant to her in an e-mail: "The WDI serves an extremely important function in the debate community that no other group can fulfill—community building across time (generations) and space (schools/teams).... The lack of a clear hierarchical division between teacher/taught means we all learn from each other's experiences, and have an opportunity to be leaders for our peers."[41] Carly Wunderlich Watson, a former Michigan State debater and NDT champion, praised the WDI in similar terms: "Debate is an activity whose culture has historically excluded women. The WDI affords women from all over the opportunity to get to know each other, build relationships and use those connections throughout the year in order to retain and grow the number of women in debate."[42] Finally, Kate Shuster, a former Emory debater and NDT champion, stressed how, for her, the WDI was about community building: "To me, the most important and interesting thing about the WDI is that it is a space for change and growth that exists largely outside of governing institutions. We're really only bound by the conventions we choose to bind us, so we're able (for example) to intentionally try to create space for the debates within debate while experimenting with different techniques to build community."[43] Reflected in all of these statements is the WDI's commitment to respect, to community building, and to keeping conversations going.

If debate is to succeed as a form of civic education, it has to normalize the existence of the outspoken, public, disagreeing woman. The WDI does that. If for only five days, participants cannot escape a space in which outspoken women are celebrated, where cismen are not numerically dominant, where disagreement is encouraged, and where women debaters are the norm. To be clear, the WDI is not some utopia where every experience is perfect, every interaction productive, and every person feels equally validated. The WDI is a place where disagreement and criticism are constants—between board members, between the community and the board, between campers and staff, and among campers. What distinguishes the WDI is its comfort with disagreement, its dedication to keeping conversations going even in the face of offense, and its commitment to intentionally build community among folks who otherwise may not see their lives, selves, and well-being as intertwined.

Ultimately, I argue that competitive debate's exclusion of women is not tied to its adversarial format as much as it is tied to gender/sex exclusions built on power differentials. Society must grapple with these power differentials if it is to achieve egalitarian forms of citizenship and rich civic engagement. So, if you want to talk about debate and speech as civic education, you also better be talking about sex and gender. As of now, the WDI is the one place where this consistently, intentionally, and systematically happens in the United States.

To really conceive of speech and debate as liberatory forms of civic education, where our community is premised on a sense of wholeness rather than oneness,[44] we need to reflect on the history of gendering/sexing/racializing debate and imagine how the radical performance of the debating woman, as well as the debating person of color, might transform how we understand debate, speech, civic engagement, and citizenship.

10

DEBATING CONVICTION:
FROM SINCERE BELIEF TO AFFECTIVE ATMOSPHERE

RONALD WALTER GREENE AND DARRIN HICKS

Between 1954 and 1966, the "debating both sides controversy" was the "most spirited and persistent controversy in speech education."[1] As the twenty-first century began, the authors of this chapter argued that it was time to revisit that controversy because it provided important lessons for how to promote the ethical capacities required for deliberative citizenship.[2] Unlike deliberative theories that avoid discussing the cultural interventions necessary to cultivate the ethical sensibilities of a deliberative citizen, the debating both sides controversy was mostly about the ethical challenges of an underappreciated cultural intervention (or cultural technology)—intercollegiate tournament debate. We argued that avoiding a discussion of the cultural interventions required for deliberative democracy allowed the universalization of discursive norms without attention to how "the techniques invented for [the internalization of these norms] have particular national and economic histories that disrupt their universal pretensions."[3] It had long been accepted by those involved with debate that learning to debate is "training for democracy; it is training for citizenship."[4] For us, however, investigating those moments when debate and its preferred practices were challenged provided an opportunity to recall the historical permutations of debate and how it was invested with productive powers to transform students into citizens.

The ethical problem that fueled the debating both sides controversy was the relationship between a student debater's convictions and the arguments he or she advanced in a given debate round for or against a policy proposal.

The growth of tournament debating had promoted the practice of switch-side debating, encouraging students to argue just as well on the affirmative as on the negative side of a resolution (balanced between an even number of affirmative and negative rounds during the preliminary stage of a tournament).[5] We made two arguments: first, that the question of conviction was resolved by shifting its location outside of the personal belief of the debater (for or against a specific policy) and toward debate as a means of democratic decision making. At the heart of this reassignment of conviction was the investment of an ethical substance—free and full expression—within debate as a procedure of democratic decision making. The political conjuncture of the Cold War, we argued, provided debate with an opportunity to align with a variant of Cold War liberalism that promoted free speech as proof of American exceptionalism.[6]

Our second argument was that the reassignment of conviction provided an antidote to those who worried that the gamification of debate hurt its political value. In contrast, the gaming of debate became an opportunity for the moral development of the student. In our words, debate became a "freedom game," as students learning switch-side debate were seen to be more empathetic and pluralistic toward minority points of view and, therefore, more open to the ethical demands of being persuaded by the force of the better argument.[7] The problem we identified about these claims was that they failed to appreciate how this form of moral development was similar to the ethical distance that cultivated the claims of legitimacy for the emerging knowledge class after World War II. Thus, advocates of debating both sides displaced the (inter)nationalist and class histories of their favorite technique of self-fashioning while promoting the universalization of liberal variants of debate.

In this chapter, we wish to return to the debating both sides controversy to acknowledge and engage those who have taken our original gambit as a point of departure. Alternative histories have been written about debate, and a new defense of debating both sides has emerged, often advancing criticisms of our earlier arguments about the role of conviction in debate. At the same time, our initial argument about how variants of liberalism are transformed by the movement of conviction toward the technology of debate has interacted with new challenges to how the debate game embeds certain racial logics of white supremacy. To account for the more recent uptake of our work and the controversy over debate tournaments becoming sites of social activism against the exclusions and normalizations of debate practices, we will advance the need for a more affective orientation toward conviction.

Continuing the debate about debate, this chapter approaches conviction as affective in nature. By that, we mean that conviction is not simply sincere belief. Rather, we contend that conviction is better understood as the affective investment in—and attachment to—a belief. Conviction, in other words, is how and how much a particular belief matters. Convictions, affectively, have an irreducibly embodied dimension; they emerge in and through sensation. Specifically, convictions, we believe, are first felt as pulsations of energy coursing through bodies as they enter into contest, or as they engage in the relational movements of attack and defense. Debates, of course, are such contests, and the convictions that animate any particular debate register on the bodies of debaters—for instance, in their vocal modulations, bodily tremors, and rhythmic breathing. Bodily responses, such as modulation, tremor, and rhythm, along with speed, volume, attraction, and repulsion, are experienced and measured in terms of their intensity, as a qualitative change in magnitude and force. This means, for us, that in a debate round, convictions are not only a property of the particular belief motivating the argument that an advocate makes. Convictions, we suggest, should be seen, instead, as a dimension of the visceral experience of debating.

The embodied nature of conviction does not mean, however, that convictions are best understood as the property of an individual body. In fact, convictions are never simply personal, because they arise in the encounter, in those moments when bodies confront and are confronted by other bodies. Convictions are relational; they are interactional and environmental properties. They form in and through the interaction of the advocates, along with all the other bodies and things present, in a round and beyond, circulating throughout the tournament space. Hence, conviction, more precisely, describes the intensity of a given encounter, the qualitative changes occurring in the moment-to-moment unfolding of contestation between advocates. Experienced and expressed as waves of intensive movement, the convictions circulating in and through a contest cannot be subtracted or divided without changing the character of that encounter.[8]

Once framed in terms of the affective intensity of an encounter, convictions are better understood as collective feelings. And as these collective feelings traverse the bodies of advocates and the spaces those bodies inhabit, they generate an "affective atmosphere" that is "impersonal," in that it belongs to "collective situations and yet can be felt as intensely personal."[9] Convictions, like all affects, are contagious. Constituted from a public stock of feelings and conceptions, convictions spread through and mobilize collective bodies to support or challenge a policy, institution, candidate, or social practice, like tournament debating.

Thus, for conviction to be treated as a problem, as it has been since the advent of modern tournament debating, entails challenging the intensity of the affective relations that animate debates, which include not only the bodies of particular debaters but how their bodies are collectivized in and through complex assemblages of practices, spaces, temporalities, and procedures into an affective atmosphere.

Fear and Faith

While there were antecedents to the debating both sides controversy during the first two decades of the twentieth century, the peculiar history of the controversy was inaugurated during the 1954–1955 national debate topic: "Resolved: That the United States should extend diplomatic recognition to the communist government of China." As Michael Bartanen and Robert Littlefield note in *Forensics in America*, the choice of recognition for the People's Republic of China as a debate topic was "a curious community decision, given the political events of the time."[10] In the midst of McCarthy's Red Scare, the service academies at West Point and Annapolis announced they would not debate the resolution. A group of teachers colleges likewise declared that they would not debate the topic, and some schools in Virginia, most notably Roanoke College, also refused. Why? Some were concerned that speaking in favor of the resolution might make debaters more open to the appeals of communist propaganda, while others argued that being in favor of the resolution would give aid and comfort to the enemy. The military academies were concerned that speaking in uniform for such a bold foreign policy reversal would position the cadets in opposition to U.S. foreign policy. Yet others suggested the topic was designed to bring out criticisms of Senator Joe McCarthy.[11] Moreover, at least one director of debate avoided affirming the resolution because he feared students and others might be misidentified—and possibly investigated—as communist sympathizers.[12]

The first semester of the 1954 debate season began after the Army-McCarthy hearings (held between March and June of 1954) and came to an end with the Senate's censure of Senator McCarthy in December 1954. In the meantime, Karl Wallace, then the president of the Speech Association of America, was encouraged to intervene to change the topic, but both he and the National

Intercollegiate Committee on Debate and Discussion refused.[13] Moreover, public luminary Edward R. Morrow "backed Wallace's position" on an episode of his *See It Now* television program in November 1954, just eight months after his famous March 9, 1954, episode discrediting Senator McCarthy.[14] With the tide turning against McCarthy, James MacGregor Burns defended the standards of argumentation in intercollegiate debate as superior to those of the politics of the time: "when questions are often dismissed with wisecracks, smears, half-truths, and the big lie."[15] Wallace's steadfast defense of the topic, Morrow's intervention, and the strong support of other debate programs for lifting the gag order on the military academies secured the "association between college debate and the First Amendment."[16] Furthermore, as others have claimed, the decision to keep debating the China topic even "may have helped rein in McCarthyism."[17]

In light of Richard Murphy's widely read ethical challenge to the practice of debating both sides (published a few years after McCarthy's exit),[18] we spent less time on McCarthy's role in the debate over debate in order to highlight the broader story about Cold War liberalism. For Murphy, requiring students to debate both sides as a precondition for tournament participation ignored how the debater's conviction might condition his or her preference to argue one side or another of the resolution.[19] Tournament debating had made an ethical imposition a precondition for participation. For Murphy, however, debate was a form of public speaking and, as such, to advocate regardless of sincere belief was to violate the rhetorical norm that a "public statement is a public commitment."[20] In contrast to Murphy's ethic that debate was a form of public speaking, the advocates of debating both sides argued that debate was a pedagogical lab, a safe space for trying on different arguments and experimenting with differing beliefs about the topic.

In crafting a more micro-history of the controversy bounded by McCarthy's decline, English and colleagues responded to our original argument by returning to how the advocates of debate valued the activity. In doing so, they provided an even more heroic story of debate's triumph over demagoguery.[21] For them, the lesson to be drawn from the earlier defense of debate was that "debating both sides encourages participants to dismantle absolutist 'us versus them' dichotomies." Thus, debate appeared less as a cultural technology of American exceptionalism, as we argued, and instead represented a "civic attitude that serves as a bulwark against fundamentalism of *all* stripes."[22] In this tale of how debate fights against fundamentalism and Manichean dichotomies, a heroic narrative displaced our intellectual history describing the connection between free speech and conviction. In fact, the heroic narrative simply conflated fundamentalism and McCarthyism, with the aversion to Manichean dichotomies working to deflect sustained reflection on the ethical problematization of conviction, both as it occurred within that historical context and in present challenges to debate practice. As we argued previously, this slippage between conviction and fundamentalism mirrored later neoconservative efforts in the State Department to resituate debate as a weapon in the War on Terror, by enlisting it as a liberal technology of Islamic reformation.[23] Here we want to focus less on the striking similarities between this heroic tale and the State Department's justifications, and, instead, seize the opportunity provided by this slippage between conviction and fundamentalism, with its concomitant historical leap from McCarthy to the War on Terror, to reconceptualize conviction as an affective relation. Put differently, the ethical problem of conviction is an affective problem of how intensely people attach themselves to particular configurations of debate.

The affective atmosphere of the McCarthy era has been generally described as one of fear. Geoffrey Stone writes, "During the McCarthy era, Americans were exhorted to fear not only Soviet agents but 'un-Americanism.' And [the United States] responded to this exhortation. [Americans] grew fearful not only about our national security but about the subversion of our religious, moral, and national values, our media, and our educational system."[24] At the time, Francis Biddle, Franklin Roosevelt's former attorney general, published *The Fear of Freedom*, arguing that the fears of the U.S. public threatened their own freedoms. Biddle wrote, "Power in America rests on public opinion, which at present seems to be approving the slow abandonment of individual freedoms, so gradually achieved, so casually disregarded." Biddle argued that the real threat to freedom was a public "in fear of an imagined peril to their institutions of freedom" demanding that they be "secured by repressions that may ultimately stifle them."[25] While the fear of communism stoked by McCarthy affected the decisions of some schools to refuse to debate the China topic, the collective response was not one of fear but faith: a faith in debate as a technique for securing free speech.

Our less heroic narrative requires an appreciation of how the value of free speech provided a means by which the ethical problem of conviction was transferred from the sanctity of a personal belief to a "fighting faith." Arthur Schlesinger Jr.'s *Vital Center*, a founding text of Cold War liberalism, provides the broader context. For Schlesinger, the threat to democracy was internal: "the rise of totalitarianism ... signifies ... an internal crisis for democratic society. There is a Hitler, a Stalin in every breast."[26] For Schlesinger, a democratic faith necessitated free discussion because it was the climate democracy requires for responsible decision. The affective response to fear was a democratic faith—a fighting faith for civil liberties, especially free speech.

What we want to extract from the controversy over switch-side debating in the McCarthy era is more than the fact that debate and free speech were tightly stitched. More importantly, the free speech defense of debate after McCarthy's exit from the public stage supports our story that free speech had emerged as a means to distinguish the United States as a "free society" from the totalitarianism of communism. The Princeton University Debate Panel called efforts to limit debate on the China topic "an invasion of free speech by civil and military authorities," arguing that to support the gag order was "an ominous imitation of the Kremlin."[27] Intercollegiate debate had become an activity worthy of fighting for and part of the moral geography that separated the United States from the Soviet Union. It was this moral geography that, we argued, supported the claims of American exceptionalism.

However, at this point in the history, conviction had not yet been reassigned to debate as a method of decision making. In fact, the debating both sides controversy was rather muted during the public controversy over the China topic. The problem of conviction in debating both sides would play out in terms of a different question: Should debaters have a conviction, or sincere belief, before they argued for or against the policy under discussion, or should debate itself be a means for creating sound convictions?[28] Recent apologists for switch-side debate continue to repeat the claims for sound conviction promoted by the critical thinking effect of debate.[29] However, this epistemic defense of debating both sides fails to account for the affective way that conviction was rewired into the defense of debate as a means of democratic decision making. The most important essay for moving conviction from a personal belief toward debate as a procedure for democratic decision making was provided by Dennis Day. As we recently summarized Day's position:

> Day argued that the real threat to democratic life was the surfeit of conviction, the rise of "true believers" to power.... The best means to combat fanaticism was to require students to argue against their convictions. Through rigorous training in debating both sides of a question, debaters became skilled in articulating the convictions of others. The result, Day argued, was a transfer of conviction: a disinvestment in the sanctity of personal belief spurring a fierce commitment to debate as a technology of democratic decision-making.... Day argued the willingness to embrace

this technology demonstrated a genuine commitment to full and free expression, the commitment that differentiates liberalism from all varieties of totalitarianism.[30]

Day did more than claim, as the Princeton Debate Panel did, that an intervention into whether teams should debate was a violation of free speech. Day made sure that conviction for debate became the precondition for one's first-order conviction for any policy option. Our point here is that this transfer of conviction should be appreciated affectively—as a move away from belief as an individual truth and toward an intense encounter with the activity of debate. The transfer of conviction works affectively to recharge the intensity one experiences in and for debate. As the advocates of debate insist, to abandon debating both sides is to abandon debate's value for correcting fundamentalism and dogmatism. Debate becomes a faith worth fighting for as it generates an affective relationship toward debate as proof of one's commitment to democracy.[31] This affective relationship is made collective through imitation and repetition every time a debater debates.

In "Lost Convictions," we described this affective relationship in class terms.[32] We began by noting the similarity between Day's central claim—that debaters must, first, detach from the affective investment (conviction) they may have in a particular belief that some act or policy (e.g., abortion) is right or wrong in order to properly participate in debate (e.g., one concerning the distribution of reproductive rights), and that debate's continued success demands, second, the debater transfer that affective investment (conviction) to the process of debate itself, to emotionally invest in playing the game, to have a fighting faith in the power of this game. This is because robust debate between open-minded and tolerant advocates is the only legitimate procedure for making decisions in a democratic polity comprised of irreducible moral difference—and the claim made by aesthetic educators that any critic-in-training must, first, learn to detach from their affective investment in the pleasure given by the content of a work of art (which is necessary to be more than a fan), and second, transfer that affective investment to the process of criticism itself, so pleasure derives from the act of assessing the work in terms of its relationship to the compositional forms and processes of perception involved in its creation and interpretation. We noted that the ability and willingness to detach and transfer conviction is not natural but must be cultivated through immersion in particular pedagogical techniques, such as those involved in aesthetic education or debate training. Given that this cultivated disposition is not evenly distributed throughout the population, but has, indeed, long served as a sign of social class, we, following Bourdieu, argued that switch-side tournament debating could be seen as a technology for cultivating the "dispositions (habitus) characteristic of different classes and class fractions."[33]

Specifically, we extended this analogy to suggest that the distance between first-order convictions (the affective investment in a particular belief) and second-order convictions (the affective investment in the power of democratic procedures) demanded by switch-side debating is similar to the way the "knowledge class" asserts its objectivity and impartiality, which allows analysts to proclaim the legitimacy and autonomy of their judgments. We concluded that the distancing effect of the game of debate participates in an educational process that aligns debating both sides with a technique of class formation.[34]

We did not argue, therefore, that debaters should argue from first-order convictions. What we think is important—and what we wish to emphasize here—is that this distancing effectively limits the range of democratic models that debate, as a social practice and pedagogical institution, can promote. To understand why some debaters argue that a genuinely liberatory form of debate demands that participants, including the judges of those debates, mute the intense affective attachment they have to the liberal values embedded in debate as a democratic procedure—something quite difficult to do, especially for those whose entire careers, as debaters and coaches, have been structured around such an affective investment—we must be willing to entertain different affective economies of conviction. This begins with the recognition that every model of debate, including both switch-side tournament debating and its performative alternatives, functions, first and foremost, as an "attunement" mechanism to calibrate one's affective relationship to debate's democratic claims.[35]

For the Love of the Game

It bears repeating that our position is not one that requires a model of technological or class determinism. It is the curious demand that debate be attached to liberal values. The work debating both sides does for the problem of conviction is, for us, historically and institutionally generated in ways that secure the liberal framework within which citizens are formed. What we are trying to emphasize here is that the debating both sides controversy is also a story of affective relations to this liberal framework. It is the affective atmosphere of a shared commitment to the liberal framework of debate that has become the site of controversy. Thus, tournament policy debate requires an affective relationship from those who participate in it. It demands a love of the game. To love the game requires an attachment to the ethical framework of debate. To do otherwise is to upset the affective atmosphere of the tournament, which produces conviction in and for debate. In this section, we turn to how the critique of debate's racial assumptions puts in relief another challenge to the affective relationship to debate's liberal framework.

In responding to our initial arguments about the history of the debating both sides controversy, some have referred to the emergence of critiques of tournament debate practices that call out U.S. policy debaters for perpetuating styles of argument that exclude and/or normalize minority participants.[36] Our historical interruption into what seemed a controversy long dead intersected a set of new criticisms of debate practices that challenged the way U.S. policy debate normalized dominant speaking practices. Writing from within the general consensus that debate should be approached as a game, Ede Warner Jr. noted that "over twenty years of various diversity efforts . . . have failed to substantially change the racial, gender, social and economic composition of interscholastic policy debate." And for Warner, "the reason is simple: [white] privilege . . . creeps into more subtle, covert spaces, like the essence of why and how people 'play the game.'"[37] Warner especially emphasized the stylistic requirements of participation: "rate of delivery, note-taking techniques, what qualifies as evidence, and other technical presentation issues."[38] The first thing one notices when watching an intercollegiate policy debate round is that participants talk very, very fast. To respond to the history of exclusion or normalization required by debate's performance barrier, Warner argued it would be necessary to allow "debates that fight for different styles and identity constructions offering different methods to access questions of policy."[39] The critique of performance styles is reminiscent of Iris Marion Young's call for a communicative democracy that prevents the exclusions and normalizations she associates with deliberative democracy.[40] If debate is a game, its rules and its presentation styles need not be treated as one and the same. If the educational value of the game is to be redeemed, debate must be open to recognizing the value of alternative performance styles.

The distancing effect required of the game of debate—a process we identified as a key element in generating cultural distinctions of class—is, for Warner, a racialized technology. Shanara Rose Reid-Brinkley described the distancing effect as a whitening: "Racially and/or ethnically different bodies must perform themselves according to the cultural norms of the debate community. . . . Students of color are performatively 'whitened.'"[41] Moreover, she describes the media coverage of urban debate initiatives as a social mobility narrative of "Ghetto Kids Gone Good"—a narrative that renders urban outreach programs to promote debate programs in communities of color as a story of educational and moral uplift.[42] More recently, Lawrence Grandpre has argued that the debate community is a microcosm of the white supremacy at the heart of liberalism.[43] Grandpre, invoking Marimba Ani, argues that debate embodies the Eurocentric philosophical tendency to remove ethical claims from lived bodies and place them within an abstract system separating word from deed.[44] This rhetorical ethic insinuates itself in the debate game as black suffering is treated as a negative or positive reason to support a policy proposal but not a reality to be engaged by the debaters themselves. What matters is how the argument of black suffering tracks to create a victory or a loss for a team. One of the ironies of this situation is that the game of debate can allow white students to use black radical traditions against the black students they were intended to empower. The separation of word and deed—and the separation of the debate round from the world the students come from and return to after the tournament—allows the debaters to advance arguments removed from their own specific histories, deploying them for competitive advantage. For Grandpre, debate, like liberalism, is ultimately structured by a politics of antiblackness that pivots around the simultaneous affective orientations of negrophobia and negrophilia. Reid-Brinkley's "Ghetto Kids Gone Good" expresses both the fear of black youth and the love of black youth debating.

One response of debaters and their coaches to the liberal demands of the activity is a more forthright rejection of the norm that affirmative teams must advocate an argument in support of the resolution. Instead, teams might challenge the resolution itself for how it requires student debaters to distance themselves from their own particularities or histories.[45] To resist affirming a policy proposal embedded in the terms of the resolution challenges what has been long treated as one of debate's essential constitutive procedures. Topicality is a reworking of the classical rhetorical stasis point of jurisdiction, which assigns and regulates the appropriate forum for arguments. To challenge topicality as an affirmative burden is not new for intercollegiate policy debate (at least it was normal to do so when we were more closely aligned with the activity as participants and coaches from the late 1970s through the mid-1990s). What is new, however, is the challenge to topicality in and through an explicit critique of debate as an exclusionary and normalizing activity. The challenge to the stock issue of topicality is part of an effort to transform the debate round into a site of social activism.

It is unclear to us whether this activist strategy is a violation of switch-side debating (where students are assigned a side) or simply a competitive tactic to displace topicality as a regulative ideal. Critics of this strategy are concerned that the refusal to affirm a policy in the language set forth by the resolution is a means for some debaters to assert that their personal experience, now formulated as a conviction-cum-ethical demand, must be given priority, which, in effect, protects that conviction from attack, in such a way that displaces the very essence of debate as a democratic procedure for critically testing the generalizability of these convictions and the implicit models of interactional justice they advance. To interpret the practice of debating without affirming the resolution misidentifies this student practice as an ethical problem of conviction. The ethical problem is not a problem of conviction but rather a problem of decorum (the appropriateness of the proper place and style for arguments). As an ethical problem of decorum, the new apologists for switch-side debating might be said to be protecting the liberal framework of policy debate as an affective regulation of how one might engage the activity of debate. If the game requires the liberal framework to be the same game for all, then the affective intensity of the debater's encounter with the game as a liberal freedom game must be enforced. To do so requires debaters to stay within the effective limit of the resolution, by affirming that resolution in its own terms. It is the desire to shield the game from a radical critique of its affective implication in antiblackness that calls forth a new round of defenses for switch-side debate.

At first blush, the challenge to the affirmative burden of topicality would seem to be allowed by the game. If an affirmative team can win the argument that the material histories of exclusion and normalization animating debate should be open to debate in the debate round, then the competitive character of the game has been rewarded. The educational value of debate gets reassociated with free and full expression without the need to traditionally affirm the resolution, because topicality is now experienced as a restriction on free and full expression. To follow Warner, transforming debate into a site of activism by challenging the procedure of topicality does not require a first-order conviction, just a desire to win the game by making its substantive and stylistic procedures open to revision in a debate round.

However, Grandpre suggests a problem with the game as played. Such a series of argumentative moves may simply expand the liberal framework of antiblackness by putting black suffering on display within an affective regime of negrophobia/negrophilia. What is needed is the rejection of the metrics of gamesmanship (wins and losses) as the only measure of success, especially for debaters of color. The motivating force or affective intensity required is to move beyond the debate tournament—and outside the debate round—to the community at large. For Grandpre, the alternative affective orientation is a fidelity to the black radical tradition that articulates debate as a project for promoting community empowerment. Debaters of color should participate in debate as a tool for "black institution building as a corrective for liberal white supremacy."[46] From this perspective of institution building, debaters can develop argumentative skills and critical knowledge they can bring to a community of activism, while the lessons learned from activism return to the debate round and to the liberal academy as a site of criticism and transformation. A different affective atmosphere—different from the motivating force of wins and loses—is being offered to debaters of color. The use of the debate round as a site for challenging the liberal framework of debate attempts to articulate debate in terms of a different affective relation than the democratic potential of debate.[47]

Conclusion

We should not rule out of order alternative affective relations to debate or foreclose the potential for those relationships to transform the encounter between the students who debate and the citizens they are becoming. The transformation of debate into a game, with pretensions of inculcating the ethical habits of deliberative citizenship, often relies on debating both sides to resituate one's conviction from a sincere belief worth debating toward debate as a method of democracy. In this chapter, we have explicated how the debate over conviction has revealed that conviction is better approached affectively. The conviction-debate relationship puts into relief the intensity of one's encounter with debate as a cultural technology. Yet this intensity is not personal. It is an atmospheric force attuning the argumentative practices of the different bodies debating to tournament debate as a practice of ethical self-fashioning. Debating conviction, through the years, provides insight into the problematizations of (or, we might say, disturbances to) the affective atmosphere of tournament debating. This atmosphere requires the motivating force of wins and losses to extract debate's educational value as a liberal technology.

A disturbance in the affective atmosphere occurs when student debaters refuse their abstraction or the requirement to distance themselves from their particular histories and communities in order to succeed at the game. The fear of demagogues, fundamentalists, and dogmatists has been, and still is, deployed to regenerate the faith in the liberal framework of debate, while negrophilia/negrophobia is covertly advanced as its affective foundation. During the Cold War, the storm generated by conviction's ethical problematization for debating both sides was resolved in practice long before it was resolved in theory. Debaters accepted the terms of the game before debating both sides was reattached to its public warrant as a democratic procedure for promoting free and full expression. This time, atmospheric disturbances may be less transient, as the liberal framework of the game becomes the stasis point of debate practice and its existential test.

II

DEBATERS AS CITIZENS:
RETHINKING DEBATE FRAMEWORKS TO ADDRESS
THE POLICY/PERFORMANCE DIVIDE

SARAH STONE WATT

Policy debate, an activity known primarily for its depth of research into public policy issues[1] and its rapid rate of speech,[2] has undergone significant changes in both style and substance. Historically restricted to a single topic and often characterized by highly technical jargon, this form of debate has recently become more malleable as debaters have taken it upon themselves to reflect not only on the policies circumscribed by the annual topic but also on how that topic was chosen, how debaters and coaches behave, and the social norms and practices of the debate community. While policy debate remains a strong training ground for aspiring lawyers and politicians, it has also become a space for students to explore their criticisms of those fields and to engage in social activism.[3] Rather than modeling behaviors suited to a courtroom or Congress, some policy debaters now engage in performances of citizenship writ large and are expanding their focus from weekend tournaments to debate as civic engagement.[4] For these debaters, citizenship is less about legal membership in a state and more about our "basic habits of interaction" on topics that affect our ability to live together.[5]

As the content of arguments has changed, so too has the form and the evidence offered as support. While debaters continue to recognize the value of law review articles and government documents, they have broadened the scope of inventional resources to include the literature of critical cultural studies, artistic expressions, and lived experience. This evolution of the activity has debaters increasingly asking questions about identity and political agency vis-à-vis the policy-making process. Their questioning and integration of different forms of evidence has made debate more creative; teams now play music, tell stories, recite poetry, and even use visual arts in performances of engagement with the political process. These developments have led to greater racial, economic, and gender diversity within the debate community while simultaneously prompting calls for stricter enforcement of the traditional rules of policy debate.[6] In short, debates over the substance and style of policy debate have become increasingly divisive.[7]

There has been considerable resistance to the performative turn within some established policy debating societies, and even a controversial attempt to create a separate policy-only league to preserve policy debate in its traditional form—as research-based debate focusing solely on policy resolutions, without all the debate about the rules or issues of identity.[8] However, all signs indicate that identity-driven debate is here to stay. Identity debaters are reaching the highest levels of policy debate, and their approaches and arguments have spilled over into other formats.[9]

The rise of what some call performance or identity-based debates is a reflection of debaters' attentiveness to larger tensions in contemporary U.S. politics.[10] These debates illustrate the political alienation and distrust among some segments of American society. Multiple studies have demonstrated decreasing levels of trust among Americans, especially African Americans, both for their government and their fellow citizens.[11] While Americans have long valued a healthy skepticism toward government, the growing lack of trust in our fellow citizens concerns some political theorists. Danielle Allen, for example, argues that our distrust "of each other" threatens to lead to "democratic disintegration." In democracies "marked by settled patterns of distrust," she argues, "citizens develop modes of political behavior designed to maintain boundaries." Such "citizenly habits," she concludes, "corrode democratic citizenship from within."[12] This type of distrust, particularly surrounding race relations, is manifested today not just in U.S. political discourse but in intercollegiate debate.

Just as our nation needs reflection and reorientation to preserve its democratic experiment, so too does the debate community need to "think patiently and directly" about how to deal with growing distrust.[13] Only then can debate serve as an educational space for learning the skills necessary for democratic engagement in our increasingly diverse and polarized society. In that spirit, this chapter borrows Allen's notion of "political friendship" to help illuminate one potential avenue through which debaters and coaches might reorient themselves to debate as citizens rather than as competitors in an academic game.

To do this, I do not think that debate must entirely forego its competitive element, but it will need to place greater emphasis on communication skills not always emphasized in the competitive model of debate: the competitors' ability to evaluate political sacrifice and promote greater levels of trust. To get there, I first elaborate on the apparent disconnect between status quo debate arguments and participants' levels of mutual understanding and trust. Then I argue that in order to overcome these problems, debaters must be taught to better comprehend the intersections of lived experience and institutional change. Finally, I highlight some changes that might be expected if political friendship—and by extension engaged citizenship—were to become a central framework in the pedagogy of intercollegiate policy debate.

Disconnection and Distrust

Traditionally, participants have come to debate expecting to take sides on controversial issues, specifically public policy issues currently being debated within the broader political culture. Typically, debaters argue over the merits of a proposed policy by reflecting on the harms of the status quo, as outlined in the affirmative case. Then debaters move to debating whether a proposed policy change will solve the problems identified and have significant advantages or disadvantages. While some debate organizations, particularly at the high school level, have fairly clear rules regarding the content of debates, the two major collegiate policy debate organizations—the National Debate Tournament (NDT) and the Cross Examination Debate Association (CEDA)—do not have clear guidelines governing what debaters may or may not talk about in their speeches. Intercollegiate debate relies on rules governing tournament logistics, such as time limits for speeches and the submission of ballots. However, what happens in any given round is largely up to the debaters. Content is most often dictated by available evidence and community norms. Debaters have long been trained to question their opponent's evidence; now, many are also questioning their opponents' reliance on the community norms themselves. At issue in many of these debates are norms that allegedly privilege white male debaters over those of other races and genders.[14]

This strategy is what has come to be known as "performance" debate, and it involves debaters describing personal experiences or invoking poetry and other modes of literary or artistic expression that reflect a different sort of civic identity. Performance debate is, in the most basic terms, a new way to talk about issues of identity and citizenship, one rooted in a radical critique of the hierarchies of power in contemporary society. Just as the introduction of any new style of argument forces debaters to adapt, the performative turn places new demands on the debate community—demands that have proven to be very controversial. Why is the performative turn in debate so different and controversial? The answer is simple: because it is so fundamentally personal.

Rather than starting from the premise that we are all similarly affected by or implicated in policy decisions, performance debaters question the drive for social homogeneity and highlight the ways in which we are all implicated in—and divided by—a system that positions some as dominant and others as subservient. Challenging the assumption that Americans are all one people working toward common goals, these arguments question the very possibility of common goals. Performance/identity teams use creative strategies to reveal the ways in which status quo policy making is a form of ritual that purports to include everyone for the benefit of all, when in fact the process requires ongoing sacrifices by some individuals for the benefit of others. For example, Ryan Wash and Elijah Smith, in their winning performances at the 2013 NDT and CEDA national tournaments, argued that debate norms had to change if historically excluded groups, such as African Americans and LGBTQ individuals, were to feel at home in the activity. In one speech, Wash emphasized how "certain individuals" associated with policy debate had been "able to determine what debate should be," while others were forced to adapt to those standards if they were to have a "home in debate."[15] Wash and Smith's arguments highlighted the fact that, in the United States, certain groups have historically been subservient to others, and they argued that the structures of policy debate reflected those larger processes that rendered some debaters/citizens invisible.

Invisibility, as Allen recognizes, is not merely the inability to be seen. Invoking Ralph Ellison's *Invisible Man*, she defines invisibility as "the experience of sacrifice without recognition or honor."[16] Debate arguments such as those of Wash and Smith highlight the ways in which the rules of debate render individuals with certain racial or sexual identities invisible by failing to recognize their contributions to debate. In 2014, for example, the Towson team of Korey Johnson and Ameena Ruffin, who became "the first black women to win a national debate championship tournament," was rendered "invisible" by some who refused to accept their defeat of a team from the University of Oklahoma in the final round of the CEDA Nationals.[17] While many in the debate community celebrated their victory, others—both in the debate community and the popular press—derided their performance as part of a shift toward a style of debate that failed to "develop high-level research skills or marshal evidence from published scholarship."[18] These criticisms ignored the fact that, in many ways, Johnson and Ruffin's performance mirrored the fast-talking, evidence-focused style of traditional debate. For the most part, Johnson and Ruffin adhered to community norms, but still their victory provoked controversy.

What was it about Johnson and Ruffin's performance that concerned the critics? Although they read published scholarship at a rapid rate (as is the norm in policy debate), their case articulated a critique of scholarship that relies on descriptions of black suffering to criticize status quo political structures. Their argument highlighted the way that images of lynching and black suffering in the scholarly literature turn that suffering into a spectacle that might prevent black Americans from imagining a future where they are not the targets of such violence.[19] Yet despite the fact that they were adhering to community norms and echoing an argument prominent scholars have made, Johnson and Ruffin found their championship at the center of the controversy surrounding performance debate and were subject to harsh criticisms of their abilities and even their intelligence. These criticisms came both from some members of the debate community and from conservative bloggers and the popular press.[20] Only after weeks of hateful articles circulating on the Internet and elsewhere did the CEDA issue an official announcement celebrating Johnson and Ruffin's accomplishment.[21] This delay was partially due to the lack of a dedicated public relations person within the organization, but it also demonstrated the failure of the organization to anticipate the controversy.[22] This moment marked Johnson and Ruffin as, paradoxically, both the center of attention and invisible.[23]

Allen, drawing on Ellison's response to the controversy surrounding racial integration in Little Rock, Arkansas, explains that what is necessary to overcome invisibility is the recognition of sacrifice. She argues that invisibility is inevitable so long as there is a lack of "language to comprehend sacrifice, or the losses and disappointments people accept" for the sake of communal agreement.[24] In Little Rock, she argues, people "on the ground" did possess the language of sacrifice, but "the public language of political theory, which can directly interact with policy, did not reflect a precise awareness of the practical sacrifices involved in the production of democratic agreement and laws."[25] Political theorist Hannah Arendt saw the struggle in Little Rock as something that should have been addressed by "reforming political institutions, ensuring their inclusiveness, and maintaining public peace by defining some questions as outside of politics."[26] However, Ellison recognized that inclusive citizenship was not possible without "addressing those aspects of democratic decision making that the dream of unity had previously hidden: loss and disappointment." As a result, "resentment and distrust" festered in Little Rock, leaving those who had sacrificed the most during the controversy largely invisible.[27]

By the same token, traditional debaters tend to be in favor of including marginalized groups within debate. They want to reform the activity, and they pledge to recruit and retain students from groups that historically have been excluded. At the same time, many persist in defining questions of identity as outside the bounds of the activity of debate itself. That is, they agree that the issue needs to be discussed; they just do not want it discussed within the space of the debate round itself. Performance debate challenges this attitude by highlighting the sacrifice of marginalized groups in both U.S. politics *and* in policy debate.[28] And it does so not just by arguing about the merits of policies that disadvantage minorities but by challenging the traditional rules and norms of the activity itself.

Lived Experience and Institutional Change

By engaging in debates about identity, some traditional debaters have come to understand that their "comforts [are] constructed out of the sacrifices of others."[29] Unfortunately, the understanding typically stops there. Lacking a full appreciation of how some debaters are rendered invisible by the rules and community norms of debate, many traditional debaters make the same criticisms of identity-based debate as political theorists make of identity politics: that it is divisive and disruptive. Meanwhile, some identity debaters present narratives of personal suffering in ways that impede collective understanding of the social hierarchies they seek to dismantle.[30] All this prevents debaters from learning more about one another and exploring mutually beneficial frameworks of political agency. Instead, debaters feel forced to choose sides in the controversy over whether debate should emphasize lived experience or public policy. Thus, rather than becoming better citizens by learning to interact with—and to comprehend the experiences of—others, some debaters become better technocrats, while others become more disdainful of the system, ultimately seeing "social death" or metaphorical suicide as the only way out.[31] The result is an increase in the number of "clash of civilizations" debates in which students fail to hear one another and instead push their side of the argument to the point of "angry verbal confrontations, broken friendships, and group segregations."[32] As in contemporary U.S. politics, the arguments become louder and more divisive but fail to engage one another.

Debaters appear to be asking the right questions, but the perpetuation of the policy-performance divide is preventing them from finding good answers. Instead of training debaters to be better citizens, intercollegiate debate may instead be perpetuating what Giroux has dubbed "the age of the disappearing intellectual"—an age in which "criticism, dialog, and thoughtfulness" are seen as a "liability."[33] Forced to choose between public policy issues and the lived experience of people, debaters feel trapped.[34] They are exposed to information relevant only to that choice, much as citizens today often limit their intake of news and information to those sources that confirm their existing views.[35] If debate is to be a space where students learn to be citizens, thinking critically and engaging their fellow citizens across socioeconomic divides, then the activity must teach students to reflect *both* on public policy issues and the lived experiences of those historically marginalized and excluded.

In short, student debaters can no longer pretend that the experiences of difference and suffering are outside the realm of intercollegiate debate. Instead, they must be encouraged to grapple with the issues of race and gender that shape—and often determine the potential for—mutual understanding across differences. Juliet Hooker explains that "political solidarity as it is generally understood . . . denotes the ability of individuals to engage in relations of trust and obligation with fellow members of a political community whom they may see as inherently 'other.'"[36] She contends that since consent is necessary in a democracy, solidarity too must be cultivated, so everybody feels that they have been treated fairly. In order to develop solidarity, "democratic strangers must recognize that they have an obligation to live with others on terms of fairness, reciprocity, and mutual respect."[37] Again, many within the debate community already may feel solidarity with those marginalized on the basis of race or gender. Yet the proliferation of intense "clash of civilizations" debates demonstrates that proclaiming solidarity is easier than enacting it. Genuine solidarity, as Hooker argues, "is more than just an emotion; it is also an ethical orientation that moves us to action."[38] If the debate community is to move toward true solidarity, all debaters must confront the ways in which the identity categories they occupy shape their "ethical-historical perspectives" and distance them from those who are differently situated.[39]

Political Friendship in Debate

In response to our increasingly divided and seemingly fragmented political culture, Danielle Allen asks, "[C]an we devise an education that, rather than teaching citizens not to talk to strangers, instead teaches them how to interact self-confidently?"[40] Following Ellison, Allen argues that we must develop means of "assessing relative levels of sacrifice but also for analyzing the intersection of social experiences and politics."[41] We must strive to be good citizens by recognizing and evaluating "nonaccidental" political loss and its attendant political emotions. Unfortunately, many debaters, like the policymakers they sometimes emulate, have become good at insulating themselves from the need to consider these losses. Many seem more concerned about some apocalyptic extinction-of-humanity scenario than about the everyday oppression experienced by some individuals. Rather than continuing to coach debaters to predict the demise of humanity, we must encourage them to attend to something far closer to their control: coping with the losses real human beings suffer for the good of the whole. This sort of understanding is at the core of citizenship, as Allen argues. In order to promote this understanding and the mutual trust it engenders, however, we must learn to empathize with suffering and sacrifice. In coming to terms with the personal sacrifice underlying performance debate, we cannot so easily disentangle reason, interest, and emotion as it is experienced in democratic practice.

In short, we must find new ways to promote what Allen calls "political friendship"—not by holding hands and eliminating competition but by evaluating competing interests and assessing political sacrifice. We must recognize that, in politics, everybody must sacrifice for the good of the whole, but some sacrifice more than others and some *groups* regularly sacrifice more than anybody. We must train debaters to demonstrate consideration for those experiencing loss and, as Hooker suggests, to "envision shared political obligations" even when "what we see and experience is radical otherness."[42] Debaters must come to grips with the fact that their subject location often prevents them from seeing what someone else is experiencing. They must learn that to advance the best argument—or even the best policy—requires not stringent adherence to their own way of seeing but the ability to empathize with the lived experiences of others. Above all, debaters need to explicitly recognize how their advocacy might require sacrifice or cause suffering among marginalized groups.

A framework of political friendship would move debates away from the "clash of civilizations" and instead force debaters to cross racialized and gendered divides to understand how their advocacy might affect the lives of those who are different from themselves. This move requires changes in the habits debaters typically rely on when crafting their arguments, as well as differing strategies during and after debates. Cases should not be constructed solely on the basis of solvency arguments, nor solely on the basis of lived experience. While these may be starting points, debaters must learn to go further, considering what their advocacy requires of their fellow citizens. Too often in "clash of civilizations" debates, the first question asked in cross-examination says, in effect, "within your framework, what can we do to win the debate?" This question is always already problematic; it assumes that each team must operate within the framework the other team has chosen. In early performance debates, for example, students would often get caught up in concerns that they might be forced to engage in the same style of debate (e.g., if one team played music, the other worried they would have to play music too) in order to win. Many debaters now recognize that they can engage one another in different styles, but questions remain about how to engage questions of identity, marginalization, and community norms. Within a framework of political friendship, debaters can better address these issues by explaining how they have considered who must sacrifice—and what they must sacrifice—if their position were to prevail.

Beyond understanding the sacrifice inherent in their advocacy, debaters operating within a framework of political friendship would need to demonstrate that they respect the "agency and autonomy" of affected groups and are committed to "ethical reciprocity."[43] Ethical reciprocity relies on the idea of "wholeness of the citizenry, rather than its oneness,"[44] meaning that citizens recognize their differing interests but are committed to shared membership in a broader community. While there may be an affective dimension to political friendship, ethical reciprocity requires going beyond mere empathy for one another and instead relies on a normative "commitment to act on behalf of others."[45] Reciprocity implies neither self-sacrifice nor the sacrifice of others but instead seeks the best possible path for all involved. This task, of course, is complicated by the fact that racialized and gendered divisions are deeply rooted, and individuals often do not realize that their perspectives are shaped by fundamentally different understandings of history and politics. Whether one comes from a dominant or a marginalized group, this sort of blind spot is what causes "clash of civilizations" debates in the first place. In order for a framework of political friendship to work, members of the dominant group must no longer "resist sacrifice and refuse to surrender unearned privilege and power."[46] Before there can be genuine reciprocity, debaters must be willing to acknowledge that the community norms of debate historically have been developed by and for the dominant group. This recognition will not completely compensate for histories of marginalization, but it can serve as one step toward reconstituting community norms "on more equitable grounds."[47]

Often, framework debates between policy teams and identity teams, or even between two identity-focused teams, are judged on the basis of their educational value. While all involved may agree that debate is an educational activity, Allen's theory of political friendship suggests a different standard—a standard rooted in how ordinary citizens evaluate and judge arguments in the realm of public controversy. Invoking Aristotle, Allen notes that Aristotle begins his treatise in the *Art of Rhetoric* by reminding speakers that "it is the business of the audience to judge, not to learn." Unlike students, who are "led to truth by a teacher," the citizen/judge operates "in the field of opinion," where decisions about the best course of action in a particular case are based on the judgment of audiences.[48] Using the framework of citizenship, a debater might successfully persuade the judge that they have done the better job debating by assessing the sacrifices of those affected by their proposal, displaying goodwill toward those who disagree, and identifying grounds of mutual consent, where even those who may not benefit from a particular decision can find reason to support it.[49]

In a framework of political friendship, debaters would not only reflect on the potential sacrifices inherent in their advocacy but also approach the debate with a willingness to listen and understand new arguments about sacrifice—and to test whether what they advocate is still defensible in light of those sacrifices. In many ways, this framework does not change how debaters advance arguments but rather how they react to arguments involving issues of identity and marginalization. In a debate where one team proposes a policy and is confronted with evidence of the sacrifice it might require, the team proposing the policy might concede the sacrifice and still consider ways in which the policy might be implemented in a spirit of ethical reciprocity. If a team cannot demonstrate that it took into account the sacrifice involved, then it deserves to lose the debate. In their assessment of who did the better debating, judges should act like enlightened citizens, assessing which team best illuminated a path toward mutual understanding and respect by carefully considering the political consequences of their advocacy. This is debate framed as political friendship.

In debate framed as political friendship, debaters would come to understand that losing is not the end of the world. Rather, they would see it as an opportunity to reconsider their position in light of what they have learned. Hooker explains that "citizens have divergent and conflicting interests, and public policy decisions will therefore inevitably generate winners and losers."[50] In debate, as in politics more broadly, we need to help people better manage loss, especially when that loss is bound up in questions of identity. A framework of political friendship provides guidance for what ought to happen within a debate by calling on debaters to ask themselves: would I treat a friend this way? Perhaps more importantly, it provides guidance for what should happen after the judge declares a winner and loser. After choosing a winner and a loser in a "clash of civilizations" debates, for example, the judge might prompt the debaters to discuss how the community as a whole might address the concerns raised by those who lost the debate. One goal of this model of debate is to stop thinking about citizenship as a zero-sum game and to instead embrace "a conception of reciprocity so fluid that even a winner doesn't expect to stay a winner for long."[51]

Finally, we would do well to continue to question and decrease—if not eliminate altogether—systems of mutually preferred judging.[52] If we are to cultivate trust, we must all have opportunities to interact with one another across ideological, material, and positional divisions. We must develop opportunities to interact with one another as citizens and to test our arguments and evaluations in front of judges with whom we disagree. In order for this to work, it is incumbent on both judges and debaters to seek to understand one another and be open to persuasion. In order for debate to be truly valuable as civic education, debaters must learn to extend goodwill and disarm distrust—a skill that has been at the core of the rhetorical tradition since Aristotle's *Rhetoric*.[53]

PART 4
CULTIVATING CIVIC SKILLS AND LITERACY

12

DEBATE ACTIVITIES AND THE PROMISE OF CITIZENSHIP

EDWARD A. HINCK

In this chapter, I attempt to show how the interests of argumentation theorists and communication theorists converge on the problem of communicating across deep disagreements. My claim is that participating in debate activities can teach students how to balance argumentative technique with a concern for others in one's community, which is a major theme in the National Task Force on Civic Learning and Democratic Engagement's vision of civic education in *A Crucible Moment: College Learning and Democracy's Future*.[1] Next, to show how participation in speech and debate activities can prepare students for citizenship, I propose a typology of advocacy skills that holds potential for personal development. Here I argue that debate activities provide a developmental experience that, at its best, moves students through a process that potentially actualizes the vision of educational reform that Mortimer Adler described in *The Paideia Proposal*.[2] However, where Adler's vision of education focuses on the acquisition of knowledge and skills, I attempt to draw attention to the ways in which debate facilitates the development of communication practices related to argumentative dialogue. In the last section of this chapter, I draw on practices from the Coordinated Management of Meaning (CMM) project to show how debate educators can teach students to manage differences with others. In the process, they can begin to acquire the compassion and skill necessary for productive argumentative dialogue—an essential practice for the development of citizenship. In this regard, I advance a rationale for speech and debate activities that goes beyond the cognitive skills of critical thinking and persuasive speaking to include personal development of a sense of humane citizenship.

Humanitas and the Problem of Coordinating Meaning

What kind of person do we hope to develop over the course of a career in competitive debate, and what kind of debate activities should we design to produce those qualities? Contemporary educators shared the same concerns as ancient teachers of rhetoric in developing students' sense of civic virtue. Adler identified three objectives for education in *The Paideia Proposal*: (1) "personal growth or self-improvement—mental, moral, and spiritual"; (2) "an adequate preparation for discharging the duties and responsibility of citizenship"; and (3) the "need to earn a living."[3] According to Adler, "all genuine learning is active, not passive. It involves the use of the mind, not just the memory. It is a process of discovery, in which the student is the main agent, not the teacher."[4] Citizenship involves working out differences with others, the messy process of arguing about issues of the day, of bringing a sense of commitment to others and the larger community, of finding ways of coordinating different meanings and interests in a community fraught with political conflict.[5]

In his exploration of the history of the idea of communication, John Durham Peters concluded that successful communication "should be measured by the successful coordination of behaviors." He framed the question in a relational way, writing that the question should not be "Can we communicate with each other?" but rather "Can we love one another or treat each other with justice and mercy?" Because it concerns larger issues of the state, thinking about citizenship, then, asks us to find ways to hold ourselves together in ethical ways. "Given our condition as mortals," Peters argues, "communication will always remain a problem of power, ethics, and art." This is "not something to lament," he argues; "it is the beginning of wisdom." Peters went on to note that great thinkers from Hegel and Marx to Dewey, Mead, Adorno, and Habermas have all recognized that "just communication" is the "index of the good society." He then concluded with his own ethical principle for that sort of community-building communication: "To treat others as we would want to be treated means performing for them in such a way not that the self is authentically represented but that the other is caringly served."[6]

Rhetorical training holds the promise for just communication in the pursuit of ethical citizenship. Aubrey Gwynn noted that for Isocrates rhetoric was "the noblest of all sciences requiring from the student long effort and much sacrifice, but giving him in return knowledge and practical wisdom that are indispensable for civic virtue."[7] Cicero's theory of the "doctus orator" bears a striking similarity to the range of subjects students draw on in preparation for debate competition: "Psychology, ethics, politics, dialectics, even physics: all these must be studied, not for their own worth, but because without them an orator may often fail in the knowledge required for his practical work."[8] Speech educators easily recognize the idea of a cultured orator—a person trained in more than just one field of knowledge. Central to Cicero's theory of education is the concept of *humanitas*. According to Gwynn, this meant "to be a man [sic] in all that is most human, and to be human in one's relations with all other men; that is Cicero's ethical and social ideal, and his educational theory is based on the same principle."[9]

Today, however, a dialectical tension seems to exist between developing technical prowess in rhetorical practices and upholding ideals that might serve citizens seeking the best for their communities. This problem was as much an issue for the ancients as it has been for modern forensics educators who try to balance concerns about competitive success with concerns about personal development. This raises the question of what it means to be educated "for life," or to deal with the problems of "power, ethics, and art" in communication, to use Peters's terms.

To address this issue, I want to draw on the work of a former national debate champion, W. Barnett Pearce, and his colleagues who have spent considerable energy trying to address the more complex, messy, and difficult problems of coordinating differences in meaning.[10] Reviewing the entire body of theory and research advancing CMM is beyond the scope of this chapter, but the relevance of these scholars' work for debate training and citizenship is worth consideration. In *Moral Conflict*, Pearce and Stephen W. Littlejohn take up the very difficult question of how to communicate when "social worlds collide."[11] Accepting the conditions of a postmodern world, they offer important ways of thinking about how to communicate and how to achieve a transcendent eloquence—a discourse featuring philosophical, comparative, dialogic, and critical qualities. They describe philosophical discourse as "attempts to uncover the assumptions about knowledge, being, and values that lie behind positions in conflict"; comparative in "attempts to create categories that can be used to compare otherwise incommensurate systems"; dialogic in "attempts to move the debate from statements designed to convince to statements designed to explore"; and critical in the sense that "it exposes the powers and limits of each side in a controversy, and, more important, it exposes them to the advocates on both sides."[12] Kimberly Pearce similarly calls for discourse practices that are "replete with caring, compassion, love, and grace"[13]—practices that CMM scholars describe as leading to better social worlds.

These ideals might seem unrelated to argumentation. Yet argumentation scholars have been concerned with the problems of deep disagreement for some time. At some point in the process of teaching about advocacy, we introduce our students to concepts of argumentative dialogue from Wayne Brockriede,[14] Henry Johnstone,[15] or Josina Makau and Debian Marty[16] in hopes that they might begin to understand how argumentation can be deployed in ethical and pragmatic ways to build relationships with others and solve difficult human problems. Some of us who have led speech and debate programs have read these works and thought about how they might be made more central to debate pedagogy. Understanding that at the end of each tournament there can be only one champion, but wanting to teach students that there is more to life than winning trophies, some of us have sought ways to make participating in speech and debate more meaningful for students. Participating in speech and debate activities offers potentially transformative learning opportunities. Such activities, directed by a professional educator with an appreciation for imparting a concern for one's community, develop not only reasoning skills but also skills needed to relate to members of one's team and, ultimately, to the larger society. Put another way, debate can teach students not just about winning or losing but about living in a world "replete with caring, compassion, love, and grace."[17] In short, debate training *can* help develop students' sense of *humanitas*.

So far I have tried to connect the problems of civic engagement with the ideals of rhetorical and argumentation training. Peters saw the goal of living with others as the problem of dealing with differences; at the heart of CMM, W. B. Pearce argued, is the problem of how to coordinate differences. Similarly, Peters sees the ideal of love and compassion as we work through differences of power, art, and ethics much as W. B. Pearce and CMM scholars see better worlds as replete with caring, compassion, and love. Peters emphasizes the goal of performing in ways that bring about these communication practices capable of sustaining us in our differences; CMM scholars discuss speech acts as the key to understanding how to build better relationships with others. Pearce and Littlejohn examined the range of programs designed to address the ways in which political differences divide communities and placed the study of communication practices at the center of managing those civic tensions; argumentation scholars have theorized ways in which dialogue can serve as a means to relate to others who inhabit very different moral worlds. Most recently, Vernon Cronen,[18] drawing on earlier work by Pearce, Johnson, and Branham,[19] has made the case that CMM can be applied to argumentation studies in productive ways.

Forensics educators can move students toward this broader idea of citizenship by developing two sets of skills, one that begins with a concern about argument technique and arrives, potentially, at techniques for cultivating a sense of community—*humanitas*. The value of debate as an example of Adler's educational vision can be found in the kind of inquisitive, active learning necessary to connect the technical reasoning skills of students with the more imaginative and generative communication skills of building relationships with others—the kinds of skills Pearce and his colleagues sought to develop with CMM. Debating can teach students to distinguish good arguments from lesser ones, but forensics educators also play an important role in showing students how to manage different social worlds. When those students become aware of the differences on a team and begin to recognize their membership in a larger debate community, they can begin to develop that sense of *humanitas*. Not all speech and debate educators share this vision, and not all students seek this kind of education. But I believe it represents a philosophy of teaching that not only facilitates academic achievement but can deliver on the promise of educating ethically responsible citizens.

From Concern with Technique to a Concern for Community

Speech and debate activities are essential to developing the higher-order skills described by Adler—an "enlarged understanding of ideas and values"—because they involve what he calls "maieutic" learning.[20] Maieutic learning is learning through questioning and active participation. To describe the unique value of forensic activities, I offer a description of levels of critical thinking and a discussion of how the context of the classroom differs from the active learning experienced through debate activities. My intention is to suggest that immersion in the "forensics laboratory"[21] creates conditions for educational dialogue that are less likely to emerge in a modern classroom format. Instead of the more general definition of *maieutic* as a process of Socratic questioning, I advocate for a sort of maieutic learning grounded in questioning strategies arising out of the CMM tradition. In the process, I demonstrate the relevance and value of these practices for debate educators interested in transformational learning, the kind of education capable of cultivating a sense of *humanitas*.

Levels of Critical Thinking About Arguments

Critical thinking skills might be described in relation to Bloom's taxonomy of increasingly more complex forms of thinking.[22] In Adler's formalization of *The Paideia Proposal*, the first and most simple form of learning is the *acquisition* of knowledge. In an introductory debate class, this might involve learning how language functions to construct claims, how claims call for evidence and different forms of reasoning, and how those forms of reasoning each have specific tests. After learning about the different types of reasoning, students would need to be able to distinguish one kind from another so that they could apply the appropriate tests. For example, cause-and-effect argument, argument from sign, argument from parallel case, and other types of reasoning all require acquired knowledge to identify the type of reasoning and the relevant tests for each type. In addition to acquiring knowledge about claims and reasoning, debate students are called on to acquire knowledge about the subject matter of the propositions they are assigned to debate.

Once students have acquired knowledge about the types and tests of reasoning, they can move to the more complex task of *applying* those tests to complex argumentative structures. Especially when considering tests for advantages or disadvantages in a policy debate, these applications of knowledge are not necessarily discussed in a formal logic text. Instead, they were developed for the purpose of comparing policies in academic debate, although they presumably reflect broader discussions of public policy. So, for example, tests of uniqueness (i.e., assessing whether a plan uniquely causes a proposed advantage or disadvantage) have emerged out of the ways in which academic debate teaches students to analyze policy effects. These methods of analysis are in turn presumably based on how various disciplines study policy making in the political realm.

Next is the ability to *compare* competing points of view on issues. It is one thing to develop an argument that proposes a time frame or attempts to calculate probability for a policy outcome. It is quite another to compare the strength of the argument—the reasoning and evidence for one's position—relative to the position of one's opponent. The debate student must understand both positions' evidentiary support and reasoning, the burdens for each competing position, and the relevant tests to apply. The student also must be able to compare complex sets of ideas to frame what is at stake for the audience on that issue. And hopefully, the debate student develops the capacity to engage in this kind of critical analysis for each of the relevant issues in a given round of debate.

The understanding that students bring to the comparison of competing points of view must overlap to some degree with understandings of both the other student advocates and the audience. The student must develop a degree of understanding that contributes to his or her ability to see the arguments and issues with a degree of objectivity and rationality capable of appealing to the audience despite the opponent's argument. In some debate coaches' parlance, this has been described as "in-round vision," referring to the capacity for a student in the heat of a debate to *take the perspective* of audience members, judges, and the opposing team. Student debaters must try to see how the arguments interact and sense the logical force of the competing positions, then array those understandings against a set of argumentative options, comparing their probabilities for persuasive success and then choosing a set of arguments likely to prevail in the debate. Arguably, this is a complex set of assessments; such understanding and capability can only be developed through repeated practice and reflection to improve one's capacity to recognize increasingly more sophisticated possibilities for advocacy and their likelihood for success.

Transforming Attitudes Toward Argument

Social constructionists often see competitive debate and argumentative dialogue as diametrically opposed.[23] Certainly, the communicative format of debate rewards competition. However, my claim is that the competitive format is not without value in facilitating the experiences and reflection needed to promote argumentative dialogue. My goal here is to show how participation in debate activities provides the possibility for reflection, leading to transformative learning.

In the classroom, we can teach a student to study specimens of argument as a way to promote critical thinking. For an illustration, let us say our goal is to impart an understanding of cause-and-effect reasoning: What does it look like or sound like when we might hear this form of reasoning used in an argument or debate? What are the appropriate tests for this type of reasoning? And how do we apply those tests when faced with an example of this type of reasoning? In this situation, the student might not be engaged in considering the outcome of the argument—that is, whether the cause-and-effect relationship under discussion seems probable or might have some bearing on the student's life. It might only be an example for consideration in class. A student can remain distant from the content of the argument since it is only a classroom example, not a question with direct relevance to real life. For students in this classroom exercise, there may not be engagement of what Richard Petty and John Cacioppo described as the central processing route,[24] where the student is motivated and able to carefully scrutinize the reasoning. In this respect, the classroom is limited as a context for learning, or as a way to stimulate the acquisition and application of knowledge.

If we change the conditions of study by placing the cause-effect relationship in the context of academic debate, the element of competition potentially changes the degree to which the student engages the content of the argument. When a student confronts a cause-effect relationship in a plan that they cannot refute with their existing knowledge or research, the student becomes motivated to study the cause-and-effect relationship more carefully. That motivation manifests itself in further researching the cause-and-effect relationship, so that the student is better prepared for a future round of debate, should the same arguments be used. In this respect, the student is motivated to study the argument more carefully so that he or she might be more successful in later debates. Competition thus serves as the impetus for engaging critical thinking processes at a deeper level.

I am trying to distinguish between two learning situations that engage different attitudes, skills, and levels of reflective awareness. In the classroom, the student might become interested in the argument as a specimen for study, but the argument lacks connection to an issue or a controversy that might motivate a student to engage in critical thinking at a deeper level. In the context of competitive debate, the student engages in that deeper critical thinking because of the desired competitive outcome. The truth value of the argument might be of secondary concern to the debater because academic debate is a specialized forum for argument—a kind of language game—where competitive success is the goal.

Of course, a third kind of situation exists beyond *both* the classroom *and* the debate tournament: the public sphere of civic life. It awaits all college students upon graduation, when they will be called on as citizens to participate in arguments about public policy controversies and other issues of shared significance. When the enterprise of arguing is undertaken to determine the best answers to these kinds of questions, the outcome directly affects the lives of the participants and their fellow citizens. In these situations, arguers have even more reason to cooperate in testing each other's arguments in the most rigorous way. Finding the best answers is no longer an academic or even a competitive exercise but a matter of making fair and prudent decisions.

In civic debate, the competitive attitude that motivates debaters to study and carefully analyze arguments can, conceivably, interfere with good decisions and the pursuit of truth. Where the stakes are higher than a mere tournament victory, a certain maturity is called for—a maturity rooted in the ability to recognize when another advocate is making a better argument and a willingness to compromise with the opponents or even concede defeat. Mature advocates have the skills needed to recognize the stronger argument and are motivated to discover the best arguments, even if that means abandoning positions they had resolved to defend. Mature advocates have the ability to adapt to changing situations, remain open-minded, and trust that opposing advocates are also committed to deliberating in good faith. Mature advocates devote the cognitive effort necessary to process complex arguments, and they sustain the psychological energy necessary to carefully evaluate all the arguments and evidence.

The elements of mature advocacy, in short, reflect many of the ideals upheld by the political and argumentation theorists noted earlier. They reflect an understanding of Johnstone's notion of tension—arguing as competently as one can but remaining open to the possibility of being persuaded.[25] They also remind us of Peters's ambition of arguing artfully but with compassion to create a more just world,[26] as well as Barber's vision of strong democracy where "talk engenders empathy, nourishes affection, and engages imagination."[27] Such civic visions reflect Pearce and Littlejohn's call for transcendent eloquence, or an eloquence that combines philosophical, dialogic, critical, and transformative qualities that transcend particular moral conflicts.[28] These are the demands of argument involving deep disagreement. We cannot teach skills that guarantee resolution of such disagreement, but we can teach our students how to build the kinds of relationships that make resolving argumentative differences in the civic world possible.

Facilitating the Development of *Humanitas*

Speech and debate educators can play an important role in facilitating the development of *humanitas*. Adler argued that to develop intellectual skills and the skills of learning itself, one has to learn outside of the classroom, "guided" by "someone more expert" than ourselves.[29] What James McBath described as the "forensics laboratory"[30] of speech and debate activities provides just that sort of learning environment. Students develop flexibility and creativity in their thinking by participating in debate, as they reflect on a range of strategies and tactics needed for competitive success. Beyond that, they learn how to relate to others between rounds of competition, from the interactions with coaches and other students. In van rides home from tournaments, it is not uncommon to hear philosophical conversations about how one should live one's life, and these conversations continue throughout one's career in speech and debate activities. For the most part, scholars of forensics pedagogy have taken this mentoring process for granted; we recognize that mentoring occurs, but it is just viewed as part of the job. More attention should be paid to the ways in which these informal conversations among forensics educators and their students relate to the kind of argumentative dialogue we need for engaged citizenship. In this last section, I return to the ideas of Pearce and his colleagues to show how CMM might inform this process of developing *humanitas*, or that sense of humane citizenship we hope to cultivate in our students.

Speech and debate educators, like athletic coaches or managers in almost any organization, must deal with human conflict. Such conflicts are unavoidable, require considerable time and energy to address, and interfere with the larger goals of educational and competitive success. Within a debate program, human conflicts are messy—as are the conflicts we all encounter as citizens—but with much less at stake. Nevertheless, they distract both the participants in the conflict and others from preparing for competition, and they often lack easy solutions. When team conflicts arise, forensics educators are called on to act wisely and, if possible, to transform the conflict into a teaching moment. But what does it mean to act wisely in these situations? And what might students learn from experiencing conflict?

Pearce notes the difficulty of finding those "bifurcation points," or openings, where intervening in a conflict might prove useful: "Sometimes we have trouble recognizing and acting wisely into bifurcation points because we are so caught up in the meaning of what is going on that we lose sight of the possibilities of changing the shape of the pattern."[31] In the context of managing conflict on a debate or forensics team, this points to an obvious challenge: Debate and forensics coaches are often called on to counsel students facing such bifurcation points, but those students may be so enmeshed in their own lived experience that they have trouble seeing alternative possibilities. During these conflicts, debate and forensics educators can draw on the practices of CMM to help assure that the conversation does not disintegrate but rather becomes a teachable moment. Here I want to discuss just two concepts from CMM that forensics educators often rely on in facilitating personal growth on the part of students: the cultivation of systemic understanding and the use of circular questioning.

Systemic Understanding

Forensics educators bring a great deal of wisdom to the enterprise of leading their teams. They have witnessed students engage in noble practices of dedication and hard work, and they have given considerable thought to the kind of communication strategies that might motivate those who need to work harder. As more mature adults, their sense of personhood has grown beyond the anxieties of young adulthood, and they tend to be more concerned with fulfilling their professional obligations, like teaching classes, scholarly activity, service to the university, and coaching. Most no longer worry about the kinds of status needs that some members of their team struggle to pursue. Generally, forensics educators are sensitive to the limits of some members of the team and the gifts and talents of other team members. Also, they hear the many stories told by students trying to make sense of their lives and their place on the team. As such, they bring a great deal of perspective to understanding how those stories shape students' behaviors and success on the team. They are in a position to develop a systemic understanding of the team and of the social world constructed by the stories told by team members.

Pearce has argued that when we take a communication perspective on human behavior, "we assume that people make and manage meaning." As such, the "interesting and useful questions" to ask about student debaters have to do with "what specific meanings they are making in given situations, how they are making those meanings, and how these meanings affect the social worlds that they are making."[32] Forensics educators understand that their students live in different social worlds, but they might not recognize that the sources of conflict preventing a team from working well together are also socially constructed. Their role as teachers, then, is to engage students in conversations that help them to see what Pearce describes as the coherence of other team members' stories. So when students bring problems to a coach or director of a program—about how the coach has been unfair to one or more team members, or about some other injustice or problem related to team behaviors or activities—that coach or team director is in a position to ask powerful questions that might help a student reframe their understanding of the conflict. The goal of these conversations is to cultivate within the student a more systemic understanding of others' stories so that they can begin to develop the reflective practices needed to resolve conflicts. In the course of doing so, student debaters learn valuable lessons in what Pearce calls building "better social worlds."[33]

Circular Questioning

The process of building better social worlds relies on an array of communication practices from CMM that are beyond the scope of this chapter. However, one example of how forensics educators might engage students in potential moments of transformational learning is through the process of circular questioning. Pearce distinguishes among three kinds of questions, describing each metaphorically. First, questions in traditional "debating" are "used as clubs to defeat an opponent." Second, there is Socratic questioning, where questions are used "as shovels to uncover that on which your current belief stands." Finally, Pearce describes "circular questioning," where questions function as "signposts, alternatively directing the listeners' attention to things they would not otherwise see," or containing "embedded suggestions," or "reframings," or simply cues to "look here."[34] It is this last sort of questioning—circular questioning—that I believe has the potential to bring about transformational learning in student debaters.

Forensics educators teach by drawing on their experience with many students over multiple seasons of competition, their different strategies for motivating them, and their compassion and respect for the ways in which young adults struggle with managing coursework, debate participation, part-time employment, family pressures, and all the other stresses of college life. They have a systemic understanding of how people might work together with compassion and appreciation for each other, and they can use circular questioning to help students who come into their offices for help to discover their own answers. In Pearce's words, they can become "artists of inquiry," or artists "appropriately considered experts" in "how to inquire, not in the results of previous inquiries." Like all artists, artists of inquiry "have studied the tools of their trade, trained their own performance ability, engaged in coached practice, [and] taken on new dimensions of practice as a result of experience and exposure to striking models of artists in other schools."[35] In short, forensics educators, as "artists of inquiry," can help debate students find their own way.

Often educators have a strong sense of what students *should* do in a particular situation, but the practice of directing action can trigger a defensive reaction on the part of some students. Instead of attempting to control the student's behavior and risking resistance in these moments, many of us have sensed the possibility of leading students to reflective thinking through circular questioning. Circular questioning involves opening up a conversation about possibilities, or asking questions that lead students to still more questions. Ultimately, the goal is to help students discover their own answers. In the process, debate educators can help students create their own vision of a better social world.

In the course of this sort of process, students hopefully will discover their own ways of making sense of difficult situations. They might begin to see the dilemmas posed by uncoordinated actions, and they might feel compelled to think more imaginatively about how to act wisely in the future. Ideally, they will also begin to develop compassion and empathy for others who inhabit different social worlds. Pearce does not directly discuss circular questioning as a pedagogy of transformative learning. But when forensics educators act as "artists of inquiry," they can channel conflict among students into critical reflection on the most basic "epistemic, sociocultural, and psychic assumptions" underlying the students' worldview.[36] In short, they can lead students to moments of transformative learning, where they begin to develop that sense of *humanitas* essential to ethical civic life in a free society.

Conclusion

CMM scholars might think that this chapter has left out too much of that tradition to achieve a coherent statement of its relevance to coaching debaters and developing citizenship. In response, it is worth noting that in 1965, the same year that John Wittig and W. Barnett Pearce won the National Debate Tournament while representing Carson-Newman College, Henry Johnstone, a philosopher of rhetoric and argumentation, offered these words regarding the problem of how to work through deep disagreements: "The open-minded person, then, is one in whom there is tension. On the one hand, he wishes to maintain himself. On the other hand, he must expose himself to the risk of change implicit in argument. Such tension is necessary to any human being who wishes to transcend the horizons of his immediate experience and inhabit a world."[37] These sentiments, of course, sound strikingly similar to the conclusions Pearce arrived at almost a half century later. In describing the kind of communication practices that make managing differences possible, Pearce wrote: "I'm using a technical sense of 'dialogue' here. I do not mean just talk. Rather I'm referring to a particular quality of communication in which a relationship is formed in which each participant remains in tension between standing your ground and being profoundly open to the others."[38] For both Johnstone and Pearce, learning how to negotiate this tension between principled disagreement and openness to persuasion is what makes it possible for human beings to construct a more humane social world.

Speech and debate programs have much to contribute to civic education. When done right, these programs offer students a highly refined set of research and critical thinking skills tempered by reflective thinking practices that increase awareness of both the possibilities and limitations of one's own "epistemic, sociocultural, and psychic assumptions."[39] This is what speech and debate training, at its best, has to offer: a kind of transformative learning that makes coordinating meanings more possible in a very complex world.

13

DELIBERATION AS CIVIC EDUCATION:
INCORPORATING PUBLIC DELIBERATION INTO
THE COMMUNICATION STUDIES CURRICULUM

SARA A. MEHLTRETTER DRURY, REBECCA A. KUEHL,
AND JENN ANDERSON

In his 1952 book on the theory and practice of public speaking, W. Norwood Brigance argued that teaching speech was critically important to maintaining a free, democratic society. While the bulk of his book focused on public speaking (particularly persuasive speeches), Brigance also devoted a chapter to democratic discussion. "It is the activity of problem-solving by thinking together and purposefully talking it out," he explained, that enables the solving of community problems.[1] Brigance's work represented an early attempt to theorize the relationship between democracy and what is now referred to as public deliberation—the careful examination of a problem and a range of solutions by a group of people in "an open, inclusive exchange that incorporates and respects diverse points of view."[2]

Incorporating public deliberation into communication studies curricula promotes civic knowledge and engagement, including engagement with public issues important to particular communities. Teaching undergraduate students through public deliberation develops the habits and practices of rhetorical citizenship, or that "set of communicative and deliberative practices that . . . allow citizens to enact and embody their citizenship."[3] The process of public deliberation includes the following stages: (1) naming and framing an issue of concern, including specifically identifying the major components of the problem and

The scholarship in this chapter was funded by a Community Innovation Grant from the Bush Foundation, the charitable arm of 3M, and by an Indiana Humanities Grant.

three or more potential approaches to addressing that problem; (2) citizens working through the issue, typically with the guidance of a trained facilitator; (3) moving toward judgment, with citizens making decisions about how best to move forward and address the problem in that particular community; and (4) reporting on the deliberation and public decision making.[4] Public deliberations often tackle "wicked problems," or problems involving a variety of stakeholders and agents with decision-making powers, or problems not easily solved by technical solutions or solutions based in the expertise of a particular field.[5] Teaching students to participate in public deliberation as facilitators and citizens fosters civic knowledge about public issues and hones deliberative skills, like the ability to participate in and moderate a small group discussion. It also teaches students how to articulate their personal and public values and helps them to realize the potential for making a difference by participating in collective public action. These sorts of skills, and the civic knowledge, values, and motivations they are built on, are essential to civic engagement in the twenty-first century, according to a recent report from the National Task Force on Civic Learning and Democratic Engagement, *A Crucible Moment: College Learning and Democracy's Future*.[6]

In this chapter, we argue that deliberation can provide students with the hands-on training for democratic citizenship called for in *A Crucible Moment*. Reporting on actual programs in civic education emphasizing *civic rhetoric*, or the skills of critical thinking, speaking, and writing needed for engaged citizenship, we argue that deliberation is an effective pedagogical tool for promoting *rhetorical citizenship*, the embodied practice of participating in deliberations and other civic activities beyond the university setting.[7] We begin by briefly examining the historical connections among the study of speech, argumentation, debate, and deliberation, and by outlining how deliberation helps develop civic knowledge and the skills of civic engagement. Next, we discuss efforts to integrate public deliberation into communication studies curricula at two different educational institutions in the Midwest, one a large public university and the other a small liberal arts college. As part of this discussion, we describe the learning objectives of deliberative events in both curricular and cocurricular communication programs. We then analyze instructor and student reactions to participating in these public deliberations, demonstrating positive outcomes across a variety of institutional settings and assessing the opportunities and challenges of deliberation as a pedagogical practice in civic education. Finally, we suggest ways to incorporate public deliberation into the communication curriculum at a variety of college-level educational institutions.

Historical Background

The idea of public deliberation has deep historical roots in U.S. political life. Writing about the United States in the early nineteenth century, Alexis de Tocqueville celebrated the political engagement and community spirit of the young nation. When faced with a problem, he observed, "neighbors" in the United States would "immediately constitute a deliberative body" and work together to solve it.[8] While de Tocqueville's account was colored by his desire to spur democratic practices in his native France, he was commenting on something that was new and unique to the United States: a strong tradition of public discussion and community forums, including New England town halls, the lyceum, the public forum movement, and public debating societies.[9]

As colleges began to offer formal instruction in oratory and speech communication in the early twentieth century, professors of speech focused on several different settings: individual speeches, debates, and group discussions.[10] Early on, public discussions were linked to debate, with debate being seen as the more formal, argumentative form of public discourse, while discussion was viewed more as a way of exploring ideas. Some early speech scholars viewed discussion as the more accessible form of public discourse, since debate tended to require knowledge of specific rules and types of evidence.[11] Unlike debate, discussion also allowed participants to keep an open mind, considering a variety of points of view rather than making the case *for* or *against* a particular perspective. This encouraged consideration of a wider range of viewpoints, as opposed to the pro-versus-con orientation of formal debate.[12]

The pedagogical value of discussion was its connection to everyday public life in a democracy. During World War II, teachers of speech argued in the *Quarterly Journal of Speech* that "public discussion" was "the cornerstone of democracy" and that the "interchange of ideas" was essential to the training of citizens for democratic society.[13] Discussion was the "means of thinking together through purposeful conversation,"[14] Brigance maintained, and he observed that "a free society is sustained by discussion and cannot be sustained without it."[15] The speech communication field took its task of educating students for civic responsibilities seriously, as Herman Cohen noted in his history of the discipline: "We cannot question the unswerving commitment to democracy held by members of the speech profession in the years preceding and during World War II."[16] In the postwar period, however, discussion became less central to pedagogy and research in the speech communication discipline.[17] With the discipline becoming more specialized and divided between humanistic and social scientific approaches,[18] discussion fell between the cracks of humanistic studies in rhetoric, argumentation, and debate, as well as social scientific work in small group communication and interpersonal communication.[19]

Recently, public discussion—now more commonly called public deliberation—has experienced a rebirth. Prior to 1995, the terms *public deliberation* or *deliberative democracy* rarely appeared in the academic literature. In the early 2000s, however, the study of democratic deliberation became common not only in communication studies but also in political science, philosophy, and other fields.[20] In the past few years, more scholars of rhetoric and argumentation have begun to seriously consider the connections among civic rhetoric, rhetorical citizenship, and public deliberation.[21] There remains, however, a need to link communication pedagogy with contemporary understandings of democratic deliberation, exploring the connection between teaching rhetoric and enacting citizenship. We have the opportunity to not only teach our students about rhetorical studies and public deliberation in our classrooms but also to train them to do the work of rhetoric in their communities through public deliberation events.

Public deliberation as a pedagogical practice encourages the development of civic knowledge, skills, values, and actions—the four categories that make up *A Crucible Moment*'s framework for twenty-first-century civic learning and democratic engagement.[22] In some ways, collective action is the culmination of the first three categories. To encourage productive public action, citizens need *knowledge* of democratic ideals and processes; *skills* of analysis, reasoning, and communication; and the *values* of empathy and open-mindedness. These factors all drive individual motivation and larger organizational efforts for *collective action*. While *A Crucible Moment* lists "deliberation" as a skill ("deliberation and bridge building across differences"), a broader understanding of *democratic deliberation* suggests that a robust pedagogy promotes not only a particular set of skills but also civic knowledge and democratic values. Ultimately, deliberation equips students for current and future collective actions on public issues in their communities.[23]

To that end, we turn our attention to examining how public deliberation enhanced student learning in communication studies courses at South Dakota State University (SDSU) and Wabash College. The examples are drawn from two campuses and four different curricular and cocurricular experiences: an intermediate-level research methods course and an introductory-level argumentation and debate course at SDSU, and an intermediate-level deliberation course and a cocurricular deliberation fellows program at Wabash. By analyzing instructor observations and student reflections, we document and categorize the civic knowledge, skills, values, and collective actions that resulted from our efforts to teach democratic deliberation to our students.

Community Contexts: Learning Argumentation Through Public Deliberation

Our analysis of the benefits of public deliberation draws on the experiences of all three coauthors at their home campuses. The authors secured external funding from the Bush Foundation (a charitable organization of 3M) and Indiana Humanities, which allowed them to hold public deliberations involving student participation. At SDSU, a large state land-grant university, students involved in the deliberation came from two courses taught in the fall of 2014. In the first course, a research methods course, students received in-class instruction on using a variety of communication research methods to implement and assess public deliberation. Students had two options for actively engaging with the public deliberation, which focused on the issue of breastfeeding in local businesses. Students received training either as a group facilitator or note-taker, and they either fulfilled that role at the event or transcribed table notes and entered survey data after the event. After completing these activities, students wrote brief reflection papers where they were asked to comment on what they learned about research methods and community-based research through the process of active engagement with the public deliberation event. Students in the second course at SDSU, an argumentation and debate course, were given an extra credit opportunity to become trained and participate in the same deliberation. Afterward, they wrote a reflection paper where they discussed how they saw different perspectives and arguments at work in the deliberation, as well as how the facilitation training or note-taking skills would be beneficial to their future career goals. Some students were concurrently enrolled in both courses.

At Wabash College, a small liberal arts college for men, student experiences with public deliberation involved participating in an intermediate-level elective course on deliberation during the spring 2014 semester and a cocurricular, yearlong Democracy Fellows program during the 2014–2015 academic year. Students in the public deliberation course examined theories of deliberative democracy and facilitation. A major component of the course was planning and facilitating public deliberation events, two of which occurred on campus, one as a partnership with Indiana University–Purdue University Fort Wayne and the other a simulation exercise in class. The student reflections from this course were drawn from journal assignments on a variety of topics, including facilitation, planning a deliberation, and reflecting on the outcomes of deliberative events.

Wabash College's cocurricular Democracy Fellows program aims to equip students to lead productive, problem-solving conversations in their local communities. One of the authors, a rhetoric faculty member with training in deliberation, directs the fellows program. After receiving training in facilitation and deliberation, the eight students in the program worked closely with stakeholders on and off campus to plan, lead, and facilitate public deliberations. Additionally, the students worked under faculty supervision to conduct research on the quality and character of public deliberation, drawing on methods of rhetorical criticism and argumentation theory. The students in the program represented a variety of majors; all had course experience with deliberation through the college's basic public speaking course, and three had completed the previously mentioned course in deliberation. In preparation for writing their essays, the fellows planned and facilitated deliberations in undergraduate science courses, hosted a campus dialogue on racial sensitivity, held a public deliberation about sustainability, and led a public deliberation on how to improve the "quality of place" in the county, which focused on citizens deliberating specific short-term and long-term planning to enrich Montgomery County, Indiana, as a place to work and live.

Across these varied community contexts and settings, public deliberation represented a practical laboratory for students to engage in the work of *doing* rhetoric, thus creating an opportunity to enhance curricular and cocurricular learning about research and argumentation.[24] The public deliberation events helped students see how community members gave reasons for their beliefs, considered alternative perspectives, and worked through what would be the most fitting solution to a public issue—a process that also promoted the learning goal of developing critical thinking skills. Preparing for a public deliberation, students considered what makes a compelling or pressing public problem for a community. In participating as a facilitator, note-taker, or participant, students took part in evaluating proposed approaches to that problem in a systematic way. After the event, reflective assignments and report writing encouraged students to think about thematic trends in public discourse, why certain arguments or perspectives succeeded while others were dropped or eliminated from the conversation, and, ultimately, how community members come to judgment. Real-world public deliberation can be a messy enterprise;

participants rarely express their value premises as clearly as they do in a formal collegiate debate round. Students can move beyond theories and examples in class and instead seek to understand how argumentation works in the robust—if somewhat messy—field of public deliberation.

Analysis: Learning Opportunities and Challenges of Public Deliberation

In public deliberation's real-world laboratory, students enhance their civic capacity by applying their knowledge, skills, and values to the collective action of deliberation over public problems. We used a variety of techniques to assess learning outcomes and to identify the challenges of public deliberation as a mode of civic education. First, students in courses at both institutions wrote reflective statements after participating in public deliberation events. Second, the Democracy Fellows at Wabash College took part in a midyear and an end-of-year reflection on their experience in the yearlong program. The supervising instructors also recorded their observations and reflections throughout the process.[25]

Transmitting and Gaining Civic Knowledge

Public deliberation events provide students with an opportunity to take what they learn in the classroom and apply that knowledge to encounters with other students and citizens in their communities. While "civic knowledge" is often portrayed as an understanding of the processes of governance, it also includes understanding the historical and contemporary aspects of democratic principles.[26] Part of understanding democratic principles is recognizing and analyzing how communication influences values, advocacy, protest, and public decision making.

In reflecting on their year in the program, the Wabash Democracy Fellows stressed how deliberation teaches the possibilities of invigorating local governance and citizen participation in democracies. One fellow reflected on how the process of deliberation represented a "novel form of political discussion" because "ordinary citizens can sit down and have a civilized discussion about matters they truly care about." Other fellows suggested that the program had demonstrated the power of citizens to impact their local community, writing that participating in the fellows program had shown how "government can be changed and improved by anyone [with] a passion and an ability to build passion in others," and that deliberation showed "how much influence community members can have on the governmental proceedings."[27] Participating as facilitators of deliberation demonstrated the potential of communication to empower community members as agents of change.

In the argumentation and debate course at SDSU, students gained civic knowledge based not just in competitive but also cooperative theories of argumentation.[28] They were then able to apply that knowledge in the real-world setting of a public deliberation about developing additional community-wide breastfeeding support. In their reflections after the event, SDSU students reflected on the practice of cooperative argument at the small group discussion tables. In facilitating small group discussions at the public deliberation events, students had to apply their knowledge about argumentation and different stakeholder perspectives to moderate different perspectives in the discussions. Similarly, Wabash students noted how taking part in planning deliberations demonstrated public argumentation, including how "analyzing and crystalizing complex opinions into succinct, coherent ideas ... enabled us to understand people's concerns and beliefs better."[29]

Transmitting civic knowledge from a communication course to the applied context of a public deliberation event is a form of experiential learning connected to a variety of measures of educational progress, including increased civic engagement.[30] However, the SDSU instructors also saw gains in civic knowledge in terms of the development of an awareness and respect for the specific community issue—in this case, business support for breastfeeding. At the public deliberation training, the students engaged in a simulation exercise where they participated in and observed a group of volunteers practice deliberating the issue of breastfeeding support. Although this is an issue that most college students do not have personal experience with, the SDSU students were willing to volunteer their thoughts and consider the perspectives of various stakeholders.

The Wabash instructor also noticed that her students became more interested and invested in the local community around campus after they took part in public deliberations. One student from Wabash explained the importance of seeking out opinions from citizens, as well as experts, when public problem solving: "It is near impossible to really identify a community and solve its problems without getting a proper proportion of the community involved."[31] Student willingness to learn from the experience and expertise of community members was itself a form of civic knowledge, in that they learned that, in a democracy, a community's citizens need to be involved if public issues are to be addressed productively.

Teaching Skills

Across each of the four pedagogical settings, student reflections demonstrate that participating in training for deliberation and facilitation or note-taking during deliberation developed the skills of critical thinking and reasoning. Taking part in a real-world deliberation allowed students to identify different strategies of argumentation in an experiential learning environment. It also taught them many of the other skills we seek to cultivate in communication studies curricula.

Serving as a facilitator encouraged students to engage in critical thinking, seek out and consider multiple perspectives, exercise their oral communication skills, and gain experience in collaborative decision making.[32] Students saw facilitation as important to guiding the public decision-making process. One Wabash student who took notes during the process commented on how the facilitator's strategies to "stop conversation, slow it down and ask people if they have additional comments ... proved to be very helpful for the conversation, as this would spark ideas and new conversations between the participants."[33] Similarly, after facilitating a public deliberation in South Dakota, another student wrote: "By allowing people to discuss problems and what we can do to fix them in small groups, it allows a greater variety of people to share their concerns and ideas."[34] Participants' sharing of experiences related to a public problem is an important first step in the process of deliberating over solutions to that problem.

Putting students into the active role of facilitator encouraged them to become more aware of how participants presented claims and how they supported their claims with reasoning and evidence.[35] In the process, students learned that people do not always provide clear support for their arguments, which might be seen as a drawback in using deliberation to teach argumentation. With proper preparation, however, students become prepared to encounter and analyze public arguments—good and bad—and to suggest how those arguments might be improved. Learning the skills of navigating differing opinions and improving the quality of argumentation among their fellow citizens is an excellent opportunity for students to apply their knowledge of argumentation theory.

In striving to be a good facilitator, the student must learn to *listen* for claims and evidence, and then very quickly recognize opportunities to ask follow-up questions so as to promote better arguments within the deliberative conversation. An SDSU student reflection on this process suggested the importance of learning how to apply questioning techniques to advance the conversation:

"Learning how to facilitate discussions through the training was very helpful, in that I learned what kind of questions to ask, when to maybe switch topics, and more."[36] Students also noted that because many participants relied on their own expertise and experiences—as educators, health care providers, scientists, or parents, for example—it was up to the facilitator to ask questions that might bring alternative perspectives to bear on the deliberation.

Across the four pedagogical settings, students stressed how the *public* nature of the deliberation activity enhanced their learning. One SDSU student wrote: "[Y]ou can read and study all you want about an activity . . . but *participating* in the activity greatly informs your paradigm of said activity." Another stressed the importance of seeing "research in action" through participating in the event.[37] A student from the Wabash deliberation course commented that "deliberation . . . [is] different from theory to practice," and that facilitating an on-campus public deliberation "was a confidence booster" because the student was able to lead the group to "important solutions."[38]

Involving students in postdeliberation assessments also facilitated experiential learning of critical thinking and analytical skills. Students who entered data for the SDSU project wrote that it helped them learn by doing. Students described how they were better able to understand the full picture of the public deliberation event and the community health topic through examining both the qualitative data (i.e., the discussion and arguments at the event) and the quantitative data (i.e., demographic information and evaluations of the event). They noted areas of both discrepancy and overlap across these different modes of data collection and analysis, and they felt that these results helped clarify the distinctions and commonalities between them. Finally, they commented on the benefits of utilizing multiple forms of communication research and action to aid in public problem solving.

After facilitating an event on sustainability, students in the Democracy Fellows program examined surveys, table notes, and transcripts of the conversations in order to draw out key themes. The resulting report highlighted focal points where good discussion had resulted in understanding and agreement. In their analysis of the deliberation transcripts, the students noted that participants saw one option "as an easier strategy to begin implementing and the one with significant impact potential," as opposed to two other approaches to the problem.[39] Public deliberation therefore provided an opportunity for these students to reflect on how the participants made tough choices, choosing between multiple desirable options, which further enhanced their understanding of the role of argumentation and deliberation in public decision making.

Emphasizing Civic Values of Open-Mindedness and Empathy

Students involved in public deliberation exercises frequently affirmed deliberation's potential for creating a more civil, collaborative environment for public decision making. Deliberation also encouraged them to explore more diverse perspectives and opinions. By exposing participants to diverse arguments, deliberation encouraged open-mindedness, consideration of multiple perspectives, and empathy for the concerns of others. Students at Wabash expressed that deliberation allowed them to come to a better understanding of different perspectives on campus issues. For example, one student wrote that leading deliberations allowed for more authentic discussion: "I feel the flash discussion [deliberation event] goes to the next level and really addresses the heart of the issue and its importance."[40] After taking part in a deliberation, SDSU students saw the embodiment of the distinction between cooperative argumentation and competitive argumentation, or debate.[41] "Ideally, everyone 'wins' a deliberation," one SDSU student explained, while another commented that the "small groups provided a safe environment for people to come together and discuss problems."[42] In discussions after the deliberation events, students at both campuses asked questions about why deliberation was not more common in government, since it appeared to be a more productive way of acknowledging differences, working through options, and moving toward public judgment.

Students noted that the cooperation and understanding evident in the deliberation they participated in did not preclude discussion of a diversity of arguments, perspectives, and ideas. The structured format that encourages viewing a problem and solutions from multiple perspectives encourages participants to move beyond their own perspective. For example, students reflected on how the public deliberation experience taught them how the process itself can "educate" participants, writing that "in some cases the exact issue is already known but in this case the deliberation helped educate the facilitators and participants of what exactly [the] problem was."[43] These viewpoints were not static, but rather the deliberative format encouraged participants to engage one another's ideas, as documented by an SDSU student: "By everyone stating things they believed could be problems, it allowed others to see things differently."[44] Even if participants at their small group table had similar views, the deliberative process of asking questions encouraged "speculative artificial clash" between ideas, which in the case of the breastfeeding deliberation led to a discussion about generational differences.[45] Whether participating, note-taking, or facilitating, student reflections confirm that deliberation brings out a wide variety of viewpoints and arguments, and that participants in the deliberation do not merely hear those arguments but engage in a consideration of different stakeholders' ideas about a given issue.

Equipping Students for Collective Action

Participating in public deliberation events inspired students to see their own future in a different light, enhancing their sense of civic responsibility. For example, taking part in the deliberation event often encouraged students to develop their opinions on a variety of issues. An SDSU student who took part in the breastfeeding deliberation wrote: "When I signed up for the facilitation, I didn't have much of an opinion on the issue, but as the discussion progressed, I began to develop my own ideas."[46] A consequence of participating in a public deliberation is that students start to develop their own thoughts on significant public problems. This prepares students to engage in a similar process of considering a problem, articulating approaches, and brainstorming solutions to other public issues in their community.

When students develop civic knowledge, use that knowledge to hone their critical thinking and communication skills, and practice deliberating with an open mind and empathy, they are well positioned to become engaged citizens who will act similarly in their communities. "Wherever I go," wrote one SDSU student, "I'll be a citizen of the area I belong [to]. . . . In order to maintain the free society in which we live today, citizens need to participate in local conversations and governments regarding decisions that affect our communities."[47] A Wabash student's reflections expressed similar themes: "I believe deliberation is a great tool for people to solve issues. I think it would be especially beneficial for politics where all voices can be heard. This could help diminish the [partisan climate] of American politics and produce a real democracy."[48] Regardless of topic, students at both institutions saw the benefits of participating in deliberation as important to their futures as citizens.

Others tied the facilitation skills to their career intentions, seeing the connection between their own vocational paths and public engagement. A Wabash Democracy Fellow commented that his postgraduation position in a company's marketing leadership was "all because of my experiences with WDPD."[49] One SDSU student explained: "I want to work directly with people, specifically in the area of health and nutrition. Deliberating is a helpful skill to learn. . . . [O]ur nation is faced with complicated problems, such as the wide spectrum of body weight. . . . A situation like this calls for complicated solutions where deliberation is definitely needed."⁵⁰ Another suggested that in their future career in business, they "will use some of these skills to better facilitate meetings."⁵¹ Just as participation in debate and forensics cultivates research and speaking skills, public deliberation contributes to the civic education of the twenty-first-century student by demonstrating how the theories and skills of argumentation, listening, and collaborative decision making are relevant to their lives, both as professionals and citizens. The primary difference is that debate is historically rooted in a competitive model of argumentation, while public deliberation often emphasizes cooperation, collaboration, and empathy for a diversity of viewpoints while engaging in public problem solving.

Public Deliberation in the Communication Studies Curriculum

Students in a variety of educational contexts—from public land-grant universities to small liberal arts colleges—stand to benefit from the practice of *doing* rhetoric through public deliberation. This type of activity fits well with many college and university missions of utilizing institutional expertise and resources to engage the community to enact positive change. It also catalyzes critical thinking and civic engagement, which are central elements of a liberal arts education. For faculty at institutions with a large commuting population, public deliberation can be a way to connect student classroom experiences to their lives in the community. Deliberation is the fusion of critical thinking and community engagement, a deep learning opportunity that serves and stretches the mission and vision of different types of institutions, departments, faculty, and students. The impact of this learning also extends beyond the classroom, as students internalize the values of civic engagement and build relationships within the community through public deliberation.

Those interested in incorporating deliberation into existing coursework on public speaking, argumentation, and other communication studies courses can find ample resources in existing textbooks, such as *Public Speaking and Civic Engagement*; *Public Speaking and Democratic Participation: Speech, Deliberation, and Analysis in the Civic Realm*; *Dialogue and Deliberation*; *Cooperative Argumentation*; and *Democracy in Small Groups: Participation, Decision-Making, and Communication*.⁵² The National Communication Association's new Public Dialogue and Deliberation Division, which began programming at the 2016 convention, also promises to be a valuable resource for research, pedagogy, and practice in public deliberation.

Participating in public deliberation events provides opportunities for students to enhance their understanding of rhetorical and argumentation theory, as they acquire the ability to recognize patterns of argument and other rhetorical choices made by participants in public deliberations. Deliberation also appears to cultivate pragmatic optimism rather than political cynicism, as students see the potential for productive civic engagement in the public sphere. Less than a decade after the revival of public deliberation as a serious topic of research and teaching in higher education, there is still much work to be done on the methods and benefits of incorporating public deliberation into the communication curriculum. From our selected experiences, however, it seems clear that reuniting speech and deliberation in the communication studies curriculum is an appropriate and fitting response to recent calls for reforming civic education to focus more on the knowledge, skills, values, and actions necessary for engaged citizenship in the United States.

14

YOUTH, NETWORKS, AND CIVIC ENGAGEMENT:
COMMUNITIES OF BELONGING AND COMMUNITIES OF PRACTICE

G. THOMAS GOODNIGHT, MINHEE SON, JIN HUANG,
AND ANN CRIGLER

Civil society plays a vital role in a democracy. Traditionally, civil society was enacted in town halls and public squares where the community could assemble. Public platforms, popular forums, and community festivals were available among neighbors. The influx of immigrants and the rise of modern, urban society in the 1920s prompted a movement to gather citizens from a variety of backgrounds, ethnic origins, and interests into the "Great Community."[1] We find the influences of the past in the present. In the past twenty years, new waves of immigration have once again fostered challenges and opportunities for the continuation and renewal of civil society. At the University of Chicago in the 1920s, collaborations between the university and the primary school were designed to produce educated citizens in a time of emergent mass media. Presently, argumentation and debate, informal logic, and critical thinking constitute the legacy of pragmatic work on civic education across the United States. Inspired by that earlier work at the University of Chicago, we have assembled a twenty-first-century intervention in Los Angeles that is designed to recenter primary schools in the education of students for civic engagement through a program of deliberative experiences that builds communication capacities.

Contemporary urban civil society poses challenges to the communicative assumptions underlying traditional models of public argument. Modern cities offer vast conduits of circulation and travel. Neighbors routinely come from different places, speak different languages, commute long distances to work, live in mixed family arrangements, and have different interests, resources, and levels of skill attainment. Mobility, messages, and lifestyles are richly mixed among friends and strangers. The result has been the steady expansion of the number, range, and intensity of groups in civil society addressing community needs for safety, cleanliness, health care, food, transport, and other issues. The proliferation of these local, sometimes transient communities, has been matched by burgeoning philanthropic efforts at the local, regional, national, and international levels.[2] We feel that primary and secondary school students can participate in civil society by learning to deliberate as individuals in community.

How can the rising generation be prepared to understand, compare, evaluate, and contribute to these civic deliberations? For a century, the humanities generally, and the communication discipline in particular, have relied on John Dewey's idea of "problem solving" to encourage learning through critical thinking and speaking.[3] The speech field was founded by ex-English teachers who emphasized discussion and debate. Forensic contests trained students in lawyer-like advocacy, where debate focused on propositions of policy.[4] Citizenship, in this paradigm, meant pragmatic argumentation by advocates who, in theory, had equal time, skills, and resources to debate propositions of policy. New practices of advocacy now exist, including parliamentary styles of debate, moot courts, and Worlds-Style debate. Yet the advocacy skills taught still remain largely defined by a forensics model of argumentation. Advocacy training disciplines critical thinking from an analytic, adversarial, and persuasive standpoint. Competition winnows the wheat from the chaff. Excellence is recognized with favorable judgment. Complex issues are reduced to a resolution, which is then debated with affirmative and negative sides vying to advance and defeat a proposed policy or proposition.

This model remains incomplete in important ways. Urban and rural educational systems are changing, adapting to new technologies in a networked society. The homogeneity of forums and scenes of discussion and debate rooted in a place-based civil society now is giving way to a pluralistic, multicultural world. Presently, migration competes with stability, schools become the assembly point for diverse populations, and a common perspective on communicative norms and values cannot be assumed. We are working with a program that focuses on material, campaign-oriented, affective education in critical thinking and deliberation. We train coaches who add to the school year seasons of moments of civic engagement through deliberation. In this program, called Penny Harvest, students deliberate over (1) community needs; (2) the construction of advocacy campaigns; (3) the appropriate individuals, groups, or institutions to reach out to and support; and (4) the acts of committing to communities of belonging and of practice.

Penny Harvest is a child philanthropy program of the Common Cents Foundation.[5] It has met with broad success with elementary and middle school students across the country in New York, Colorado, Florida, Ohio, and Washington. Between 2010 and 2012, students collected almost $1.4 million in pennies and distributed more than 3,432 grants to local, national, and international organizations.[6] We added to its Los Angeles version leadership conferences that brought together students from five local schools. In the fall, small mixed groups of students shared stories about the activities and findings from their home schools. Also, they discussed the campaigns under way. In the spring, students talked about how to decide on who to fund, where to volunteer, and how to celebrate.

Our project has been under way in the schools for four years. We work as a small interdisciplinary group of faculty and staff from political science, communication, engineering, and education with support by USC Civic Engagement.[7] Penny Harvest has been adapted to several charter, public, and private elementary and middle schools in Boyle Heights and South East Los Angeles. The project extends USC's commitment of faculty and students to these schools in service-learning projects with the development of networking competencies. What makes the Penny Harvest distinctive is a carefully designed nine-month program that requires participation and support from the whole school community. The program works with the principal, teachers, parents, and a group of selected student leaders. These leaders create a philanthropy roundtable that identifies community issues. Then they work with the student body to discuss local problems, gather pennies in their neighborhoods, connect with community-based organizations, participate in neighborhood service, and ultimately make monetary grants. In the fall, students deliberate and assemble a "wheel of caring" that visualizes community needs. Deliberation also takes place as they discuss motivations, plans, and strategies for the campaign. In the spring, deliberation continues, with the leadership group debating how to define a school's commitment to community action. The spring also offers opportunities to discuss personal commitments to local organizations and plan a legacy event for the program.

The goal of this chapter is to outline a preliminary model for youth training in public communication and democratic participation relevant to an increasingly pluralistic society of the twenty-first century. We use the example of the Penny Harvest program to illustrate our theoretical underpinnings of *network pragmatics* and how it might guide current and future civic education for school-aged children in multiethnic urban contexts. Whereas "forensics" frames training as a contest over a proposition with divided participants, "network pragmatics" emphasizes the deliberative processes involved in identifying needs by talking with community members, gathering resources, making ties, evaluating a mix of potential interventions, and volunteering. Generally, forensics models of debate are propositional, discursive, analytic, and reductive. Debate is a tool for decision making. Conversely, network pragmatics focuses on acquiring communication capacities by providing alternative spaces and activities for deliberating. For youth, the school is one such example of an alternative to household spaces. Penny Harvest is an example of an activity that involves deliberation. We argue that students taking part in the Penny Harvest program learn and practice network pragmatics through deliberative experiences focusing on identifying needs, critical thinking, affective development, and campaigning. These experiences build connections between communities of belonging and communities of practice.

This chapter has three parts. First, we start by bringing to the surface and discussing several challenges to forensic models of democratic participation. We argue that the forensics model is incomplete because it fails to take into account the heterogeneous norms of communication in a diverse society, the different affective orientations for addressing community needs, and the discontinuities of urban groups, agencies, and institutions. Second, we sketch a theory of learning, communication, and engagement that identifies *network pragmatics* as an alternative way to cultivate civic capacities through a sequence of deliberative moments (communicating needs, resources, alternatives, and commitments). Third, we describe how the Penny Harvest program works to build *communities of belonging* in the first semester, then *communities of practice* in the second. Penny Harvest models a program that develops civic capacities through engaging students in acts of discovery, personal expression, critical thinking, and community discussion. Thereby, it promotes a commitment to community building and legacy creation through enacting a series of deliberative moments.

Challenges to Forensic Models

In the tradition of John Dewey, the pragmatists of the early twentieth century viewed critical thinking and debate as useful tools for educating recent immigrants and ethnic groups for citizenship in a democracy. For the pragmatists, diversity was a difficulty to be overcome rather than an asset to be developed. While we value the pragmatists' tools of argumentation and debate, we hold that cultural diversity is a resource than can be developed across primary and secondary schools through programs that cultivate community-building deliberative capacities. In general, we hold to Aristotle's understanding of deliberative argument as the process through which communities speak to questions of future action.[8] In the following discussion, we illustrate how we extend speech programs to develop habits of deliberative practice among youths in diverse communities.

The Heterogeneity of Communication Norms and Values

Today's diverse communities of argument and the broader groups constituting civil society reflect and advance cultural change. Not only language but culture writ large can explain many of the ways in which people relate to others and to the world around them. Culture operates within formal and informal, institutionalized and everyday practices of living. These ways of sense making shape how one thinks and communicates thoughts. In addition to the language they use, people differ in how they relate to knowledge and information, perceive the current state of things, and form ideas about how events invite response. Studies show that the culture in which one matures influences one's cognition, emotion, and motivation,[9] and communication styles reflect culture as well.[10] Culture can be a powerful predictor of variability in individual behaviors.[11] Cultural practices and cognitive processes are also very much interconnected and work to reinforce each other.[12] Group affiliations based on one's ethnic or national origins can motivate collective and political action.[13] Conventions for expression vary. Norms regulating communication differ. We propose that positive, pragmatic networking experiences encourage and build a sense of hope, affiliation, altruism, and capacity. Networks augment civil society, and civic engagement is realized through networks.

Culturally based cognitive processes have real-life consequences that impact one's quality of democratic life. Public opinion surveys, for example, are concerned with measuring and theorizing about "what people think." Sometimes they are used to predict behavior. Survey research also feeds back into policy decisions. Accurately describing the processes of opinion formation, expression, and exchange—and how each of these steps actually works at the individual and collective levels—is a major challenge for scholars of politics and democracy. Scholars agree that the ability to communicate one's opinions and to move freely between thought and talk are important to having one's opinion "count" in survey research. Whether taking part in opinion surveys or participating in public deliberation, the mechanisms for publicly stating one's interests should therefore be recognized as an instrument of power, giving voice to the otherwise "inarticulate majority" and allowing the average citizen to participate in the process of governing.[14]

As Heejung Kim and David Sherman remind us, however, "talking as a good tool for better thinking" is very much a Western idea. In other words, the value of talking through—and of publicly stating one's views—may not be readily apparent to citizens who do not share such "culturally specific beliefs and assumptions."[15] The act of self-expression holds merit only when it is socially legitimized by the culture in which that self-expression is taking place.[16] As such, not all individuals in our ethnically diverse society might be acculturated to some of the most important requirements for democratic engagement and community building: genuine interaction, communication, and collective persuasive efforts with neighbors or strangers.[17] If we hope to engage the diversity of individuals in our society, young people need to learn how to communicate successfully with those who are *un*like themselves.

Despite increased efforts from community organizations and leaders, genuine challenges remain if we hope to overcome miscommunication and misunderstandings (or even the lack of communication) across "lingua-cultural" differences.[18] Language itself is culturally constructed and can be a direct cause of problems in intrapersonal communication and in conversations with others. In a pluralistic society, culturally homogeneous forums and scenes of discussion and debate must be transformed to accommodate the mixed communication practices and norms of diverse communities. In the twenty-first century, migration competes with stability, schools are becoming assembly points for diverse populations, and we can no longer assume a common perspective on communicative norms and values. Yet, at the same time, urban environments present complex webs of personal, professional, and social traffic that invite new forms and forums of discussion and debate.

Developing Emotional Capacities and Affective Bonds

Before the bar or in public deliberations, forensic debate is an activity in which contesting advocates hope to convince a judge, jury, or citizens that something is true or untrue, just or unjust, right or wrong, or wise or unwise in a particular case. Even in competitive advocacy, debaters play within and against common understandings of what it means to argue, as well as understandings of what constitutes effective and ethical advocacy. Within this context, emotions can be strategically framed as appeals, but underlying such maneuvers are the conventions and practices that constitute shared cultural commitments. Before there can be debate, these commitments, as well as shared affective bonds, must be established through successful engagement in communication.

What kind of affective bonds can be created in modern urban communities, among people of different backgrounds who come and go from different places? Network theories encourage us to research social structures and to theorize about those connective spaces where shared affective bonds might be discovered and cultivated. In a networked society, social movements may harness the energy of emotions—such as disgust and anger, or hope and enthusiasm—but those shared affective bonds with others must first be discovered and articulated.[19] By motivating students to self-organize their own communities and to travel into new and different communities of belonging and practice, the context of their education is broadened. By anticipating, crafting, and working within these broadened cultural networks, common efforts become possible. Through this process, students with different feelings about their communities develop shared affective bonds. When this works successfully, the whole may exceed the sum of its parts.

In the 1920s, training in citizenship was a pragmatic project, where argumentation and critical thinking were taught as methods of problem solving. According to Dewey, communities could become democratic to the extent that they set aside traditional ethnic differences and preferences and addressed common problems of security, safety, and progress. Schools were key to democratic progress.[20] Debate was taught as a form of advocacy, with a proposition or resolution dividing those supporting change from those opposing it. Network pragmatics starts with a more basic premise: namely, that one's sense of self and other affective dimensions of one's identity must be shared and articulated through a community-building campaign before debate can be introduced productively. We feel that community engagement presupposes an investment in affective networking in civil society. Penny Harvest takes schools through a deliberative process in which students are invited to discover affinities, seek ties, make connections, work with others, prioritize needs, generate resources, and make a commitment to strengthen and change their community.

Civic Engagement, Institutional Contexts, and Youth

The courtroom and the pulpit offered two models for the expression of free, democratic citizenship in the early twentieth century. Today's models of public address are more numerous and complicated; cooperation cannot be assumed, nor does advocacy remain the only model of practical or critical thinking. The challenge now is to develop communicative orientations that students can deploy and practice within the changing boundaries of traditional institutions and across causes championed by new start-ups oriented to specific problems. We are working on providing communicative training that would make the "outside" (i.e., traditional and start-up groups) connect with activities inside the classroom.

Civic skills normally include language skills taught in primary schools, such as vocabulary and grammar, reading and writing, typing, and computer proficiency. They also include organizational skills, such as how to work in group settings, organize meetings, prepare an agenda, and delegate responsibilities.[21] These civic skills represent the foundation of Verba and colleagues' civic voluntarism model, which emphasizes "the communication and organizational abilities that allow citizens to use time and money effectively in political life."[22] Once individuals acquire civic skills, of course, they still need to develop confidence and be given opportunities to engage in community activities.

The likelihood that civic skills will lead to engagement depends on whether individuals are given opportunities to develop and practice deliberative exchange. Confirming much of what de Tocqueville and Putnam observed in very different historical periods, Verba and colleagues argue that the "civic skills that facilitate participation" in civic life "are cultivated in the major secondary institutions of adult life, including churches, non-political organizations, and the workplace."[23] More so than socioeconomic differences, these institutional contexts explain much of the variation in the types and levels of civic skills among individuals. These are the places where individuals tap into interpersonal and social networks, which may potentially lead to recruitment into civic activities.

Nina Eliasoph has studied the practices of community-based youth organizations (CBYOs). She observes that the structural and interpersonal dynamics *within* CBYOs might actually create barriers to the attainment of civic life.[24] Furthermore, the ability of young people to identify actual social problems and actively participate in the larger society was limited by the existing repertoire of specific projects, discourse frames, vocabularies, and modes of functioning within particular organizations. Others have voiced similar concerns about how CBYOs sometimes fail to overcome obstacles to youth engagement. Interpersonal relationships and power dynamics within CBYOs tend to be more egalitarian in general.[25] However, some of the practices within such organizations "may actually marginalize some young people by insisting that they assimilate to a majority culture."[26] Active participation in school activities does not even prevent marginalized youths from being bullied in some cases.[27] Youths lacking the skills to socialize, both within and outside of the dominant culture's institutions, are still more likely to experience peer rejection and even bullying.[28]

Although we acknowledge that both skills development and institutional participation are important factors contributing to civic engagement, we must be aware of the limitations of existing models in regard to diversity. Thus, it is incumbent upon us to explore the communication competencies, experiences, and reflective training that might create fresh possibilities for connection, collaboration, and identity formation within urban contexts. Critical thinking in the forensic/deliberative model aspired to be analytic, reductive, and objective. Debate does indeed prepare students to analyze and engage the issues central to mainstream politics. Additional sensibilities, skills, and training are needed for students in contemporary urban environments, however. Civic engagement in urban environments requires understanding and interaction across more diverse populations. In the remainder of this chapter, we focus on how the Penny Harvest project has helped students acquire communicative orientation, and network pragmatics, needed for democratic participation in a pluralistic culture.

Penny Harvest and Civic Engagement

Following John Dewey's insight into the formation of the public sphere, we agree that the school can serve as a critical training ground for civic education.[29] Dewey believed that schools could teach deliberative skills, but he later grew frustrated by the bigger challenge of forging engaged communities or "publics."[30] Absent a sense of community, deliberation suffers; people are distracted from civic affairs. Thus, it is important that students learn not only the skills of argumentation and deliberation but also of identity formation and community building. Civic education that goes beyond the forensic model includes a deliberative orientation that promotes a sense of self-worth built on identification and informed doing. Deliberative training has long been part of the rhetorical tradition, but to reimagine it in contemporary form requires that we cultivate the material, affective, and networking practices that situate and shape students into active members of a community.

Throughout their youth, children learn to participate in and identify with communities through communication. A community may be viewed as a network of relationships among individuals where interaction or exchange occurs. Sometimes this involves interaction between intimates who share the bonds of family or friends; at other times, it involves strangers who share the broader spaces of civil society, such as schools or community groups. The program we are developing undertakes to identify self-subscribed communities of belonging and, through intervention, extends students' participation in communities of practice where they learn to network with strangers. In particular, we identify possible local civic networks near students who live within an urban community. Civic groups are invited to speak to Penny Harvest students about community needs and resources. The hope is that involvement with civic organizations will have positive pragmatic outcomes for students, increasing their abilities and comfort with communication.

The overall goal of the Penny Harvest project is to develop a sense of civic capacity and neighborhood participation by engaging teachers and students in philanthropic fund-raising. The idea is to help participating students develop an increased awareness of social issues and the values of service to the community. Participation in philanthropy roundtable discussions about community needs or strategic planning increases students' deliberative and decision-making capacities. At the same time, the program engages the whole school community of students, teachers, and parents. The parents become more interested in community issues as they engage with their child in discussions of neighborhood challenges and fund-raising strategies. Teachers incorporate lessons from Penny Harvest into their curriculum and classroom activities.

The Los Angeles program recruits college students to expand classroom learning by working with grade and middle school students. Participation of USC undergraduates takes many forms, with some serving as Penny Harvest coaches who work with the student leaders. Others conduct a Leadership Conference, where they work with student participants on their communication and networking skills. These activities provide USC students with opportunities for intergenerational sharing and learning. Many of our undergraduates enjoy volunteer work, but their participation in this program has been limited.

The project's reach ultimately extends to traditional and start-up local civil society organizations. These individuals and groups reach beyond the schools.

They have the human and material resources necessary to strengthen the capacity of neighborhoods. Selected schools in East and South Central Los Angeles are taking part in our pilot study of Penny Harvest's impact on youth civic engagement. The term we gave to practices of civic engagement, that we hoped to promote, is *network pragmatics*. Network pragmatics comprises an open-ended array of communication activities constituting acting, connecting, doing, making, belonging, and becoming.

Network Pragmatics and Deliberation

Network pragmatics involves constructive learning experiences. Penny Harvest is designed to cultivate comfort with discussion, information exchange, making requests of strangers, and community participation. Management theory confirms the usefulness of networking as a trained ability. Skilled individuals are more likely to network with others who possess needed information.[31] They also are more likely to offer assistance to others.[32] Such skills increase the chances of individuals engaging in social networking activities for the purposes of constructing and maintaining social relationships.[33] The aim of Penny Harvest is to move beyond questions of skill development, however, and to develop capacities for civic engagement.

In order to develop strong social ties in civil society, young people must be encouraged and trained from an early age to initiate communication and participate in deliberative events. Deliberative argument builds positive emotions that are self-reinforcing when networking succeeds. Networking creates sustainable and productive interpersonal relations and encourages cooperative effort in a common cause. Communication in a networked context functions as a capacity-building activity that generates trust and relational resources over time; individuals engage in positive interactions and support one another.[34] Even if the social ties are not deep, the act of communicating with others may be sufficient to elicit participation, inspire creativity, and build connections within a community.[35] From a communicative standpoint, the term *ties* is a metaphor for *relationships*. The ties of intimacy are rooted in habits learned from one's earliest communities of belonging. Social life is not limited to a personal sphere but extends outward to communities of practice. Such groups assemble around a range of ongoing projects. As a student matures, their ties to communities of belonging and practice change, as do the contexts themselves. Networking is a never-ending process of expanding and contracting—joining and severing—these ties through communication.

We propose *communities of belonging* and *communities of practice* as means for understanding the relationship between emotional and social support networks and the capacities and skills for youth civic engagement. The links between communities of belonging and communities of practice revolve around (1) the emotional or affective dimensions of civic participation and (2) the experiences gained from exercises in coordinated civic activities. In our conceptualization of the terms, communities of belonging and communities of practice go hand in hand and are constituted within a model of youth civic engagement that unfolds over the course of a school year.

Penny Harvest promotes that model sequentially. In the fall, we ask students to develop and discover a wider community of belonging by expressing what they see as common problems, working with peers to identify resources, and contacting civic groups in their area to solicit cooperation. Penny Harvest activities then move from belonging to practice, gradually shifting the emphasis to making decisions about how to distribute funds, encourage an ongoing school commitment, promote continuing volunteerism, and leave a civic legacy.

Initially, children involved in Penny Harvest learn to deliberate through participation in networks that engage family and friends. The resulting communities of belonging reflect varied ethnic norms, economic circumstances, and cultural customs. Communities of belonging offer to the child an identity-constructing communication network. From family, lessons are learned about when, how, and with whom to deliberate. Communities of practice are then made available through the more numerous and varied institutions of civil society, including schools, churches, and community groups. These groups provide new and different opportunities for volunteering, learning, and working together. Communities of belonging and communities of practice, although they frequently overlap, offer distinctive communicative experiences for students and teach different lessons.

Communities of Belonging

Communities of belonging are constituted by networks that center on a student's interpersonal relationships. They are grounded in social institutions such as family, where the student already has a sense of attachment, belonging, and trust. Family represents a core group where a child learns to communicate through observation, imitation, and play. Friends and neighbors may represent a similar but distinct network outside the family. In either case, these primary groups are ones with which individuals are likely to identify. The "I" becomes "we" in these communities of belonging. Feelings of empathy and compassion come from being deeply committed to communities of belonging. These feelings deepen the bonds of networks, even while they may mandate weak ties with those not inside the primary group.

Communities of belonging may also be characterized by alternative referents that signal a sense of place. These indicate different forms of self-identification, such as "student at a school," "child in a family," or "resident of a neighborhood." The referent may also be cultural or ethnic, such as "American," "Latino," or "Chinese American." Communities of belonging are important for civic engagement in that they provide an emotional and social "safe place" where capacity-building and communicative experiences may occur. At the same time, feelings of belonging, compassion, and empathy may transfer from these more intimate sites to other communities.

Communication experiences may act as motivators for developing relationships with others who share a commitment to civic engagement. It is possible that increases in networking activities can enhance and extend feelings of belonging. This may occur, for example, even where home relationships are weak. Increasing facility with networking may extend the reach of initial belonging communities, thereby motivating students to participate more easily in pragmatic communities of practice. Philanthropy is such a community that involves collaboration with others who share similar substantive interests, even while having different experiences, points of view, skills, and time for commitment.

Communities of Practice

A community of practice is a social group that requires engagement with others outside of their communities of belonging. In addition to the intimate norms of family and peer groups, a community of practice is defined by its purposes, routines, and events, and requires special relationships, skills, and activities to be successful. A community of practice is likely to extend a young person's experiences to unfamiliar communities, new forms of communication, and challenging events. Over time, a community of practice may evolve into a network similar to a community of belonging. Yet, initially, civic engagement requires communicating with people who may belong to very different primary communities. Networking with others demands learning about the issues of concern to an assembled group, as well as discussion, discovery, and the exercise of advocacy and compromise skills. Pragmatic exchange requires students to find ways to take account of the motivations and constraints of others and to commit to the group's judgment and decisions. Cities have numerous communities of practice that are supported by the state, other established institutions, or neighborhood councils and start-ups.

Civic engagement connects young people with communities of practice. A social group may take up a particular task, involving its members and extending work beyond the horizon of internal group activities. Civic engagement is brought about through a series of events: initial identification of needs, interests, and capacity for common action by the group; the development of a plan to gather resources and involve others; the organizational efforts to stage events or other group activities; and celebration and passing on the legacy. Civic engagement is an evolutionary process involving the creation, expansion, integration, and termination of networks of commitment among individuals. We hold that the disciplined experience of civic events at an early age prepares students for successful engagement later. Like swimming, the communication habits required for engagement are best learned by immersing students in situations where those communication practices are required, developed, and refined through active participation.

Keeping in mind that school-aged youths have more constrained social environments than professional adults, we have sponsored an intervention that encourages students to develop a variety of communication skills that make them feel comfortable with expanding their networks of belonging to more varied and extended networks of practice.[36] Network communication practices are necessary to the integrated development of urban civil society, as well as interactions between urban and rural communities. We argue that such network pragmatics enables students to forge local relationships with others in discussions of community needs, identification of relevant work, campaigning for resources, and deliberation over alternatives. Finally, we hold that teaching network pragmatics enhances learning in other core areas of the curriculum by using civic engagement as a context for cognitive development in math, reading, writing, and critical thinking.

Conclusion

Penny Harvest is a successful youth philanthropy program. It was developed initially in New York schools and over the years has spread across the country. Penny Harvest asks students to identify community needs, form a leadership group, get the school involved in collecting pennies, decide how to allocate those funds, and then celebrate the year and create a legacy for the program. The genius of the program lies in its premise that giving matters—for everyone. The effort is what counts. When organized into campaigns, individual efforts can have significant results. In a sense, Penny Harvest was ahead of its time; it anticipated the crowdsourcing now used to raise funds through social media networks. The unique element of Penny Harvest is its focus on schools as a site of civic engagement. In this respect, Penny Harvest demonstrates how learning may be combined with practical action to make a difference in communities.

Network pragmatics focus on building hope, trust, empathy—a web of positive affects promoting civic capacity and care. The program complements, yet makes a turn away from, forensic models of advocacy that feature analysis, argumentation, and judgment on deliberative propositions. Our program features deliberation over needs, material resources, allocating funds, and other issues, but it also emphasizes affective ties and community building. We feel that such training in primary and middle school is useful, particularly in urban contexts. One cannot assume that cities are populated by citizens who have uniform speech norms, access to civic organizations, opportunities for engagement, or experiences across schools. The pragmatists of the early twentieth century did not see great virtue in cultural diversity. In the twenty-first century, however, we need deliberative models that emphasize communication and culture as important features of education for citizenship.

Penny Harvest animates critical thinking through hosting deliberative events that connect people and expose them to constructive engagement with the community. Involvement with this sort of philanthropic effort gives students experience with communication skills useful not only in school but in civic organizations. Civic engagement in urban spaces requires network pragmatics, and those communication skills are best learned in a positive, constructive environment early in life. That is what Penny Harvest is all about: cultivating the abilities of networking and civic engagement in diverse, urban populations of young people.

The Penny Harvest project is under way in the Los Angeles area. USC students are working with Penny Harvest leadership groups in several schools, bringing together students otherwise separated by freeways and other barriers dividing neighborhoods. In 2015 and 2016, the program hosted leadership conferences involving USC students and Penny Harvest students from East and South Central Los Angeles. At their first meeting, participants of a school's leadership group discussed community needs and resources. In later meetings, they began to plan their campaigns and develop publicity for the effort. At leadership conferences, we bring together as many as eighty Penny Harvest students to talk among themselves and work together in common cause. We believe that this sort of project, emphasizing civic engagement, network pragmatics, and deliberative experience, can be adapted to local traditions, resources, and social connections within and across schools in urban areas around the globe.

From the project, we are beginning to learn how to involve college students in philanthropy by adapting traditional models of forensic debate and deliberation to the needs of local communities with diverse populations. We are transforming the study of argumentation and deliberation from a contested space of competitive debate to a more affective range of activities that build trust, empathy, and hope for productive critical thinking and civic engagement. Such efforts, we believe, will enhance the self-worth and sense of efficacy among students who come from diverse educational and cultural backgrounds, providing them from an early age with the network communication skills they need for social coordination, civic commitment, and personal success.

15

PATHWAYS TO CIVIC EDUCATION:
URBAN DEBATE LEAGUES AS COMMUNITIES OF PRACTICE

MELISSA MAXCY WADE

Civic education that includes advocacy skills has experienced a resurgence in recent years. As a path to reinvigorating our deliberative democracy, and as an antidote to uncivil discourse and partisan gridlock, advocacy-based civic education has been endorsed by educators, civic leaders, and others concerned with the civic health of the nation. Many argue that civic engagement curriculum should include interaction among students who are different from each other, as well as participation in evidence-based argument about relevant topics.[1] Yet others have pointed out that civic education is still largely neglected in socioeconomically challenged secondary school populations.[2] This neglect threatens the long-term prospects for civic engagement among America's youth. Developing civic education initiatives that enfranchise those neglected populations and encourage conversations across socioeconomic divides is thus imperative.

This chapter examines the role of Urban Debate Leagues (UDLs) in contributing to civic education among underserved populations. UDLs have helped level the playing field through creation of multigenerational and activist communities of practice. Former U.S. Secretary of Education Arne Duncan observed the potential of UDLs, arguing that "competitive urban debate is

The epigraphs to this chapter's sections are derived from Edward Lee, "Memoir of a Former Urban Debate League Participant," *Contemporary Argumentation & Debate* 19 (1998): 93–96.

almost uniquely suited to building... the 'Four C's' of 21st century skills—critical thinking, communication, collaboration, and creativity. And to that list I might add a fifth 'C'—for civic awareness and engagement."[3]

In this chapter, I elaborate and extend on Duncan's endorsement, showing how UDLs work to empower underserved student populations with civic knowledge and skills. I begin by reflecting on the UDL as a helpful addition to current educational practices.

Urban Debate Leagues

[T]he Atlanta Urban Debate League... provided [me] the opportunity to question the nefarious rites of passage (prison, drugs, drinking) that seem to be uniquely debilitating to individuals in poor urban communities.... The solution is to offer people a choice beyond minimum wage or prison. Urban Debate Leagues provide that. Debating delivers a galaxy of alternatives... for those who are only offered hopelessness and despair.... Debating forces us to abandon predetermined notions of correctness in light of well-reasoned alternatives. I am left wondering what would occur if debate became as compulsory in inner-city educational culture as football and basketball. Imagine graduating from high school each year millions of underprivileged teenagers with the ability to articulate their needs, the needs of others, and the ability to offer solutions. I am convinced that someone would be forced to listen.

—Edward Lee

Edward Lee, in "Memoir of a Former Urban Debate League Participant," powerfully illustrates the potential for debate as a site of resistance to the status quo in education. As the UDL approaches thirty years of age, it is appropriate to evaluate its trajectory—from the assumptions made at its founding, to the different kinds of scholarship on the program over the years, to the lessons learned from regular reflection and the lived experience of its participants. My primary argument is that debate participation creates multigenerational communities of practice, which are one path to a liberating civic education for all participants: students, teachers, parents, administrators, educational policymakers, community stakeholders, academic interns, and volunteers. The UDL offers an opportunity to bring different voices together toward a common goal of problem solving, skill development, and dialogue that promotes increased contact between different racial, ethnic, religious, and socioeconomic groups for participatory learning and civic education.

The Need for Change

There is a unique synergy between the lack of funding and anachronistic pedagogical practices creating what can only be described as a chronic educational crisis. . . . Instead of teaching the art of questioning, students are instructed to conform to dominant social paradigms. Instead of breeding creativity, free and independent thought is discouraged.

—Edward Lee

The statistics in education are sobering. The social and economic future of the United States is clouded by an educational system that is failing millions of American students. Some reports suggest the high school graduation rate has increased substantially over the past decade, from 71.7 percent in 2001 to 81 percent in 2012.[4] As the U.S. prison population continues to rise, however, these statistics substantially underestimate the depth of the dropout crisis. After accounting for incarcerated young adults, the high school dropout rate for young black males rises by 40 percent, and the reported narrowing of the black-white graduation gap since 1990 disappears entirely.[5] A 2012 U.S. Department of Education study estimated black and Hispanic graduation rates at just 60 percent and 58 percent, respectively, and found that some states graduate as few as 62 percent of their students.[6] Dismal statistics have led the *New York Times* editorial board to lament "the dropout crisis," concluding that current trends "present a clear danger to national prosperity."[7]

Failure to earn a high school diploma incurs enormous costs to both the dropout and society at large. After adjusting for unemployment, high school dropouts earn an average of just $8,358 per year.[8] In 2012, the low employment rate for high school dropouts (48 percent vs. 64 percent for high school graduates and 87 percent for college graduates) ignores the 6.7 million young adults neither working nor in school, representing $93 billion in lost revenues and social services costs.[9] High school dropouts incur significant social costs as well. The Alliance for Excellent Education finds that high school graduates live longer and healthier lives and are more likely to raise healthy, educated children.[10] The influence of a high school diploma on incarceration is particularly striking: on a given day, almost one in ten high school dropouts will be incarcerated. For African American males who drop out of high school, almost one in four will be incarcerated and will cost taxpayers $292,000 in various cost indexes.[11]

The current education system does not promote equality. Jonathan Kozol persuasively argues that there is compulsory unequal schooling in the United

States and that our nation operates in a system of educational apartheid.[12] Educational disparity has implications for political, social, and economic well-being, and leads to physical aggression, gang membership, high dropout rates, and a furthering of the digital divide in a society increasingly dependent on technology for success.[13] The UDL was conceived and currently functions to resist educational apartheid and liberate those caught in its oppressive web. It also functions as a formidable vehicle to level the playing field in civic education.

A Plan for Change

[bell hooks's Homeplace] is any institution created to shelter and empower people to speak out against their oppression and the subordination of others.... Resistance to a pedagogy based on forced indoctrination in a classist, sexist, and racist culture can only be seen as a logical act of self-preservation.... A pedagogy that instills talking to without listening, commands without allowing dissent, and unwavering loyalty to repressive regimes prepares its constituency for... either a lifetime of... alienating... jobs or a lifetime in the penal system.... The Urban Debate League provides a space for us to learn what justice is because it forces us to learn from those disproportionately affected by injustice.

—Edward Lee

One method for teaching the critical thinking and advocacy skills required for civic engagement is competitive tournament debating. The personal testimony and career trajectories of thousands of privileged American leaders speak to the power of debate. Training in critical listening and thinking is also a strategy for rethinking current school training. Competitive debate is supported by decades of scholarly work on its pedagogical power to teach critical thinking outside a classroom through the laboratory of tournament competition.[14]

Because competitive interscholastic debate requires funding for computer access, research materials, travel to tournaments, and training at summer institutes, the primary population that has historically participated can be characterized as white, male, and affluent. It is not surprising that many U.S. presidents, national and state legislators, executives, corporate officers, and military leaders have been trained in debate. Committed to changing this demographic and using debate to nurture the potential for all children in the American educational system, the UDL offered an opportunity for conversation across the socioeconomic divide that would nourish and educate *all* participants. Dialogue and debate has the potential to disrupt stereotypes at all levels and advance an aspirational vision of treating one another as siblings in the human family. Civic education is built on a foundation of participatory learning involving students who are different from one another and who are empowered for long-term civic engagement.[15] Competitive debate functions as a participatory community of practice, which delivers civic education and encourages civic engagement.

The seminal work on communities of practice is that of Jean Lave and Etienne Wenger, who argued that learning "crucially involves *participation* as a way of learning—of both absorbing and being absorbed in—the 'culture of practice.'"[16] As the work of Wenger and colleagues progressed, the notion of building vibrant communities of practice around regular meetings for members with common activities became the pedagogical norm.[17] Building communities of practice through debate competitions, with their attendant after-school meetings, research sessions, parent and stakeholder involvement, and student-teacher partnerships, is a logical application of this pedagogical theory.

In the world of academic debate, it is a foundational tenet that competition motivates critical thinking. On a highly functioning debate team, competition motivates individuals to cooperate for the good of the community as well as for individual achievement. The exploration of ideas and research gives rise to both individual and group ownership of learning. Teachers and students work together in ways that encourage partnerships for learning similar to educational philosopher Paulo Freire's path to a liberating education, one that encourages democratic dialogue and critical thinking.[18]

Democratic dialogue is a powerful antidote to traditional education's emphasis on deference to authority, where students "rehearse their futures as passive citizens and workers by learning that education means listening to teachers tell them what to do and what things mean."[19] Teachers and students engaging in competitive debate collaborate so that both experience the self-discovery inherent in participatory learning.

UDLs work because the student-teacher partnership forms the foundation of participatory learning in a community of practice. The concept is simple. Students are paired in teams, given topics, and asked to present arguments in favor of (affirmative) or against (negative) a particular resolution in a specified time limit in front of a judge/critic/teacher. Student engagement is high as they brainstorm with each other and their teacher/coaches, add research to their positions (both teacher guided and student discovered), write up their positions, practice with peers in front of their teacher/coaches, rewrite their positions anticipating their opponents' arguments, and perform the debate in a tournament or classroom setting against students/peers from other schools. The student speaks, questions opponents, critically evaluates the ideas (and research), and engages in complex analysis and synthesis of argument over the course of time frames from fifteen minutes to two hours. The judge/teacher critiques the debate through commentary, questions, and dialogue with the participants with the goal of refining positions of advocacy. The judge uses the role of authority not to impose a truth about the issue but to facilitate a liberating discussion of the process, content, and evolution of the arguments. Since one topic is traditionally debated over a whole year in interscholastic competition, the ideas, research, and collaborations are rigorously advanced through a series of tournaments. Participants engage many sides of an issue and regularly push the boundaries of conventional social wisdom. The resulting community of practice becomes a dynamic and empowered entity engaged in robust problem analysis that leads to civic awareness and delivers the skills necessary for civic engagement.

No less a figure than Malcolm X articulated the empowerment that results from debating:

> But I will tell you that, right there in the prison, debating, speaking to a crowd, was as exhilarating to me as the discovery of knowledge through reading had been. Standing up there, the faces looking up at me, the things in my head coming out of my mouth, while my brain searched for the next best thing to follow what I was saying, and if I could sway them to my side . . . then I had won the debate—once my feet got wet, I was *gone* on debating. Whichever side of the selected subject was assigned to me, I'd track down and study everything I could find on it. I'd put myself in my opponent's place and decide how I'd try to win if I had the other side; and then I'd figure a way to knock down those points.[20]

Malcolm X found the transformative power of debate at Norfolk Prison through debating people of privilege from Harvard and Yale.[21] The potential exists for millions of children to experience the power of community created by the debate activity. Creating such communities for secondary school students invites participation and community membership.

How UDLs Work to Educate, Empower, and Transform Lives

UDLs offer a pedagogical tool that simultaneously opens the mind to alternatives and empowers students to take control of their lives. Half of the time, students are disseminating information and forming arguments about complex philosophical and political issues. In the other half, they answer the arguments of others. Self-reflexivity is an inherent part of the activity.... The ability to question subjectivities presented as objective truth makes debate uniquely empowering for individuals disenfranchised by the current system. It teaches students to interrogate their own institutionalized neglect and the systemic unhindered oppression of others.

—Edward Lee

The first UDL began in 1985 in Atlanta as a local project involving a small number of university and secondary school faculty and staff in three socioeconomically challenged high schools. Through time, many missteps, and significant negotiation of privilege through practice, the local project became a community of practice and, ultimately, launched a national movement. In 1996, the Open Society Institute (now called the Open Society Foundations) partnered with the Barkley Forum of Emory University and began seeding UDLs in other cities based on the Atlanta model.[22] Today, there are UDLs in various stages of development in 24 cities, and 8,452 students (86 percent minority, 76 percent low income) from urban school districts participated in 2014. Sponsors have invested $11 million to support the programs in more than five hundred secondary schools.[23] UDLs work. The National Association for Urban Debate Leagues assessed independent peer-reviewed research to conclude that 90 percent of urban debaters graduate on time, and 86 percent enroll in college. Urban debaters are 80 percent more likely to graduate from college.[24] A 2013 study of Atlanta UDL participants (using propensity score matching) yielded statistically significant results for female participants in grades 6 through 10: participants had increased standardized math and reading test scores, reduced tardiness, and increased reading proficiency and fluency.[25] Research on the UDL as a site for prejudice reduction is also promising.[26]

UDLs help level the playing field in education and have the potential to be key players in promoting civic education. In Atlanta, the dialogue between people of privilege and people in challenge has resulted in profound transformations over the past thirty years. Curriculum has been informed and led by listening to students. The original high school program expanded to include middle school and elementary school programs after younger siblings expressed a desire to participate in the wake of attending tournaments, often with their parents. The result was elementary school participants being mentored by middle school debaters, who were judged by high school debaters mentored by college students, many of whom were UDL graduates. Secondary school teachers served as coaches and collaborated with students on building and refining arguments for competition. University faculty and administrators functioned as teachers, coaches, and judges; trained parents and community stakeholders as judges; conducted academic assessments; and generated resources. These conversations across socioeconomic divides have grown multigenerational communities of practice that have transformed all participants.

The transformations take many forms. First, UDL teachers have been empowered to take competitive debate practices into the academic classroom. Debate is a pedagogical tool that can be employed as a class curriculum, a multidisciplinary instructional method, and a cocurricular intramural activity, in addition to its usual role as an extracurricular competitive program. Collaborative debate experiences within the curriculum can address many causal factors leading to the decision to drop out: disengagement, boredom, and lack of challenge. Imagine a classroom where students do most of the speaking as they debate in front of classmates who are taking notes to form questions for their own opportunities to enter the debate, with a teacher facilitating group cross-examination and fostering group critique of the ideas being debated.[27] A recent study of 326 high school teachers from the National Speech and Debate Association's member rolls strongly correlated Debate Across the Curriculum instructional methods with implementation of Common Core State Standards, which build critical thinking skills.[28] Classroom debates allow students to grow and develop a powerful sense of self and voice, a belief that learning matters, and a conviction that their actions can make a difference. In Atlanta, UDL teachers were transformed and empowered to use debate in classrooms in multiple academic disciplines, promoting critical thinking and civic education for all students, not just those on the extracurricular debate team.

Second, UDL students were motivated to develop the necessary academic skills to participate in competition. They quickly saw *their* participation in debate as a critique of traditional debate as an elite learning ground for children of privilege. Their empowered voices changed the conventional menu of policy argumentation. For example, debate arguments about privilege, vernacular language, cycles of oppression, social movements, patriarchy, racism, heterosexism, and speaking for the "other" became as standard as more traditional debate arguments about nuclear deterrence, political capital, and energy policy. Environmental debates came to include discussions of environmental racism and "not in my backyard" movements, in contraposition to more traditional arguments about America's energy policies or dependence on foreign oil. One result in Atlanta, after ten years of listening to the arguments of UDL participants, was that the traditional and UDL communities truly came together when three top local private schools petitioned to join the UDL middle school league.

Third, privileged college student debaters and graduate students working as volunteers and academic interns in UDL programs began to deconstruct their own privilege in the face of the level educational playing field and through dialogue with UDL students over debate arguments. They began to understand Kozol's arguments about what it means to be winners in a rigged game.[29] These students increasingly changed their career trajectory from law school to Teach for America programs, graduate programs in education, international debate projects to seed literacy in impoverished areas, and participation in local activist projects such as community gardens and Freedom University, a Georgia-based education program for undocumented college-age students.

Fourth, parents and community partners were transformed to support the UDL. In Atlanta, the Atlanta Housing Authority (AHA), Boys and Girls Clubs of Metro Atlanta, TechBridge, Atlanta Public Schools, and local churches have provided much more than funding or meeting space, with group members becoming tournament judges, mentors, emergency transportation facilitators, volunteers, and, most importantly, social activists advocating for healthy communities. Parents, seeing the transformation in their children, have become judges and trainers at tournaments, and special recognitions acknowledge their contributions. Many parents became effective advocates for retaining and expanding debate programs in the wake of the Atlanta Public Schools test cheating scandal. Turner Broadcasting System's legal department became an engaged partner. What started as a volunteer group of judges became a sustained commitment by the legal department to assist with programming, including public debates by their attorneys while UDL middle school students judged the debates on issues of civic importance in the legal community. The robust postdebate discussions gave students exposure to careers in law, while the attorneys were exposed to the significant results of critical thinking training for young students. The potential exists for students to work on civic projects with community partners as the result of membership in a multigenerational community of practice.

Fifth, UDL alumni—both participants and volunteers—became more involved citizens. While a great deal of research has been done on the effect of debate participation on scholarship, academic achievement, and other indicators of personal and professional success, there is no known research assessing the impact that participation in debate as a community of practice has on alumni participants. A 2011–2013 internal assessment of 346 Emory University debate alumni who worked in the UDL documented significant ongoing civic activism and engagement, which they directly attributed to their participation in the Atlanta UDL program.[30] The results of this survey indicate a strong relationship between service opportunities afforded through the Atlanta UDL and a strong commitment to civic engagement later in life: "Nearly half of all students who initially participate in debate . . . remain actively engaged alumni after 'retiring' from competition. 44% agreed . . . Atlanta UDL service influenced their career path. 71% agreed their experience increased their personal commitment to community service beyond their professional career."[31] There seem to be clear links to participation in the Atlanta UDL and commitment to long-term community service. One respondent noted the significance of communities of practice: "Everyone was involved in debate community service—everyone. . . . Service became routinized. Everyone was busy, but everyone found time to share skills and time. I've never before been in a community like Emory debate . . . where each member was competitive in his or her own way, pursued his or her own interests, but also expected that service of themselves and each other. Once you are in a place like that for four years, it is difficult not to expect that of yourself ten years later."[32] The experience of Emory debate alumni, while not statistically generalizable, suggests participation in UDL programs strongly influences long-term commitment to civic engagement and continued participation in activist communities of practice.

An Ethnographic Case Study

Debate allows students to take control of their educational destiny and at once make it a site of resistance. It allows those saddled with the baggage of poverty, racism, and sexism to construct their personal strategy for liberation.
—Edward Lee

Ethnographic studies offer much promise for assessing the impact of UDL programs as engaged communities of practice.[33] One such program, Computer Assisted Debate (CAD), was launched in 2003 in Atlanta, targeting middle school children living in AHA communities, the most socioeconomically challenged cohort in the city. CAD students participated in the Atlanta UDL and were supported by after-school instructional programs and summer training workshops. Studies of CAD, which demonstrated participant absences dropping 44 percent, disciplinary referral and suspensions dropping 45 percent, and reading proficiency scores rising two and a half grade levels in one year,[34] prompted the Bush administration to identify CAD as the premier education program in the Helping America's Youth Initiative.[35] The U.S. Department of Justice named CAD one of five programs that work in the national Weed and Seed Program.[36] The Institute for Law and Justice identified CAD as one of two school-based programs recommended for national replication as an antigang youth development program.[37]

A yearlong academic ethnographic study of CAD concluded that the program promoted student empowerment through literacy skill development and became an activist community of practice.[38] Student achievement was significantly augmented when African American Vernacular English was used as the initial primary "language" of instruction before moving, in partnership with students, to more conventional forms of Standard English.[39] The study offered support for evaluating literacy as a gateway to participation in democracy as a result of student empowerment, specifically pointing to academic engagement through student-driven curriculum, student-teacher collaboration, and student ownership of learning. The work also persuasively argued that CAD was a powerful example of Wenger's notion of communities of practice.

CAD graduates who moved on to high school debate programs in Atlanta renamed their program the Community Activist Debates in ownership of their experience. Graduates persuaded Renee Glover, then CEO of the AHA, to allow them to serve as an advisory group to help with drug reduction efforts in their communities. They recruited more than two hundred parents to attend public debates on drug and gang issues facing AHA communities. CAD graduates continue to serve as junior faculty in elementary and middle school summer programs offered by area colleges, following a job application process that includes interviews with program administrators and evaluation by the students. Many CAD students now serve as teachers and volunteers in UDL programs and other forms of civic activity in various cities.

CAD's success as a community of practice privileges culturally relevant pedagogies engaged with respect. One of the founding teachers speaks with passion about respect as the foundation for community membership for all participants, teachers, and students: "One of the premises of the program . . . we've tried to emphasize over time for the teachers and the instructors is that you . . . meet the students where they are. . . . [M]y most critical assessment . . . of [traditional] educational methods is . . . the arrogant assumption that the student needs to meet you where you are. . . . In short, the CAD project demands of itself the one commitment it asks from its students: respect."[40]

Concluding Reflections

Thank you to all those who gave me the gift of resistance. I once read "the cry of the poor is not always just, but if you don't listen to it, you will never know what justice is."

—Edward Lee

Inviting underserved populations to the world of debate has changed all who participate, causing us to rethink traditional debate communities of practice. The conversation across the socioeconomic divide is a powerful, mutually nourishing dialogue. Intercollegiate debate has been transformed, often painfully, from the infusion of UDL students into the college ranks, which now regularly engages in arguments interrogating privilege in competition practices in addition to the traditional policy arguments that have long characterized competition. College debate programs have become more activist outside the competitive arena, and their communities of practice have grown to embrace participation in prison debate programs, community gardens, Freedom University, and other forms of civic engagement.

University staff and students teach debate in profoundly different ways than we were taught, having been guided by UDL students seeking changes in instructional method, curriculum, and the language of respect. We constantly revise and renegotiate our relationships with each other, and with various actors in the university, public school, and community setting in service to the powerful children we find attracted to debate. Over the past five years, an upper-level undergraduate psychology class at Emory could elect to judge at four UDL middle school tournaments as part of their program of study. When middle school students from the CAD program asked if they could judge the psychology students in *their* final classroom debates on solutions to community problems, the beginning of a dialogue that far exceeded an academic exercise truly began. Because of the empowered voice of UDL middle school debaters, many of the psychology students became long-term members of the Atlanta UDL community of practice. All participants benefit.

None of us initially working in the UDL program in Atlanta thirty years ago foresaw the directions our work would ultimately be taking. A small after-school instructional and monthly tournament program for thirty high school students, three secondary teachers, and a few graduate students generated a profound dialogue that became a one-thousand-member multigenerational community of practice engaged in respect, listening, critical thinking, activism, and, often, forgiveness. The community of practice sought engagement with traditional competition circuits populated with people of privilege and was formed and transformed through the process of bringing new ideas to tournament dialogue.

The dialogue has often been painful and challenging, but the resulting transformation has been a powerful engine of social change and civic engagement as exemplified in the exceptional voices of Leaders of a Beautiful Struggle (LBS). LBS is a Baltimore community activist group founded by alumni of the Baltimore UDL, many of whom were national intercollegiate debate champions. LBS has demonstrated profound influence in national media through commentary on police practices in Ferguson, Baltimore, New York, and Texas, in addition to so many other examples of structural racism and majority privilege deeply woven in the fabric of the United States. LBS is a multigenerational activist community of practice that takes civic engagement to nationally significant outcomes.

The UDL continues to develop through a process of trial and error, dialogue, and partnership. But there is no question that UDL communities of practice have transformed our appreciation for the power of debate education and the depth of competitive tournaments as laboratories for participatory learning, empowerment, civic education, and activism.

PART 5
INTERNATIONAL COLLABORATION
AND INTERCONNECTIONS IN DEBATE

16

COMPARING ARGUMENT AND DEBATE MODES TO INVOKE STUDENT CIVIC ENGAGEMENT: LEARNING FROM "THE BEN"

ALLAN D. LOUDEN AND TAYLOR W. HAHN

Tell me and I forget. Teach me and I remember. Involve me and I learn.

In this chapter, we propose that the Benjamin Franklin Transatlantic Fellows Summer Institute (BFTF) offers a rich pedagogical model for coupling civic engagement with classroom-based argument and debate training. Since 2006, the BFTF, a U.S. Department of State institute sponsored through the Bureau of Educational and Cultural Affairs, has hosted high school students, ages sixteen to eighteen, representing the post-Soviet states, Western Europe, and the United States.[1] During the monthlong program, fellows develop skills centering on international collaboration, diplomacy, civic engagement, and political advocacy, blending courses in argument and debate with civic outreach. Periodically, the institute has incorporated various prototypes to test innovative approaches for promoting civic engagement. These adaptations, developed by staff, alumni, and Department of State representatives, allow for a "lived assessment" of potential models for civic engagement and democracy promotion. This chapter shares discoveries from the BFTF for training students in civic *praxis*, integrating classroom-based learning with community-based civic engagement applications.

The epigraph to this chapter is commonly attributed to Benjamin Franklin and is used as an unofficial motto for the institute. See "BFTF at Wake Forest University," Benjamin Franklin Transatlantic Fellows Summer Institute, http://www.bftf.org/ (accessed March 2, 2016).

Debate and Civic Engagement Within and Across the Curriculum

Questions of how best to promote productive argument and debate, both in the classroom and in society, have been broadly discussed across a variety of contexts. Joseph Bellon and Alfred Snider and Maxwell Schnurer have demonstrated the value of debate within multiple educational contexts, arguing for debate across the curriculum and promoting the study of argumentation as a gateway to improved interpersonal relationships and collective problem solving.[2] These works show how argument and debate can do more than prepare students vocationally and competitively. Indeed, there is a growing consensus that debate offers students a flexible toolbox of skills applicable in a variety of everyday contexts.[3] This is demonstrated by Ede Warner and Jon Bruschke, who champion debate's utility as a tool of empowerment that traffics beyond classroom learning into public spheres.[4] This potential for empowerment has been shown to extend into the digital realm as well, offering individuals a means of critically engaging one another respectfully across a wide variety of mediums.[5] While each of these scholars has pointed toward the potential for debate and deliberation to positively impact students, there remains little comparative data that assess how varying debate pedagogies interact with real-world modalities. This chapter approaches the question "How do various methods employed to teach debate and deliberation work as modes of civic education?"

Translation of classroom instruction to actualized modes of civic engagement requires attention toward the multifaceted and culturally contingent nature of community and identity. This recognition has fostered an exploration of how civic engagement might be conceptualized within both American and European cultures. In this article, we build on previous research on the BFTF as a site for deliberative training with a steady focus on networking and intraintertrainational civic engagement.[6]

Since antiquity, debate and discussion has found its purposive roots in the public civic forum. As part of a working group on alternative debate models at the 2009 National Developmental Debate Conference held at Wake Forest University, Theodore Albiniak defined civic engagement within the context of argument and debate, showing that debate offers skills "essential to advocating and adjudicating issues in democratic deliberation."[7] Much of the legwork needed to demonstrate debate's role in civic engagement has already been performed. What remains is the presentation of diverse models of praxis-based pedagogy that offer differing perspectives on how to instill the study of argumentation with a civic mission. What follows is a temporally organized exploration of various models utilized by the BFTF to teach debate as a means of promoting civic and community engagement.

Argument, Debate, and Civic Engagement at the BFTF

The BFTF is organized in three distinct segments: classwork, study trip, and applied civic engagement.[8] In the initial week of classwork, BFTF fellows enroll in courses designed to develop debate and advocacy skills utilizing, in part, a focus on deliberation-based simulations. Logically, many people would expect an institute sponsored by the State Department (their goal being, in part, future international cooperation) to utilize simulations as a means of fostering democracy promotion. However, the BFTF has purposely *not* focused on democracy promotion, recognizing such an emphasis would result in cross-cultural exchanges filtered through a U.S. lens. Our choice to avoid democracy promotion is intended to foster respect for the cultures and practices represented among the fellows. More fundamentally, this choice is based on the shared belief that discussion and discovery is better fostered with minimal authoritative overlay—that our task is not to proselytize but to enable. We want fellows to achieve their own proprietorship of civic engagement, focused less on ideology and more on the processes of decision making, debating, and deliberation. Through this model, the BFTF's staff members constantly remind themselves that fellows must work outside a U.S.-centric framework, operating within contexts in their homelands that may or may not be based on a democratic model.

In addition to simulation-based training in the classroom, the BFTF takes fellows into the community for short-term volunteer opportunities, primarily working with a broad range of educational and community centers. This part of the program follows a weeklong study trip and is intended to develop a sense of solidarity among the fellows and the surrounding Winston-Salem community. This quick emersion in the surrounding area is similar to that seen in much larger programs, such as the American Democracy Project, that utilize volunteerism and service learning to engage students with local communities.[9]

We are under no illusion that this "drive-by" exposure fully prepares fellows for long-term civic engagement when they return home. Civic engagement that does not acknowledge the individual needs of students and their home communities provides little more than an ephemeral sense of helping others. At the same time, we believe that the institute does inculcate skills and provide firsthand experiences that are key prerequisites to long-term community involvement.

Another guiding principle at the BFTF is a focus toward individualized education. The multicultural and cross-cultural nature of the BFTF amplifies the importance of the differing cultural assumptions, competencies, and skills underlying argumentation across cultures, what James Crosswhite refers to as an implicit aspect of argument that contains cultural assumptions, competencies, and skills.[10] Living with students from other cultures, fellows are rapidly exposed to cross-cultural exchanges that can problematize cultural assumptions, paving the way for deliberative exchange between otherwise distant cultures and communities. These cross-cultural exchanges expose underlying assumptions and skill sets, prompting students to not only deliberate but also to question some of the underpinnings of their own presumptions about argumentation and debate.[11] At the BFTF, deliberative abilities are developed during the first week in such courses as Comparative Constitutionalism and Citizenship and Conflict.[12] These courses are designed as "debating forums," where fellows test the merits of various governmental archetypes and develop competencies in deliberating with peers from other nations and backgrounds. Fellows reported that these exercises were not only informative but also increased their optimism about the potential for resolving international and cross-cultural conflicts. As one student wrote in an exit survey after the 2011 institute: "This class was so great we learn to be leaders and try to make an agreement with all country for a better world. I wish that adult can think like the youth and maybe there will be no war that's why we should teach the new generation about peace about environment and stuff they should make more programs like this."[13] The combination of these models—formalized debate and small group deliberative exchanges—familiarized fellows with the tools necessary to positively engage one another throughout and, more importantly, *following* the institute. These skills were further cultivated during later civic engagement opportunities, training fellows to apply their critical thinking skills to real-world problems. While the short courses and general layout of civic engagement opportunities are a continuing aspect of the BFTF, the nuances of the civic engagement segment have changed over time in accordance to fellow's needs, the strengths of the institute's staff, application of "lessons learned," and deliberative innovations. As the following sections illustrate, the BFTF has utilized diverse pedagogical tools to promote internal and external deliberation, prompting a cyclical relationship among argument, debate, and civic engagement opportunities over the years.

The 2007–2008 BFTF

The BFTF has a long history of prompting its staff to utilize skill sets developed through competitive collegiate debate. As a result, the 2007–2008 model, as a reflection of staffing expertise, directly taught argumentation and debate skills. By tapping into the know-how of debate faculty, graduate students, and undergraduates, the BFTF organized around formal classes, practice debates, and approaching civic engagement from a more detached perspective—a traditional civics approach.

Anyone involved in debate knows that the activity provides portable skills with a lifetime of applications, but we also recognize that format and context can dramatically impact pedagogic results. In 2007, the BFTF envisioned teaching "civic engagement" by creating venues where students could refine their debate skills. To this end, students selected topics, conducted research, and staged public debates on campus and in the surrounding community. This public debate model included events at Winston-Salem City Hall and other venues where the debates could be geared toward community organizations as audience members. The venues, when possible, reflected the tangible interests of the host group, and broader community needs were also reflected in the debate topics. In addition, on-campus debates were presented to invited critics with expertise in the topic area. These events motivated the fellows to speak, research, and test ideas, both within a traditional classroom setting and in a more public forum similar to the public debates some American debate programs utilize to extend their teams' experiences beyond the tournament context.

In understanding debate as a form of civic engagement, the fellows' intellectual focus on particular topic areas was grounded in the assumption that this model would encourage skill acquisition that would transfer to other topics and contexts. Upon reflection, this was a defensible model for debate training, although some fellows later reported that their training was not readily translatable to other contexts. The assumption that a weeklong training would ingrain skills and a critical stance useful in inventing and managing community deliberations and problem solving in other cultural contexts proved overly optimistic.

Efforts to invigorate the fellows' commitment to civic engagement and constructive deliberation on returning home were supplemented by exercises in volunteerism. In addition to the aforementioned events, the 2007–2008 BFTF institutes took fellows into the surrounding Winston-Salem community for a day of "direct civic engagement." For example, the 2008 fellows spent an afternoon cleaning local streams and assisting community partners with litter-control initiatives. Fellows were asked to perform volunteer opportunities for local organizations primarily to comply with grant requirements; initially, these efforts were not central to the institute's pedagogy. Engagement with community partners proved to be a positive experience for many of the fellows, but it was not adequately integrated into the teaching model of the institute. Fellows seemingly did not have sufficient context to appreciate the interplay of deliberation, debate, civic engagement, and volunteerism. Upon reflection, we recognized that we had yet to resolve the question of how to connect the study of argumentation and debate with a practical understanding of civic engagement—that is, how to best assure the transference of skills to practice.

The 2011 BFTF

The curriculum at the 2011 BFTF sought to resolve the disconnect of argument training and civic participation evident in the 2007–2008 institute by changing the ratios of debate and civic engagement. Debating exercises were used to interrogate the foundational assumptions, both organizational and philosophical, underlying the volunteer and community outreach activities. Pedagogical choices aligned with what psychologist Daniel Willingham has written about deep learning: "The ability to think critically depends on having adequate content knowledge; you can't think critically about topics you know little about or solve problems that you don't know well enough to recognize and execute."[14] In his explanation of how critical thinking skills align with debate, Willingham argues that when learners "see both sides of an issue," they are more likely "to spontaneously think 'I should look at both sides of this issue.'"[15] In 2011, the institute focused on developing critical skills prior to civic engagement, in the hope that enhanced prior understanding of the civic issues and locations would provide the fellows with the content knowledge they needed for more fully formed ideas and self-persuasion.

The 2011 BFTF restructured its civic engagement opportunities toward these ends, asking fellows to select a controversy area that they felt was important to themselves and their own communities. These topic areas included: environment and sustainability, economics and poverty, arts, child welfare and education, and documentary film studies and journalism. Fellows were placed in groups according to their preferred area of interest, and then discussed their topic, examining the nuances of the issues involved and how controversies over those issues affected their own communities. For example, fellows in the environment and sustainability group quickly discovered that recently proposed clean energy initiatives, while perhaps popular within their own nations of origin, were not universally endorsed. A fellow who spoke in favor of a hydroelectric dam quickly discovered that nations downstream were strongly opposed to the initiative, arguing that the project would be ecologically devastating. By asking fellows to self-select their working group's controversy areas, we created learning spaces where students were often exposed to impassioned viewpoints. This approach to civic controversy exposed students to more alternative perspectives, challenging their preconceptions in a learning environment where they might develop collective knowledge of the potential ramifications of various ideas and proposals. Importantly, it also sensitized the fellows to the community-based projects they would later visit, adding depth and empathy to their understanding of the issues facing public service organizations.

Exposing fellows to controversial issues and diverse viewpoints was intended to promote openness toward new opinions and critical assessment of both their own opinions and the positions of others in their group. In their interest groups, fellows interrogated the actions and philosophies of real-world organizations working within their topic area. By deliberating among themselves in a loosely structured environment, they engaged in assessment of ongoing crises and perspectives that affected the lives of their own families and communities. As a result, there was greater buy-in for the civic engagement aspect of the program and less focus on fellows' own unique perspective and opinions. The fellows began to take more custody of their own decision making.

In addition to deliberation within each group, all fellows took part in a short course on argumentation and debate. This course was structured to facilitate deliberative exchange when faced with multiple interests that appeared to be mutually exclusive. To demonstrate how these conflicts unfolded and to offer road maps for future resolution, fellows worked together to frame debate topics that juxtaposed interest groups, finding relevant overlap. One such topic was formulated between the arts and economics groups. These groups came together to debate if community art was a reasonable expenditure of public funds. Because groups were implicitly tasked with problematizing each other's assumptions, the arts group could not simply argue that "more art is always good," nor could the economics group only consider the "bottom line." While the initial arguments in these intergroup debates were spirited and oppositional, they did eventually expose areas of common ground, opening potential avenues of deliberation and compromise.[16] These debates were useful for exposing the blind spots in various positions, revealing how and why audiences might fail to support their proposals due to their commitments to other priorities.

By questioning the assumptions underlying various outreach activities they participated in, fellows began to probe the forms and functions of community organizations. This process often elicited appreciation for the complexity of civic engagement, making the constraints faced by civic groups apparent and prompting deeper thought about how projects were presented and interpreted by the community. Reflection was further facilitated through the debating experience, as the fellows gained greater understanding of both their own positions and the many other positions that could conceivably be held by other stakeholders affected by civic programs. Debating also enriched the outreach encounters themselves by encouraging the fellows to form and take ownership of their own opinions. This focus on debate and critical reflection also illuminated the relationship between debate and civic engagement as a developmental process where preengagement argumentation can enhance one's appreciation and self-capacity for civic purpose.

The process also has implications for cultural integration. By teaching fellows how to engage groups and individuals with divergent priorities, the debate exercises promoted fellows' reflection on their own interpersonal differences. This was demonstrated in multiple survey responses where fellows indicated that, upon becoming comfortable talking about serious and controversial issues, they utilized the free time in their schedule to build better relationships with their peers. These informal interactions, as one participant put it, "really let each individual speak for his- or herself" and better allowed "the group to bond."

The success of the 2011 BFTF's approach to debate and civic engagement is demonstrated by the fellows' shift in attitude toward deliberation and civic engagement. Of the sixty-two fellows who completed an exit survey, 54 percent reported their commitment to being involved in civic or political life in their own country had "highly increased." Interactions on social media also reflected the success of the institute, as BFTF Facebook traffic patterns over the following year shifted from primarily social interactions to more substantive content, including information seeking and sharing, professional networking, and development of BFTF-inspired projects. Participation in these interactions was also sustained over a long period of time and indicated a deep understanding of and commitment toward civic outreach.[17] Increasing numbers of projects—some approaching the magnitude of the BFTF itself—were developed, promoted, joined, and funded through the work of the program's alumni.[18] Arguably, this broader and more sustained impact resulted from the changes in instructional assumptions and approaches described previously.

The 2014 BFTF

In 2014, the BFTF continued to explore how best to promote the interconnectivity between argument and civic engagement. During this institute, the pedagogic focus was on investing in the fellows' capacity to *independently* translate classroom instruction to real-world scenarios. Previous years at the institute had demonstrated the capacity for fellows to utilize classroom instruction in real-world scenarios. However, the capacity of the fellows to effect this translation with minimal prompting from staff remained unexplored. Self-actualization on the fellows' part was a core tenet of the 2014 BFTF. The curricular revision experimented with reversing the order of applied argument and civic engagement. Fellows were immersed in civic engagement opportunities, and then prompted to deliberate on their experiences utilizing the argument and debate skills previously developed during their classroom curriculum.

Debate and deliberation among fellows was prompted through simple, conversational instigation from staff members. For example, while returning from an outreach opportunity with a local food bank, a small group of fellows was asked: "Do you think the resources and energy dedicated to food banks could be better utilized through community gardening initiatives?" These types of questions were presented to fellows in a way that was informal, but with little effort they could be translated into a pro-con debate. Posing questions that implied debatable propositions functioned as conversational fuel, often leading to animated and creative debates. These discussions, naturally, varied in levels of formality, intensity, and length; some groups elected not to engage questions of civic engagement in an argumentative forum, while others spent much of their free time in discussion of pros and cons. This pedagogical strategy was intended to encourage realistic democratic deliberation, equipping individuals with the capacity to engage one another but allowing circumstance to shape the nature of those exchanges.[19] William Rehg shows that this type of exercise is a useful way to teach debate and civic engagement, as it may prompt otherwise inert actors to "present public arguments in a cooperative, dialogical spirit."[20] The 2014 BFTF served as an application of Rehg's model, showing how argument and debate can be practiced cross-culturally and demonstrating that only minimal preliminary instruction is necessary to promote meaningful exchange.

Despite the institute's success, shifting away from concurrent debate and civic engagement activities was not without risk. In 2014, the BFTF explored civic engagement as a fertile ground for argumentative praxis, testing whether and how fellows might self-realize the utility of debate upon leaving the classroom.[21] Because this was unexplored territory for the institute's staff, a broad spectrum of possible impetuses for dialogue were tested. As in previous years, for example, the 2014 fellows visited nonprofit organizations in the Winston-Salem area, volunteering at food distribution centers, community gardens, and environmental conservation projects. These visits were structured to offer fellows the opportunity to communicatively engage peers during acts of physical labor, prompting real-time analysis of volunteer activities and illuminating the physical, sometimes grueling, nature of community outreach initiatives. Both during and after outreach opportunities, fellows deliberated on the strengths and weaknesses of various engagement models. However, fellows self-reported that discussions conducted simultaneously with volunteer activities were comparatively ineffective. Those deliberations that occurred immediately following volunteer events were considered richer and more fruitful because fellows were able to focus more on the discussion.

Asking fellows to critically examine and debate the merits of volunteer activities while engaged in those activities produced mixed results. While some fellows did succeed in deliberating while working, others elected to ignore deliberative prompts. Still others became so focused on the discussion that they stopped engaging in the volunteer activities. What we have found, then, is that deliberating immediately following outreach opportunities works better, and that delaying the promotion of these exchanges does not diminish the quality of the fellows' insights. In fact, fellows have shown that, even immediately after returning from a strenuous volunteer activity, they are capable of self-identifying moments of potential conflict or intercultural friction. They also are capable of deploying deliberative skill sets learned earlier in the institute. One fellow demonstrated this deeper understanding of socially contingent engagement opportunities, reporting: "It's always great to have hands-on experience with other projects and 'steal' inspiration. The visit to the Second Harvest Food Bank, for instance, also portrayed cultural and economic differences between European countries and the U.S. You have definitely a bigger gap between people's economic situations, but you have also more volunteerism." The successful deployment of critical thinking skills when deliberating about civic engagement, social needs, and cultural differences was likely due, in part, to the fellows' cohabitation throughout the institute. By rooming with one another for an extended period, fellows grew comfortable enough to speak their minds while also having enough time and opportunity to engage their peers in unstructured, self-prompted dialogue. The merger of social, informal, and formal interactions primed fellows to comfortably engage in deliberation without further instruction from staff members. This refocusing of civic engagement at the BFTF opened space for increased social outreach, creating a cyclical interaction in which more outreach opportunities provided the fellows with additional topics for deliberation.

Conclusion

In this chapter, we examined three examples of debate-based pedagogy and their effects on civic engagement within intercultural contexts. Based on our findings, we have isolated four important points for the educator interested in civic instruction. First, our experience reinforces a belief that exercises based on debate and deliberation offer translatable skill sets, allowing students to deploy classroom learning in real-world situations with little or no prompting. However, the translatability of these capacities is more fully realized when students are conversant with the rationales behind the civic landscapes they occupy. This approach, when combined with an instructor's hands-off mindset, allows students to develop their own solutions to—and take ownership of—ongoing community needs. A model of pedagogy that combines formal instruction in deliberation with more indirect ways of prompting actual deliberations enables students to apply these skills on their own, often with more creative solutions.

Second, we found that debate promotes and facilitates the development of better norms and practices in civic engagement. This view is informed by student responses that indicate an enhanced ability to critically assess not only outreach organizations but also their relative effects in addressing community needs. Furthermore, fellows indicated an increased capacity to meaningfully articulate their own beliefs. By organizing students into cohesive groups during debate instruction and outreach opportunities, educators can help students develop a stronger sense of how civic engagement initiatives operate theoretically and practically. This dovetailed approach toward civic engagement—treating civic engagement as both a philosophical and a practical concept—fosters leadership skills through classroom discussion and deliberation while also fostering an appreciation for volunteerism through outreach opportunities.

Third, continued innovation at the BFTF demonstrates that the relationship between argumentative engagement and civic outreach is strong enough to allow experimentation. Based on our collective experience, we conclude that were these interests not deeply integrated, our ongoing pedagogical experimentation would likely have derailed the learning process. Rather than the "yelling matches" we too often witness in public political argument, the fellows learned to disagree amicably, despite their limited formal training in the skills and norms of democratic deliberation. Their view of energized "confrontations of ideas" as productive and collaborative rested on their acquired experience and mutual respect. The BFTF demonstrates that debate instruction is readily translatable to diverse pedagogic formats, including multicultural, multinational contexts.

Our final conclusion is informed by an observation made by David Zarefsky in the foreword to this volume. Zarefsky argues that debate's utility is not (and cannot be) fully realized unless it is juxtaposed with an appreciation of civic responsibility and engagement. Since classical Athens, debate's orientation toward *dissoi logoi* has functioned as a means of eliciting public deliberation, working to illuminate better norms and practices within civic society. As such, educating students on the direct applicability of debate to issues outside the classroom is essential to promote positive transformations in civil society.

In closing, the benefits of approaching debate and civic engagement as mutually reinforcing activities is demonstrated by the diverse pedagogical frameworks offered at the BFTF over the past nine years. In its early years (2007–2008), we showed the capacity for debate to function as a form of civic engagement, bringing voice to community concerns by facilitating public deliberation. Later (2011), we showed that argument and debate skill sets promote critical inquiry into the norms, standards, expectations, successes, and failures of previous, ongoing, and yet-developed civic engagement initiatives. And more recently (2014), the BFTF has demonstrated that practical civic engagement opportunities can provide the impetus for fellows to deploy more formally learned argument skill sets, independently fostering space for critical inquiry and debate.

The format of the BFTF has varied considerably, yet the skills acquired by fellows have remained constant. These skills have included the intellectual dexterity that the study of argumentation and debate provides for thinking through an issue, an appreciation of the synergy between the theory and practice (*praxis*) of argumentation and debate, and the faith that critical thought and vigorous debate does not hamper but rather strengthens social and political progress.

The results of the BFTF continue to speak for themselves. Alumni of the institute have gone on to hold internships and other positions at embassies and other governmental offices in their home countries. Others attend leading universities (including many Ivy League schools), and still others have helped develop civic projects, large and small, in nearly all of the countries participating in the program. In a number of cases, former fellows have used their talents to develop large-scale youth programs mirroring the formats and methods of the BFTF. Although it is impossible to catalog the experiences of each and every fellow, the core results of the institute can be summarized succinctly. In the words of one fellow, "BFTF made me who I am. It transformed [me] from a person who likes to design projects to help the community to a confident person who knows that no matter the problem, there is a way to break it down and get it done. And there are 43 other individuals who are as eager as you are to help. BFTF shapes one's personality and their future." The networking skills cultivated through the civic outreach and collective deliberation activities of the BFTF have benefited many students. So too have the habits of open-minded yet critical thinking encouraged by the program. Continuing to cultivate these qualities in students will be an important and evolving mission of the institute in its coming years. Providing new and rich opportunities for students from around the world, the BFTF will continue to be a leader in developing debate and civic engagement pedagogies for an increasingly global society.

17

THE WORLDS-STYLE DEBATE FORMAT: PERFORMING GLOBAL CITIZENSHIP

UNA KIMOKEO-GOES

In 2013, *Time* declared today's youth "the me, me, me!" generation. Journalists, teachers, and parents worry about the part millennials might play as the new century unfolds. An important part of that drama will be how they enact citizenship. Since college is where students develop many of their habits of citizenship, universities are particularly invested in teaching students how to live a life of civic purpose. Debate programs often justify their mission in just these terms. Indeed, the conference that gave rise to this volume rests on the presumption that there is a natural relationship between debate and civic life. This chapter explores how that relationship is manifested and reinforced by participation in a particular form of debate: Worlds-Style debate (also called British Parliamentary debate). The lessons about citizenship encouraged by Worlds-Style debate expand the idea of citizenship to a global perspective, and they stress the need to become aware of international issues and accountable to diverse communities. By participating in Worlds-Style debate, students come to understand citizenship not as a fixed concept but as something that is *performed* every day. In Worlds-Style debate, students are given opportunities to perform and practice their civic roles with students from other cultures.

My personal experience with the China Debate Education Network (CDEN) helped me better realize the connections between debate and civic education.

I am greatly indebted to Teresa Green, grant coordinator for the China Debate Education Network, who helped me formulate some of the concepts of this chapter.

While I had to travel six thousand miles to fully appreciate these lessons, they should be evident to anybody involved with competitive debate programs and other organizations that promote public advocacy and the discussion of political and social issues. J. Michael Hogan discusses the need to cultivate the "habits and skills of civic participation," which should include "how to speak, how to argue, and how to deliberate in a diverse, technologically advanced society."[1] While these may be worthy goals within the United States, their relevance to China and other countries with no tradition of democratic participation might not be so clear. Thus, it is important that we reflect on the pedagogical value of debate in our increasingly global society. In this chapter, I argue that even in countries without strong democratic traditions, students participating in Worlds-Style debate learn valuable skills and habits of civic engagement in a global context.

Defining Citizenship

The *Oxford English Dictionary* defines a citizen as a "legally recognized subject or national of a state, commonwealth, or other polity, either native or naturalized, having certain rights, privileges, or duties."[2] This definition suggests that citizenship and civic responsibilities are best defined in terms of particular nation-states, or within the context of the duties and rights ascribed to citizens of those states. Those of us in the United States may think of civic education as primarily geared toward teaching students about our system of government and how to participate in its formal institutions, such as the court system, state and national legislatures, or the electoral process. This view has significant limitations. First, many people live in countries where they are not afforded the same opportunities, and even if they do have opportunities for civic engagement, those may be different or limited by the nature of their government and how it functions. Secondly, this view of civic education assumes that people's responsibilities and connections are best understood at the level of the nation-state. Civic values need not be defined solely in national terms. Debate encourages students to explore public issues that transcend institutional and national boundaries.

Scholars generally study citizenship as a set of skills and examine the spaces where citizenship is enacted. Many scholars focus on the nation-state as the primary site where citizenship is enacted, yet countless theories of the public sphere recognize practices of citizenship that take place outside arenas of formal governance. In Jürgen Habermas's conception of the public sphere, citizens debate matters of common interest, but that sphere is not defined by national boundaries. Theories of "counterpublics" have gone even further, suggesting that citizens often create their own spaces for practicing citizenship. Michael Warner clarifies: "The existence of a public is contingent on its members' activity... and not on its members' categorical classification, objectively determined position in the social structure, or material existence. In the self-understanding that makes them work, publics thus resemble the model of voluntary association that is so important to civil society."[3]

Nancy Fraser and others have elaborated on how these counterpublics form and how they relate to issues of access, deliberative engagement, and opinion formation.[4] Some scholars also have begun to reflect on the implications of such theories for how we teach speech and debate. As Robert Asen and Daniel Brouwer have argued in the introduction to a collection of essays titled *Counterpublics and the State*, work in this area has encouraged rhetorical theorists to think of the public as a "multiplicity of dialectically related public spheres rather than a single, encompassing arena of discourse."[5] So if we are to think of college classrooms as "protopublic spaces," as Rosa Eberly suggests,[6] we need to take into account the variety of ways in which both publics and counterpublics are constituted and engaged, not just in the United States but in cultures with very different traditions and forms of government.

Public sphere theory is useful for understanding practices of citizenship, but we also need to study those practices themselves. Asen and others have defined *citizenship* as "a process"[7] and have investigated "the habits, attitudes, or orientations of those comprising actual communities."[8] This approach treats citizenship as "a discursive phenomenon in the sense that important civic functions take place in deliberation among citizens," as Christian Kock and Lisa Villadsen have written. In this view, "discourse is not prefatory to real action but is in many ways constitutive of civic engagement."[9] Defining citizenship as a discursive phenomenon focuses attention on the variety of ways that deliberation and debates themselves function to constitute citizenship. From a theoretical standpoint, this approach provides a more useful way of understanding citizenship in an increasingly diverse world than a static definition that merely catalogs citizens' rights and responsibilities under different governmental regimes.

Debate provides both a set of procedures and a forum for students to constitute and practice citizenship, whatever their national or cultural background or traditions. Angela Ray has shown this to be historically true, examining antebellum men's debating clubs as "places where participatory citizenship was produced rhetorically, through word and ritual."[10] Today, debates are organized around topics of wide-ranging political or social importance, and competitive debate formats attract students from diverse backgrounds and give them opportunities to practice the habits of citizenship. Worlds-Style debate can be uniquely valuable for teaching those habits and for learning more broadly about the rights and responsibilities of citizenship in a global context.

Worlds-Style Debate

Worlds-Style debate gets its name from the fact that it is practiced all over the globe, and debate programs are turning to the format with "stunning rapidity."[11] From 2011 to 2015, the annual Worlds-Style championships have been held in Botswana, the Philippines, Germany, India, and Malaysia. While I believe debate generally helps develop advocacy and critical thinking skills,[12] Worlds-Style debate has the advantage of providing a more accessible venue for student debaters to discuss issues of public importance. Teams are required to create all of their arguments without the help of any coaches or other outside advisors, and they cannot consult online sources. The debate format is modeled after the British parliamentary system, with four teams of two speakers in each round—two teams supporting the proposition and two opposing it. Usually, teams receive their topics just fifteen minutes before the debate, and topics are related to current events and social issues. At the end of the debate, a chair and two panelists rank the teams, one through four. Worlds-Style debate is adjudicated through consensus judging; the chair and the two panelists must agree on the ranking of the teams. Adjudicators are asked to "confer in a spirit of cooperation and mutual respect," and they communicate their rankings to the debaters immediately after the debate.[13] The format involves the judges in civic deliberations as well, as they are expected to make well-reasoned cases for their assessment of the debate and be willing to listen to alternative views and compromise as they decide the final outcome.

Worlds-Style debate, especially internationally, tends to be open to wider public audiences, not just other debate participants. As opposed to more specialized forms of debate, such as National Debate Tournament (NDT) and Cross Examination Debate Association (CEDA) policy debate or the National Parliamentary Debate Association in the United States, Worlds-Style debate is specifically geared to ordinary citizens and is judged by the standards of "an average reasonable person."[14] Some see the rising popularity of Worlds-Style debate as part of a backlash against "the perceived over-formulism of parliamentary as well as policy debate."[15] Most events involve only those competing and judges who are experienced with competition. However, the United States Universities Debating Championship (USUDC), held in Alaska in 2015, sold more than 350 tickets to the general public for its final debate.[16] More than 170 teams participated in the event, representing more than 40 institutions across North America. Other Worlds-Style debates, such as the European Universities Debating Championship in Vienna in 2015 and the World Universities Debating Championship (WUDC) in Malaysia in 2015, were covered by local and national media and streamed live over the Internet. The Internet has generally expanded the reach of Worlds-Style debate both through live streaming and through Skype debates between teams from different nations.

The diversity of participants is one of the unique features of Worlds-Style debate. The first official WUDC was held in Scotland in 1981 and included just over 40 teams from 7 nations.[17] Last year's event in Malaysia hosted more than 370 teams from more than 50 counties in Africa, Asia, Europe, and North America. No other form of debate has the international reach of Worlds-Style debate. With such a wide variety of countries represented, debaters cannot simply assume that their competitors or their judges will be familiar with their examples, so they must work harder to find material that will be relevant to their audience. Debaters also must read widely to be prepared for a variety of arguments. Similarly, judging in Worlds-Style debate demands more careful preparation and a broader perspective. Because judging is done by consensus, adjudicators cannot simply assume that their preferences for particular arguments or styles of debate will be shared; they must instead articulate specifically what they find most effective. While debating norms still exist (as I will explain later in this chapter), the diversity of the participants helps correct for some of the regional "echo" effects common in other forms of debate, where debaters and judges have preconceived notions of which arguments, delivery styles, or even universities should win.

Worlds-Style debate is not only practiced globally, but the topics debated are usually global in nature. Some topics ask debaters to consider many countries' interests, such as: "This House believes that the United States and the European Union should seek to promote peace by heavily subsidizing Israeli businesses who invest in the Palestinian territories" (a topic from Malaysia's WUDC in 2015). Often, the debaters themselves are in a position to determine who "This House" might be—that is, who the decision-making agent should be. For example, when debating another Worlds-Style debate topic, "This House would prohibit the media from reporting on the mental illness of those accused of crimes," the debaters themselves might decide whether "This House" should refer to a government or some other entity. Debaters also cannot think just in terms of their own country's government, as arguments relevant only to their home nation are generally frowned upon as limiting the debate.

While Worlds-Style debate does not have one governing body that oversees and dictates all of its events, one dominant rule helps sustain the broad, global perspective of the activity: the rule that opening speeches cannot be "place set unfairly"—that is, they cannot "restrict the debate so narrowly to a particular geographical or political location that a participant of the tournament could not reasonably be expected to have knowledge of the place."[18] Debaters are thus discouraged from framing their arguments in ways that make sense only for a particular country—unless, of course, the topic itself calls for that. The expectation is that debaters will offer arguments that are accessible and meaningful to a variety of audiences. For hosts crafting debate setting motions for Worlds-Style debate events, Steve Llano suggests that "any motion must be grounded in public deliberation." That means, in Llano's words, that "there must be a test to see if reasonable, interested people could get access to a variety of sources of public debate on the topic."[19] For the most part, this policy results in topics that are comparatively more public and accessible than the topics in some other styles of debate.

Beyond requiring debaters to think broadly and globally about topics, Worlds-Style debate encourages debaters to engage social issues that are not usefully understood in terms of the nation-state. Unlike other U.S. debate formats, which focus on actions the state might take (e.g., "The U.S. Federal Government should . . ."), many Worlds-Style debate topics do not presume a single state actor, or even a governmental actor at all. One topic from the Malaysia WUDC in 2015, for example, focused not on governments but on families: "This House regrets the decline of tightly integrated families." Similarly, a topic from the USUDC in Alaska the same year emphasized a moral choice rather than governmental action: "This House believes that adults who wish to have children and are financially able have a moral obligation to adopt rather than have biological children." In both these cases, the issues involved are not usefully understood in terms of a governmental actor but are nevertheless relevant and important social concerns. Indeed, because the topics do not call on government actors, some debaters find them more relevant to their own lives. The topics may not require debaters to think much about the government, but they do confront them with serious questions about the importance of family and family values.

Other topics in Worlds-Style debate have asked debaters to think seriously about social movements that transcend national boundaries. During the Malaysia debates in 2015, for example, one resolution asked debaters to reflect on what some scientists consider to be the most pressing issue of our time: "This House believes that environmental movements should support climate engineering that fundamentally alters the environment, in an attempt to combat Global Warming." At a Worlds-Style debate competition at Oxford University in 2014, another topic focused on Grindr, a geosocial networking application: "This House, as the gay community, regrets the existence of Grindr." While these sorts of issues relate to civic and social concerns of interest to many college students, they are not framed (and sometimes cannot be usefully framed) as state decisions. As such, they expand debaters' conceptions of citizenship and civic responsibilities. By engaging competitors from different nations on issues not necessarily regulated by the state, debaters are pushed to consider their responsibilities to broader communities, transcending narrow definitions of "citizenship." Debaters are pushed to consider how their everyday actions (e.g., participation in social media) might have an impact on others around the world, or they might be encouraged to become more invested in social movements that transcend national boundaries.

The China Debate Education Network

I believe Worlds-Style debate promotes civic virtue and engaged citizenship in many different contexts, but it was my work in China that most clarified the relationship between the format and citizen training. Robert Asen argues for "citizenship as a mode of public engagement,"[20] and Worlds-Style debate has proven an effective tool for teaching my students how their own understanding of "public engagement" both resembles and differs from the idea of civic education in China.

In 2012, Willamette University was awarded a three-year, three-million-dollar grant from the Open Society Foundations to expand university-level debate in China and "to create a sustainable network for debate, active discussion, and civic engagement."[21] Five other U.S. universities partnered with Willamette University on the grant establishing the CDEN, with each American university assuming responsibility for a different region in China. The grant recipients partnered with Chinese educators and hosted training sessions on how to teach debate and argumentation, and the grant helped fund regional tournaments and even national events, including an annual tournament that regularly included more than 250 teams. From 2012 to 2015, more than two hundred Chinese universities, nearly three thousand debaters, and some seven hundred teachers participated in the program.[22] The grant was premised on the notion that debate is citizenship training, and that citizenship training promotes democratic ideals. As Robert Trapp wrote in the CDEN grant proposal itself: "This project assists in global society, contributing to the development of communities of citizens articulate in civic matters and artful in engaging critical needs of the community."[23] The CDEN is not alone in advancing debate in China. Other programs are engaged in similar pursuits.

China is a prime example of a country in which citizenship cannot be measured through traditional U.S.-European standards of democratic engagement. Yet through debate, Chinese students performed different *kinds* of citizenship, and American educators and students learned about more global perspectives on what it means to be a citizen. China's government system has only one party, and yet debate requires students to argue both for and against particular positions on issues, giving them a new appreciation for oppositional views in a nation that has no meaningful political opposition. Within the debates themselves, freedom of expression is promoted, so speakers have a (relatively) safe space to explore issues of public importance. While China does not have open public elections like Western democracies, Chinese students who aspire to leadership within the Communist Party still benefit from the skills developed in debate, such as confidence in public speaking and the ability to organize one's ideas. Members of the party recognize these connections between debate and party leadership, and both the Communist Youth League and the Central Committee of the Chinese Communist Party have supported debating competitions, and members frequently serve as judges.

Party members may value debate as leadership training, but evidence suggests that Chinese students participate in debate for many of the same reasons as their Western counterparts. As part of our evaluation of the grant's success, we solicited qualitative and quantitative data from debaters who were new to the activity regarding their experiences with the CDEN. Debaters were asked to clarify in their own words how debate helped to "improve your public speaking skills." Many students responded in predictable yet reassuring ways, noting how debate improved not only their speaking but their critical thinking skills. One student, identified only as KM, wrote: "It is a way to improve my critical thinking." Another student, LH, also mentioned critical thinking but then added: "It hones my English skills. And it helps me to realize how to utilize body language to express." Self-expression is especially valuable in an educational culture that depends mostly on mass lectures. Perhaps ZK, another student respondent, was imagining giving such lectures him- or herself when he or she wrote: "I improved very much by debating. I can speak loudly in front of a lot of people."[24]

The ability to break down arguments and think critically about messages was a common theme in the responses, and those skills, of course, are useful in multiple arenas. Even if Chinese students never participate in democratic elections, self-confidence and the ability to speak in front of large audiences prepares them for personal success in educational or business environments. The CDEN's 2015 report notes that "civic engagement particular to CDEN in China is rooted first in critical thinking and individual transformation. With each debate round, students practice with one another not just their English capabilities, but their ability to identify a stance worth arguing and subsequently carrying out."[25] This emphasis on critical thinking among Chinese students parallels the chief benefit cited by American students who participate in debate. From a 2001 survey of U.S. debaters, the authors concluded: "The development of critical thinking skills should be the primary benefit proposed in efforts to reach out to new students and publics."[26]

Although individual growth is valuable in-and-of-itself, Chinese debaters involved with the CDEN also saw larger connections between their skills and the broader society. When asked what they "believe to be the value of debate participation," many wrote about China's growing influence in the world and the future challenges of globalization. "The Chinese young generation will benefit from it," one student wrote while also noting that today's students would shape the "future world." Another wrote at some length about China's growing influence in the world and the need to prepare today's young people for the challenges of globalization: "Mainland China is a nation with a huge population. Our homeland is now facing a lot of challenges and opportunities and there are hundreds of thousands of social problems and conflicts lying ahead and calling for national discussions of all kinds. Debate teaches us not to obey authority but to the truth, and that's truly crucial to our society's development." Of course, the CDEN did not set out to teach Chinese students "not to obey authority," and comments like these could be a little unsettling in a country that does not protect free speech. Yet the basic sentiment behind these remarks—that debate encourages students to think deeply about social issues—was echoed in many of the responses. Another student, NS, said much the same thing in a less provocative way: "After exposed to different ideas, I may have a deeper understanding of certain social affairs. I believe that the ideas having being discussed can benefit the society more. Although I will not preach to other people about my ideas or try to civilize people, I will try conveying the ideas to people discussing social affairs with me."[27]

Chinese youth clearly saw their debate skills as relevant to their civic lives and their nation's growing role in world affairs. They articulated anxieties about China's place in the global arena and described ways debate could prepare them to respond to future demands. KM, for example, wrote that debating with students from different cultures was of "great importance" and concluded: "I am looking forward to communicating with different people about global issues. This kind of communication will benefit all." Cross-cultural communication of this sort is most likely to occur at larger international events, but even at local tournaments students engaged global issues. Debaters also saw the competitions as spaces for practicing skills relevant to citizenship, such as understanding both sides of a controversial issue. OQ, for example, called debate a "stage" where he or she could not only "show myself to others" but also "understand people from other side" or even "stand for the side which I do not want" and still "fight for it without hesitation."

Not all voices were so optimistic about the larger cultural or intercultural benefits of debate. BW conceded that the "experience did help me as a individual. For example, it incentivized me to read more and question more." But he or she was not so sure "it benefited my community or country." Noting that debate originated in the West, where a democratic system already existed, BW observed that in China people "do not really have a say in the whole procedure of making a policy." Although debate pushed Chinese students to "know more and think deeper," BW opined that it would not have much of an effect on a "whole community and country without democracy." Although Asian cultures have their own rich histories of exchanging ideas, debate as an intercollegiate activity is more closely associated with the Western liberal arts tradition. As Steven Johnson has argued, "the preeminent place given argument in Western educational traditions is grounded in a vision of argument not as an unpleasant consequence of human interaction but as the very foundation of human knowledge."[28] Liberal arts programs in the West especially stress dialogue and discussion as pedagogical tools, but those tools may seem alien to some Chinese students.

BW's critique extended to the topics debated at Worlds-Style events. First, according to BW, the motions debated were almost always about "western ideas" and "movements happening in developed countries." Second, even those relevant to China would be "hard for us to debate," given the government's control over information and the lack of governmental transparency. Third, even if they *could* debate important and relevant issues, Chinese students had no "channel to speak out for ourselves." BW concluded, "So I don't think BP debate benefit my community and country."[29]

BW had a point about the topics. Motions from the Chinese national tournament in 2015 included: "This House believes that satirists have the 'right to offend' in their works" and "This House would cancel permanent membership on the UN Security Council." Neither of these topics is particularly relevant to young people in China. At the very least, both would produce a very different debate in China than they might in the United States. Despite the fact that the event was targeted toward Chinese debaters and the topics were written by Chinese educators, no topic from the China Open Debate Tournament asked debaters to evaluate Chinese governmental actions, nor did the topics address issues unique to China. While these broad topics may have encouraged the debaters to take a global perspective, they failed to engage them in debate over the most difficult and controversial issues facing their own country.

BW's criticism points to the chief obstacle to debate teaching citizenship skills in China. In promoting performing citizenship through debate, one must also take seriously the national restrictions that constrain the actions that might arise from such conversations. The involvement of the Communist Youth League and the Central Committee of the Communist Party in Chinese debate events also raises questions about what topics may be off limits, and it may even have a chilling effect on the debates. If the CDEN does nothing more than develop skills of personal expression and provide a space for practicing civic engagement, however, it still seems worth the effort.

Worlds-Style debate also has benefits for the Western debaters and coaches who participate in the activity. Participants felt engaged in a civic enterprise simply from their exposure to different people and cultures, and it offered them new ways of thinking about argumentation and debate. Involvement with Chinese debate also helps U.S. debaters and educators better understand the limitations on intercollegiate debate within their own country. In the United States, for example, debate programs are ordinarily male-dominated, and debaters come mostly from the disciplines of political science, law, or economics. Ironically, that means that the students already most interested in and represented in politics are receiving the most citizenship training. Conversely, in China, the debaters were mostly women, and many were interested in becoming teachers. Education and the languages were their major fields of study. With debate in the United States still dominated by men,[30] Worlds-Style debate is at least beginning to take actions to make women feel more welcome. For several years, the Worlds' schedule has included the North American Women's Debating Championships, and women's tournaments have also been held throughout the United Kingdom and Ireland. By cultivating women's debate skills and providing networking opportunities, these events certainly assist in equalizing the representation of women in debate. But debate programs in the United States could still do more to reach out to international students in the United States, as well as teachers and students across disciplines, in an effort to broaden the appeal of debate and promote diversity among debaters.

Including new voices might require debate communities to rethink preferences for argument construction, types of evidence, and styles of delivery. The preference for deductive, claim-oriented argumentation is well established in Worlds-Style debate, although this style may not be suited to debaters from other cultures. Ge Gao explains that Chinese students, for example, value an indirect approach to communication that "emphasizes what is implied or not said rather than what is said, thus compensating for the inadequacy of words."[31] It is difficult to conceive of a debate style that would focus more on what is left unsaid, but stressing listening skills and attentiveness to implicit claims might be one way to better accommodate diverse participants and strengthen debate in general.

Conclusion

As I have already suggested, there are some limitations to Worlds-Style debate as education for citizenship. While the activity is not bound by national borders, it does have linguistic barriers. The vast majority of tournaments are held in English. The limited exposure I have had to tournaments held in other languages (Spanish and Mandarin) suggests that there are norms unique to these communities. For example, while the English-speaking division of the CDEN tends to include more women and has a more publicly oriented style, the Mandarin division is more formal, male-dominated, and aggressive. Indeed, Mandarin debate in China more closely resembles debate in the United States and other Western countries. Spanish-language Worlds-Style debating events are expanding both in the United States and throughout Latin America. At this time, international Spanish competitions tend to be more oratorical and performative in nature, although they are still evolving.

The linguistic preference for English in Worlds-Style debate also affects how debaters and adjudicators are ranked. Nonnative speakers and judges often receive lower rankings than native speakers of English, suggesting that while the community attempts to expand globally, vestiges of power differentials remain. In a survey of more than one thousand debaters in 2013, 46 percent said they had witnessed some form of cultural bias in the debates. These included:

- Racist language and/or jokes in debates or at socials.
- Judges giving unfair or poorly explained decisions, explicitly, or perceived to be, on the basis of immutable characteristics.
- Adjudicators complaining about the quality of their debates, conflating "ESL debates" with "bad debates."
- Teams dismissing outright, or giving insufficient response to, teams of an ESL or EFL background.[32]

The survey also found that more than 50 percent of ESL debaters agreed or strongly agreed with statements about feeling intimidated and "looked down on" by native English speakers. Similar biases against nonnative speakers are present on many college campuses, where complaints about ESL instructors are common. Still, it is an issue that needs to be addressed if Worlds-Style debate is going to provide a valuable space for practicing global citizenship.

In addition to linguistic biases, Worlds-Style debate still suffers from underrepresentation of traditionally disempowered groups. Recruiting efforts can help address this problem, but debate historically has been associated with those who have power and resources. Angela Ray's observation about the history of debate still rings true today: "Debating clubs operated by the socially, economically, and politically dominant buttressed their power as individuals and as a collective."[33] Harvard, Yale, Oxford, and Cambridge still regularly feature in the finals of Worlds-Style debate competitions (prestigious Australian universities are also very competitive but tend to attend fewer international events). Competitive debate in the United State has shown concern for the diversity of participants for more than twenty years, and Worlds-Style debate has taken some significant strides.[34] But challenges remain.

One way that the debate community has addressed the problem of elite domination is by including topics that are especially relevant to marginalized groups. At the Malaysia WUDC in 2015 for example, one motion focused on a policing doctrine employed primarily in poor neighborhoods: "This House believes that the African-American community should oppose 'broken windows policies.'"

At the North American Universities Debating Championship in 2014, another motion encouraged debate over the privileging of English itself: "This House believes that authors who belong to historically oppressed peoples should only write in their native languages." Ray's historical study of antebellum men's debating clubs suggests that allowing debaters from marginalized group to debate topics of concern to their own communities—in the language of those communities—might help educate and empower them to effect social change. In those antebellum debating clubs, as Ray notes, "the debating format—and the desire for individuals to appear to advantage in performance—also meant that discourses of challenge were rehearsed and implicitly legitimated as potential choices."[35] Considering the diversity of participants in Worlds-Style debate, we should do more to encourage such "discourses of challenge."

Although Worlds-Style debate encourages participants from positions of privilege to think deeply about issues they might not otherwise engage, those same issues can create difficulties for debaters of color.[36] Topics focusing on the challenges faced by marginalized groups sometimes lead to overgeneralizations about those groups, even stereotyping. For a student of color, such language can create visceral reactions, and engaging those stereotypes are psychologically difficult. During the Debaters of Colour Forum held at the Vienna European Universities Debating Championship in 2015, one student commented: "It's also hard for us as people of colour to call out because it's harder. It's easy for white people to 'be offended,' but for us there's an emotional impact. We don't get to confront these issues on the level of an intellectual chat. It can cause other conflicts for us."[37] The forum called for additional training of debaters and adjudicators on how to appropriately grapple with issues of race and for an expansion of such topics so that debaters would be more prepared to engage them in a respectful way.

If Worlds-Style debate is to become even more useful for citizenship training, we must find new ways to include those voices that historically have been absent from debate. The debate community is concerned with inclusivity, as the Debaters of Colour Forum shows. And, clearly, some progress has been made. The final round at the United States Universities Debating Championship in 2015, for example, had a majority of students of color and included three black debaters, two of whom were from Morehouse College, the historically black and all-male college that also hosted the United States Universities Debating Championship in 2016. Yet the other three colleges in the final round were Brown, Harvard, and Yale, and there was only one woman among the finalists. At least in the United States, Worlds-Style debate still appears to be dominated by elite universities, and too few women debaters appear in finals.

Worlds-Style debate is thus far from a perfect space for practicing citizenship. Yet despite its limitations, it creates a useful arena for students to practice and perform the habits and skills of citizenship, especially students from countries whose governments limit their democratic rights. As universities prioritize international exposure for their students, Worlds-Style debate also provides students with opportunities to engage people from other countries on global issues. This experience with cross-cultural communication will be increasingly important in the years to come, as will the knowledge and experience gained from debating issues that transcend national boundaries, such as world trade, climate change, or refugee crises. In addition, Worlds-Style debate has the potential to engage broader public audiences, helping bridge the gap between student debating skills and real-world public advocacy. In the recent centennial issue of the *Quarterly Journal of Speech*, Robert Asen called on scholars of rhetoric and deliberation to broaden their research and teaching to engage more "people and sites across the globe."[38] Worlds-Style debate, particularly as it is practiced internationally, provides one way to answer this call.

18

SUZHI JIAOYU, DEBATE, AND CIVIC EDUCATION IN CHINA

LORAND LASKAI, DAVID WEEKS, AND TIM LEWIS

This chapter explores the lessons we have drawn from running the largest English-language debate league in China. We attempt to sketch out the case for debate—and a conceptual framework for debate—in a nondemocratic setting. We do not argue that debate is a way to promote democratic values in an illiberal country like China. In fact, we do the opposite: we separate debate from its explicitly democratic undertones and show the adaptability of the practice in multiple contexts.

The National High School Debate League of China (NHSDLC) is the biggest English-language debate league in China, running more than eighty tournaments every year in nearly forty cities across mainland China. Starting with a few loosely organized tournaments in a few large coastal cities, we quickly discovered that a decentralized model of engagement—providing free debate training and gaining the support of local teachers and administrators—could greatly expand the reach of debate in China.

We ascribe debate's enormous popularity in China in large part to its deep resonance with the reformist Chinese discourse of *suzhi jiaoyu* (素质教育), which indirectly translates as "quality" or "character" education. *Suzhi jiaoyu* stands as a counterpoint to education based on standardized testing (应试教育) and has become a focal point for various attempts to overcome the deficiencies of traditional Chinese education. As this chapter illustrates, *suzhi jiaoyu* has a tangled genealogy linked to China's Confucian and Marxist past. The contemporary meaning and goals of *suzhi jiaoyu* are diverse and incongruous, and largely based on context rather than on a specific definition.

These ambiguities aside, *suzhi jiaoyu* in many regards mirrors the discourse in the West about "21st century skills" and the need to create a modern workforce—that is, a workforce that can compete and innovate in an interconnected, globalized marketplace. We also find a strong connection between *suzhi jiaoyu* and the skills and traits commonly associated with debate: creativity, critical thinking, logical argumentation, and the ability to express one's self with confidence.

In reflecting on the concept of *suzhi jiaoyu*, we sense additional connections to debates over civic education and engagement. Civic education, broadly understood, entails teaching students how to engage with the political and social structures that govern their lives. Because many political systems lack participatory democracy, civic education, especially in places like China, cannot simply mirror traditional Western conceptions of civic engagement. The Leninist state apparatus that rules China makes it difficult or impossible to engage in *any* form of civic participation without joining the party. Nevertheless, creating "quality people" who are socially and morally conscious of their connections to one another (even if they are not directly engaged in the political process) is important to the overall cohesion and civic health of a society—especially one like China, which is quickly developing and changing. We assert that just as debate is important in fostering civic values in the West, debate in China can play a role in creating the "quality" people that *suzhi jiaoyu* aspires to produce.

Overview of the Debate Scene in China

Debate has existed in China for hundreds of years, but only among elites and in a form unlike its Western counterpart. While in the West the development of a strong middle class and a free and vibrant public sphere encouraged the democratization of public discourse, debate in China remained limited to the elite, upper echelons of the governing mandarin until early in the twenty-first century. Today, debate is on the roster of extracurricular activities for most Chinese high school and college students, although the format, which features four people on each side of a debate question, severely limits the amount of clash. In addition, topics remain purposely vague and apolitical. Examples of Chinese debate topics include: "It is not acceptable to tell lies"; "It is best to never jump on the bandwagon"; and "It is more important to do rather than say."

Thus, debate in China tends toward waxing philosophically, even poetically, about questions not really conducive to the sort of concrete analysis and critical engagement typical of policy debate in the West.

The major advances in Chinese debate over the past five years have come from abroad. At the college level, a robust Worlds-Style debate (also called British Parliamentary debate) scene has percolated into the country and taken hold at more than 160 Chinese colleges. At the high school level, one type of American-style debate (美式辩论)—specifically, Public Forum debate—has spread at public schools across the country.

The popularity of these Western forms of English-language debate reflect the growing international orientation of the country. As more students go abroad to study, they build international connections through debate and help popularize the activity back home. Debating in English also creates something of a buffer against the typical constraints of the Chinese state education system. Given the language barriers, debating in English allows more freedom to engage with contemporary issues of social and political importance. This is not to say that English-language debate enables students to debate controversial or politically sensitive topics; boundaries still exist.[1] Nevertheless, debating in English allows more space for real debate.

The Current Landscape of Chinese Education

The Chinese political system is notable for its long, unbroken spell of dynastic rule, dating back to 2100 BCE and concluding with the fall of Qing dynasty in 1912. During dynastic rule, the educational system in China adhered to a central form: reliance on Confucian texts and strenuous examinations to determine merit. The Imperial Examination (科举), used to select candidates for the state bureaucracy, was notorious both for its difficulty and its importance as a means of social mobility. Scholars looking to enter the higher ranks of government would spend decades studying and mastering archaic subsets of knowledge and techniques, such as composing the tedious "eight-legged essay."[2] Many never passed the exam and returned home in shame.

As China's Qing dynasty foundered under the weight of internal contradiction and a failure to modernize in the face of Western influences, the Imperial Examination and the Confucian values it enshrined—the value of rote memorization over creativity, form over practicality, deference over individual thought—became targets of Chinese social reformers. Most elite scholars in

China knew little about practical matters, and they had little ability to grapple with and absorb Western ideas and techniques. Reformers rightfully blamed the system for hampering creativity and promoting stuffy deference to traditional sources, arguing that the status quo educational system failed to teach moral responsibility and suffocated innovation. In a famous short story, "Madman's Diary," Lu Xun weaved this critique into a fantasy world in which humans cannibalized their young. The story stood as an extended metaphor for the destructive effects that traditional Chinese culture and education were having on young people. As the Qing dynasty slid into decline, the Imperial Examination was abolished, but it was too late. The Qing dynasty fell and China descended into disorder and civil war.

When the Chinese Communist Party founded the People's Republic of China in 1949, it took a new approach to most aspects of Chinese culture. Confucius was condemned. Lu Xun was deified. Education was also approached differently: practical skills in engineering and agriculture were valued; a "critical consensus" against intense examination and rote memorization arose.[3] In practice, however, many teachers, left to their own devices, stuck to their old ways. A culture of testing persisted, especially as education became more accessible to the masses and competition for space at China's top-tier universities became increasingly fierce. Over the years, the Chinese education system solidified into a system in which, in the words of one scholar, "teaching is geared to the examinations; teachers focus on academically promising students and ignore others; rote learning dominates classroom teaching and students are weighed down by excessive homework and examination pressure."[4] The resulting system emphasized merit but arguably rewarded the wrong type of merit. Students were incentivized to conform and memorize, not express themselves or develop deep understanding of their subjects. In recent years, these shortcomings have led to much discussion of a "creativity gap" and an "innovation gap" in China.[5]

Although it would be an exaggeration to say that Chinese education has regressed back to its premodern past, some of the old ways persist. Chinese people, often with pride, draw comparisons between the Imperial Examination and China's notoriously difficult and competitive entrance exam for university students. Students' scores on the Gaokao (which translates as the National Higher Education Entrance Exam) decide not only which university they will attend but also their major and future earning potential. Moreover, the Gaokao typifies the worst of Chinese practices: students are required to memorize large amounts of esoteric facts on various subjects. At best, the Gaokao incentivizes rote memorization over developing creative and critical faculties. At worst, the test actively normalizes a culture of cheating. In one village, riots broke out on testing day when local police unexpectedly cracked down on cheating. Villagers saw the crackdown as breaking an implicit agreement between the state and the people.[6]

Yong Zhao, author of *Who's Afraid of the Big Bad Dragon?*, argues that the Chinese educational system cannot easily reform because it is a product of the country's long tradition of authoritarianism and enforced hierarchy.[7] He says that the system has no problem incentivizing creativity and excellence, but that it often encourages the wrong *type* of creativity. He cites examples of Chinese creativity in skirting regulation, fabricating research, and climbing the rungs of a broken system. "The authoritarian spirit of absolute obedience to authority seems to direct creativity to risky cheating in order to realize the wishes of the high authority, which may or may not be shared by the people."[8] Whether Zhao is right about the system's inability to reform in more positive ways, he makes a compelling point about how the Chinese system ultimately incentivizes the wrong type of competencies. In the following discussion, we will look into the growing discourse surrounding reform of the Chinese educational system and how debate might fit into that effort.

The Discourse of *Suzhi Jiaoyu*

In a 1970 issue of the *American Political Science Review*, Giovanni Sartori, a student of comparative politics, wrote about "conceptual stretching," which he defined as "the distortion that occurs when a concept, applied to new cases, does not fit the new cases." This process leads to "vague, amorphous conceptualization," which muddies the meaning of terms when they are applied across differing cultural contexts.[9] Many terms utilized in this chapter might be subject to "conceptual stretching," including *civic education*, *twenty-first-century skills*, and *global competency*. However, no term better illustrates Sartori's concern than *suzhi jiaoyu*.

Suzhi jiaoyu roughly translates as "character education," although the full breadth of the concept hardly translates precisely. Other possible translations include "competence education," "quality education," or "essential qualities-oriented education." The ambiguity behind the concept arises from the term *suzhi*, which by one count has been translated into thirty-two different English terms.[10] Harkening back to Confucian education and the norms surrounding the cultivation of moral character in ancient Chinese society, the concept of *suzhi* refers to a person's holistic moral and mental qualities—or lack thereof.[11]

To this day, it is a common refrain in Chinese society to blame an individual's moral failings or lack of manners on the low quality of their *suzhi*.

In ancient times, *suzhi* referred to intractable, inborn characteristics, in contrast to *suyang* (素养), which denotes characteristics derived from upbringing and environment. State modernization in the mid-twentieth century blurred the dichotomy between *suzhi* and *suyang*, turning *suzhi* into an amorphous, all-encompassing term that denoted an intrinsic quality, both mutable and immutable. The term also became central to the propaganda surrounding the Chinese Communist Party's modernization drive, as efforts to instill the habits and practices of modern citizenship were framed as a struggle to raise the people's *suzhi*.

The concept of *suzhi* in its modern context still conforms to the perspective of traditional Chinese philosophy on the relationship between governing institutions and people. In Chinese philosophy and rhetoric, institutions are of secondary importance, as ultimately people shape institutions, not vice versa. The seminal philosopher of China's modern era, Liang Qichao, famously wrote in the midst of the decline of the Qing dynasty that the struggle for creating a new nation should center on creating new people, not institutions. Another prominent Chinese scholar from the same time period, Yan Fu, likewise wrote that improving the quality of people had to be the basis for saving the nation; the vitality of institutions was but an external indicator of the nation's health.[12]

The 1980s, and the "opening up" of the Chinese economy (改革开放), brought the discourse of *suzhi* more prominently into discussions of China's educational system. Discontent grew over an educational system that pitted students against each other in competition for scarce resources. Critics also complained that it was failing to prepare Chinese students for the modern era. In the 1990s, *suzhi jiaoyu* gained still more steam as a counterpoint to an educational curriculum that was still overly standardized and centered on test taking. More than twenty years later, however, the implications of *suzhi jiaoyu* for Chinese educational policy remain unclear. In theory, *suzhi jiaoyu* promotes stress reduction for students, increased space for individual creativity, and a deemphasis on rote memorization—in short, a more liberal, character-building education. The specifics of how that sort of education is best implemented, however, remain clouded in ambiguity.

American education scholar Andrew Kipnis has reported on one visit he made to a Chinese class purportedly grounded in *suzhi jiaoyu*. Although the curriculum was supposedly designed to promote creativity, students were still forced to memorize Tang dynasty poetry. Even if the students did not enjoy the raw rote memorization of Tang poems now, the teacher argued, "they would appreciate them after they grew up," and "it would make the students more creative." Some schools in China also still emphasize ideological character education (政治思想素质), which promotes support of the party, love of one's country, and other forms of patriotic indoctrination.[13] Examples such as this may signify local resistance (as in the former case) or bureaucratic misalignment with government policy (in the latter). Nevertheless, they demonstrate the difficulty of implementing a coherent national educational policy in China today. With characteristic equivocation, Chinese education minister Zhou Ji pledged in a 2005 interview to "fully implement the Party's educational policies," which revolve around *suzhi jiaoyu*, while dismissing various concerns and criticisms that had been raised as merely theoretical debates.

As a popular Chinese saying goes, "suzhi jiaoyu is an empty frame, you can fit many things within it" (素质教育是一个旷, 什么多往里面放).[14] As is explained in the following section, that "empty frame" includes certain aspects of *suzhi jiaoyu* that comport well with similar reform efforts in the West—the discourse about "21st century skills."

Suzhi Jiaoyu, Twenty-First-Century Skills, and the Value of Debate

The key to understanding the meaning and purpose of *suzhi jiaoyu* is the nationalistic sentiment that motivates it. The point of educating "high-quality" people is to promote not personal fulfillment but the needs of the state. The ultimate goal of *suzhi jiaoyu* is "national strength," writes Belinda Dello-Iacovo, a Chinese education scholar.[15] The overwhelming priority of the People's Republic of China over the past thirty years has been modernization and enhancing the power of the state. Primarily, this means succeeding economically in an increasingly globalized market.

Since as far back as the 1990s, top Chinese ministers and government officials have said that fostering talent and creativity were critical to China's future success. In 1999, education minister Chen Zhili declared that China would rise or fall based on the country's ability to meet the demands of the twenty-first-century economy.[16] But China's problem of human capital is rooted in more than a failure to promote a modern workforce. A 2005 McKinsey Global Institute survey found that fewer than 10 percent of Chinese job candidates had the skills and talents they would need to work for foreign companies.[17] These talents and skills include more than technical competencies; they also include the ability to communicate and collaborate with a diversity of other workers.

In this regard, *suzhi jiaoyu* maps neatly onto the discourse, coming primarily from the West, about "21st century skills." Conceived in the 1980s as an attempt to draw attention to structural shifts in the economy and changes in the skill sets needed to compete in an increasingly globalized world, twenty-first-century skills represents a comprehensive plan for adapting education to a rapidly changing world. *A Nation at Risk*, a report published by the National Commission on Excellence in Education in the 1980s, summarized the chief exigency behind this movement to reform education: "[America's] once unchallenged preeminence in commerce, industry, science, and technological innovation is being overtaken by competitors throughout the world."[18] While China's discourse of *suzhi jiaoyu* does not reflect the same fear of decline, it rests on a similar assumption: that economic globalization dictates systemic educational reform. "History is not kind to idlers," concluded *A Nation at Risk*. Educational reformers in China are motivated by precisely the same sentiment.

The concept of "21st century skills" centers its platform for educational reform on the so-called Four Cs—critical thinking, communication, collaboration, and creativity. Together, the Four Cs presumably encompass all the competencies necessary to navigate a fluid, ever-changing environment while also helping students to anticipate and adapt to new challenges.

Debate, more than most cocurricular or extracurricular activities, cultivates all four Cs of the twenty-first-century skills. It promotes creativity and critical thinking as debaters research their topics and design their cases. It promotes communication through its emphasis on public speaking and argumentation, and it demands collaboration as debaters work together to prepare and present their cases. Debate develops the ability to understand issues from a variety of perspectives, and it turns students from passive collectors of knowledge to active participants in their learning. While celebrated for cultivating research skills, debate does much more than that. It also requires that participants apply what they have learned in new and creative ways.

In the Chinese educational system, debate has assumed the form of a grassroots movement to promote the development of these same sorts of skills. Debate introduces students to a completely new academic environment, where creativity and critical thought are rewarded. Unlike an exam-centric model, debate is fluid instead of static, hinging on extemporaneous thought and human interaction rather than solitary study. Chinese students participating in a debate tournament for the first time—especially those from deeply traditional schools—often find the activity disconcertingly unnatural at first. As they grow more comfortable, however, they often become passionately committed to debate, as the activity allows for a kind of self-expression that traditional Chinese education inhibits. Many Chinese students participate in debate simply because they enjoy it.

Thus, debate in China has become one way to modernize Chinese education short of comprehensive educational reform. It is one tool reformers use to counterbalance a sclerotic educational system that appears unable to adjust on its own accord. Relying on a critical combination of teacher and administration support and student enthusiasm, debate might be brought into a Chinese school by reformist elements within the administration, using extra credit or official invitation letters to attract students. Equally often, however, student interest, in the form of a club or informal community, pushes administrators and teachers to take a greater interest in debate activities. Since competitive success reflects well on teachers and administrators, there is usually strong interest in supporting debate once its full potential is known.

Critical in either case is a strong network of support to foster and nurture students' interest and passion for debate. This allows debate to take root in an environment still largely inhospitable to extracurricular activities. In test-based education systems like China, there's never enough time: even twenty years after administrators and officials began limiting the amount of time students spend in the classroom, the school day itself still consumes a huge portion of students' time. Chinese schools often hold classes from 7:30 a.m. until well past 6:00 p.m. And this does not include supposedly optional self-study sessions at night, which many students treat as mandatory. Many students also attend weekend study sessions, which, again, are not mandatory but may be seen as necessary to succeed in this fiercely competitive environment.

For all these reasons, the NHSDLC is not an ordinary debate club. We also engage in outreach, doing hundreds of free training and informational sessions at schools every year. In addition, we court local teachers and school officials, making the case for debate, and we maintain a robust online presence, fully integrating debate into our participants' social media. All of this is required to foster and maintain interest, cultivate talent, and ensure that student interest does not dwindle under the weight of the countless other responsibilities of a Chinese student.

Creating "Quality" People

During the annual dinner for the National Association for Urban Debate Leagues, former U.S. Education Secretary Arne Duncan, a past debater himself, said, "In a number of respects, competitive urban debate is almost uniquely suited to building what's been called the 'Four C's' of 21st century skills—critical thinking, communication, collaboration, and creativity. And to that list I might add a fifth 'C'—for civic awareness and engagement."[19] In China, that implicit nexus between work skills and citizenship is laid out in the concept of *suzhi jiaoyu*. More explicitly than the parallel discourse in the West, *suzhi jiaoyu* underscores the importance of educating students to be good or "quality" people.

After years of chaotic, fast-paced modernization, China faces a potential moral crisis as brutal competition and the drive to get ahead has produced an epidemic of apathy and selfishness. In 2011, when a two-year-old girl was run over on a busy street in Foshan, twelve pedestrians walked by without assisting the gravely injured child. By the time a street cleaner finally took her to a hospital, the little girl was dead. The incident prompted a lot of soul-searching in China,[20] although similar incidents of apathy and neglect occurred afterward with startling frequency.[21]

Many Chinese fear that their country is losing its moral compass and falling victim to rampant materialism. And unlike in Western countries, where democratic processes and civil society are natural mechanisms for exercising the moral and civic aptitude of people, there are few similar mechanisms of civic habituation in China. Moreover, the educational system does little to counteract the ill effects of civic apathy. Courses in politics are intended to raise students' political and moral consciousness, but many classes are taught in a stiff, rigid manner that have the effect of breeding still more deference to authority, political and social apathy, and disengagement from civic life.

Debate has the obvious effect of raising civic awareness and increasing students' knowledge of contemporary events. In China, student debaters regularly debate topics ranging from the morality of the death penalty, to how best to overcome poverty, to the benefits and drawbacks of China's modernization.[22] Topics like these bring students into touch with the factors and forces that bind them together. Debate also promotes what Hannah Arendt called "thoughtfulness"— that is, the process of understanding the ethical implications of one's actions.[23]

China's leaders have often feared that exposure to Western ideas might foster dissent against a regime that has, in the past, sought to limit those ideas. In our experience promoting debate in China, the primary impact of the activity has *not* been to foment antigovernment dissent. Living in a society where participating in public discourse is not the norm, students in China rarely articulate their opinions on political or social issues outside of a controlled, educational setting like debate. Debate, at least at the high school level, is thus more of an exercise in coming to terms with one's own identity than a political act. With the goal of developing more informed beliefs on important issues, students in China still view debate mostly as an educational tool, not a political act. Nevertheless, debate in China does important civic work, promoting common understandings and a shared sense of identity among Chinese students. By creating a space for collective engagement with important issues, debate in China helps bind students together as citizens of their country.

Conclusion

This chapter has looked to the thriving debate scene in China for lessons, and we find two lessons worth emphasizing. First, debate has become an important mechanism for counteracting the harmful effects of the traditional Chinese educational system and instilling in students the Chinese equivalent of "21st century skills." Second, debate can play a role in fostering a sense of citizenship even in nondemocratic countries. By creating a space for students to develop an understanding of their common identity as members of society, debate helps counteract apathy and promote a collective moral conscience.

While this chapter focuses on China and the discourse of *suzhi jiaoyu*, the lessons learned no doubt have relevance to other countries as well. The problems facing China—an overly standardized educational system and a weakly developed sense of collective citizenship—are not unique to the country. As Yong Zhao points out in *Who's Afraid of the Big Bad Dragon?*, even the United States has been heading in the direction of more standardized testing. As Americans grapple with the repercussions of these policies, we might look both at China and toward debate as a possible remedy to the problems associated with a testing regime. Similarly, we see debate as counteracting the growing polarization in American politics. Although debate certainly does not prevent people from disagreeing, it does help build common understandings and shared identity that might help us resolve disagreements more productively. Debate is all about disagreement, but it teaches students how to disagree with reason, civility, and an eye toward the common good.

Ultimately, the problems faced by both China and the United States are not unique. We believe debate provides a powerful educational tool not only for promoting twenty-first-century workforce skills but also for building more civic-minded societies.

NOTES

Introduction

1. Bernard K. Duffy and Richard W. Leeman, eds., *American Voices: An Encyclopedia of Contemporary Oratory* (Westport, Conn.: Greenwood Press, 2005), xi–xxv.
2. See Wynton C. Hall, "The Invention of 'Quantifiably Safe Rhetoric': Richard Wirthlin and Ronald Reagan's Instrumental Use of Public Opinion Research in Presidential Discourse," *Western Journal of Communication* 66 (2002): 319–46.
3. David T. Z. Mindich, *Tuned Out: Why Americans Under 40 Don't Follow the News* (New York: Oxford University Press, 2005), 6.
4. Barack Obama, "Remarks of President Barack Obama—State of the Union Address as Delivered," *The White House*, January 13, 2016, https://www.whitehouse.gov/the-press-office/2016/01/12/remarks-president-barack-obama-%E2%80%93-prepared-delivery-state-union-address.
5. David Mathews, *Politics for People: Finding a Responsible Public Voice*, 2nd ed. (Urbana: University of Illinois Press, 1999), 1–2.
6. See J. Michael Hogan, "Rhetorical Pedagogy and Democratic Citizenship: Reviving the Traditions of Civic Engagement and Public Deliberation," in *Rhetoric and Democracy: Essays in the Tradition of William Norwood Brigance*, ed. David M. Timmerman and Todd F. McDorman (East Lansing: Michigan State University Press, 2008), 75–97.
7. Duffy and Leeman, *American Voices*, xxiii.
8. Robert D. Putnam, *Bowling Alone: The Collapse and Revival of American Community* (New York: Simon and Schuster, 2000).
9. Ibid., 43.
10. Robert Putnam, "Bowling Together," *American Prospect*, February 11, 2002, 20–22.
11. See Associated Press, "Turnout in Presidential Elections Hit 40-Year High," *Politico*, December 15, 2008, http://www.politico.com/story/2008/12/turnout-in-presidential-elections-hit-40-year-high-016576.
12. Michael P. McDonald, "Voter Turnout in the 2012 Presidential Election," *Huffington Post*, February 11, 2013, http://www.huffingtonpost.com/michael-p-mcdonald/turnout-in-the-2012-presi_b_2663122.html.
13. Michael P. McDonald, "National General Election VEP Turnout Rates, 1789–Present," *United States Election Project*, last updated June 11, 2014, http://www.electproject.org/national-1789-present.
14. International Institute for Democracy and Electoral Assistance, "International Voter Turnout, 1991–2000," *Fair Vote*, http://archive.fairvote.org/turnout/intturnout.htm (accessed March 31, 2016).
15. Michael X. Delli Carpini, "Gen.com: Youth, Civic Engagement, and the New Information Environment," *Political Communication* 17 (2000): 341–43.
16. Kei Kawashima-Ginsberg et al., *Millennials Civic Health Index* (Washington, D.C.: National Conference on Citizenship, 2013), 4.

17. Ibid.

18. Abby Kiesa et al., *Millennials Talk Politics: A Study of College Student Political Engagement* (College Park, Md.: Center for Information and Research on Civic Learning and Engagement, 2007), 4, 24–27.

19. W. Lance Bennett, "The UnCivic Culture: Communication, Identity, and the Rise of Lifestyle Politics," *PS: Political Science and Politics* 31 (1998): 741–61.

20. Russell J. Dalton, *The Good Citizen: How a Younger Generation Is Reshaping American Politics* (Washington, D.C.: CQ Press, 2008), 17.

21. Commission on Youth Voting and Civic Knowledge, *All Together Now: Collaboration and Innovation for Youth Engagement* (Medford, Mass.: Center for Information and Research on Civic Learning and Engagement, 2013), 19–20. Available online at: http://civicyouth.org/wp-content/uploads/2013/09/CIRCLE-youthvoting-individualPages.pdf (accessed March 30, 2016).

22. W. Lance Bennett, "Introduction: Communication and Civic Engagement in Comparative Perspective," *Political Communication* 17 (2000): 308.

23. Theda Skocpol, *Diminished Democracy: From Membership to Management in American Civic Life* (Norman: University of Oklahoma Press, 2003), 174.

24. Barack Obama, "'Notre Dame Commencement Address' (17 May 2009)," *Voices of Democracy*, http://voicesofdemocracy.umd.edu/obama-notre-dame-commencement-address-speech-text/.

25. National Task Force on Civic Learning and Democratic Engagement (NTFCLDE), *A Crucible Moment: College Learning and Democracy's Future* (Washington, D.C.: Association of American Colleges and Universities, 2012).

26. Ibid., 69.

27. Ibid., 2.

28. Ibid.

29. For a collection of essays reflecting on the contributions of classical rhetoric—and especially Isocrates—to civic education, see Takis Poulakos and David Depew, eds., *Isocrates and Civic Education* (Austin: University of Texas Press, 2004).

30. Kevin Mattson, *Creating a Democratic Public: The Struggle for Urban Participatory Democracy During the Progressive Era* (University Park: Penn State University Press, 1998), 45.

31. Meira Levinson, *No Citizen Left Behind* (Cambridge, Mass.: Harvard University Press, 2012).

32. Hogan, "Rhetorical Pedagogy and Democratic Citizenship," 89–92.

33. John Dewey, *The Public and Its Problems* (1927; repr., Athens, Ohio: Swallow Press, 1991), 208.

34. Hogan, "Rhetorical Pedagogy and Democratic Citizenship," 90. For more on speech, debate, and discussion, see also University of Wisconsin Extension, *Wisconsin Extension Manual of Debate* (Madison: University of Wisconsin, 1913), https://babel.hathitrust.org/cgi/pt?id=hvd.32044096984554;view=1up;seq=7.

35. For more detailed discussions of speech, debate, and discussion programs in the Progressive Era, see William M. Keith, *Democracy as Discussion: Civic Education and the American Forum Movement* (Lanham, Md.: Lexington Books, 2007), and Pat J. Gehrke, *The Ethics and Politics of Speech: Communication and Rhetoric in the Twentieth Century* (Carbondale: Southern Illinois University Press, 2009).

36. William Hawley Davis, "Is Debating Primarily a Game?," *Quarterly Journal of Public Speaking* 2 (1916): 171.

37. Herman Cohen, *The History of the Speech Communication: The Emergence of a Discipline, 1914–1945* (Annandale, Va.: Speech Communication Association, 1994), xi.

38. William Norwood Brigance, *Speech: Its Techniques and Disciplines in a Free Society*, 2nd ed. (New York: Appleton-Century-Crofts, 1961), 1, 4–5.

39. Quintilian, *Institutio Oratoria: The Orator's Education*, ed. and trans. Donald A. Russell, Loeb Classical Library 124 (Cambridge, Mass.: Harvard University Press, 2002), 187.

40. Scott Varda, "Isocratic Citizenship: Toward a Pedagogy of Citizen Orators," in *The Functions of Argument and Social Context*, ed. Dennis Gouran (Washington, D.C.: National Communication Association, 2010), 523–28.

41. Obama, "State of the Union Address."

42. Jeffrey R. Young, "Colleges Call Debate Contests Out of Order," *Chronicle of Higher Education*, October 3, 2008, http://chronicle.com/article/Colleges-Call-Debate-Contests/6808.

43. See ibid.

44. See, for example, Peter Loge, "Black Participation in CEDA Debate: A Quantification and Analysis," *CEDA Yearbook* 12 (1991): 79–87; Jack Rogers, "Interrogating the Myth of Multiculturalism: Toward Significant Membership and Participation of African Americans in Forensics," *Forensic of Pi Kappa Delta* 80, no. 4 (1995): 21–30; Jack Rogers, "A Community of Unequals: An Analysis of Dominant and Subdominant Culturally Linked Perceptions of Participation and Success Within Intercollegiate Competitive Debate," *Contemporary Argumentation & Debate* 18 (1997): 1–22; Pamela Stepp, "Can We Make Intercollegiate Debate More Diverse?" *Argumentation and Advocacy* 33 (1997): 176–91; and Mike Allen et al., "Diversity in United States Forensics: A Report on Research Conducted for the American Forensic Association," *Argumentation and Advocacy* 40 (2004): 173–84.

45. For more on the Urban Debate League and other debate programs designed for students of color, see Kenneth Broda-Bahm, ed., "Voices from the Ideafest: The Open Society Institute and Urban Debate in the U.S.," *Contemporary Argumentation & Debate* 19 (1998): 58–96; Ede Warner and Jon Bruschke, "'Gone on Debating': Competitive Academic Debate as a Tool of Empowerment," *Contemporary Argumentation & Debate* 22 (2001): 1–21; Briana Mezuk, "Urban Debate and High School Educational Outcomes for African American Males: The Case of the Chicago Debate League," *Journal of Negro Education* 78 (2009): 290–304; M. Leslie Wade Zorwick, Melissa M. Wade, and Dietlinde P. Heilmayr, "Urban Debate and Prejudice Reduction: The Contact Hypothesis in Action," *Contemporary Argumentation & Debate* 30 (2009): 30–51; and Richard Pineda and Chris Salina, "Model Proposal: Increasing Latina/o Involvement in Policy Debate Through Summer Debate Workshops," *Contemporary Argumentation & Debate* 30 (2009): 114–29.

46. See, for example, Sheryl A. Friedley and Bruce B. Manchester, "An Analysis of Male/Female Participation at Select National Championships," *National Forensic Journal* 3 (1985): 1–12; Carrie Crenshaw, "Dominant Form and Marginalized Voices: Argumentation About Feminism(s)," *CEDA Yearbook* 14 (1993): 72–79; Jon Bruschke and Ann Johnson, "An Analysis of Differences in Success Rates of Male and Female Debaters," *Argumentation and Advocacy* 30 (1994): 162–73; Robert Greenstreet and Tracy Frederick, "The Sounds of Silence: The Gender-Based Experiences of Women in Intercollegiate Forensics," *Forensic of Pi Kappa Delta* 85, no. 3 (2000): 25–36; Pamela L. Stepp, "Sexual Harassment in Communication Extra-curricular Activities: Intercollegiate Debate and Individual Events," *Communication Education* 50 (2001): 34–50; and Chris Harper, "Gender and Competitive Equity: The 2007 and 2008 National Parliamentary Debate Association National Tournaments," *Forensic of Pi Kappa Delta* 94, no. 1 (2009): 1–12.

47. Amanda Wilkins and Jeffrey Hobbs, "A Feminist Critique of Intercollegiate Debate," *Contemporary Argumentation & Debate* 18 (1997): 57–67; Kenneth Broda-Bahm, ed., "Invitational Debate," special issue, *Contemporary Argumentation & Debate* 21 (2000): 74–115; Carol K. Winkler, C. Kevin Fortner, and Sara Baugh-Harris, "Overcoming Challenges to Women in At-Risk Communities Through Urban Debate Leagues," *Forum on Public Policy* 2013, no. 1 (2013): 1–22.

48. Michael W. Shelton and Cynthia K. Matthews, "Extending the Diversity Agenda in Forensics: Invisible Disabilities and Beyond," *Argumentation and Advocacy* 38 (2001): 121–31.

49. See, for example, Shanara Rose Reid-Brinkley, "The Harsh Realities of 'Acting Black': How African-American Policy Debaters Negotiate Representation Through Racial Performance and Style" (Ph.D. diss., University of Georgia, 2008); Shanara Rose Reid-Brinkley, "Ghetto Kids Gone Good: Race, Representation, and Authority in the Scripting of Inner-City Youths in the Urban Debate League," *Argumentation and Advocacy* 49 (2012): 77–99; Tiffany Y. Dillard-Knox, "Against the Grain: The Challenges of Black Discourse Within Intercollegiate Debate" (master's thesis, University of Louisville, 2014); and Luis M. Andrade and Jon Bruschke, "Cultural Pedagogy as Motivation and the Role of 'Institutional Agents' in Intercollegiate Debate," in *Disturbing Argument*, ed. Catherine H. Palczewski (New York: Routledge, 2014), 407–13.

50. Brittney Cooper, "'I Was Hurt': How White Elite Racism Invaded a College Debate Championship," *Salon*, May 13, 2014, http://www.salon.com/2014/05/13/%E2%80%9Ci_was_hurt%E2%80%9D_how_white_elite_racism_invaded_a_college_debate_championship/.

51. See Jessica Carew Kraft, "Hacking Traditional College Debate's White-Privilege Problem," *The Atlantic*, April 16, 2014, http://www.theatlantic.com/education/archive/2014/04/traditional-college-debate-white-privilege/360746/, and Krissah Thompson, "Redefining the Word," *Washington Post*, November 9, 2014, http://www.washingtonpost.com/sf/national/2014/11/09/teams-strategy-unsettles-some-in-the-collegiate-debate-community/.

52. E. J. Dionne Jr., *They Only Look Dead: Why Progressives Will Dominate the Next Political Era* (New York: Touchstone Books, 1997), 261.

53. "About Us," *Atlanta Urban Debate League*, http://www.atlantadebate.org/about-us/ (accessed March 20, 2016).

54. Karin Fischer, "To Appeal to American Universities, Chinese Students Embrace the Art of Argument," *Chronicle of Higher Education*, October 18, 2015, http://chronicle.com/article/To-Appeal-to-American/233796.

55. See, for example, Stanley Fish, *Save the World on Your Own Time* (New York: Oxford University Press, 2008), and William J. Bennett and David Wilezol, *Is College Worth It?* (Nashville: Thomas Nelson, 2013).

56. Quoted in Scott London, *Doing Democracy: How a Network of Grassroots Organizations Is Strengthening Community, Building Capacity, and Shaping a New Kind of Civic Education* (Washington, D.C.: Kettering Foundation, 2010), iv.

57. Stephen Macedo et al., *Democracy at Risk: How Political Choices Undermine Citizen Participation, and What We Can Do About It* (Washington, D.C.: Brookings Institution, 2005), 166.

Chapter 1

1. H., "A Trip from Charleston to Columbia," *Christian Recorder* (Philadelphia), July 9, 1885, 2; Katherine Smedley, *Martha Schofield and the Re-education of the South, 1839–1916* (Lewiston, N.Y.: Edwin Mellen Press, 1987), 118–19.

2. "The Black Republican Radicals: The Meeting on Saturday," *Daily Constitutionalist* (Augusta, Ga.), April 16, 1867, 2. See B. F. Witherspoon, "The Rev. T. [sic] W. Beaird," *Southwestern Christian Advocate* (New Orleans), January 24, 1895, 5, and Ronald E. Butchart, *Schooling the Freed People: Teaching, Learning, and the Struggle for Black Freedom, 1861–1876* (Chapel Hill: University of North Carolina Press, 2010), 21.

3. Clionian Debating Society (Charleston, S.C.), Proceedings, 1847–1851, Charleston Library Society, Charleston, S.C. (hereafter CDS-CLS); Clionian Debating Society (Charleston, S.C.), Proceedings, 1851–1858, David M. Rubenstein Rare Book and Manuscript Library, Duke University, Durham, N.C. (hereafter CDS-Duke). Other known groups were the Euterpean and the Utopian Debating Societies, both mentioned in the Clionian proceedings.

4. CDS-CLS, October 2, 1850. These notes usually give dates when debates were held; questions were chosen at earlier meetings.

5. CDS-CLS, December 26, 1849; CDS-Duke, January 1, 1852; CDS-CLS, June 20, 1849, September 18, 1848.

6. CDS-Duke, January 14, 1858; Edmund L. Drago, *Charleston's Avery Center: From Education and Civil Rights to Preserving the African American Experience*, rev. and ed. W. Marvin Dulaney (Charleston, S.C.: History Press, 2006), 38–44; Michael P. Johnson and James L. Roark, *Black Masters: A Free Family of Color in the Old South* (New York: Norton, 1984), 153–94.

7. Catherine R. Squires, "Rethinking the Black Public Sphere: An Alternative Vocabulary for Multiple Public Spheres," *Communication Theory* 12 (2002): 459, 460.

8. Isadore A. Hyames, Compiled Military Service Records, for Co. D, 8th New York State Militia; and Conrad D. Ludeke, Compiled Military Service Records, for Co. B, 82nd New York Infantry, Co. C, 90th New York Infantry, and Co. C, 1st New Orleans Infantry, all in Records of the Adjutant General's Office, 1780s–1917, Record Group 94, National Archives and Records Administration, Washington, D.C.

9. Eric Foner, *Freedom's Lawmakers: A Directory of Black Officeholders During Reconstruction*, rev. ed. (Baton Rouge: Louisiana State University Press, 1996), 40, 226.

10. School report of Simeon W. Beaird, January 1, 1866, M799, reel 20, Records of the Superintendent of Education for the State of Georgia, Bureau of Refugees, Freedmen, and Abandoned Lands, 1865–1870, Record Group 105, National Archives and Records Administration; Heather Andrea Williams, *Self-Taught: African American Education in Slavery and Freedom* (Chapel Hill: University of North Carolina Press, 2005), 128; H. M. Turner, "Georgia Correspondence," *Christian Recorder* (Philadelphia), October 5, 1867, 1; "Black Republican Radicals"; *Journal of the Proceedings of the Constitutional Convention of the People of Georgia* (Augusta, Ga.: E. H. Pughe, 1868); "Washington," *New York Tribune*, March 17, 1870, 1; Witherspoon, "Rev. T. W. Beaird." Readers should beware: secondary sources often confuse Simeon W. Beaird with Thomas P. Beard (1837–1918), an African American newspaper editor and politician in postwar Augusta. I am grateful to Elena Rodina for her assistance in disentangling the histories of the two men.

11. Squires, "Rethinking the Black Public Sphere," 460.

12. "Black Republican Radicals."

13. Mary Kelley, "'A More Glorious Revolution': Women's Antebellum Reading Circles and the Pursuit of Public Influence," *New England Quarterly* 76 (2003): 163–96; Angela G. Ray, "The Permeable Public: Rituals of Citizenship in Antebellum Men's Debating Clubs," *Argumentation and Advocacy* 41 (2004): 1–16.

14. Emma Jones Lapsansky, "'Discipline to the Mind': Philadelphia's Banneker Institute, 1854–1872," in *A Question of Manhood: A Reader in U.S. Black Men's History and Masculinity*, ed. Darlene Clark Hine and Earnestine Jenkins, vol. 1 (Bloomington: Indiana University Press, 1999), 399–414; Elizabeth McHenry, *Forgotten Readers: Recovering the Lost History of African American Literary Societies* (Durham, N.C.: Duke University Press, 2002); Shirley Wilson Logan, *Liberating Language: Sites of Rhetorical Education in Nineteenth-Century Black America* (Carbondale: Southern Illinois University Press, 2008).

15. CDS-CLS, November 9, 1847.

16. Drago, *Charleston's Avery Center*; Bernard E. Powers Jr., *Black Charlestonians: A Social History, 1822–1885* (Fayetteville: University of Arkansas Press, 1994), esp. 36–72; Amrita Chakrabarti Myers, *Forging Freedom: Black Women and the Pursuit of Liberty in Antebellum Charleston* (Chapel Hill: University of North Carolina Press, 2011).

17. Larry Koger, *Black Slaveowners: Free Black Slave Masters in South Carolina, 1790–1860* (Jefferson, N.C.: McFarland, 1985); Loren Schweninger, *Black Property Owners in the South, 1790–1915* (Urbana: University of Illinois Press, 1990). See Myers, *Forging Freedom*, 122–28.

18. CDS-CLS, October 14, 1850; CDS-Duke, October 6, 1851; CDS-CLS, May 17, 1848.

19. In 1855, James N. McElligott would recommend that debating societies debate the details of constitutions and bylaws, for greater precision of thought and greater understanding of legal procedure; McElligott, *The American Debater: Being a Plain Exposition of the Principles and Practice of Public Debate* (New York: Ivison and Phinney, 1855), 129.

20. Most library holdings were acquired in 1849–51.

21. CDS-CLS, October 8, December 26, 1849, April 17, May 1, 1850.

22. CDS-CLS, August 14, December 2, 1850.

23. Ray, "Permeable Public," 5n5.

24. CDS-CLS, January 6, 1851.

25. CDS-CLS, December 1, 1847. The records state simply, "The debate opened by the regular debatants, and was sustained principally on the negative. It was then decided in the negative. The question for the next evening's debate was chosen."

26. Drago, *Charleston's Avery Center*, 36; Powers, *Black Charlestonians*, 52. Drago lists nine questions debated by the Clionian Debating Society alongside similar questions debated by the Chrestomathic Literary Society at the college. Yet in only one case (question 6) did the collegians debate the question prior to the Clionians' debate. Compare CDS-CLS and Books 1, 2, and 3 (#173/4, 5, 6), Chrestomathic Literary Society Minute Books, College of Charleston Archives, Charleston, S.C. Records of the other College of Charleston debating society of the time, the Cliosophic Society, are not extant.

27. Theodore Dwight, *President Dwight's Decisions of Questions Discussed by the Senior Class in Yale College, in 1813 and 1814, from Stenographic Notes, by Theodore Dwight, Jun.* (New York: J. Leavitt, 1833), 7, 341. I am grateful to Eric Fuchs for calling my attention to this book.

28. Charles Morley, *A Guide to Forming and Conducting Lyceums, Debating Societies, &c, with Outlines of Discussions and Essays, and an Appendix, Containing an Epitome of Rhetoric, Logic, &c.* (New York: A. E. Wright, 1841), 26, 49.

29. Frederic Rowton, *The Debater: A New Theory of the Art of Speaking; Being a Series of Complete Debates, Outlines of Debates, and Questions for Discussion* (London: Longman, Brown, Green, and Longmans, 1846); McElligott, *American Debater*.

30. CDS-CLS, December 26, 1848, June 23, 1851; CDS-Duke, March 28, 1854.

31. Angela G. Ray, "How Cosmopolitan Was the Lyceum, Anyway?" in *The Cosmopolitan Lyceum: Lecture Culture and the Globe in Nineteenth-Century America*, ed. Tom F. Wright (Amherst: University of Massachusetts Press, 2013), 30–32.

32. Ronald J. Zboray and Mary Saracino Zboray, "Women Thinking: The International Popular Lecture and Its Audience in Antebellum New England," in Wright, *Cosmopolitan Lyceum*, 46.

33. One society secretary noted, positively, "the usual share of interest that historical questions generally afford"; CDS-Duke, June 14, 1852.

34. CDS-CLS, July 31, October 14, 1850.

35. On Regulus, see CDS-CLS, November 4, 1850. On Washington and Alexander, see CDS-CLS, February 23, 1848. On Napoleon, see CDS-CLS, March 1, April 5, June 7, 1848, March 21, 1849, March 31, 1851; CDS-Duke, October 25, 1852; Angela G. Ray, "Learning Leadership: Lincoln at the Lyceum, 1838," *Rhetoric & Public Affairs* 13 (2010): 362.

36. CDS-CLS, November 5, 1849; CDS-Duke, December 8, 29, 1851.

37. CDS-Duke, June 2, 1856, February 2, 1857.

38. Ray, "Permeable Public," 12; Richard L. Weaver II, "Forum for Ideas: The Lyceum Movement in Michigan, 1818–1860" (Ph.D. diss., Indiana University, 1969), 164; see entries for December 19, 1849, in Book 1 (#173/4), February 21, 1855, in Book 2 (#173/5), October 8, 1856, February 11, April 22, June 3, 1857, in Book 3 (#173/6), Chrestomathic Literary Society Minute Books, College of Charleston Archives.

39. CDS-CLS, November 23, 1847, September 18, 1848; CDS-Duke, December 13, 1852.

40. Drago, *Charleston's Avery Center*, 40.
41. CDS-CLS, July 5, 1849; CDS-Duke, June 8, 22, 1853; Ray, "Permeable Public," 12; Ray, "Learning Leadership," 383n48.
42. Drago, *Charleston's Avery Center*, 38.
43. CDS-Duke, April 26, 1852; CDS-CLS, July 8, 1850; CDS-Duke, December 16, 1852. See Ray, "Permeable Public," 11.
44. CDS-Duke, December 29, 1851.
45. CDS-Duke, November 23, 1853. See CDS-CLS, March 14, 1849, May 22, 1850.
46. CDS-CLS, May 17, 1848.
47. "Young Men's Pacific Congress," *Daily Evening Bulletin (San Francisco)*, December 18, 1856, 3.
48. Margaret Malamud, "Black Minerva: Antiquity in Antebellum African American History," in *African Athena: New Agendas*, ed. Daniel Orrells, Gurminder K. Bhambra, and Tessa Roynon (Oxford: Oxford University Press, 2011), 72; CDS-CLS, January 7, 1850.
49. W. E. B. Du Bois, *The Souls of Black Folk* (1903; repr., New York: Bantam, 1989), 76.
50. Darlene Clark Hine and Earnestine Jenkins, "Black Men's History: Toward a Gendered Perspective," in Hine and Jenkins, *Question of Manhood*, 1:2.

Chapter 2

1. This chapter reflects the preliminary observations of what is an ongoing effort. While I am the sole researcher responsible for the development of this project, I have received invaluable support from my research assistants Natalie Barnett and Izik Dery. They will continue to play an important role as we work to build a robust dataset that can be made accessible for future collaboration with other scholars. I would also like to especially thank David Zarefsky, Angela Ray, Brian Lain, and Wayne Kraemer for their constructive feedback and suggestions during the early formative stages of this process.
2. Charles Sears Baldwin, "Intercollegiate Debate," *Educational Review* 42 (December 1911): 481.
3. Egbert Ray Nichols, *Intercollegiate Debates*, vol. 4 (New York: Hinds, Noble and Eldredge, 1914). The third volume of this series, though harder to locate, also contains similar material.
4. David Potter, *Debating in the Colonial Chartered Colleges: An Historical Survey, 1642 to 1900* (New York: Teachers College, Columbia University Bureau of Publications, 1944).
5. See, for example, Michael D. Bartanen and Robert S. Littlefield, *Forensics in America: A History* (Lanham, Md.: Rowman and Littlefield, 2014), 28–33.
6. Potter, *Debating in the Colonial Chartered Colleges*, 94.
7. Ibid., 96–98.
8. Ibid., 119.
9. The earliest of these intercollegiate debate exchanges can be traced back to a series of "friendly contests" that were held between various literary societies from Northwestern University and the University of Chicago. These began in 1872 and continued until at least 1877. This particular series accounts for roughly half of the thirteen debates we have documented prior to 1892.
10. Carl Vrooman, "College Debating," *The Arena*, June 1984, 682.
11. Ralph Curtis Ringwalt, "Intercollegiate Debating," *The Forum*, January 1897, 633.
12. Vrooman, "College Debating," 680.
13. There is some fragmentary evidence that certain oratorical associations included activities that they labeled as "debates" in their competitions. However, these appear to have been much more limited forms of the activity and were rare occurrences. Furthermore, the

bifurcation of debate from oratorical activities at the intercollegiate level was widespread and especially pronounced in virtually all of the student publications we examined.

14. "Orators, Attention!," *Ariel*, December 9, 1899, 141.

15. Arthur E. Holt, "Debating in Yale," *Colorado Collegian*, March 16, 1899, 7.

16. It is important to note that the issue of coaching was far from settled during this period. Even in instances in which faculty became more involved in the administration of debate activities on campus, this did not necessarily mean that they took an active role in coaching the team. In fact, there appears to be a great deal of disagreement among educators and students as to the appropriateness of coaching. While some saw it as necessary to help improve the quality of the debates, others saw it as a corrupting influence that risked creating debaters who simply "parroted" what they had been told.

17. Cecil Frederick Bacon, "Intercollegiate Debating," *The Forum*, October 1898, 225.

18. Ibid.

19. "Editorial," *Vassar Miscellany*, May 1903, 368.

20. O. W. Firkins, "Wisconsin-Minnesota Debate," *Ariel*, May 8, 1897, 6.

21. Marion Mills Miller, "Debate in American Colleges," *The Bachelor of Arts*, January 1896, 213.

22. To be clear, we did not find examples of anyone invoking Aristotle or that phrasing. The comparison to Aristotle is mine alone.

23. Baldwin, "Intercollegiate Debate," 481.

24. George P. Baker, "Oratory and Debating: Intercollegiate Debating," in *Proceedings of the 14th Annual Convention of the Association of Colleges and Preparatory Schools of the Middle States and Maryland 1900* (Albany: University of the State of New York Press, 1901), 104.

25. Our survey suggests that Baker was not alone in this regard. A number of other educators associated with debate had similar concerns about the future of the activity.

26. Henry D. Sheldon, *Student Life and Customs* (New York: D. Appleton, 1901), 209.

Chapter 3

1. See, for example, L. Leroy Cowperthwaite and A. Craig Baird, "Intercollegiate Debating," in *History of Speech Education in America*, ed. Karl Wallace (New York: Appleton-Century-Crofts, 1954), 259–76; William M. Keith, *Democracy as Discussion: Civic Education and the American Forum Movement* (Lanham, Md.: Lexington Books, 2007); Jarrod Atchison and Edward Panetta, "Intercollegiate Debate and Speech Communication: Historical Developments and Issues for the Future," in *The Sage Handbook of Rhetorical Studies*, ed. Andrea A. Lunsford, Kirt H. Wilson, and Rosa A. Eberly (Thousand Oaks, Calif.: Sage Publications, 2009), 317–33; and Michael D. Bartanen and Robert S. Littlefield, *Forensics in America: A History* (Lanham, Md.: Rowman and Littlefield, 2014), 19–21. The National Communication Association's centennial anniversary in 2014 also prompted reflection on the ongoing importance of this relationship, as communication departments continue to house debate programs and communication scholars lend their expertise to formalized electoral debates and more informal debating practices in the public sphere. See Kathleen Hall Jamieson, "The Discipline's Debate Contributions: Then, Now, and Next," *Quarterly Journal of Speech* 101 (2015): 85–97, and Darrin Hicks and Ronald Walter Greene, "Managed Convictions: Debate and the Limits of Electoral Politics," *Quarterly Journal of Speech* 101 (2015): 99–112.

2. As Keith details, debates about debating authored by faculty in speech dominated the first ten years of the *Quarterly Journal of Public Speaking* (now, the *Quarterly Journal of Speech*), in *Democracy as Discussion*, 67.

3. Frank Hardy Lane, "Faculty Help in Intercollegiate Contests," *Quarterly Journal of Public Speaking* 1 (1915): 9–16, especially 14.

4. On the importance of archival research into historical gendered relationships, see Susan Zaeske and Sarah Jedd, "From Recovering Women's Words to Documenting Gender Constructs: Archival Research in the Twenty-First Century," in *The Handbook of Rhetoric and Public Address*, ed. Shawn J. Parry-Giles and J. Michael Hogan (Oxford: Wiley-Blackwell, 2010), 184–202.

5. Bartanen and Littlefield, *Forensics in America*, 271.

6. Although women certainly took part in debating exercises earlier, the honor of the first college women's debating society at a coeducational institution in the United States is usually attributed to the Oberlin Collegiate Institute (now Oberlin College). Oberlin's Young Ladies' Association, later known as the Ladies' Literary Society, was founded in 1835.

7. Donald Orrin Olson, "Debating at the University of Nebraska" (master's thesis, University of Wisconsin, 1947), 71–74.

8. Egbert Ray Nichols, "A Historical Sketch of Intercollegiate Debating: III," *Quarterly Journal of Speech* 23 (1937): 259.

9. Mildred Freberg Berry, "A Survey of Intercollegiate Debate in the Mid-West Debate Conference," *Quarterly Journal of Speech* 14 (1928): 90.

10. The total number of women enrolled in U.S. colleges increased over this period, though their percentage of the total student body varied. This surge in enrollment numbers included students of more diverse racial, ethnic, religious, and economic backgrounds. See Barbara Miller Solomon, *In the Company of Educated Women: A History of Women and Higher Education in America* (New Haven: Yale University Press, 1985), 62–63.

11. For details about enrollment during this period, see Carol Sonenklar, *We Are a Strong, Articulate Voice: A History of Women at Penn State* (University Park: Penn State University Press, 2006), 56.

12. "Years of Coaching Included in Career," *Centre Daily Times*, January 19, 1972, 5.

13. "A Summary Report Showing the Growth of Women's Debate at the Pennsylvania State College, 1931 to 1937," 1937, document, Clayton H. Schug Papers, Group #282, Box 1, Folder: Women's Debate Annual Report, 1931–1947, Penn State University Archives, University Park, Pa. (hereafter cited as Schug Papers).

14. "Varsity Debaters (Did They Ever Look Like This, Boys?)," *Penn State Alumni Magazine*, April 1945, 3; "Coed Finds a Way for Talking All She Wants," *Centre Daily Times*, December 19, 1952, 11.

15. Marjorie Witsel Gemmill to Clayton H. Schug, November 10, 1971, in scrapbook, Schug Papers, Group #282, Box 3.

16. Ruth Zang Potts to Clayton H. Schug, November 5, 1971, in scrapbook, Schug Papers.

17. Florence Watkins Patrick to Clayton H. Schug, November 8, 1971; Rosalind Schnitzer Miller to Clayton H. Schug, November 5, 1971; and Elsie Douhett Withey to Clayton H. Schug, October 25, 1971, in scrapbook, Schug Papers.

18. Lois Notovitz Goldberg to Clayton H. Schug, undated, in scrapbook, Schug Papers.

19. Helen Dickerson Wise to Clayton H. Schug, December 1971, in scrapbook, Schug Papers.

20. Harriet Morgan Knauff to Clayton H. Schug, undated, in scrapbook, Schug Papers.

21. "Varsity Debaters," 4.

22. Sara Bailey Wagner to Clayton H. Schug, November 3, 1971, in scrapbook, Schug Papers.

23. Miller to Schug.

24. Patrick to Schug.

25. G. G. Rosen Michelson to Clayton H. Schug, December 5, 1971, in scrapbook, Schug Papers.

26. Miller to Schug.

27. Withey to Schug.

28. Michelson to Schug.

29. Joan Huber to William W. Hamilton, October 23, 1971, in scrapbook, Schug Papers.

30. Huber to Schug.

31. Ina Rosen Friedman to Clayton H. Schug, November 9, 1971, in scrapbook, Schug Papers.

32. Jean Hootman Eisenhower to Clayton H. Schug, November 10, 1971, in scrapbook, Schug Papers.

33. Thorrel B. Fest, "A Survey of College Forensics," *Quarterly Journal of Speech* 34 (1948): 168–73; Emogene Emery, "Rehabilitating Women's Debate," *Southern Speech Journal* 17 (1952): 186–91.

34. Emery, "Rehabilitating Women's Debate," 187.

35. Mimi Barash Coppersmith, interview with the author, State College, Pa., August 13, 2013.

36. Amy Gutmann, "Civic Education and Social Diversity," *Ethics* 105 (1995): 557–79. As Gutmann argues, "teaching toleration, mutual respect, and deliberation does not homogenize children or deny the value of genuine differences that are associated with diverse ways of individual or communal life. Quite the contrary, teaching these civic virtues supports the widest range of social diversity that is consistent with the ongoing pursuit of liberal democratic justice. The same civic education also supports individuality and autonomy, as best they can be supported by any public educational authority" (579).

37. Margaret Nash and Lisa Romero, "'Citizenship for the College Girl': Challenges and Opportunities in Higher Education for Women in the United States in the 1930s," *Teachers College Record* 114, no. 2 (2012): 1–35. Madeline Arnot's review identifies the critique of citizenship as a male-dominated narrative and historical studies of women's quest for citizenship through education as two prominent feminist perspectives in the literature. See her "'Gendered Citizenry': New Feminist Perspectives on Education and Citizenship," *British Educational Research Journal* 23 (1997): 275–95.

38. Sasha Roseneil, *Beyond Citizenship? Feminism and the Transformation of Belonging* (New York: Palgrave Macmillan, 2013), 1.

39. Social justice allies may be defined as "members of dominant social groups (e.g., men, Whites, heterosexuals) who are working to end the system of oppression that gives them greater privilege and power based on their social-group membership." See Ellen M. Broido, "The Development of Social Justice Allies During College: A Phenomenological Investigation," *Journal of College Student Development* 41 (2000): 3.

40. For an overview of the literature on the gender, racial, and ethnic diversity in contemporary debate, see Rae Lynn Schwartz-Dupre, "Women in Debate: From Virtual to Material," *Contemporary Argumentation & Debate* 27 (2006): 106–20. Catherine H. Palczewski, "Beyond Peitho: The Women's Debate Institute as Civic Education," in this volume. Emma Pierson's analysis demonstrates that the problem of sexism is not limited to one geographical location or one type of debate in contemporary competitive communities in "Men Outspeak Women: Analysing the Gender Gap in Competitive Debate," *Monash Debating Review* 11 (2013): 8–15.

41. See Shaun R. Harper and Stephen John Quaye, "Making Engagement Equitable for Students in U.S. Higher Education," in *Student Engagement in Higher Education: Theoretical Perspectives and Practice Approaches for Diverse Populations*, ed. Stephen John Quaye and Shaun R. Harper (New York: Routledge, 2015), 1–14. For discussions of debate as a tool of empowerment for women students, Urban Debate Leagues, and HBCUs, see Palczewski, "Beyond Peitho"; Ede Warner Jr. and Jon Bruschke, "'Gone on Debating': Competitive Academic Debate as a Tool of Empowerment," *Contemporary Argumentation & Debate* 22 (2001): 1–21; Melissa Maxcy Wade, "The Case for Urban Debate Leagues," *Contemporary Argumentation & Debate* 19 (1998): 60–65; and Timothy M. O'Donnell, "'The Great Debaters':

A Challenge to Higher Education," *Inside Higher Education*, January 7, 2008, https://www.insidehighered.com/views/2008/01/07/odonnell.

Chapter 4

1. Thomas Merton, *No Man Is an Island* (San Diego, Calif.: Harcourt, 1955), 127.
2. Michael D. Bartanen and Robert S. Littlefield, *Forensics in America: A History* (Lanham, Md.: Rowman and Littlefield, 2014).
3. Ibid., 44.
4. Chaïm Perelman and Lucie Olbrechts-Tyteca, *The New Rhetoric: A Treatise on Argumentation*, trans. John Wilkinson and Purcell Weaver (Notre Dame: University of Notre Dame Press, 1969), 31–35.
5. Shirley Mullen, "The Links Among Civic Engagement and Cultural Values," in *Civic Provocations*, ed. Donald W. Harward (Washington, D.C.: Bringing Theory to Practice, 2012), xi.
6. Carol Geary Schneider, foreword to Eric L. Dey, Cassie L. Barnhardt, Mary Antonaros, Molly C. Ott, and Matthew H. Holsapple, *Civic Responsibility: What Is the Campus Climate for Learning?* (Washington, D.C.: Association of American Colleges and Universities, 2009), ix.
7. Carol Geary Schneider, "To Democracy's Detriment: What Is the Current Evidence, and What If We Fail to Act Now?" in Harward, *Civic Provocations*, 9.
8. Corey Keyes, "The Eudeamonic and the Civic," in Harward, *Civic Provocations*, 21.
9. Dey et al., *Civic Responsibility*, 1.
10. Bartanen and Littlefield, *Forensics in America*, 62–63.
11. William Hawley Davis, "Is Debate Primarily a Game?," *Quarterly Journal of Public Speaking* 2 (1916): 171.
12. William M. Keith, *Democracy as Discussion: Civic Education and the American Forum Movement* (Lanham, Md.: Lexington Books, 2007), 66.
13. Ibid., 69.
14. A. Craig Baird, "Shall American Universities Adopt the British System of Debating?," *Quarterly Journal of Speech Education* 9 (1923): 220–21.
15. R. O. T. Hollister, "Faculty Judging," *Quarterly Journal of Public Speaking* 3 (1917): 235.
16. Bartanen and Littlefield, *Forensics in America*, 103.
17. Michael D. Bartanen and Robert S. Littlefield, "Competitive Speech and Debate: How Play Influenced American Educational Practice," *American Journal of Play* 7 (2015): 160.
18. Perlman and Olbrechts-Tyteca, *The New Rhetoric*, 31–35.
19. C. Thomas Preston Jr., "The Interconnectedness Between Intercollegiate Policy Debate and the Urban Debate Leagues: From a Distance, Five Years and Change Later," *Contemporary Argumentation & Debate* 27 (2006): 157–72.

Chapter 5

1. For a discussion of the rise of academic debate, see William M. Keith, *Democracy as Discussion: Civic Education and the American Forum Movement* (Lanham, Md.: Lexington Books, 2007).
2. Michael D. Bartanen and Robert S. Littlefield, *Forensics in America: A History* (Lanham, Md.: Rowman and Littlefield, 2014), 8, 40.
3. E. C. Robbins, *The High School Debate Book*, 2nd ed. (Chicago: A. C. McClurg, 1912), 1, 4.
4. See, for example, Austin J. Freeley, *Argumentation and Debate: Rational Decision Making*, 4th ed. (Belmont, Calif.: Wadsworth Publishing, 1976), 2, 3, and Douglas Ehninger and

Wayne Brockriede, *Decision by Debate* (1949; repr., New York: International Debate Education Association, 2008), 25. Many other examples could be cited.

5. Mitchell Thomashow, "The Virtues of Controversy," *Bulletin of Science, Technology & Society* 9 (1989): 66.

6. Thomas Christiano, "The Significance of Public Deliberation," in *Deliberative Democracy: Essays on Reason and Politics*, ed. James Bohman and William Rehg (Cambridge, Mass.: MIT Press, 1997), 248.

7. Gordon S. Wood, "Mr. Madison's Weird War," *New York Review of Books*, June 21, 2012, 65.

8. Samuel Kernell, "Introduction: James Madison and Political Science," in *James Madison: The Theory and Practice of Republican Government*, ed. Samuel Kernell (Stanford: Stanford University Press, 2003), 3.

9. Richard K. Matthews, *If Men Were Angels: James Madison and the Heartless Empire of Reason* (Lawrence: University Press of Kansas, 1995), 1, 3.

10. James Madison, *Writings* (New York: Library of America, 1999), 167. In all cases where italics are used, this reflects Madison's usage. Also note that Madison's spelling does not always match modern norms, but it was correct at the time.

11. Colleen A. Sheehan, *James Madison and the Spirit of Republican Self-Government* (New York: Cambridge University Press, 2009), 10.

12. *Federalist* 10 in *Writings*, 161, 163.

13. *Federalist* 62 in *Writings*, 343; emphasis original.

14. *Federalist* 48 in *Writings*, 285.

15. *Federalist* 10 in *Writings*, 163.

16. *Federalist* 10 in *Writings*, 162.

17. *Federalist* 37 in *Writings*, 194.

18. *Federalist* 62 in *Writings*, 341.

19. Sheehan, *James Madison*, 5.

20. Amy Gutmann and Dennis Thompson, *Why Deliberative Democracy?* (Princeton: Princeton University Press, 2004), 3.

21. John Rawls, "The Idea of Public Reason," in Bohman and Rehg, *Deliberative Democracy*, 93.

22. Bruce Ackerman and James S. Fishkin, *Deliberation Day* (New Haven: Yale University Press, 2004).

23. Matthews, *If Men Were Angels*, 22.

24. Daniel Kahneman, *Thinking, Fast and Slow* (New York: Farrar, Straus and Giroux, 2011), 13.

25. Ibid., 85, 103.

26. Ibid., 417.

27. Jonathan Haidt, *The Righteous Mind: Why Good People Are Divided by Politics and Religion* (New York: Pantheon, 2012), 40, 46, 47.

28. "Public Knowledge: Senate Legislative Process a Mystery to Many," *Pew Research Center*, January 28, 2010, http://pewresearch.org/pubs/1478/political-iq-quiz-knowledge-filibuster-debt-colbert-steele; "Well Known: Clinton and Gadhafi; Little Known: Who Controls Congress," *Pew Research Center*, March 31, 2011, http://www.people-press.org/2011/03/31/well-known-clinton-and-gadhafi-little-known-who-controls-congress/.

29. Gabriel S. Lenz, *Follow the Leader? How Voters Respond to Politicians' Policies and Performance* (Chicago: University of Chicago Press, 2012), 10, 15, 226.

30. *Federalist* 49 in *Writings*, 287, 288, 290; emphasis original.

31. "Consolidation," *National Gazette*, December 5, 1791, in *Writings*, 500.

32. Robert C. Grady, *Restoring Real Representation* (Urbana: University of Illinois Press, 1993), 21.

33. *Federalist* 51 in *Writings*, 295.

34. *Federalist* 41 in *Writings*, 230.

35. Madison's belief that better ideas would emerge in free and open debate can be seen as quite similar to John Stuart Mill's support of the free marketplace of ideas in *On Liberty*. See John Stuart Mill, *Utilitarianism, Liberty, and Representative Government* (New York: E. P. Dutton, 1910).

36. See Stephen Toulmin's enormously influential book, *The Uses of Argument* (New York: Cambridge University Press, 1958). A number of the books on debate pedagogy cited earlier reflect this approach. Other contemporary approaches to argument, including the informal logic tradition that was developed at the University of Windsor and pragma-dialectics developed by Frans van Eemeren of the University of Amsterdam and his many colleagues and students, are other variants of modern pragmatic argumentation theory that could be used to support a Madisonian view of practical reason.

37. Kahneman, *Thinking*, 361.

38. See *Federalist* 53 and 56 in *Writings*. For example, in *Federalist* 53, Madison asked, "How can foreign trade be properly regulated by uniform laws, without some acquaintance with the commerce, the ports, the usages and the regulations of the different states? How can the trade between the different states be duly regulated without some knowledge of their relative situations in these and other points? How can taxes be judiciously imposed and effectually collected if they be not accommodated to the different laws and local circumstances relating to these objects in the different states?" (307). After citing additional examples indicating the need for expert knowledge, he added: "These are the principal objects of federal legislation, and suggest most forceably, the extensive information which the representatives ought to acquire" (307).

39. "Public Opinion," *National Gazette*, December 19, 1791, in *Writings*, 500, 501.

40. Matthews, *If Men Were Angels*, 19. It is important to note that Matthews sees this commitment to reason as a flaw in Madison's thinking and particularly criticizes him for a "passionless notion of reasonable liberal politics [that] ultimately precludes the possibilities of the 'benevolence and brotherly affection' that his rhetoric sometimes suggests he also wanted" (9). What Matthews fails to understand is that Madison did not see reason as a substitute for passion or in modern language values but as a means for choosing among values through the rough-and-tumble of debate in the public square in order to serve the needs of all citizens.

41. Star A. Muir, "A Defense of the Ethics of Contemporary Debate," *Philosophy & Rhetoric* 26 (1993): 285.

42. Ibid., 290.

43. Iris Marion Young, "Difference as a Resource for Democratic Communication," in Bohman and Rehg, *Deliberative Democracy*, 400, 402.

44. See Chaïm Perelman and Lucie Olbrechts-Tyteca, *The New Rhetoric: A Treatise on Argumentation*, trans. John Wilkinson and Purcell Weaver (Notre Dame: University of Notre Dame Press, 1969).

45. *Federalist* 51 in *Writings*, 295.

Chapter 6

1. On the significance of Malcolm X's debating experience in the Norfolk Prison Colony, see Robert James Branham, "'I Was Gone on Debating': Malcolm X's Prison Debates and Public Confrontations," *Argumentation and Advocacy* 31 (1995): 117–37. Regarding Nixon's debating experience, Roger Morris notes in *Richard Milhous Nixon: The Rise of an American Politician* that "more than any academic experience, it was college debating that seemed to foreshadow and ever shape his later entry into national politics" (New York: Henry Holt,

1991), 129. The formative influence of Hillary Clinton's debating experience at Maine South High School in Park Ridge, Illinois, is discussed in Amy Chozick, "In Debate, Hillary Clinton Will Display Skills Honed Over a Lifetime," *The New York Times*, October 9, 2015, http://www.nytimes.com/2015/10/11/us/politics/in-debate-hillary-clinton-will-display-skills-honed-over-a-lifetime.html?_r=0.

2. William Rehg, "The Argumentation Theorist in Deliberative Democracy," *Controversia: An International Journal of Debate and Democratic Renewal* 1 (2002): 18–42.

3. Ibid., 25.

4. Jeffery Maynes, "Critical Thinking and Cognitive Bias," *Informal Logic* 35 (2015): 184–204.

5. Frans H. van Eemeren and Rob Grootendorst, *A Systematic Theory of Argumentation: The Pragma-Dialectical Approach* (Cambridge: Cambridge University Press, 2004).

6. Dan M. Kahan, "Ideology, Motivated Reasoning, and Cognitive Reflection," *Judgment and Decision Making* 8 (2013): 407–24.

7. Albert H. Hastorf and Hadley Cantril, "They Saw a Game: A Case Study," *Journal of Abnormal Psychology and Social Psychology* 49 (1954): 129–34.

8. Jonathan J. Koehler, "The Influence of Prior Beliefs on Scientific Judgments of Evidence Quality," *Organizational Behavior and Human Decision Processes* 56 (1993): 28–55.

9. Hart Blanton and Meg Gerrard, "Effect of Sexual Motivation on Men's Risk Perception for Sexually Transmitted Disease: There Must Be 50 Ways to Justify a Lover," *Health Psychology* 16 (1997): 374–79.

10. Ryan L. Claassen and Michael J. Ensley, "Motivated Reasoning and Yard-Sign-Stealing Partisans: Mine Is a Likable Rogue, Yours Is a Degenerate Criminal," *Political Behavior* 38 (2016): 317–35.

11. A wide-ranging review of the experimental data on motivated reasoning is made in Patrick W. Kraft, Milton Lodge, and Charles S. Taber, "Why People Don't Trust the Evidence: Motivated Reasoning and Scientific Beliefs," *Annals of the American Academy of Political and Social Science* 658 (2015): 121–33.

12. Sungjong Roh, Katherine A. McComas, Laura N. Rickard, and Daniel J. Decker, "How Motivated Reasoning and Temporal Frames May Polarize Opinions About Wildlife Disease Risk," *Science Communication* 37 (2015): 340–70.

13. James N. Druckman and Toby Bolsen, "Framing, Motivated Reasoning, and Opinions About Emergent Technologies," *Journal of Communication* 61 (2011): 659–88.

14. Mark Fischle, "Mass Response to the Lewinsky Scandal: Motivated Reasoning or Bayesian Updating?," *Political Psychology* 21 (2000): 135–59.

15. Bill Bishop, *The Big Sort: How the Clustering of Like-Minded America Is Tearing Us Apart* (New York: Houghton Mifflin, 2008).

16. Daniel Kahneman, *Thinking, Fast and Slow* (New York: Farrar, Straus and Giroux, 2011).

17. Maynes, "Critical Thinking," 186.

18. Gregory Schraw, "Promoting General Metacognitive Awareness," *Instructional Science* 26 (1998): 113–25.

19. Maynes, "Critical Thinking," 196–97.

20. Ibid., 199–200.

21. Kenneth Burke, *A Rhetoric of Motives* (Berkeley: University of California Press, 1969), 23.

22. Brendan Nyhan and Jason Reifler, "When Corrections Fail: The Persistence of Political Misperceptions," *Political Behavior* 32 (2010): 303–30.

23. Sol Hart and Erik C. Nisbet, "Boomerang Effects in Science Communication: How Motivated Reasoning and Identity Cues Amplify Opinion Polarization About Climate Mitigation Policies," *Communication Research* 39 (2012): 701–23.

24. Sahara Byrne and Philip S. Hart, "The 'Boomerang' Effect: A Synthesis of Findings and a Preliminary Theoretical Framework," *Communication Yearbook* 33 (2009): 3–38, quote on 22.

25. Stephan Lewandowsky, Ullrich K. H. Ecker, Colleen M. Seifert, Norbert Schwarz, and John Cook, "Misinformation and Its Correction: Continued Influence and Successful Debiasing," *Psychological Science in the Public Interest* 13 (2012): 122.

26. Michael Mendelson, *Many Sides: A Protagorean Approach to the Theory, Practice and Pedagogy of Argument* (Dordrecht, Netherlands: Kluwer, 2002).

27. This doctrine is based on Protagoras's fragment: "Man is the measure of all things: of things which are, that they are, and of things which are not, that they are not." For commentary on various translations and their implications, see Edward Schiappa, *Protagoras and Logos: A Study in Greek Philosophy and Rhetoric* (Columbia: University of South Carolina Press, 1991).

28. Alan Bailey, *Sextus Empiricus and Pyrrhonean Scepticism* (Oxford: Clarendon Press, 2002); Benson Mates, *The Skeptic Way: Sextus Empiricus's Outlines of Pyrrhonism* (Oxford: Oxford University Press, 1996).

29. See Cicero, *Academica*, trans. H. Rackham (London: William Heinemann, 1933): 2.104; Mendelson, *Many Sides*, 142; R. J. Hankinson, *The Sceptics* (London: Routledge, 1995), 92–115; and Richard Bett, "Carneades' Pithanon: A Reappraisal of Its Role and Status," in *Oxford Studies in Ancient Philosophy*, ed. Julia Annas, vol. 7 (Oxford: Clarendon Press, 1989), 59–94.

30. Cicero, *On the Republic*, trans. Clinton W. Keyes (Cambridge, Mass.: Harvard University Press, 1928): 3.9.

31. Mendelson, *Many Sides*, 143. Regarding Carneades's influence on Cicero, see also J. G. F. Powell, "Introduction: Cicero's Philosophical Works and Their Background," in *Cicero the Philosopher*, ed. J. G. F. Powell (Oxford: Clarendon Press, 1995), 1–35.

32. Mendelson, *Many Sides*, 137.

33. Ibid., 247–54; on *controversia* declamations as the "crowning exercise" of Roman rhetorical study, see Quintilian, *Intitutio Oratoria*, trans. H. E. Butler (Cambridge, Mass.: Harvard University Press, 1966).

34. Michael A. Gilbert, *Coalescent Argumentation* (Mahwah, N.J.: Lawrence Erlbaum Associates, 1997), 105.

35. Ibid., 109.

36. Ibid., 112; see also David M. Godden, "Arguing at Cross-Purposes: Discharging the Dialectical Obligations of the Coalescent Model of Argumentation," *Argumentation* 17 (2003): 219–43.

37. Lewandowsky et al., "Misinformation and Its Correction," 117.

38. See Nick Chater and Paul Vitányi, "Simplicity: A Unifying Principle in Cognitive Science?," *Trends in Cognitive Sciences* 7 (2003): 19–22.

39. David J. Hardisty, Eric J. Johnson, and Elke U. Weber, "A Dirty Word or a Dirty World? Attribute Framing, Political Affiliation, and Query Theory," *Psychological Science* 21 (2010): 86–92.

40. For example, see Deborah Tannen, *The Argument Culture: Moving from Debate to Dialogue* (New York: Random House, 1998).

41. Josina M. Makau and Debian L. Marty, *Cooperative Argumentation: A Model for Deliberative Community* (Prospect Heights, Ill.: Waveland Press, 2001), 88.

42. Ibid., 107.

43. On manufactured controversies, see Gordon R. Mitchell, "Whose Shoe Fits Best? Dubious Physics and Power Politics in the TMD Footprint Controversy," *Science Technology and Human Values* 25 (2000): 52–86, and Leah Ceccarelli, "Manufactured Scientific Controversy: Science, Rhetoric, and Public Debate," *Rhetoric & Public Affairs* 14 (2011): 195–228.

44. Susan Jarratt offers a feminist perspective on this point in her "Feminism and Composition: The Case for Conflict," in *Contending with Words: Composition and Rhetoric in a*

Postmodern Age, ed. Patricia Harkin and John Schilb (Boston, Mass.: Bedford/St. Martin's, 1991), 105–23; see also Gerald Graff, *Clueless in Academe: How Schooling Obscures the Life of the Mind* (New Haven: Yale University Press, 2003), 81–95.

Chapter 7

1. Michael D. Bartanen and Robert S. Littlefield, *Forensics in America: A History* (Lanham, Md.: Rowman and Littlefield, 2014).
2. George Pierce Baker, *The Principles of Argumentation* (Boston: Ginn, 1895).
3. Karen Armstrong, *The Battle for God*, 1st ed. (New York: Alfred A. Knopf, 2000), xvi–xvii; Phil Zuckerman, *Living the Secular Life: New Answers to Old Questions* (New York: Penguin, 2014).
4. William Schweiker, "How's the Weather in Rome?," *Martin Marty Center for the Advanced Study in Religion*, July 2, 2015, http://divinity.uchicago.edu/sightings/hows-weather-rome.
5. Michael Specter, "Pope Francis and the GOP's Bad Science," *The New Yorker*, November 14, 2014, http://www.newyorker.com/news/daily-comment/pope-francis-gop-s-bad-science.
6. Kenneth Burke, *The Philosophy of Literary Form: Studies in Symbolic Action* (Baton Rouge: Louisiana State University Press, 1941), 293.
7. Henry W. Johnstone Jr., *Philosophy and Argument* (University Park: Penn State University Press, 1959); Chaïm Perelman and Lucie Olbrechts-Tyteca, *The New Rhetoric: A Treatise on Argumentation* (Notre Dame: University of Notre Dame Press, 1969).
8. Douglas G. Jacobsen and Rhonda Hustedt Jacobsen, *No Longer Invisible: Religion in University Education* (New York: Oxford University Press, 2012).
9. Michael Walzer, *The Paradox of Liberation: Secular Revolutions and Religious Counterrevolutions* (New Haven: Yale University Press, 2015).
10. Ibid., 122.
11. Ibid., 17.
12. Ibid., 10.
13. See the research summarized by J. Warner Wallace, "Are Young People Really Leaving Christianity?," *Cold Case Christianity*, September 30, 2016, http://coldcasechristianity.com/2016/are-young-people-really-leaving-christianity/.
14. See David A. Frank and Michelle Bolduc, "From *Vita Contemplativa* to *Vita Activa*: Chaïm Perelman and Lucie Olbrechts-Tyteca's Rhetorical Turn," *Advances in the History of Rhetoric* 7 (2004): 71–87.
15. Kenneth Liberman, *Dialectical Practice in Tibetan Philosophical Culture: An Ethnomethodological Inquiry into Formal Reasoning* (Lanham, Md.: Rowman and Littlefield, 2004).
16. Michael J. Perry, *Religion in Politics: Constitutional and Moral Perspectives* (New York: Oxford University Press, 1999), 45.
17. Ibid.
18. George M. Fredrickson, *Racism: A Short History* (Princeton: Princeton University Press, 2009), 56.
19. "About Us," Whitefield Academy, https://www.whitefieldacademy.com/AboutUs/ (accessed August 5, 2015).
20. "Mission Statement," Liberty University, http://www.liberty.edu/aboutliberty/?PID=6899 (accessed August 5, 2015).
21. "Mission Statement," University of Oregon, https://uoregon.edu/our-mission (accessed August 11, 2015).
22. "About Us," Whitefield Academy.
23. Ibid.

24. Jim Selby (dean of Whitefield Academy), phone interview with the author, July 29, 2015, and August 11, 2015.

25. Zev Chafets, "Ministers of Debate," *New York Times*, March 19, 2006, http://www.nytimes.com/2006/03/19/magazine/319debate.html?_r=0.

26. Ibid.

27. Ibid.

28. Michael Hall (director of debate, Liberty University), phone interview with the author, June 29, 2015.

29. Chafets, "Ministers of Debate."

30. George Alexander Kennedy, *Classical Rhetoric and Its Christian and Secular Tradition from Ancient to Modern Times*, 2nd ed. (Chapel Hill: University of North Carolina Press, 1999).

31. Sonia Scherr, "College Campuses See Rising Anti-Semitic Sentiment," *Southern Poverty Law Center*, August 29, 2008, https://www.splcenter.org/fighting-hate/intelligence-report/2008/college-campuses-see-rising-anti-semitic-sentiment.

32. Burke, "The Rhetoric of Hitler's Battle," in *The Philosophy of Literary Form*.

33. Scherr, "College Campuses See Rising Anti-Semitic Sentiment."

34. Perry, *Religion in Politics*, 45; emphasis added.

35. David Tracy, *Plurality and Ambiguity: Hermeneutics, Religion, Hope* (San Francisco: Harper and Row, 1987), 76.

36. Perry, *Religion in Politics*, 46.

37. Hannah Arendt, *The Origins of Totalitarianism*, new ed. (New York: Harcourt, Brace and World, 1966), 471–73.

38. Zuckerman, *Living the Secular Life*, 38.

Chapter 8

1. CEDA, "2013–2014 Controversy Announcement," College Policy Debate Forums, May 13, 2013, http://www.cedadebate.org/forum/index.php/topic,4823.0.html.

2. Kelly Young, John Koch, Bruce Najor, Ali Hiland, Jacob Justice, Brad Meloche, and Taylor Slaw, "Restoring the Balance: Restricting Presidential War Powers," College Policy Debate Forums, April 21, 2013, 10, http://www.cedadebate.org/forum/index.php/topic,4800.msg10523.html#msg10523.

3. Mark Mazzetti and Michael S. Schmidt, "Ex-Worker at C.I.A. Says He Leaked Data on Surveillance," *New York Times*, June 9, 2013, http://www.nytimes.com/2013/06/10/us/former-cia-worker-says-he-leaked-surveillance-data.html.

4. James Madison to W. T. Barry, August 4, 1822, in *The Writings of James Madison*, ed. Gaillard Hunt (New York: G. P. Putnam's Sons, 1910), 9:103.

5. The National Task Force on Civic Learning and Democratic Engagement (NTFCLDE), *A Crucible Moment: College Learning and Democracy's Future* (Washington, D.C.: Association of American Colleges and Universities, 2012).

6. Ibid., 31.

7. "Who We Are," Opportunity Nation, https://opportunitynation.org/who-we-are/ (accessed November 2, 2015).

8. "Connecting Youth and Strengthening Communities: The Data Behind Civic Engagement and Economic Opportunity," Opportunity Nation, September 2014, 6, http://www.pointsoflight.org/sites/default/files/resources/files/opportunity_nation_civic_engagement_report_2014.pdf.

9. See, for example, Wilbur E. Gilman, "Can We Revive Public Interest in Intercollegiate Debates?," *Quarterly Journal of Speech* 14 (1928): 553–63; James Leonard Highsaw,

"Interscholastic Debates in Relation to Political Opinion," *Quarterly Journal of Speech* 2 (1916): 365–82; Gordon R. Mitchell, "Pedagogical Possibilities for Argumentative Agency in Academic Debate," *Argumentation and Advocacy* 35 (1998): 41–60; and Anjali Vats, "Civic Engagement Through Policy Debate: Possibilities for Transformation," in *Navigating Opportunity: Policy Debate in the 21st Century*, ed. Allan D. Louden (New York: International Debate Education Association, 2010), 242–50.

10. William Keith, "Keynote Address: A New Golden Age—Intercollegiate Debate in the Twenty-First Century," in Louden, *Navigating Opportunity*, 20.

11. See, for example, Michael Davis and Peter Bsumek, "The Public Debate Writing Assignment: Developing an Academically Engaged Debate Audience," *Contemporary Argumentation & Debate* 32 (2013): 92–97; Matthew Gerber, "Toward Public Sphere Intercollegiate Policy Debate: The Path to Participation?," *Contemporary Argumentation & Debate* 30 (2009): 79–92; Allan Louden and Theodore Albiniak, "Alternative Debate Models: Working Group Summary," in Louden, *Navigating Opportunity*, 236–41; Timothy O'Donnell, "A Rationale for Intercollegiate Debate in the Twenty-First Century," in Louden, *Navigating Opportunity*, 27–56; Sarah T. Partlow-Lefevre, "Arguing for Debate: Introducing Key Components for Assessment of Intercollegiate Debate Programs," *Contemporary Argumentation & Debate* 33 (2012): 31–74; Gordon Stables, "Suggested Guidelines for Controversial Area Papers," *Contemporary Argumentation & Debate* 31 (2010): 71–77; and Carly Woods, Matthew Brigham, Brent Heavner, Takuzo Konishi, John Rief, Brent Saindon, and Gordon R. Mitchell, "Deliberating Debate's Digital Futures," *Contemporary Argumentation & Debate* 27 (2006): 81–105.

12. Vats, "Civic Engagement Through Policy Debate," 242.

13. Partlow-Lefevre, "Arguing for Debate"; O'Donnell, "A Rationale for Intercollegiate Debate."

14. Davis and Bsumek, "The Public Debate Writing Assignment"; Woods et al., "Deliberating Debate's Digital Futures."

15. Mitchell, "Pedagogical Possibilities," 6.

16. Stables, "Suggested Guidelines for Controversial Area Papers," 74–75. See also Gordon Stables, "2010 Controversy Paper Submission Information and Dates," College Policy Debate Forums, March 30, 2010, http://www.cedadebate.org/forum/index.php/topic,742.msg1337.html#msg1337, and Gordon Stables, "Guidelines for Controversial Area Papers," CEDA Debate, October 2007, http://topic.cedadebate.org/node/8.

17. Eric Morris, "CEDA-Miller Center Public Debate Series," College Policy Debate Forums, August 22, 2013, http://www.cedadebate.org/forum/index.php/topic,4928.msg11067.html#msg11067.

18. Morris, "CEDA-Miller Center."

19. "About the Miller Center," the Miller Center, http://millercenter.org/about (accessed June 30, 2015).

20. Madison Cup, "About," James Madison University, http://www.jmu.edu/debate/madison-cup/about.shtml (accessed November 2, 2015).

21. Tim Kaine, "A Better Approach to War Powers," *Prism* 5, no. 1 (2014): 6–7.

22. "National War Powers Commission," the Miller Center, https://millercenter.org/issues-policy/foreign-policy/national-war-powers-commission (accessed November 2, 2015).

23. See, for example, Jarrod Atchison, Brendon Bankey, Mitch Hagney, Kevin Kuswa, and Jacob Uzman, "2010–2011 Immigration Controversy Paper Proposal," College Policy Debate Forums, April 20, 2010, http://www.cedadebate.org/forum/index.php/topic,773.msg1490.html#msg1490; Gordon Stables, "Supporting the Arab Spring: Democracy Assistance in the Middle East and North Africa," College Policy Debate Forums, April 25, 2011, http://www.cedadebate.org/forum/index.php/topic,2380.msg4481.html#msg4481; and Young et al., "Restoring the Balance."

Chapter 9

1. The construction sex/gender emphasizes the interrelation between the concepts of sex (typically understood as biological) and gender (typically understood as cultural). I use this construction to make clear that even the category of *woman* is not stable. Ciswomen, transwomen, and genderqueer folk all face distinct sex/gender challenges in debate, where being white, male, and cisgender are privileged and normative. Tracked along simplistic binary sex lines, men are statistically overrepresented in debate and speech participation. Women make up 56 percent of college students (a figure that is increasing), while women's participation in debate and forensics remains relatively static. Mark Hugo Lopez and Ana Gonzalez-Barrera, "Women's College Enrollment Gains Leave Men Behind," *Pew Research Center*, March 6, 2014, http://www.pewresearch.org/fact-tank/2014/03/06/womens-college-enrollment-gains-leave-men-behind/; Daniel Borzellaca, "The Male-Female Ratio in College," *Forbes*, February 16, 2012, http://www.forbes.com/sites/ccap/2012/02/16/the-male-female-ratio-in-college/. Departing from a binary approach, one can still rightly say cisgender men are statistically overrepresented in debate and speech.

2. Kimberlé Crenshaw, "Demarginalizing the Intersection of Race and Sex: A Black Feminist Critique of Antidiscrimination Doctrine, Feminist Theory and Antiracist Politics," *University of Chicago Legal Forum* 140 (1989): 139–67; Adrien Katherine Wing, ed., *Critical Race Feminism: A Reader* (New York: New York University Press, 1997).

3. bell hooks, *Talking Back* (Boston: South End Press, 1989).

4. Barbara Welter, *Dimity Convictions: The American Woman in the Nineteenth Century* (Athens: Ohio University Press, 1976).

5. Here, I echo Campbell's analysis in Karlyn Kohrs Campbell, "The Rhetoric of Women's Liberation: An Oxymoron," *Quarterly Journal of Speech* 59 (1973): 74–86.

6. Charles Morris III and Catherine H. Palczewski, "Sexing Communication: Associations of Sex/Gender and Sexuality," in *The Unfinished Conversation: 100 Years of Communication Studies*, ed. Pat J. Gehrke and William Keith (Washington, D.C.: Routledge, 2014), 128–65.

7. Helen F. North, "Emblems of Eloquence," *Proceedings of the American Philosophical Society* 137 (1993): 408; see also Amy C. Smith, "Athenian Political Art from the Fifth and Fourth Centuries BCE: Images of Political Personifications," in *Dēmos: Classical Athenian Democracy*, ed. C. W. Blackwell (The Stoa, 2003), 1–28, http://www.stoa.org/projects/demos/home (accessed January 10, 2016).

8. "Peitho," *Theoi Greek Mythology*, last updated 2011, http://www.theoi.com/Daimon/Peitho.html (accessed January 10, 2016). For more on Peitho, see Carly S. Woods and Michele Kennerly, "Rhetorica's Figures: Female Personifications and Their Place in Feminist Historiography," paper presented at the 15th Biennial Rhetoric Society of America Conference, San Antonio, Tex., May 2014.

9. Most likely from Tacitus's "Eloquence, the harlot of the arts," as cited in Donald C. Bryant, *The Rhetorical Idiom* (Ithaca: Cornell University Press, 1958), 130; also used in John Louis Lucaites and Celeste Michelle Condit, introduction to *Contemporary Rhetorical Theory*, ed. John Louis Lucaites, Celeste Michelle Condit, and Sally Caudill (New York: Guilford Press, 1999), 6, and Martin J. Medhust, "Editor's Welcome," *Rhetoric & Public Affairs* 1 (1998): iii.

10. Ernest J. Enchelmayer, "Rhetoric in the Visual Arts," *Conference of the International Journal of Arts and Sciences* 1, no. 19 (2009): 59–79, http://openaccesslibrary.org/images/AUS182_Ernest_J._Enchelmayer.pdf.

11. C. Jan Swearingen, *Rhetoric and Irony: Western Literacy and Western Lies* (New York: Oxford University Press, 1991), 228.

12. Michael Burgoon, "Instruction About Communication: On Divorcing Dame Speech," *Communication Education* 38 (1989): 303.

13. Ibid., 304–5.

14. Ibid., 305.

15. Michelle A. Mazur, "Women in Parliamentary Debate: An Examination of Women's Performance at the National Parliamentary Debate Association's National Tournament," *Journal of the NPDA* 8 (2001): 31–36.

16. Women's Debate Institute, *Women in Debate: A Best Practices Manual*, last modified October 2014, http://womensdebateinstitute.org/wp-content/uploads/2014/10/WDI-Best-Practices.pdf.

17. Katie Donovan, "The Success Gap," *National Forensic Journal* 30 (2012): 42–46.

18. Victoria P. DeFrancisco, Catherine Helen Palczewski, and Danielle Dick McGeough, *Gender in Communication: A Critical Introduction* (Los Angeles: Sage Publications, 2014), 64–67.

19. Glenna Matthews, *The Rise of Public Woman: Woman's Power and Woman's Place in the United States, 1630–1970* (New York: Oxford University Press, 1992), 3; Mary P. Ryan, *Women in Public: Between Banners and Ballots, 1825–1880* (Baltimore: Johns Hopkins University Press, 1990), 3.

20. Matthews, *The Rise of Public Woman*; Alison Piepmeier, *Out in Public: Configurations of Women's Bodies in Nineteenth-Century America* (Chapel Hill: University of North Carolina Press, 2004); Ryan, *Women in Public*.

21. Carolyn Eastman, *A Nation of Speechifiers: Making an American Public After the Revolution* (Chicago: University of Chicago Press, 2009), 54.

22. Ibid., 55.

23. Catherine Helen Palczewski, "The Male Madonna and the Feminine Uncle Sam: Visual Argument, Icons, and Ideographs in 1909 Anti-Woman Suffrage Postcards," *Quarterly Journal of Speech* 91 (2005): 365–94.

24. 56 *Cong. Rec.* H787 (daily ed. January 10, 1918) (statement of Rep. Gray).

25. Ibid.

26. 56 *Cong. Rec.* H786 (daily ed. January 10, 1918) (statement of Rep. Clark).

27. E. R. Thompson, "Development and Validation of an International English Big-Five Mini-Markers," *Personality and Individual Differences* 45 (2008): 542–48; P. T. Costa and R. R. McCrae, *NEO Personality Inventory Professional Manual* (Odessa, Fla.: Psychological Assessment Resources, 1992); L. A. Jensen-Campbell and W. G. Graziano, "Agreeableness as a Moderator of Interpersonal Conflict," *Journal of Personality* 69 (2001): 323–61.

28. See, for example, Jennifer Coates, "One-at-a-Time: The Organization of Men's Talk," in *Language and Masculinity*, ed. Sally Johnson and Ulrike Hanna Meinhof (Oxford: Basil Blackwell, 1997), 107–29; Sara Mills, *Gender and Politeness* (Cambridge: Cambridge University Press, 2003); Deborah Tannen, *You Just Don't Understand: Women and Men in Conversation* (New York: William Morrow, 1990); and Julia Wood, *Gendered Lives: Communication, Gender and Culture*, 10th ed. (Boston: Wadsworth, 2013).

29. For the link between civic education and civility, see Jack Crittenden and Peter Levine, "Civic Education," in *The Stanford Encyclopedia of Philosophy*, ed. Edward N. Zalta, last updated May 30, 2013, http://plato.stanford.edu/archives/sum2013/entries/civic-education/, explaining how civility is a central virtue taught by civic education: "Civic dispositions identified by the Center for Civic Education include civility, respect, individual responsibility, self-discipline, civic-mindedness, open-mindedness, compromise, toleration of diversity, patience and persistence, compassion, generosity, and loyalty to the nation and its principles," citing *Civitas: A Framework for Civic Education* (Calabasas, Calif.: Center for Civic Education, 1991), in "Revitalizing Civic Learning in Our Schools," *A Position Statement of National Council for the Social Studies*, approved by the NCSS Board of Directors 2013, http://www.socialstudies.org/positions/revitalizing_civic_learning (accessed January 10, 2016).

30. Don Waisanen, "Toward Robust Public Engagement: The Value of Deliberative Discourse for Civil Communication," *Rhetoric & Public Affairs* 17 (2014): 288.

31. Ibid.

32. Dreama Moon, "White Enculturation and Bourgeois Ideology: The Discursive Production of 'Good (White) Girls,'" in *Whiteness: The Communication of Social Identity*, ed. Thomas K. Nakayama and Judith N. Martin (Thousand Oaks, Calif.: Sage Publications, 1999), 192.

33. Kate Davy, "Outing Whiteness: A Feminist/Lesbian Project," *Theatre Journal* 47 (1995): 198. See Moon, "White Enculturation and Bourgeois Ideology," 181 for an extension of this discussion.

34. bell hooks, *Outlaw Culture: Resisting Representations* (New York: Routledge, 1994), 79.

35. Ronald C. Arnett and Pat Arneson, *Dialogic Civility in a Cynical Age* (Albany: State University of New York Press, 1999).

36. Ibid., 54.

37. Ibid., 284.

38. Ibid., 285.

39. This is a play on Gayatri Spivak's conception of strategic essentialism. And, like strategic essentialism, the separatism is intentionally political and temporary, constantly reflecting on what the separatist location can, and cannot, do. See Gayatri Chakravorty Spivak, *The Spivak Reader*, ed. Donna Landry and Gerald MacLean (New York: Routledge, 1996). The boundaries of this separation are always in discussion, as the WDI's trans inclusion policy makes clear. "Trans Inclusion Policy," *Women's Debate Institute*, March 2014, https://womensdebateinstitute.org/wp-content/uploads/2014/10/Trans-Inclusion-Policy.pdf.   For details about the camp, see http://womensdebateinstitute.org/ (accessed February 14, 2016).

40. "Why the WDI Is Important," *Women's Debate Institute*, last updated August 31, 2015, http://womensdebateinstitute.org/.

41. Beth Mendenhall, e-mail message to the author, October 30, 2014.

42. Carly Wunderlich Watson, e-mail message to the author, October 30, 2014.

43. Kate Shuster, e-mail message to the author, October 30, 2014.

44. Danielle S. Allen, *Talking to Strangers* (Chicago: University of Chicago Press, 2004), 12–20.

Chapter 10

1. Dennis G. Day, "The Ethics of Democratic Debate," *Central States Speech Journal* 17 (1966): 12–13.

2. Darrin Hicks and Ronald Walter Greene, "Debating Both Sides: Argument Pedagogy and the Production of the Deliberative Citizen," in *Argument at Century's End: Reflecting on the Past and Envisioning the Future*, ed. Thomas Hollihan (Annandale, Va.: National Communication Association, 2000), 300–307, and Ronald Walter Greene and Darrin Hicks, "Lost Convictions: Debating Both Sides and the Self-Fashioning of Liberal Citizens," *Cultural Studies* 19 (2005): 100–126.

3. Greene and Hicks, "Lost Convictions," 120.

4. Dallas C. Dickey, "Debate Training and Citizenship," *Southern Speech Journal* 8 (1943): 79.

5. Not all tournaments required switch-side debating; some tournaments allowed teams to debate only one side of the resolution (affirmative or negative) consisting of four debaters (often referred to as "four-man" [*sic*] debate), but this required an even number of affirmative and negative teams to efficiently run a tournament.

6. Greene and Hicks, "Lost Convictions," 112–17.

7. Ibid., 117–20.

8. We are borrowing this conception of intensity from Gilles Deleuze, *Difference and Repetition*, trans. Paul Patton (New York: Columbia University Press, 1994), 232–38.

9. Ben Anderson, "Affective Atmospheres," *Emotion, Space and Society* 2 (2009): 80.

10. Michael D. Bartanen and Robert S. Littlefield, *Forensics in America: A History* (Lanham, Md.: Rowman and Littlefield, 2014), 103.

11. For a review of some of the popular arguments against debating the China topic, see Eric English et al., "Debate as a Weapon of Mass Destruction," *Communication and Critical/Cultural Studies* 4 (2007): 222. It should be noted there were vigorous responses from debate programs in the Ivy League asking schools to reconsider their decision to opt out of the topic. The primary argument was free speech. See Jonas Schultz, "Murrow Show to Deal With Debate Question," *Columbia Spectator*, November 23, 1954, 1, 4, and "Princeton Wires Dulles," *New York Times*, November 16, 1954, 15.

12. Schultz, "Murrow Show," 1, 4, and "Fearful Colleges Ban Debate on Recognition of Red China," *The Harvard Crimson*, June 17, 1955, http://www.thecrimson.com/article/1955/6/17/fearful-colleges-ban-debate-on-recognition/.

13. "Red China Topic Stands," *New York Times*, November 30, 1954, 16.

14. English et al., "Debate as a Weapon of Mass Destruction," 222.

15. James MacGregor Burns, "Debate Over Collegiate Debates," *New York Times*, December 5, 1954, SM12.

16. Bartanen and Littlefield, *Forensics in America*, 104.

17. English et al., "Debate as a Weapon of Mass Destruction," 222.

18. Richard Murphy, "The Ethics of Debating Both Sides," *Speech Teacher* 6 (1957): 1–9.

19. Ibid., 2.

20. Ibid.

21. We previously recognized the value of English et al.'s historical focus in Darrin Hicks and Ronald Walter Greene, "Conscientious Objections: Debating Both Sides and the Cultures of Democracy," in *The Functions of Argument and Social Context*, ed. Dennis Gouran (Washington, D.C.: National Communication Association, 2010), 172–78.

22. English et al., "Debate as a Weapon of Mass Destruction," 222, 224.

23. Hicks and Greene, "Conscientious Objections," 175–79.

24. Geoffrey R. Stone, "Free Speech in the Age of McCarthy: A Cautionary Tale," *California Law Review* 93 (2005): 1404.

25. Francis Biddle, *The Fear of Freedom* (New York: Doubleday, 1951), 7.

26. Arthur M. Schlesinger Jr., *The Vital Center: The Politics of Freedom* (1949; repr., New York: De Capo Press, 1988), 250.

27. "Princeton Wires Dulles," 15.

28. A. Craig Baird, "The College Debater and the Red China Issue," *Central States Speech Journal* 6 (1955): 5–7. We provide a comprehensive story about how conviction moved from a first-order belief for or against a policy proposal toward a second-order belief in debate as a procedure in Greene and Hicks, "Lost Convictions," 102–12.

29. Casey Harrigan, "Against Dogmatism: A Continued Defense of Switch-Side Debate," *Contemporary Argumentation & Debate* 29 (2008): 37–66.

30. Darrin Hicks and Ronald Walter Greene, "Managed Convictions: Debate and the Limits of Electoral Politics," *Quarterly Journal of Speech* 101 (2015): 102.

31. On the role of political argument in constituting the "affective relations of democracy," see Zornitsa Keremidchieva and Vera Sidlova, "Political Argument and the Affective Relations of Democracy: Recovering Vaclav Havel's Theory of Associated Living," in *Proceedings of the 8th International Conference of the International Society for the Study of Argumentation*,

ed. Bart Garssen, David Godden, Gordon Mitchell, and Francisca Snoeck Henkemans (Amsterdam: Sic Sat, 2015), 722–28.

32. Greene and Hicks, "Lost Convictions," 100–126.

33. Pierre Bourdieu, *Distinction: A Social Critique of the Judgment of Taste*, trans. Richard Nice (Cambridge, Mass.: Harvard University Press, 1979), 6.

34. William M. Keith has asked how different the debate over debating both sides was in the early twentieth century from the one we tell during the Cold War. One answer is that the argument that debating both sides can transfer conviction to debate as a method of democratic decision making had not occurred, so the affective relationship between conviction and debate in the earlier debate was worked out in favor of debate as a game and not as debate as a democratic method. However, the peculiarity of the game debate at this time might reveal more nuanced answers. Conversely, the gamification move does participate in the class formation of the emerging middle classes. One might argue that O'Neill's defense of debate as an "intellectual sport" was also a defense of the speech discipline as a rightful partner in the educational development of the professional middle class and a claim to a class interest of autonomy by the speech profession as part of this emerging knowledge class. See William Keith, *Democracy as Discussion: Civic Education and the American Forum Movement* (Lanham, Md.: Lexington Books, 2007), 209, and James O'Neill, "A Disconcerted Editor and Others," *Quarterly Journal of Public Speaking* 1 (1915): 80. For a broader discussion of the earlier version of the debating both sides controversy in the first two decades of the twentieth century, see Keith, *Democracy as Discussion*, 68–70, and Hicks and Greene, "Managed Conviction," 99–101.

35. Thomas Rickert, *Ambient Rhetoric: The Attunements of Rhetorical Being* (Pittsburgh: University of Pittsburgh Press, 2013), 8–11.

36. Harrigan, "Against Dogmatism," 37–66; Kelly M. Young, "Impossible Convictions: Convictions and Intentionality in Performance and Switch-Side Debate," *Contemporary Argumentation & Debate* 32 (2011): 1–44.

37. Ede Warner Jr., "Go Homers, Makeovers or Takeovers? A Privilege Analysis of Debate as a Gaming Simulation," *Contemporary Argumentation & Debate* 1 (2003): 68.

38. Ibid., 66.

39. Ibid., 77.

40. Iris Marion Young, "Communication and the Other: Beyond Deliberative Democracy," in *Democracy and Difference: Contesting the Boundaries of the Political*, ed. Seyla Benhabib (Princeton: Princeton University Press, 1996), 120–36.

41. Shanara Rose Reid-Brinkley, "The Harsh Realities of 'Acting Black': How African-American Policy Debaters Negotiate Representation Through Racial Performance and Style" (Ph.D. diss., University of Georgia, 2008), 69.

42. Shanara Rose Reid-Brinkley, "Ghetto Kids Gone Good: Race, Representation, and Authority in the Scripting of Inner-City Youths in the Urban Debate League," *Argumentation and Advocacy* 49 (2012): 77.

43. Lawrence Grandpre, "The Negrophobia/Negrophilia Paradox and Liberal (Academic) White Supremacy," in *The Black Book: Reflections from the Baltimore Grassroots*, ed. Lawrence Grandpre and Dayvon Love (Baltimore: Leaders of a Beautiful Struggle, 2014), 41–110.

44. Ibid., 55–60.

45. Young provides a description of this argumentative tactic within a discussion of "performance debate." See Young, "Impossible Convictions," 3–7. It should be noted that the affective turn in this chapter shares with Young his concerns about the ability to locate convictions within a personalized notion of sincere belief as opposed to their iteration in practice. We want to describe this iteration in affective terms to highlight how the debate over conviction is more about the intensity of attachments to debate and its affective atmospheres.

46. Grandpre, "The Negrophobia/Negrophilia Paradox," 109.

47. We recently aligned this activist turn in debate toward the assignment of conviction to debate's technological form as a means of social justice; see Hicks and Greene, "Managed Convictions," 107.

Chapter 11

1. Austin J. Freeley and David L. Steinberg, *Argumentation and Debate: Critical Thinking for Reasoned Decision Making*, 13th ed. (Boston: Wadsworth Cengage Learning, 2014), 134.

2. Jay Caspian King, "High School Debate at 350 WPM," *Wired*, January 20, 2012, http://www.wired.com/2012/01/ff_debateteam/.

3. Darren Hicks and Ronald Walter Greene, "Managed Convictions: Debate and the Limits of Electoral Politics," *Quarterly Journal of Speech* 101 (2015): 98–112; Ede Warner and John Bruschke, "'Gone on Debating': Competitive Academic Debate as a Tool of Empowerment," *Contemporary Argumentation & Debate* 22 (2001): 7.

4. Anjali Vats, "Civic Engagement Through Policy Debate: Possibilities for Transformation," in *Navigating Opportunity: Policy Debate in the 21st Century*, ed. Allan D. Louden (New York: International Debate Education Association, 2010), 242.

5. Danielle S. Allen, *Talking to Strangers: Anxieties of Citizenship Since Brown v. Board of Education* (Chicago: University of Chicago Press, 2004), 5. In this chapter, I refer to citizenship as that process of public interaction in relationship to the political, rather than as a definition of who is conferred legal status as a citizen of the United States. Citizenship, as it is conceived here, is the practice of engagement with the state and the people living in it rather than a legal title.

6. See Tiffany Y. Dillard-Knox, "Against the Grain: The Challenges of Black Discourse Within Intercollegiate Debate" (master's thesis, University of Louisville, 2014), and Shanara Rose Reid-Brinkley, "The Harsh Realities of 'Acting Black': How African-American Policy Debaters Negotiate Representation Through Racial Performance and Style" (Ph.D. diss., University of Georgia, 2008). Dillard-Knox argues that many of the performative developments in debate coincide with the increased emphasis on diversifying the debate community. Many of the performative styles debaters are employing, she explains, "are derived from a set of Black discourse practices, values, and perspectives. Unfortunately, most of the members of the Intercollegiate Policy Debate community are unwilling or underprepared to fully understand the functionalities of these new methods," which is part of what has caused increasing divisions between traditional policy debaters and performance debaters.

7. Reid-Brinkley, "The Harsh Realities of 'Acting Black,'" 126.

8. Jessica Carew Kraft, "Hacking Traditional College Debate's White Privilege Problem," *The Atlantic*, April 16, 2014, http://www.theatlantic.com/education/archive/2014/04/traditional-college-debate-white-privilege/360746/; Patrick Speice and Jim Lyle, "Traditional Policy Debate: Now More Than Ever," *WFU Debater's Research Guide*, 2003, http://groups.wfu.edu/debate/MiscSites/DRGArticles/SpeiceLyle2003htm.htm.

9. For more information on the success of performative teams, see Hicks and Greene, "Managed Convictions," 102–4, and Adam J. Jackson, "Do Articles About 'Alternative Debate' Reinforce White Supremacy?," *Leaders of a Beautiful Struggle*, April 17, 2014, http://lbsbaltimore.com/do-articles-about-alternative-debate-reinforce-white-supremacy/.

10. Identity and performance debates are often grouped together because teams who use more artistic styles, such as poetry, music, and art, typically make arguments about identity. However, there are also debaters who engage issues of identity without using the performative

style. Still, they are often grouped with performance debaters because of their integration of personal narratives.

11. Allen, *Talking to Strangers*, xv; Dan Balz and Scott Clement, "On Racial Issues, America Is Divided Both Black and White and Red and Blue," *Washington Post*, December 27, 2014, https://www.washingtonpost.com/politics/on-racial-issues-america-is-divided-both-black-and-white-and-red-and-blue/2014/12/26/3d2964c8-8d12-11e4-a085-34e9b9f09a58_story.html?utm_term=.8cbfebd5975e; Marc J. Hetherington, *Why Trust Matters: Declining Political Trust and the Demise of American Liberalism* (Princeton: Princeton University Press, 2005); Juliet Hooker, *Race and the Politics of Solidarity* (New York: Oxford University Press, 2009); Shayla C. Nunnally, *Trust in Black America: Race, Discrimination, and Politics* (New York: New York University Press, 2012).

12. Allen, *Talking to Strangers*, xvi, xix–xx.

13. Ibid., xx.

14. Dillard-Knox, "Against the Grain"; Hicks and Greene, "Managed Convictions," 104. These sources focus primarily on the element of race, but I include gender because it is represented in a growing number of these debates.

15. Ryan Wash, "NDT 2013 Finals—Emporia SW vs Northwestern LV," YouTube video, 2:15:47 (see especially 12:50), from the final round of the 2013 National Debate Tournament on April 2, 2013, posted by "Debate Stream," April 2, 2013, https://www.youtube.com/watch?v=RZrWfDIediU.

16. Allen, *Talking to Strangers*, 35.

17. Carrie Wells, "Towson University Students Win National Debate Championship," *Baltimore Sun*, March 27, 2014, http://articles.baltimoresun.com/2014-03-27/news/bs-md-towson-debate-champions-20140326_1_towson-debate-team-national-debate-championship-towson-university.

18. Carew Kraft, "Hacking Traditional College Debate."

19. See Korey Johnson, "Never Meant to Survive the Debate: Sapphire Reclaims Her Performance," *Out of Nowhere* (blog), May 8, 2014, https://outofnowhereblog.wordpress.com/2014/05/08/never-meant-to-survive-the-debate-sapphire-reclaims-her-performance/.

20. Carew Kraft, "Hacking Traditional College Debate"; Brittany Cooper, "'I Was Hurt': How White Elite Racism Invaded a College Debate Championship," *Salon*, May 13, 2014, http://www.salon.com/2014/05/13/%E2%80%9Ci_was_hurt%E2%80%9D_how_white_elite_racism_invaded_a_college_debate_championship/; Rod Dreher, "How to Speak Gibberish and Win a National Debate Title," *The American Conservative*, May 10, 2014, http://www.theamericanconservative.com/dreher/how-to-speak-gibberish-win-a-national-debate-title/; Johnson, "Never Meant to Survive the Debate."

21. Paul Mabrey, "History Made at College National Debate Tournament," Cross Examination Debate Association, April 29, 2014, http://www.cedadebate.org/node/1088.

22. The leadership of CEDA is comprised of professional debate coaches and professors. After the national tournament, most of these individuals are responsible for either preparing their own students for the NDT and/or returning to teach at their home university.

23. See Johnson, "Never Meant to Survive the Debate," for an explanation of the experience of hypervisibility and invisibility.

24. Allen, *Talking to Strangers*, 35.

25. Ibid.

26. Ibid.

27. Ibid., 35–36.

28. Dillard-Knox, "Against the Grain"; Reid-Brinkley, "The Harsh Realities of 'Acting Black.'"

29. Allen, *Talking to Strangers*, 45.

30. For further consideration of the ways in which identity politics that emphasize individual suffering may reify existing power structures, see Lauren G. Berlant, *The Queen of America Goes to Washington City: Essays on Sex and Citizenship* (Durham: Duke University Press, 2002); Wendy Brown, *States of Injury: Power and Freedom in Late Modernity* (Princeton: Princeton University Press, 1995); and Eve Tuck and K. Wayne Yang, "R-Words: Refusing Research," in *Humanizing Research: Decolonizing Qualitative Inquiry with Youth Communities*, ed. Django Paris and Maisha T. Winn (Thousand Oaks, Calif.: Sage Publications, 2014), 223–47.

31. Debaters articulate these alternatives in a variety of ways too nuanced to convey here. For more on the topic, see Jared Sexton, "The Social Life of Social Death: On Afro-Pessimism and Black Optimism," *InTensions Journal* 5 (Fall/Winter 2011): 1–47.

32. Reid-Brinkley, "The Harsh Realities of 'Acting Black,'" 126. Reid-Brinkley is writing specifically about the Louisville Project, but I believe her account accurately characterizes the responses to identity and performance strategies more broadly.

33. Henry A. Giroux, "The Disappearing Intellectual in an Age of Economic Darwinism," *Truthout*, July 13, 2010, http://truth-out.org/archive/component/k2/item/90639:henry-a-giroux—the-disappearing-intellectual-in-the-age-of-economic-darwinism.

34. This forced choice not only has consequences within the debate community but also for those advancing identity-based arguments in public debate. For a vivid illustration of the consequences of public officials facing a similar forced choice during the debate over the government's response to Hurricane Katrina, see Michael Ignatieff, "The Broken Contract," *New York Times Magazine*, September 25, 2005, http://www.nytimes.com/2005/09/25/magazine/the-broken-contract.html?_r=0.

35. W. Lance Bennett and Shanto Iyengar, "A New Era of Minimal Effects? The Changing Foundations of Political Communication," *Journal of Communication* 58 (2008): 720.

36. Hooker, *Race and the Politics of Solidarity*, 21.

37. Ibid., 4.

38. Ibid., 26.

39. Ibid., 9.

40. Allen, *Talking to Strangers*, 165.

41. Ibid., 46.

42. Hooker, *Race and the Politics of Solidarity*, 6.

43. Ibid., 30.

44. Allen, *Talking to Strangers*, 20.

45. Hooker, *Race and the Politics of Solidarity*, 30. I do not mean to imply an obligation to act, or speak, *for* others but rather an obligation to consider the needs of others when acting.

46. Ibid., 48–49.

47. Ibid., 53.

48. Allen, *Talking to Strangers*, 141.

49. Ibid., 155.

50. Hooker, *Race and the Politics of Solidarity*, 29.

51. Allen, *Talking to Strangers*, 118.

52. Mutually preferred judging is a system designed to improve the quality of judging for debates by allowing teams to assign a rank to everyone in the judging pool prior to the tournament. When assigning judges to a debate, tournament staff use software that helps them identify judges that have been ranked similarly by both teams in a given debate. Ideally, judges assigned to a debate are ranked highly by both teams. However, when there are a limited number of highly ranked judges, some debates will be assigned judges that both teams ranked equally low. For more information on mutual preference judging and its criticisms, see Jenny Heidt, "The Case Against Mutual Preference Judging," *Rostrum*, May 2003, https://debate.uvm.edu/NFL/rostrumlib/policy200305heidt.pdf.

53. Allen, *Talking to Strangers*, 150.

Chapter 12

1. National Task Force on Civic Learning and Democratic Engagement (NTFCLDE), *A Crucible Moment: College Learning and Democracy's Future* (Washington, D.C.: Association of American Colleges and Universities, 2012).
2. Mortimer J. Adler, *The Paideia Proposal: An Educational Manifesto* (New York: Macmillan, 1982).
3. Ibid., 16–17.
4. Ibid., 50.
5. See Benjamin R. Barber, *Strong Democracy: Participatory Politics for a New Age* (Berkeley: University of California Press, 1984).
6. John Durham Peters, *Speaking Into the Air: A History of the Idea of Communication* (Chicago: University of Chicago Press, 2000), 268–69.
7. Aubrey O. Gwynn, *Roman Education from Cicero to Quintilian* (New York: Russell and Russell, 1964), 48.
8. Ibid., 113.
9. Ibid., 120.
10. See W. Barnett Pearce, *Making Social Worlds: A Communication Perspective* (Malden, Mass.: Blackwell, 2007).
11. W. Barnett Pearce and Stephen W. Littlejohn, *Moral Conflict: When Social Worlds Collide* (Thousand Oaks, Calif.: Sage Publications, 1997): x.
12. Ibid., 157–67.
13. Quoted in Em Griffin, Andrew Ledbetter, and Glenn Sparks, *A First Look at Communication Theory* (New York: McGraw-Hill, 2015), 75.
14. Wayne Brockriede, "Arguers as Lovers," *Philosophy and Rhetoric* 5 (1972): 1–11.
15. Henry W. Johnstone, "Some Reflections on Argumentation," in *Philosophy, Rhetoric, and Argumentation*, ed. Maurice Natanson and Henry Johnstone (University Park: Penn State University Press, 1965), 1–9.
16. Josina M. Makau and Debian L. Marty, *Cooperative Argumentation: A Model for Deliberative Community* (Long Grove, Ill.: Waveland Press, 2001).
17. Kimberly Pearce quoted in Griffin, Ledbetter, and Sparks, *A First Look at Communication Theory*, 75.
18. Vernon E. Cronen, "CMM, Argumentation, and Moral Force," in *The Coordinated Management of Meaning*, ed. Stephen W. Littlejohn and Sheila McNamee (Teaneck: Fairleigh Dickinson University Press, 2014), 51–76.
19. W. Barnett Pearce, Deborah K. Johnson, and Robert J. Branham, "A Rhetorical Ambush at Reykjavik: A Case Study of the Transformation of Discourse," in *Reagan and Public Discourse in America*, ed. Michael Weiler and W. Barnett Pierce (Tuscaloosa: University of Alabama Press, 1992), 163–82.
20. Adler, *The Paideia Proposal*, 23.
21. James H. McBath, *Forensics as Communication: The Argumentative Perspective* (Skokie, Ill.: National Textbook Company, 1975), 11.
22. Benjamin S. Bloom, *Taxonomy of Educational Objectives: The Classification of Educational Goals*, vol. 1, *Cognitive Domain* (New York: David McKay, 1956).
23. See, for example, Barber, *Strong Democracy*; Cronen, "CMM, Argumentation, and Moral Force," 52–53; Makau and Marty, *Cooperative Argumentation*, 83–87; Pearce and Littlejohn, *Moral Conflict*, 22; and Pearce, *Making Social Worlds*, 61–65.
24. Richard Petty and John T. Cacioppo, *Communication and Persuasion: Central and Peripheral Routes to Attitude Change* (New York: Springer-Verlag, 1986).
25. Johnstone, "Some Reflections on Argumentation," 4–5.
26. Peters, *Speaking Into the Air*, 268–69.

27. Barber, *Strong Democracy*, 202.
28. Pearce and Littlejohn, *Moral Conflict*, 157–67.
29. Adler, *The Paideia Proposal*, 52–53.
30. McBath, *Forensics as Communication*, 11.
31. Pearce, *Making Social Worlds*, 93.
32. Ibid., 96.
33. Ibid., xi.
34. Ibid., 62.
35. Ibid.
36. Ibid., 193.
37. Johnstone, "Some Reflections on Argumentation," 4.
38. Pearce, *Making Social Worlds*, 215.
39. Ibid., 193.

Chapter 13

1. W. Norwood Brigance, *Speech: Its Techniques and Disciplines in a Free Society* (New York: Appleton-Century-Crofts, 1952), 442–43.
2. John Gastil, *Political Communication and Deliberation* (Los Angeles: Sage Publications, 2008), xi.
3. William Keith and Paula Cossart, "The Search for 'Real' Democracy: Rhetorical Citizenship and Public Deliberation in the United States," in *Rhetorical Citizenship and Public Deliberation*, ed. Christian Kock and Lisa S. Villadsen (University Park: Penn State University Press, 2010), 46.
4. For definitions of public/democratic deliberation, see Robert Asen, "Deliberation and Trust," *Argumentation and Advocacy* 50 (2013): 5; John Gastil and Laura W. Black, "Public Deliberation as the Organizing Principle of Political Communication Research," *Journal of Public Deliberation* 4, no. 1 (2008): 1–47; and Tina Nabatchi, "An Introduction to Deliberative Civic Engagement," in *Democracy in Motion: Evaluating the Practice and Impact of Deliberative Civic Engagement*, ed. Tina Nabatchi, John Gastil, G. Michael Weiksner, and Matt Leighninger (New York: Oxford University Press, 2012), 6–7. For a discussion of the stages of deliberation and deliberative inquiry, see Martin Carcasson and Leah Sprain, "Beyond Problem Solving: Reconceptualizing the Work of Public Deliberation as Deliberative Inquiry," *Communication Theory* 26 (2016): 41–63.
5. For the theory of wicked problems, see Horst W. J. Rittel and Melvin M. Webber, "Dilemmas in a General Theory of Planning," *Policy Sciences* 4 (1973): 155–69; for discussions of wicked problems and deliberation, see Martin Carcasson, "Facilitating Democracy Through Passionate Impartiality," *Spectra* (September 2011): 3–7.
6. The National Task Force on Civic Learning and Democratic Engagement (NTFCLDE), *A Crucible Moment: College Learning and Democracy's Future* (Washington, D.C.: Association of American Colleges and Universities, 2012), 4.
7. Rebecca A. Kuehl, "Extending Civic Rhetoric: Valuing the Rhetorical Dimensions of Global Citizenship in Civic Education," in *Contemporary Rhetorical Citizenship: Purposes, Practices, and Perspectives*, ed. Christian Kock and Lisa Villadsen (Leiden: Leiden University Press, 2014), 292.
8. Alexis de Tocqueville, *Democracy in America*, trans. Henry Reeve (New York: George Adlard, 1839), 186.
9. See William M. Keith, *Democracy as Discussion: Civic Education and the American Forum Movement* (Lanham, Md.: Lexington Books, 2007), and Angela Ray, *The Lyceum and*

Public Culture in the Nineteenth-Century United States (East Lansing: Michigan State University Press, 2005).

10. Patrick J. Gerhke and William M. Keith, eds., *A Century of Communication Studies: The Unfinished Conversation* (New York: Routledge, 2015).

11. Keith, *Democracy as Discussion*, 115–23.

12. Robert Allison, "Changing Concepts in the Meaning of Group Discussion," *Quarterly Journal of Speech* 25 (1939): 118–19.

13. Evelyn Konigsberg, Elizabeth A. Douris, Charles F. Edgecomb, Phyllis M. Hofmann, and Muriel G. Leahy, "Teaching Public Discussion During the War," *Quarterly Journal of Speech* 29 (1943): 13–18.

14. W. Norwood Brigance, *Speech Communication: A Brief Textbook* (New York: Appleton-Century-Crofts, 1947), 141.

15. Ibid., 442–43.

16. Herman Cohen, *The History of Speech Communication: The Emergence of a Discipline, 1914–1945* (Washington, D.C.: National Communication Association, 1994), 152.

17. Keith, *Democracy as Discussion*, 193–208.

18. Pat J. Gehrke, *The Ethics and Politics of Speech: Communication and Rhetoric in the Twentieth Century* (Carbondale: Southern Illinois University Press, 2009), 67.

19. See Wolfgang Donsbach, "The Identity of Communication Research," *Journal of Communication* 56 (2006): 437–48.

20. Kasper Moller Hansen, "Deliberative Democracy: Mapping Out the Deliberative Turn in Democratic Theory," in Kock and Villadsen, *Rhetorical Citizenship*, 20–21.

21. See Robert Asen, "Critical Engagement Through Public Sphere Scholarship," *Quarterly Journal of Speech* 101 (2015): 132–44; Kuehl, "Extending Civic Rhetoric," 292; and Kock and Villadsen, *Contemporary Rhetorical Citizenship*.

22. NTFCLDE, *A Crucible Moment*, 4.

23. Ibid., 4, 53.

24. Rebecca A. Kuehl, Sara A. Mehltretter Drury, and Jenn Anderson, "Civic Engagement and Public Health Issues: Community Support for Breastfeeding Through Rhetoric and Health Communication Collaborations," *Communication Quarterly* 63 (2015): 513.

25. The South Dakota State University reflections are cited as: (1) SDSU-A, Student # for the argumentation course, and (2) SDSU-RM, Student # for the research methods course. The Wabash College surveys are represented in notes as (1) WDPD 2014–2015 End of Year Survey and (2) WDPD DF Reflection, Fall 2014. The Wabash College Deliberation elective course reflections are noted by student number, Wabash-D, Student #.

26. Jonathan Gould, ed., *Guardian of Democracy: The Civic Mission of Schools* (Philadelphia: Leonore Annenberg Institute for Civics of the Annenberg Public Policy Center at the University of Pennsylvania, 2011), 16; NTFCLDE, *A Crucible Moment*, 4.

27. WDPD 2014–2015 End of Year Survey.

28. Josina M. Makau and Debian L. Marty, *Cooperative Argumentation: A Model for Deliberative Community* (Prospect Heights, Ill.: Waveland Press, 2001).

29. WDPD 2014–2015 End of Year Survey.

30. For a discussion of experiential learning and civic engagement, see Anne Colby, Thomas Ehrlich, Elizabeth Beaumont, and Jason Stephens, *Educating Citizens: Preparing America's Undergraduates for Lives of Moral and Civic Responsibility* (San Francisco: Jossey-Bass/Wiley, 2003), 131–66.

31. WDPD 2014–2015 End of Year Survey.

32. Learning outcomes are taken from the "skills" noted in NTFCLDE, *A Crucible Moment*, 4.

33. Wabash-D, Student 7.

34. SDSU-A, Student 6.

35. Brian E. Adams, "Reason-Giving in Deliberative Forums," *Journal of Public Deliberation* 10, no. 2 (2014): 20.

36. SDSU-A, Student 1.

37. SDSU-RM, Student 7; SDSU-RM, Student 8.

38. Wabash-D, Student 9.

39. Sara A. Mehltretter Drury, Adam Burtner, and Macallister Norton, *"Sustaining Ourselves" in Urbana, Illinois: Public Deliberation Report* (Crawfordsville, Ind.: Wabash Democracy and Public Discourse, December 2014).

40. WDPD DF Reflection, Fall 2014, Student 2.

41. Makau and Marty, *Cooperative Argumentation*.

42. SDSU-A, Student 2 and Student 6.

43. Quotation from Wabash-D, Student 3; SDSU-RM, Student 5 expressed similar ideas.

44. SDSU-A, Student 6.

45. SDSU-A, Student 2.

46. SDSU-RM, Student 6.

47. SDSU-RM, Student 5.

48. Wabash-D, Student 5.

49. WDPD 2014–2015 End of Year Survey.

50. SDSU-A, Student 4.

51. SDSU-A, Student 5.

52. J. Michael Hogan, Patricia Hayes Andrews, James R. Andrews, and Glen Williams, *Public Speaking and Civic Engagement*, 4th ed., 2017 (Boston: Pearson/Allyn and Bacon, 2014); Jennifer Y. Abbott, Todd F. McDorman, David M. Timmerman, and L. Jill Lamberton, *Public Speaking and Democratic Participation: Speech, Deliberation, and Analysis in the Civic Realm* (New York: Oxford University Press, 2016); Josina M. Makau and Debian L. Marty, *Dialogue and Deliberation* (Long Grove, Ill.: Waveland Press, 2013); Makau and Marty, *Cooperative Argumentation*; and John Gastil, *Democracy in Small Groups: Participation, Decision Making, and Communication*, 2nd ed. (State College, Pa.: Efficacy Press, 2014), Kindle e-book.

Chapter 14

1. John Dewey, *The Public and Its Problems* (New York: Henry Holt, 1927), 119.

2. Scott London, "Civil Society and the New Global Order," http://www.scottlondon.com/articles/civilsociety.html (accessed January 27, 2016).

3. John Dewey, *How We Think* (Boston: D. C. Heath, 1910).

4. See, for example, Austin Freeley and David Steinberg, *Argumentation and Debate: Critical Thinking for Reasoned Decision Making*, 12th ed. (Boston: Wadsworth, 2009); Albert Craig Baird, *Public Discussion and Debate* (Boston: Ginn, 1928); Glenn Richard Capp and Thelma Robuck Capp, *Principles of Argumentation and Debate* (Englewood Cliffs, N.J.: Prentice Hall, 1965); and Douglas Ehninger and Wayne Brockriede, *Decision by Debate* (New York: Dodd Mead, 1963).

5. For more information about the Penny Harvest, see "Penny Harvest: A Program of Common Cents," https://www.commoncents.org/; for information about the USC program, see "Projects," USC Penny Harvest, last updated June 25, 2014, http://www.uscpennyharvest.com/#!aboutus/csgz.

6. Nora Gross, "2010–2012 Annual Report: Special Two Year Edition," Common Cents, June 2014, http://www.guidestar.org/ViewEdoc.aspx?eDocId=2906955&approved=True.

7. "USC Penny Harvest," USC Civic Engagement, last updated June 5, 2014, https://communities.usc.edu/partnerships/pennyharvest/.

8. Aristotle, *On Rhetoric: A Theory of Civic Discourse*, trans. George Kennedy (New York: Oxford University Press, 1991), 47–48.

9. Hazel Rose Markus and Shinobu Kitayama, "Culture and the Self: Implications for Cognition, Emotion, and Motivation," *Psychological Review* 98 (1991): 224–53.

10. William B. Gudykunst, Yuko Matsumoto, Stella Ting-Toomey, Tsukasa Nishida, Kwangsu Kim, and Sam Heyman, "The Influence of Cultural Individualism-Collectivism, Self Construals, and Individual Values on Communication Styles Across Cultures," *Human Communication Research* 22 (1996): 510–43.

11. Daphna Oysermann, Heather M. Coon, and Markus Kemmelmeier, "Rethinking Individualism and Collectivism: Evaluation of Theoretical Assumptions and Meta-Analyses," *Psychological Bulletin* 128 (2002): 3–72.

12. Richard E. Nisbett and Ara Norenzayan, "Culture and Cognition," in *Stevens' Handbook of Experimental Psychology*, vol. 2, *Memory and Cognitive Processes*, ed. Hal Pashler and Douglas Medin, 3rd ed. (New York: John Wiley and Sons, 2002), 561–97; Richard E. Nisbett, *The Geography of Thought* (New York: Free Press, 2003).

13. Taeku Lee, "From Shared Demographic Categories to Common Political Destinies: Immigration and the Link from Racial Identity to Group Politics," *Du Bois Review* 4 (2007): 433–56.

14. Sarah E. Igo, *The Averaged American: Surveys, Citizens, and the Making of a Mass Public* (Cambridge, Mass.: Harvard University Press, 2008); Michael X. Delli Carpini and Scott Keeter, *What Americans Know About Politics and Why It Matters* (New Haven: Yale University Press, 1996).

15. Heejung S. Kim, "We Talk, Therefore We Think? A Cultural Analysis of the Effect of Talking on Thinking," *Journal of Personality and Social Psychology* 83 (2002): 839.

16. Heejung S. Kim and David K. Sherman, "'Express Yourself': Culture and the Effect of Self-Expression on Choice," *Journal of Personality and Social Psychology* 92 (2007): 1–11.

17. Michael X. Delli Carpini, "Race and Community Revitalization: Communications Theory and Practice," *Aspen Institute Roundtable on Comprehensive Community Initiatives*, October 15, 1998, http://repository.upenn.edu/asc_papers/5/; William B. Gudykunst, *Bridging Differences: Effective Intergroup Communication*, 2nd ed. (Thousand Oaks, Calif.: Sage Publications, 1994).

18. Michael H. Agar, *Language Shock: Understanding the Culture of Conversation* (New York: Perennial, 1994).

19. Manuel Castells, *Networks of Outrage and Hope: Social Movements in the Internet Age*, 2nd ed. (Malden, Mass.: Blackwell, 2015).

20. John Dewey, *Democracy and Education: An Introduction to the Philosophy of Education* (New York: Macmillan, 1916).

21. Sidney Verba, Kay Lehman Schlozman, and Henry E. Brady, *Voice and Equality: Civic Voluntarism in American Politics* (Cambridge, Mass.: Harvard University Press, 1995); Nina Eliasoph, *Making Volunteers: Civic Life after Welfare's End* (Princeton: Princeton University Press, 2011).

22. Verba, Lehman Schlozman, and Brady, *Voice and Equality*, 304.

23. Alexis de Tocqueville, *Democracy in America*, ed. J. P. Mayer, trans. George Lawrence (Garden City, N.Y.: Doubleday, 1969); Robert D. Putnam, "Bowling Alone: America's Declining Social Capital," *Journal of Democracy* 6 (1995): 65–78; Verba, Lehman Schlozman, and Brady, *Voice and Equality*, 366.

24. Eliasoph, *Making Volunteers*.

25. Constance Flanagan, "Developmental Roots of Political Engagement," *PS: Political Science and Politics* 36 (2003): 257–61.

26. Constance Flanagan, "Volunteerism, Leadership, Political Socialization and Civic Engagement," in *Handbook of Adolescent Psychology*, ed. Richard M. Lerner and Laurence Steinberg, 2nd ed. (New York: John Wiley and Sons, 2004), 729.

27. Kelly Champion, Eric Vernberg, and Kimberly Shipman, "Nonbullying Victims of Bullies: Aggression, Social Skills, and Friendship Characteristics," *Journal of Applied Developmental Psychology* 24 (2003): 535–51; Dorothy L. Espelage, Melissa K. Holt, and Rachael R Henkel, "Examination of Peer Group Contextual Effects on Aggressive Behavior During Early Adolescence," *Child Development* 74 (2003): 205–20; Melissa K. Holt and Dorothy L. Espelage, "Perceived Social Support Among Bullies, Victims, and Bully-Victims," *Journal of Youth and Adolescence* 36 (2007): 984–94; Anthony D. Pellegrini, Maria Bartini, and Fred Brooks, "School Bullies, Victims, and Aggressive Victims: Factors Relating to Group Affiliation and Victimization in Early Adolescence," *Journal of Educational Psychology* 91 (1999): 216–24.

28. Wendy M. Craig, "The Relationship Among Bullying, Victimization, Depression, Anxiety, and Aggression in Elementary School Children," *Personality and Individual Differences* 24 (1998): 123–30; Paul R. Smokowski and Kelly Holland Kopasz, "Bullying in School: An Overview of Types, Effects, Family Characteristics, and Intervention Strategies," *Children & Schools* 27 (2009): 101–10.

29. John Dewey, *The School and Society* (Chicago: University of Chicago Press, 1899).

30. Dewey, *The Public and Its Problems*.

31. Suzanne C. de Janasz and Monica L. Forret, "Learning the Art of Networking: A Critical Skill for Enhancing Social Capital and Career Success," *Journal of Management Education* 32 (2008): 629–50.

32. Alvin W. Gouldner, "The Norm of Reciprocity: A Preliminary Statement," *American Sociological Review* 25 (1960): 161–78.

33. Gerald R. Ferris, Darren C. Treadway, Pamela L. Perrewé, Robyn L. Brouer, Ceasar Douglas, and Sean Lux, "Political Skill in Organizations," *Journal of Management* 33 (2007): 290–320; Hans-Georg Wolff, Klaus Moser, and Andreas Grau, "Networking: Theoretical Foundations and Construct Validity," in *Readings in Applied Organizational Behavior from the Lüneburg Symposium: Personality at Work*, ed. Jürgen Deller (Mehring, Germany: Rainer Hampp Verlag, 2008), 101–18.

34. Wayne Baker, *Achieving Success Through Social Capital: Tapping the Hidden Resources in Your Personal and Business Networks* (San Francisco: Jossey-Bass, 2000).

35. Mark Granovetter, *Getting a Job: A Study of Contacts and Careers* (Cambridge, Mass.: Harvard University Press, 1974).

36. Gerhard Blickle, James A. Meurs, and Christine Schoepe, "Do Networking Activities Outside of the Classroom Protect Students Against Being Bullied? A Field Study With Students in Secondary School Settings in Germany," *Violence and Victims* 28 (2013): 832–48.

Chapter 15

1. Jonathan Gould, ed., *Guardian of Democracy: The Civic Mission of Schools* (Philadelphia: Leonore Annenberg Institute for Civics of the Annenberg Public Policy Center at the University of Pennsylvania, 2011), http://civicmission.s3.amazonaws.com/118/f0/5/171/1/Guardian-of-Democracy-report.pdf (accessed January 25, 2016).

2. Krista Hesdorfer, "The State of Civic Education," *Hamilton College News*, August 1, 2013, http://www.hamilton.edu/news/story/the-state-of-civic-education; Michael Gerson et al., in Gould, *Guardian of Democracy*.

3. Arne Duncan, "The Power of Debate—Building the Five 'C's' for the 21st Century," keynote speech at the annual dinner of the National Association for Urban Debate Leagues, April 12, 2012, http://www.ed.gov/news/speeches/power-debate%E2%80%94building-five-cs-21st-century.

4. Robert Balfanz et al., *Building a Grad Nation: Progress and Challenge in Ending the High School Dropout Epidemic (2014)*, April 28, 2014, http://gradnation.org/resource/building-gradnation-progress-and-challenge-ending-high-school-dropout-epidemic-2014.

5. Becky Pettit, *Invisible Men: Mass Incarceration and the Myth of Black Progress* (New York: Russell Sage Foundation, 2012).

6. Balfanz et al., *Building a Grad Nation*.

7. Editorial, "The Dropout Crisis," *New York Times*, May 8, 2009, http://www.nytimes.com/2009/05/09/opinion/09sat2.html?_r=0.

8. Balfanz et al., *Building a Grad Nation*.

9. Ibid.

10. Jason Amos, *Dropouts, Diplomas, and Dollars: U.S. High Schools and the Nation's Economy* (Washington, D.C.: Alliance for Excellent Education, 2008), http://all4ed.org/wp-content/uploads/2008/08/Econ2008.pdf.

11. Andrew Sum, Ishwar Khatiwada, and Joseph McLaughlin, *The Consequences of Dropping Out of High School: Joblessness and Jailing for High School Dropouts and the High Cost for Taxpayers* (Boston: Northeastern University Center for Labor Market Studies, 2009), https://repository.library.northeastern.edu/downloads/neu:376324.

12. See Jonathan Kozol, *Savage Inequalities: Children in America's Schools* (New York: Harper Perennial, 1991), and Jonathan Kozol, *The Shame of the Nation: The Restoration of Apartheid Schooling in America* (New York: Crown Publishers, 2005).

13. Melissa Wade, "The Case for Urban Debate Leagues," *Contemporary Argumentation and Debate* 19 (1998): 60–65.

14. Mike Allen et al., "A Meta-Analysis of the Impact of Forensics and Communication Education on Critical Thinking," *Communication Education* 48 (1999): 18–30.

15. Gould, *Guardian of Democracy*.

16. Jean Lave and Etienne Wenger, *Situated Learning: Legitimate Peripheral Participation* (New York: Cambridge University Press, 1991), 95.

17. Etienne Wenger, Richard McDermott, and William M. Snyder, *Cultivating Communities of Practice: A Guide to Managing Knowledge* (Boston: Harvard Business School Press, 2002).

18. Paulo Freire, *Pedagogy of the Oppressed* (New York: Herder and Herder, 1970).

19. Ira Shor, "Education Is Politics: Paulo Freire's Critical Pedagogy," in *Paulo Freire: A Critical Encounter*, ed. Peter Leonard and Peter McLaren (New York: Routledge, 1993), 29.

20. Malcolm X and Alex Haley, *The Autobiography of Malcolm X* (New York: Ballantine Books, 1987), 86–87; emphasis added.

21. Robert James Branham, "'I Was Gone on Debating': Malcolm X's Prison Debates and Public Confrontations," *Argumentation and Advocacy* 31 (1995): 121.

22. Beth Breger, "Overview of the Urban Debate Program," *Rostrum* 75 (2000): 14, 51.

23. "Urban Debate QuickFacts," *The Aspen Institute*, 2013, http://www.aspendrl.org/portal/browse/DocumentDetail?documentId=1789&download (accessed May 6, 2017).

24. "Our Results," NAUDL.

25. Carol K. Winkler, C. Kevin Fortner, and Sara Baugh-Harris, "Overcoming Challenges to Women in At-Risk Communities Through Urban Debate Leagues," *Forum on Public Policy* 2013, no. 1 (2013): 1–22.

26. M. Leslie Wade Zorwick, Melissa M. Wade, and Dietlinde P. Heilmayr, "Urban Debate and Prejudice Reduction: The Contact Hypothesis in Action," *Contemporary Argumentation & Debate* 30 (2009): 30–51.

27. James M. Wade and Leslie Wade Zorwick, "Assigned Advocacy, Argumentation, and Debate in High School Classrooms," *Rostrum* 83, no. 8 (2009): 13–15.

28. James M. Wade and Leslie Wade Zorwick, "Making the Case for Assigned Advocacy, Argument, and Debate Across the Curriculum," paper presented at the Speech and Debate as Civic Education Conference, University Park, Pa., March 6, 2015.

29. Kozol, *Savage Inequalities*.

30. William Newnam, "Barkley Forum Alumni Survey: Debate as Community Service" (part 1 of assessment report prepared for Emory University, 2011), 1–19.

31. Ibid., 6.

32. William Newnam, "Barkley Forum Alumni Survey: Debate in Career Service" (part 2 of assessment report prepared for Emory University, 2013), 1–33.

33. Isaac Wolf, "You Gotta Use Your Words: A Pilot Study of the Computer Assisted Debate Project," presentation at the Annual Conference of the National Council of Teachers of English, New York, N.Y., March 21–24, 2007; Susan Hughes, "Historical Perspectives on Debate in Atlanta: A Case Study of the Atlanta Urban Debate League," presentation at the Annual Conference of the National Council of Teachers of English, New York, N.Y., March 21–24, 2007; Patrick Wade, "The Promise of Ethnographic Methodologies in Evaluating Urban Debate Leagues," presentation at the National Communication Association Annual Convention, Chicago, November 15–18, 2007.

34. Carol Winkler, "Extending the Benefits of Debate: Outcomes of the Computer Assisted Debate Project," in *Concerning Argument*, ed. Scott Jacobs (Annandale, Va.: National Communication Association, 2009), 792–800; Carol Winkler, "To Argue or to Fight: Improving At-Risk Students' School Conduct Through Urban Debate," *Controversia* 7 (2011): 76–90.

35. Winkler, "Extending the Benefits of Debate."

36. Winkler, "To Argue or to Fight."

37. Marti Kovener, *Engaging Youth in Gang Prevention: A Research Guide for Project Safe Neighborhoods* (Williamsburg, Va.: Institute for Law and Justice, 2009), http://www.ilj.org/publications/docs/Engaging_Youth_in_Gang_Prevention.pdf.

38. Wolf, "You Gotta Use Your Words."

39. Ibid.

40. Ibid., 95–96.

Chapter 16

1. The institute is currently held at Wake Forest University and Purdue University. George Mason University also hosted for three years. There are two parallel programs each summer. The Wake Forest edition of the Benjamin Franklin Transatlantic Fellows Summer Institute (BFTF) has hosted more than four hundred fellows from Eurasia and America.

2. Joseph Bellon, "A Research-Based Justification for Debate Across the Curriculum," *Argumentation and Advocacy* 36 (2000): 161–75; Alfred Snider and Maxwell Schnurer, *Many Sides: Debate Across the Curriculum* (New York: International Debate Educational Association, 2006).

3. For a summary of research on debate's effects, see Timothy O'Donnell, "A Rationale for Intercollegiate Debate in the Twenty-First Century," in *Navigating Opportunity: Policy Debate in the 21st Century*, ed. Allan D. Louden (New York: International Debate Education Association, 2010), 27–56, and Sarah Spring, Joseph Packer, and Timothy O'Donnell, "Debate in Research, Practice, and History: An Annotated Bibliography," in Louden, *Navigating Opportunity*, 363–75.

4. Ede Warner and Jon Bruschke, "'Gone on Debating': Competitive Academic Debate as a Tool of Empowerment," *Contemporary Argumentation & Debate* 22 (2001): 1–21.

5. Alfred C. Snider, "New Models for Debating: The USA Learns from the World," in Louden, *Navigating Opportunity*, 341–48.

6. Alessandra Beasley Von Burg, Ron Von Burg, Gordon R. Mitchell, and Allan D. Louden, "Emerging Communication Technologies and the Practices of Enhanced Deliberation: The Experience of Benjamin Franklin Transatlantic Fellows Summer Institute," *Journal of Public Deliberation* 8, no. 1 (2012): 1–8; Ron Von Burg, Allan Louden, Alessandra Von Burg, and Bronwen Gainsford, "Debate, Civic Engagement and Post-Training Social Networking," in *Argumentation, Rhetoric, Debate and Pedagogy: Proceedings of the 2013 4th International Conference on Argumentation, Rhetoric, Debate, and Pedagogy*, ed. Abdel Latif Sellami (Doha: QatarDebate Center, 2013), 227–38.

7. Theodore Albiniak, "Alternative Debate Models: Working Group Summary," in Louden, *Navigating Opportunity*, 249. Albiniak's analysis focuses on alternative models of argument within intercollegiate policy debate, but his observations offer insight into the general capacity for debate as a dynamic form of communication to serve as a catalyst for civic engagement.

8. The "study trip" segment takes a weeklong excursion to Philadelphia and Washington, D.C. Fellows visit sites and host lectures designed to bring place and expertise to the first week's classes.

9. Zompetti and Williams provide the example of the *American Democracy Project*, which operates on hundreds of U.S. campuses. Joseph P. Zompetti and David C. Williams, "Democratic Civic Engagement and Pedagogical Pursuits: Using Argumentation and Debate to Energize Concerned Citizens," in *Concerning Argument*, ed. Scott Jacobs (Washington, D.C.: National Communication Association, 2009), 819–28.

10. See James Crosswhite, *The Rhetoric of Reason: Writing and the Attractions of Argument* (Madison: University of Wisconsin Press, 1996).

11. Ibid.

12. In "Comparative Constitutionalism," fellows engage in shortened policy-format debates regarding the desirability of other nations emulating the U.S. Constitution. Meanwhile, in "Citizenship and Conflict," fellows participate in a role-playing activity among fictional nation-states seeking to resolve ongoing conflict.

13. Student comments were anonymous. English was the second language for fellows, with variance among participants reflected in their written feedback. This quote comes from an anonymous survey prompt as part of a postinstitute exit survey in 2011.

14. Daniel T. Willingham, "Critical Thinking: Why Is It so Hard to Teach?," *American Educator* (Summer 2007): 12.

15. Ibid., 13.

16. This microcosm demonstrating the utility deliberation-through-debate is supported by Gerald Graff's observations regarding the utility of interdisciplinary research initiatives in academic settings. Gerald Graff, "Two Cheers for the Argument Culture," *Hedgehog Review* 2 (2000): 53–71.

17. Von Burg et al., "Debate, Civic Engagement."

18. Scores of projects funded by the State Department, U.S. Embassies, the European Union, other European and Central Asia governments, and smaller grants from a number of NGOs fueled the fellows' initiatives. Major project examples include one cohosted in Moldova and Ukraine; see "Peacebuilding in Eastern Europe 2.0," Youth Ambassadors Summer Institute, July 23, 2014, https://youthambassadorssummerinstitute.wordpress.com/2014/07/23/peacebuilding-in-eastern-europe-2-0-application-period-is-now-open/. For another hosted in Armenia, see "Who Are We?," Youth in Charge Civic Engagement Seminar, last updated August 9, 2011, https://youthincharge.wordpress.com/who-are-we/.

19. William Rehg, "The Argumentation Theorist in Deliberative Democracy," *Controversia* 1 (2002): 18–42.

20. Ibid., 21.

21. This was, in part, to test how debate skills were applied by fellows when not prompted as they were in previous instances of the institute.

Chapter 17

1. J. Michael Hogan, "Rhetoric and Communication Studies as Education for Citizenship," *Communication Currents*, April 1, 2011, http://www.natcom.org/communication-currents/rhetoric-and-communication-studies-education-citizenship.
2. *Oxford English Dictionary Online*, s.v. "citizen," www.oed.com/view/Entry/33513.
3. Michael Warner, *Publics and Counterpublics* (New York: Zone Books, 2002), 88.
4. Nancy Fraser, "Rethinking the Public Sphere: A Contribution to the Critique of Actually Existing Democracy," *Social Text* 25/26 (1990): 56–80.
5. Robert Asen and Daniel C. Brouwer, eds., introduction to *Counterpublics and the State* (Albany: State University of New York Press, 2001), 6.
6. Rosa A. Eberly, "From Writers, Audiences, and Communities to Publics: Writing Classrooms as Protopublic Spaces," *Rhetoric Review* 18 (1999): 174.
7. Robert Asen, "A Discourse Theory of Citizenship," *Quarterly Journal of Speech* 90 (2004): 191.
8. Scott R. Stroud, "The Orientational Transformation in Any Public Sphere: Deweyan Thoughts on Habermas, Habits, and Free Communication," *Argumentation and Advocacy* 49 (2012): 148.
9. Christian Kock and Lisa S. Villadsen, "Introduction: Citizenship as a Rhetorical Practice," in *Rhetorical Citizenship and Public Deliberation*, ed. Christian Kock and Lisa S. Villadsen (University Park: Penn State University Press, 2012), 1.
10. Angela G. Ray, "The Permeable Public: Rituals of Citizenship in Antebellum Men's Debating Clubs," *Argumentation and Advocacy* 41 (2004): 1.
11. Stephan M. Llano, "One if by Land, Two if by Sea, Three if by Format: British Debate Is Coming," *Contemporary Argumentation & Debate* 33 (2012): 172.
12. An early article on American Parliamentary Debate outlines virtues debate teaches students that are equally applicable to Worlds-Style debate, including developing argumentation skills, thinking "on your feet," and exposure through travel. Many APDA debaters are very successful in the Worlds-Style debate format. See Theodore F. Sheckels Jr. and Annette C. Warfield, "Parliamentary Debate: A Description and a Justification," *Argumentation and Advocacy* 27 (1990): 1–15.
13. Neill Harvey Smith, *The Practical Guide to Debating, Worlds Style/British Parliamentary Style* (New York: International Debate Education Association, 2011), 177.
14. Ibid.
15. Christopher Ruane, "College Debate in the United Kingdom: What Might U.S. Debate Programs Learn?," *Forensic of Pi Kappa Delta* 86, no. 3 (2001): 8.
16. Steve Johnson (director of debate at University of Alaska), e-mail to the author, August 23, 2015.
17. Smith, *The Practical Guide*, 4.
18. Ibid., 171.
19. Stephen M. Llano, "Setting Motions," *Monash Debating Review* 12 (2014): 5.
20. Asen, "A Discourse Theory of Citizenship," 191.
21. Robert Trapp, "Open Society Youth Initiative," grant proposal submitted to the Open Society Foundation, 2009, 5.
22. "Participation Data for Chinese Debate Education Network," assessment of CDEN for the Open Society Foundation, 2015.
23. Trapp, "Open Society Youth Initiative," 8.

24. Shawna M. Margesson, ed., "Interim Report, 6 Month Review for Year 2 OS Grant," assessment of the CDEN for the Open Society Foundation, 2014.

25. Shawna M. Margesson, "Appendix Two: Assessment Robert: Summative Narrative Report for Final Year, Open Society Foundation Grant," assessment of CDEN for the Open Society Foundation, 2015.

26. David E. Williams, Brian R. McGee, and David S. Worth, "University Student Perceptions of the Efficacy of Debate Participation: An Empirical Investigation," *Argumentation and Advocacy* 37 (2001): 205.

27. Margesson, "Interim Report."

28. Steven L. Johnson, *Winning Debates: A Guide to Debating in the Style of the World Universities Debating Championships* (New York: International Debate Education Association, 2009), 5.

29. Margesson, "Interim Report."

30. Harry McEvansoneya, "WUDC Chennai 2014 Gender Analysis: Speakers," Infogr.am, January 26, 2014, https://infogr.am/wudc-chennai-2014-gender-analysis.

31. Ge Gao, "'Don't Take My Word for It'—Understanding Chinese Speaking Practices," *International Journal of Intercultural Relationships* 22 (1998): 170.

32. Gemma Buckley, "Language, Culture, and Religious Discrimination in Debating: An Empirical Study," *Monash Debating Review* 11 (2013): 4. ESL is the abbreviation for English as a Second Language. EFL is the abbreviation for English as a Foreign Language.

33. Ray, "The Permeable Public," 7.

34. See Pamela L. Stepp and Beth Gardner, "Ten Years of Demographics: Who Debates in America," *Argumentation and Advocacy* 38 (2001): 69–83.

35. Ray, "The Permeable Public," 13.

36. Shanara Rose Reid-Brinkley discusses similar concerns for including students of color in debate by examining the Urban Debate League in the United States. See Shanara Reid-Brinkley, "Ghetto Kids Gone Good: Race, Representation, and Authority in the Scripting of Inner-City Youths in the Urban Debate League," *Argumentation and Advocacy* 49 (2012): 77–99.

37. "Debaters of Colour Forum, Vienna EUDC 4 August 2015," Europe and IONA Debating, *Facebook* (group), August 12, 2015, https://www.facebook.com/groups/705783169539180/820368001414029/.

38. Robert Asen, "Critical Engagement Through Public Sphere Scholarship," *Quarterly Journal of Speech* 101 (2015): 141, 142.

Chapter 18

1. For more information on the limits of debate in China, see David Weeks and Zhang Chengming, "Treading Carefully: Debate Topic Selection in China," *Monash Debating Review* 11 (2013): 58–64.

2. The "eight-legged essay" imposed a rigid structure on scholarly writing and tested the writer's knowledge of classical texts and idioms. The structure strictly limited the number of sentences and words each point of the essay could use to express a given thought, lending toward an emphasis on technique over substance. For more on the "eight-legged essay" and how it is composed, see Qi Gong, Zhang Zhongxin, and Jin Kemu, *Discussions on the Eight-Legged Essay* (Beijing: Zhonghua Book Company, 1993), 8.

3. Susan Pepper, *Radicalism and Education Reform in 20th-Century China: The Search for an Ideal Development Model* (New York: Cambridge University Press, 1996), 57–64.

4. Stig Thogerson, *Secondary Education in China After Mao: Reform and Social Conflict* (Aarhus: Aarhus University Press, 2000), 2–3.

5. Belinda Dello-Iacovo, "Curriculum Reform and Quality Education in China: An Overview," *International Journal of Education Development* 29 (2009): 241–49.

6. Malcolm Moore, "Riot After Chinese Teachers Try to Stop Pupils Cheating," *Telegraph* (London), June 20, 2013, http://www.telegraph.co.uk/news/worldnews/asia/china/10132391/Riot-after-Chinese-teachers-try-to-stop-pupils-cheating.html.

7. Yong Zhao, *Who's Afraid of the Big Bad Dragon? Why China Has the Best (and Worst) Education System in the World* (San Francisco: Jossey-Bass, 2014).

8. Yong Zhao, "Fooling the Emperor: How Is Creativity Misapplied in China," China-US Focus, October 23, 2014, http://www.chinausfocus.com/culture-history/fooling-the-emperor-how-is-creativity-misapplied-in-china/.

9. Giovanni Sartori, "Concept Misformation in Comparative Politics," *American Political Science Review* 64 (1970): 1034.

10. Andrew Kipnis, "Suzhi: A Keyword Approach," *China Quarterly* 186 (2006): 296.

11. *Suzhi* is a character compound of *su* 素 and *zhi* 质. *Su* meanings include "unbleached," "white," and "element," while *zhi* translates as "nature," "character," or "substance." The word's etymology dates as far back as the classic work *Guanzi* (管子), more than two thousand years ago.

12. Jie Sizhong, *Zhongguo guomin suzhi weiji* [The Quality Crisis of Our Nation] (Beijing: Zhongguo chang'an chubanshe, 2004), 3, quoted in Kipnis, "Suzhi," 66.

13. Andrew Kipnis, *Governing Educational Desire: Culture, Politics, and Schooling in China* (Chicago: University of Chicago Press, 2011), 73.

14. Kipnis, "Suzhi," 66.

15. Dello-Iacovo, "Curriculum Reform and 'Quality Education.'"

16. Thogerson, *Secondary Education in China After Mao*, 3.

17. Diana Farrell and Andrew Grant, "Addressing China's Looming Talent Shortage," McKinsey Global Institute, October 2005, http://www.mckinsey.com/insights/china/addressing_chinas_looming_talent_shortage.

18. National Commission on Excellence in Education, *A Nation at Risk: The Imperative for Educational Reform* (Washington, D.C.: U.S. Department of Education, 1983), http://www.ed.gov/pubs/NatAtRisk/index.html.

19. Arne Duncan, "The Power of Debate—Building the Five 'C's' for the 21st Century," keynote speech at the annual dinner of the National Association for Urban Debate Leagues, April 12, 2012, http://www.ed.gov/news/speeches/power-debate%E2%80%94building-five-cs-21st-century.

20. A Chinese author's reflections to this effect can be found here: Yajun Zhang, "Shocking Foshan Incident Reveals an Unspoken Illness at China's Core," *Guardian*, October 19, 2011, http://www.theguardian.com/commentisfree/2011/oct/19/foshan-incident-unspoken-illness-china.

21. For other prominent examples of this perceived lack of social conscience, see Seungjoon Lee, "Trucker Runs Over Boy Again to Be Sure He'd Died," *Korea Times*, October 25, 2011, https://www.koreatimes.co.kr/www/news/nation/2015/03/501_97273.html, and "China Baby Hatch Suspended After Hundreds Abandoned," BBC, March 17, 2014, http://www.bbc.com/news/world-asia-china-26607505.

22. See a list of NHSDLC topics here: http://nhsdlc.ning.com/page/topics.

23. Arendt contrasted "thoughtfulness" with "thoughtlessness," which she asserts allows people to participate in structures of evil and injustice without fully comprehending the moral implications of their actions. See Hannah Arendt, *The Life of the Mind* (New York: Harcourt, 1978), 5.

SELECTED BIBLIOGRAPHY

Abbott, Jennifer Y., Todd F. McDorman, David M. Timmerman, and L. Jill Lamberton. *Public Speaking and Democratic Participation: Speech, Deliberation, and Analysis in the Civic Realm.* New York: Oxford University Press, 2016.
Ackerman, Bruce, and James S. Fishkin. *Deliberation Day.* New Haven: Yale University Press, 2004.
Adler, Mortimer J. *The Paideia Proposal: An Educational Manifesto.* New York: Macmillan, 1982.
Agar, Michael H. *Language Shock: Understanding the Culture of Conversation.* New York: Perennial, 1994.
Allen, Danielle S. *Talking to Strangers: Anxieties of Citizenship Since Brown v. Board of Education.* Chicago: University of Chicago Press, 2004.
Allen, Mike, Sandra Berkowitz, Steve Hunt, and Allan Louden. "A Meta-Analysis of the Impact of Forensics and Communication Education on Critical Thinking." *Communication Education* 48 (1999): 18–30.
Allen, Mike, Mary Trejo, Michael Bartanen, Anthony Schroeder, and Tammie Ulrich. "Diversity in United States Forensics: A Report on Research Conducted for the American Forensic Association." *Argumentation and Advocacy* 40 (2004): 173–84.
Andrade, Luis M., and Jon Bruschke. "Cultural Pedagogy as Motivation and the Role of 'Institutional Agents' in Intercollegiate Debate." In *Disturbing Argument*, edited by Catherine H. Palczewski, 407–13. New York: Routledge, 2014.
Asen, Robert. "Critical Engagement Through Public Sphere Scholarship." *Quarterly Journal of Speech* 101 (2015): 132–44.
———. "Deliberation and Trust." *Argumentation and Advocacy* 50 (2013): 2–17.
Atchison, Jarrod, and Edward Panetta. "Intercollegiate Debate and Speech Communication: Historical Developments and Issues for the Future." In *The Sage Handbook of Rhetorical Studies*, edited by Andrea A. Lunsford, Kirt H. Wilson, and Rosa A. Eberly, 317–34. Thousand Oaks, Calif.: Sage Publications, 2009.
Baird, A. Craig. "The College Debater and the Red China Issue." *Central States Speech Journal* 6 (1955): 5–7.
———. "Shall American Universities Adopt the British System of Debating?" *Quarterly Journal of Speech Education* 9 (1923): 215–22.
Barber, Benjamin R. *Strong Democracy: Participatory Politics for a New Age.* Berkeley: University of California Press, 1984.
Bartanen, Michael D., and Robert S. Littlefield. "Competitive Speech and Debate: How Play Influenced American Educational Practice." *American Journal of Play* 7 (2015): 155–73.
———. *Forensics in America: A History.* Lanham, Md.: Rowman and Littlefield, 2014.
Bellon, Joseph. "A Research-Based Justification for Debate Across the Curriculum." *Argumentation and Advocacy* 36 (2000): 161–75.
Bennett, W. Lance, ed. "Communication and Civic Engagement in Comparative Perspective." *Political Communication* 17, no. 4 (2000): 307–12.

Bohman, James, and William Rehg, eds. *Deliberative Democracy: Essays on Reason and Politics*. Cambridge, Mass.: MIT Press, 1997.
Branham, Robert James. "'I Was Gone on Debating': Malcolm X's Prison Debates and Public Confrontations." *Argumentation and Advocacy* 31 (1995): 117–37.
Broda-Bahm, Kenneth, ed. "Invitational Debate." Special issue, *Contemporary Argumentation & Debate* 21 (2000): 74–115.
———. "Voices from the Ideafest: The Open Society Institute and Urban Debate in the U.S." Special issue, *Contemporary Argumentation & Debate* 19 (1998): 58–96.
Bruschke, Jon, and Ann Johnson. "An Analysis of Differences in Success Rates of Male and Female Debaters." *Argumentation and Advocacy* 30 (1994): 162–73.
Buckley, Gemma. "Language, Culture, and Religious Discrimination in Debating: An Empirical Study." *Monash Debating Review* 11 (2013): 29–38.
Carcasson, Martin, and Leah Sprain. "Beyond Problem Solving: Reconceptualizing the Work of Public Deliberation as Deliberative Inquiry." *Communication Theory* 26 (2016): 41–63.
Ceccarelli, Leah. "Manufactured Scientific Controversy: Science, Rhetoric, and Public Debate." *Rhetoric & Public Affairs* 14 (2011): 195–228.
Colby, Anne, Thomas Ehrlich, Elizabeth Beaumont, and Jason Stephens. *Educating Citizens: Preparing America's Undergraduates for Lives of Moral and Civic Responsibility*. San Francisco: Jossey-Bass/Wiley, 2003.
Cowperthwaite, L. Leroy, and A. Craig Baird. "Intercollegiate Debating." In *History of Speech Education in America*, edited by Karl Wallace, 259–76. New York: Appleton-Century-Crofts, 1954.
Crenshaw, Carrie. "Dominant Form and Marginalized Voices: Argumentation About Feminism(s)." *CEDA Yearbook* 14 (1993): 72–79.
Dalton, Russell J. *The Good Citizen: How a Younger Generation Is Reshaping American Politics*. Washington, D.C.: CQ Press, 2008.
Davis, Michael, and Peter Bsumek. "The Public Debate Writing Assignment: Developing an Academically Engaged Debate Audience." *Contemporary Argumentation & Debate* 32 (2013): 92–97.
Davis, William Hawley. "Is Debate Primarily a Game?" *Quarterly Journal of Public Speaking* 2 (1916): 171–79.
Day, Dennis G. "The Ethics of Democratic Debate." *Central States Speech Journal* 17 (1966): 5–14.
DeFrancisco, Victoria P., Catherine Helen Palczewski, and Danielle Dick McGeough. *Gender in Communication: A Critical Introduction*. Los Angeles, Calif.: Sage Publications, 2014.
Dey, Eric L., Cassie L. Barnhardt, Mary Antonaros, Molly C. Ott, and Matthew H. Holsapple. *Civic Responsibility: What Is the Campus Climate for Learning?* Washington, D.C.: Association of Colleges and Universities, 2009.
Dickey, Dallas C. "Debate Training and Citizenship." *Southern Speech Journal* 8 (1943): 77–79.
Dillard-Knox, Tiffany Y. "Against the Grain: The Challenges of Black Discourse Within Intercollegiate Debate." M.A. thesis, University of Louisville, 2014.
Druckman, James N., and Toby Bolsen. "Framing, Motivated Reasoning, and Opinions About Emergent Technologies." *Journal of Communication* 61 (2011): 659–88.
Duncan, Arne. "The Power of Debate—Building the Five 'C's' for the 21st Century." Keynote speech at the Annual Dinner of the National Association for Urban Debate Leagues, April 12, 2012. http://www.ed.gov/news/speeches/power-debate%E2%80%94building-five-cs-21st-century/.
Eastman, Carolyn. *A Nation of Speechifiers: Making an American Public After the Revolution*. Chicago: University of Chicago Press, 2009.

Eberly, Rosa A. "From Writers, Audiences, and Communities to Publics: Writing Classrooms as Protopublic Spaces." *Rhetoric Review* 18 (1999): 165–78.
Ehninger, Douglas, and Wayne Brockriede. *Decision by Debate*. New York: Dodd Mead, 1963.
Emery, Emogene. "Rehabilitating Women's Debate." *Southern Speech Journal* 17 (1952): 186–91.
English, Eric, Stephen Llano, Gordon R. Mitchell, Catherine E. Morrison, John Rief, and Carly Woods. "Debate as a Weapon of Mass Destruction." *Communication and Critical/Cultural Studies* 4 (2007): 221–25.
Fest, Thorrel B. "A Survey of College Forensics." *Quarterly Journal of Speech* 34 (1948): 168–73.
Flanagan, Constance. "Developmental Roots of Political Engagement." *PS: Political Science and Politics* 36 (2003): 257–61.
Frank, David A. "Arguing with God, Talmudic Discourse, and the Jewish Countermodel: Implications for the Study of Argumentation." *Argumentation and Advocacy* 41 (2004): 71–86.
Fraser, Nancy. "Rethinking the Public Sphere: A Contribution to the Critique of Actually Existing Democracy." *Social Text* 25/26 (1990): 56–80.
Friedley, Sheryl A., and Bruce B. Manchester. "An Analysis of Male/Female Participation at Select National Championships." *National Forensic Journal* 3 (1985): 1–12.
Gastil, John. *Political Communication and Deliberation*. Los Angeles, Calif.: Sage Publications, 2008.
Gastil, John, and Laura W. Black. "Public Deliberation as the Organizing Principle of Political Communication Research." *Journal of Public Deliberation* 4, no. 1 (2008): 1–47.
Gerber, Matthew. "Toward Public Sphere Intercollegiate Policy Debate: The Path to Participation?" *Contemporary Argumentation & Debate* 30 (2009): 79–92.
Gerhke, Pat J. *The Ethics and Politics of Speech: Communication and Rhetoric in the Twentieth Century*. Carbondale: Southern Illinois University Press, 2009.
Gerhke, Pat J., and William M. Keith, eds. *A Century of Communication Studies: The Unfinished Conversation*. New York: Routledge, 2015.
Gilbert, Michael A. *Coalescent Argumentation*. Mahwah, N.J.: Lawrence Erlbaum Associates, 1997.
Gilman, Wilbur E. "Can We Revive Public Interest in Intercollegiate Debates?" *Quarterly Journal of Speech* 14 (1928): 553–63.
Godden, David M. "Arguing at Cross-Purposes: Discharging the Dialectical Obligations of the Coalescent Model of Argumentation." *Argumentation* 17 (2003): 219–43.
Gould, Jonathan, ed. *Guardian of Democracy: The Civic Mission of Schools*. Philadelphia, Pa.: The Leonore Annenberg Institute for Civics, 2011. http://civicmission.s3.amazonaws.com/118/f0/5/171/1/Guardian-of-Democracy-report.pdf.
Greene, Ronald Walter, and Darrin Hicks. "Lost Convictions: Debating Both Sides and the Self-Fashioning of Liberal Citizens." *Cultural Studies* 19 (2005): 100–126.
Greenstreet, Robert, and Tracy Frederick. "The Sounds of Silence: The Gender-Based Experiences of Women in Intercollegiate Forensics." *Forensic of Pi Kappa Delta* 85, no. 3 (2000): 25–36.
Gutmann, Amy. "Civic Education and Social Diversity." *Ethics* 105 (1995): 557–79.
Gutmann, Amy, and Dennis Thompson. *Why Deliberative Democracy?* Princeton: Princeton University Press, 2004.
Harper, Chris. "Gender and Competitive Equity: The 2007 and 2008 National Parliamentary Debate Association National Tournaments." *Forensic of Pi Kappa Delta* 94, no. 1 (2009): 1–12.
Harrigan, Casey. "Against Dogmatism: A Continued Defense of Switch-Side Debate." *Contemporary Argumentation & Debate* 29 (2008): 37–66.
Harward, Donald W., ed. *Civic Provocations*. Washington, D.C.: Bringing Theory to Practice, 2012.

Hetherington, Marc J. *Why Trust Matters: Declining Political Trust and the Demise of American Liberalism.* Princeton: Princeton University Press, 2005.

Hicks, Darrin, and Ronald Walter Greene. "Conscientious Objections: Debating Both Sides and the Cultures of Democracy." In *The Functions of Argument and Social Context*, edited by Dennis Gouran, 172–78. Washington, D.C.: National Communication Association, 2010.

———. "Debating Both Sides: Argument Pedagogy and the Production of the Deliberative Citizen." In *Argument at Century's End: Reflecting on the Past and Envisioning the Future*, edited by Thomas A. Hollihan, 300–307. Annandale, Va.: National Communication Association, 2000.

———. "Managed Convictions: Debate and the Limits of Electoral Politics." *Quarterly Journal of Speech* 101 (2015): 98–112.

Highsaw, James Leonard. "Interscholastic Debates in Relation to Political Opinion." *Quarterly Journal of Public Speaking* 2 (1916): 365–82.

Hogan, J. Michael. "Rhetoric and Communication Studies as Education for Citizenship." *Communication Currents*, April 1, 2011. https://www.natcom.org/communication-currents/rhetoric-and-communication-studies-education-citizenship.

———. "Rhetorical Pedagogy and Democratic Citizenship: Reviving the Traditions of Civic Engagement and Public Deliberation." In *Rhetoric and Democracy: Essays in the Tradition of William Norwood Brigance*, edited by David M. Timmerman and Todd F. McDorman, 75–97. East Lansing: Michigan State University Press, 2008.

Jamieson, Kathleen Hall. "The Discipline's Debate Contributions: Then, Now, and Next." *Quarterly Journal of Speech* 101 (2015): 85–97.

Kahneman, Daniel. *Thinking, Fast and Slow.* New York: Farrar, Straus and Giroux, 2011.

Keith, William M. *Democracy as Discussion: Civic Education and the American Forum Movement.* Lanham, Md.: Lexington Books, 2007.

Kiesa, Abby, Alexander P. Orlowski, Peter Levine, Deborah Both, Emily Hoban Kirby, Mark Hugo Lopez, and Karlo Barrios Marcelo. *Millennials Talk Politics: A Study of College Student Political Engagement.* College Park, Md.: Center for Information and Research on Civic Learning and Engagement, 2007.

Kock, Christian, and Lisa S. Villadsen, eds. *Rhetorical Citizenship and Public Deliberation.* University Park: Penn State University Press, 2010.

Lee, Edward. "Memoir of a Former Urban Debate League Participant." *Contemporary Argumentation & Debate* 19 (1998): 93–96.

Levinson, Meira. *No Citizen Left Behind.* Cambridge, Mass.: Harvard University Press, 2012.

Llano, Stephan M. "One if by Land, Two if by Sea, Three if by Format: British Debate Is Coming." *Contemporary Argumentation & Debate* 33 (2012): 171–86.

Loge, Peter. "Black Participation in CEDA Debate: A Quantification and Analysis." *CEDA Yearbook* 12 (1991): 79–87.

Louden, Allan D., ed. *Navigating Opportunity: Policy Debate in the 21st Century.* New York: International Debate Education Association, 2010.

Macedo, Stephen, Yevette Alex-Assensoh, Jeffrey M. Berry, Michael Brintnall, David E. Campbell, Louis Ricardo Fraga, Archon Fung, et al. *Democracy at Risk: How Political Choices Undermine Citizen Participation, and What We Can Do About It.* Washington, D.C.: Brookings Institution, 2005.

Makau, Josina M., and Debian L. Marty. *Cooperative Argumentation: A Model for Deliberative Community.* Prospect Heights, Ill.: Waveland Press, 2001.

Mathews, David. *Politics for People: Finding a Responsible Public Voice.* 2nd ed. Urbana: University of Illinois Press, 1999.

Mendelson, Michael. *Many Sides: A Protagorean Approach to the Theory, Practice and Pedagogy of Argument.* Dordrecht, Netherlands: Kluwer, 2002.

Mezuk, Briana. "Urban Debate and High School Educational Outcomes for African American Males: The Case of the Chicago Debate League." *Journal of Negro Education* 78 (2009): 290–304.
Mindich, David T. Z. *Tuned Out: Why Americans Under 40 Don't Follow the News*. New York: Oxford University Press, 2005.
Mitchell, Gordon R. "Pedagogical Possibilities for Argumentative Agency in Academic Debate." *Argumentation and Advocacy* 35 (1998): 41–60.
Muir, Star A. "A Defense of the Ethics of Contemporary Debate." *Philosophy & Rhetoric* 26 (1993): 277–95.
Murphy, Richard. "The Ethics of Debating Both Sides." *Speech Teacher* 6 (1957): 1–9.
Nabatchi, Tina, John Gastil, G. Michael Weiksner, and Matt Leighninger, eds. *Democracy in Motion: Evaluating the Practice and Impact of Deliberative Civic Engagement*. New York: Oxford University Press, 2012.
Nash, Margaret, and Lisa Romero. "'Citizenship for the College Girl': Challenges and Opportunities in Higher Education for Women in the United States in the 1930s." *Teachers College Record* 114, no. 2 (2012): 1–35.
National Task Force on Civic Learning and Democratic Engagement. *A Crucible Moment: College Learning and Democracy's Future*. Washington, D.C.: Association of American Colleges and Universities, 2012.
Partlow-Lefevre, Sarah T. "Arguing for Debate: Introducing Key Components for Assessment of Intercollegiate Debate Programs." *Contemporary Argumentation & Debate* 33 (2012): 31–74.
Perelman, Chaïm, and Lucie Olbrechts-Tyteca. *The New Rhetoric: A Treatise on Argumentation*. Translated by John Wilkinson and Purcell Weaver. Notre Dame: University of Notre Dame Press, 1969.
Pierson, Emma. "Men Outspeak Women: Analysing the Gender Gap in Competitive Debate." *Monash Debating Review* 11 (2013): 8–15.
Pineda, Richard, and Chris Salina. "Model Proposal: Increasing Latina/o Involvement in Policy Debate Through Summer Debate Workshops." *Contemporary Argumentation & Debate* 30 (2009): 114–29.
Preston, C. Thomas, Jr. "The Interconnectedness Between Intercollegiate Policy Debate and the Urban Debate Leagues: From a Distance, Five Years and Change Later." *Contemporary Argumentation & Debate* 27 (2006): 157–72.
Putnam, Robert D. "Bowling Alone: America's Declining Social Capital." *Journal of Democracy* 6 (1995): 65–78.
———. *Bowling Alone: The Collapse and Revival of American Community*. New York: Simon and Schuster, 2000.
Ray, Angela G. "The Permeable Public: Rituals of Citizenship in Antebellum Men's Debating Clubs." *Argumentation and Advocacy* 41 (2004): 1–16.
Rehg, William. "The Argumentation Theorist in Deliberative Democracy." *Controversia* 1 (2002): 18–42.
Reid-Brinkley, Shanara Rose. "Ghetto Kids Gone Good: Race, Representation, and Authority in the Scripting of Inner-City Youths in the Urban Debate League." *Argumentation and Advocacy* 49 (2012): 77–99.
———. "The Harsh Realities of 'Acting Black': How African-American Policy Debaters Negotiate Representation Through Racial Performance and Style." Ph.D. diss., University of Georgia, 2008.
Rogers, Jack. "A Community of Unequals: An Analysis of Dominant and Subdominant Culturally Linked Perceptions of Participation and Success Within Intercollegiate Competitive Debate." *Contemporary Argumentation & Debate* 18 (1997): 1–22.

———. "Interrogating the Myth of Multiculturalism: Toward Significant Membership and Participation of African Americans in Forensics." *Forensic of Pi Kappa Delta* 80, no. 4 (1995): 21–30.

Schwartz-Dupre, Rae Lynn. "Women in Debate: From Virtual to Material." *Contemporary Argumentation & Debate* 27 (2006): 106–20.

Sheckels, Theodore F., Jr., and Annette C. Warfield. "Parliamentary Debate: A Description and a Justification." *Argumentation and Advocacy* 27 (1990): 1–15.

Shelton, Michael W., and Cynthia K. Matthews. "Extending the Diversity Agenda in Forensics: Invisible Disabilities and Beyond." *Argumentation and Advocacy* 38 (2001): 121–31.

Skocpol, Theda. *Diminished Democracy: From Membership to Management in American Civic Life*. Norman: University of Oklahoma Press, 2003.

Snider, Alfred C., and Maxwell Schnurer. *Many Sides: Debate Across the Curriculum*. New York: International Debate Educational Association, 2002.

Stepp, Pamela L. "Can We Make Intercollegiate Debate More Diverse?" *Argumentation and Advocacy* 33 (1997): 176–91.

———. "Sexual Harassment in Communication Extra-curricular Activities: Intercollegiate Debate and Individual Events." *Communication Education* 50 (2001): 34–50.

Stepp, Pamela L., and Beth Gardner. "Ten Years of Demographics: Who Debates in America." *Argumentation and Advocacy* 38 (2001): 69–83.

Tannen, Deborah. *The Argument Culture: Moving from Debate to Dialogue*. New York: Random House, 1998.

Toulmin, Stephen. *The Uses of Argument*. New York: Cambridge University Press, 1958.

Varda, Scott. "Isocratic Citizenship: Toward a Pedagogy of Citizen Orators." In *The Functions of Argument and Social Context*, edited by Dennis Gouran, 523–28. Washington, D.C.: National Communication Association, 2010.

Verba, Sidney, Kay Lehman Schlozman, and Henry E. Brady. *Voice and Equality: Civic Voluntarism in American Politics*. Cambridge, Mass.: Harvard University Press, 1995.

Von Burg, Alessandra Beasley, Ron Von Burg, Gordon R. Mitchell, and Allan D. Louden. "Emerging Communication Technologies and the Practices of Enhanced Deliberation: The Experience of Benjamin Franklin Transatlantic Fellows Summer Institute." *Journal of Public Deliberation* 8, no. 1 (2012): 1–8.

Von Burg, Ron, Allan Louden, Alessandra Von Burg, and Bronwen Gainsford. "Debate, Civic Engagement and Post-Training Social Networking." In *Argumentation, Rhetoric, Debate and Pedagogy: Proceedings of the 2013 Fourth International Conference on Argumentation, Rhetoric, Debate, and Pedagogy*, edited by Abdel Latif Sellami, 227–38. Doha: QatarDebate Center, 2013.

Wade, James M., and Leslie Wade Zorwick. "Assigned Advocacy, Argumentation, and Debate in High School Classrooms." *Rostrum* 83, no. 8 (2009): 13–15.

Wade, Melissa Maxcy. "The Case for Urban Debate Leagues." *Contemporary Argumentation & Debate* 19 (1998): 60–65.

Waisanen, Don. "Toward Robust Public Engagement: The Value of Deliberative Discourse for Civil Communication." *Rhetoric & Public Affairs* 17 (2014): 287–322.

Warner, Ede, Jr. "Go Homers, Makeovers or Takeovers? A Privilege Analysis of Debate as a Gaming Simulation." *Contemporary Argumentation & Debate* 1 (2003): 65–80.

Warner, Ede, Jr., and Jon Bruschke. "'Gone on Debating': Competitive Academic Debate as a Tool of Empowerment." *Contemporary Argumentation & Debate* 22 (2001): 1–21.

Weeks, David, and Zhang Chengming. "Treading Carefully: Debate Topic Selection in China." *Monash Debating Review* 11 (2013): 58–64.

Wilkins, Amanda, and Jeffrey Hobbs. "A Feminist Critique of Intercollegiate Debate." *Contemporary Argumentation & Debate* 18 (1997): 57–67.

Williams, David E., Brian R. McGee, and David S. Worth. "University Student Perceptions of the Efficacy of Debate Participation: An Empirical Investigation." *Argumentation and Advocacy* 37 (2001): 198–209.

Winkler, Carol. "To Argue or to Fight: Improving At-Risk Students' School Conduct Through Urban Debate." *Controversia* 7 (2011): 76–90.

———. "Extending the Benefits of Debate: Outcomes of the Computer Assisted Debate Project." In *Concerning Argument*, edited by Scott Jacobs, 792–800. Annandale, Va.: National Communication Association, 2009.

Winkler, Carol, C. Kevin Fortner, and Sara Baugh-Harris. "Overcoming Challenges to Women in At-Risk Communities Through Urban Debate Leagues." *Forum on Public Policy* 2013, no. 1 (2013): 1–22.

Women's Debate Institute. *Women in Debate: A Best Practices Manual*. Published October 2014. http://womensdebateinstitute.org/wp-content/uploads/2014/10/WDI-Best-Practices.pdf.

Woods, Carly, Matthew Brigham, Brent Heavner, Takuzo Konishi, John Rief, Brent Saindon, and Gordon R. Mitchell. "Deliberating Debate's Digital Futures." *Contemporary Argumentation & Debate* 27 (2006): 81–105.

Young, Kelly M. "Impossible Convictions: Convictions and Intentionality in Performance and Switch-Side Debate." *Contemporary Argumentation & Debate* 32 (2011): 1–44.

Zompetti, Joseph P., and David C. Williams. "Democratic Civic Engagement and Pedagogical Pursuits: Using Argumentation and Debate to Energize Concerned Citizens." In *Concerning Argument*, edited by Scott Jacobs, 819–28. Washington, D.C.: National Communication Association, 2009.

Zorwick, M. Leslie Wade, Melissa Maxcy Wade, and Dietlinde P. Heilmayr. "Urban Debate and Prejudice Reduction: The Contact Hypothesis in Action." *Contemporary Argumentation & Debate* 30 (2009): 30–51.

CONTRIBUTORS

Jenn Anderson is an assistant professor of communication studies at South Dakota State University. Her research, which focuses on community-based projects to improve women's health, has appeared in *Health Communication*, *Journal of Health Communication*, *Qualitative Health Research*, and *Journal of Applied Communication Research*. Her work on community breastfeeding advocacy also has been covered by local, regional, and national news outlets.

Michael D. Bartanen is a professor emeritus of communication at Pacific Lutheran University. He received his Ph.D. from the University of Southern California. He is the author or coauthor of five books and numerous articles and convention papers on forensics history or pedagogy. He most recently coauthored *Forensics in America: A History* (2014), with Robert Littlefield. He was a past national officer in CEDA and Pi Kappa Delta, and has received numerous awards for contributions to forensics education.

Michael J. Bergmaier is a visiting assistant professor of communication studies at Ball State University. He received his Ph.D. from the Pennsylvania State University, where he was previously a dissertation fellow with the Center for Democratic Deliberation and a summer resident with the Institute for the Arts and Humanities. His research explores how rhetoric expands and contracts the potential of democratic deliberation over contemporary national security policy. His work on debate pedagogy and paradigm collaboration received a grant from the McCourtney Institute for Democracy.

Ann Crigler is a professor of political science in the Price School of Public Policy and the Annenberg School for Communications at the University of Southern California. After receiving her B.A. from Wellesley College and her Ph.D. from the Massachusetts Institute of Technology, she taught at Wellesley College, Tufts University, and MIT before joining the faculty at USC. Her current research and teaching focus on the role of social media in U.S. elections, youth civic engagement, and emotions and political decision making.

Sara A. Mehltretter Drury is an associate professor of rhetoric at Wabash College. She also directs the Wabash Democracy and Public Discourse initiative, an interdisciplinary program that involves undergraduate students in community deliberations and problem solving. Her research and teaching focus on rhetoric, deliberation, and democratic theory, and her work has appeared in outlets such as *Communication Quarterly*, *Argumentation and Advocacy*, and *Journal of Public Deliberation*. She received her B.A. from Boston College and her M.A. and Ph.D. from the Pennsylvania State University.

David A. Frank is a professor of rhetoric and former dean of the Robert D. Clark Honors College at the University of Oregon. Professor Frank has published on the history of twentieth-century rhetorical theory, forensic education, the rhetoric of the Israeli-Palestinian conflict, and the rhetoric of Barack Obama. With Michelle Bolduc, he has been awarded a grant from the National Endowment for the Humanities for research on the "new rhetoric" of Chaïm Perelman and Lucie Olbrechts-Tyteca. Professor Frank directed the forensics program at the University of Oregon for thirty-three years.

G. Thomas Goodnight is a professor in the Annenberg School of Communication and Journalism at the University of Southern California. While at Northwestern University, he coached NDT debate and directed the graduate program. At USC, he directed the doctoral program and teaches in the areas of argumentation, public address, and rhetoric and civil society. Goodnight is a Senior Fulbright Specialist in communication studies.

Ronald Walter Greene is a professor and chair in the Department of Communication Studies at the University of Minnesota, where he also serves on the graduate faculty in American Studies, Comparative Studies in Discourse and Society, and Writing Studies. He is the recipient of the Distinguished Scholar Award from the Critical/Cultural Studies Division of the National Communication Association, NCA's Charles H. Woolbert Research Award, and the Daniel Rohrer Memorial Outstanding Research Award from the American Forensic Association, among others.

Taylor W. Hahn is the assistant director of the master's in communication program at Johns Hopkins University. He received his Ph.D. from the University of Pittsburgh. He studies argumentation, civic engagement, and debate, and he is a coauthor of the internationally recognized textbook *Finding Your Voice:*

A Comprehensive Guide to Collegiate Policy Debate. He has coached Lincoln-Douglas debate, intercollegiate policy debate, and a variety of public debate events. He is the director of civic engagement at the Benjamin Franklin Transatlantic Fellows Summer Institute, a U.S. State Department program that annually hosts students from more than forty countries.

Darrin Hicks is a professor and the director of debate at the University of Denver. He has published extensively on argumentation, community collaboration, rhetorical theory, and debate pedagogy. His research has appeared in such journals as the *Quarterly Journal of Speech, Rhetoric and Public Affairs, Journal of Public Administration Research and Theory, Evaluation Review*, and *Argumentation*.

Edward A. Hinck is a professor of communication at Central Michigan University. He is the author of *Enacting the Presidency: Political Argument, Presidential Debates, and Presidential Character* and coauthor of *Politeness in Presidential Debates*. He has been recognized with multiple awards from Pi Kappa Delta, the national honor society for collegiate speech and debate, including the E. R. Nichols Award, the Golden Gavel Award, and the John Shields Award for Outstanding Contributions to Pi Kappa Delta. In 2013, he was recognized by the Central States Communication Association for outstanding contributions to the Argumentation and Forensics Interest Group.

J. Michael Hogan, the Edwin Erle Sparks Professor Emeritus of Rhetoric at the Pennsylvania State University, is a visiting professor and chair of communication studies at Davidson College. He is a founding director of the Center for Democratic Deliberation at Penn State and the codirector of Voices of Democracy, an educational website funded by the National Endowment for the Humanities. Hogan is the author, coauthor, or editor of eight books and more than sixty articles, book chapters, and reviews. He has won a number of scholarly awards, including the National Communication Association's Distinguished Scholar Award.

Jin Huang has degrees in journalism and marketing and studied communication management at the National University of Singapore. After receiving her master's degree in public relations from the University of Southern California, she worked for a global PR firm on corporate communication, social media, and crisis communication. She currently is a Ph.D. candidate in communication at

USC, working on privacy and disclosure, dialogic communication, and narrative engagement. Her work on online community building has appeared in *New Media & Society* and *Public Relations Review*.

Jeremy D. Johnson is a dissertation fellow with the Center for Humanities and Information at the Pennsylvania State University. His research includes digital rhetoric, democratic engagement, and forensics theory and practice. As a coach for the Penn State Speech & Debate Society, his background in forensics includes extensive experience in competitive speech and debate.

Una Kimokeo-Goes received her doctoral degree in rhetoric from the Pennsylvania State University. She teaches in the Civic Communication and Media department at Willamette University, and she is the assistant director of the Willamette University Debate Union. She also is a founding member of the Chinese Debate Education Network. In addition to argumentation and debate, her research interests include the history of U.S. imperialism and rhetoric and public memory.

Rebecca A. Kuehl is an associate professor of communication studies at South Dakota State University. Her scholarship focuses on rhetorical citizenship and public deliberation, civic rhetoric and education, and women's health discourses. Her scholarship has appeared in edited volumes such as *Rhetoric: Concord and Controversy* and *Contemporary Rhetorical Citizenship* as well as in journals such as *Southern Communication Journal, Communication Quarterly, Communication Design Quarterly*, and *Journal of Human Lactation*.

Jessica A. Kurr is a postdoctoral fellow at the Pennsylvania State University, where she also received her Ph.D. and previously served as the director of debate from 2013 to 2017. She has organized more than twenty public deliberation events and developed a summer workshop for Chinese high school students at Penn State. Her scholarly research focuses on public address, argumentation, and economic rhetoric, and she has received awards and grants to support her work from various scholarly organizations, including the Gerald R. Ford Presidential Foundation, the Center for Democratic Deliberation, the American Society for the History of Rhetoric, and the History of Economics Society.

Lorand Laskai is a lead researcher at Danwei, an internet and media research service of the *Financial Times*. He graduated from Swarthmore College in 2013, where he debated on the APDA circuit. After graduating, he combined his love of debating and his interest in China to help build and expand the National High School Debate League of China. He is proficient in both spoken and written Chinese.

Tim Lewis received his B.A. in history from Bard College and his master's in education from Harvard University. He taught history and debate at the Bronx High School of Science, and he also served as the academic director of the National High School Debate League of China. He founded the Bard College Parliamentary Debate Union, and he has coached high school debate. While at Harvard, Lewis worked with the Boston Debate League, co-organizing the Debate Across the Curriculum initiative in the Boston Public Schools.

Robert S. Littlefield is a professor and the director of the Nicholson School of Communication at the University of Central Florida. He is the author, coauthor, or editor of six books and has published more than seventy-five journal articles. From 2013 to 2015, he served as editor of *Communication Studies*, the journal of the Central States Communication Association. He is coauthor of *Forensics in America: A History*. He served as president of Pi Kappa Delta, the national forensics honorary society, from 1991 to 1993 and was inducted into Pi Kappa Delta's Hall of Fame in 2007.

Allan D. Louden is a professor and chair of the Department of Communication at Wake Forest University. His research focuses on argumentation theory, political communication, and debate. He has published his research in several journals, including *Argumentation and Advocacy* and *Journal of Public Deliberation*, and he has worked on political campaigns as a communication consultant. He also received a U.S. State Department grant for the Benjamin Franklin Transatlantic Fellows Summer Initiative, a debate-oriented educational program that hosts students from forty countries.

Paul E. Mabrey III has a Ph.D. in strategic leadership studies and is the coordinator of the Communication Center at James Madison University, where he also previously served as the assistant director of debate. He is on the editorial board of *Contemporary Argumentation & Debate* and was formerly president of the Cross Examination Debate Association.

Jamie McKown is the James Russell Wiggins Chair of Government and Polity at the College of the Atlantic in Bar Harbor, Maine. As an active participant in the educational debate community for more than a decade, he is now involved in an ongoing research project to document the emergence of intercollegiate debate as a practice in the United States during the late nineteenth century. He received his B.A. in political science from Emory University, his M.A. in public communication from Georgia State University, and his Ph.D. in communication from Northwestern University.

Gordon R. Mitchell is an associate professor of communication and assistant dean of the University Honors College at the University of Pittsburgh. Mitchell's research program focuses on rhetoric, argumentation, and debate. He is the author of the award-winning book *Strategic Deception* and has published more than forty articles and book chapters in leading scholarly outlets. Mitchell has also presented his work at the World Policy Institute and the Belgian Royal Defence College, and his work on intelligence analysis has been featured in nationally syndicated op-eds and official government reports.

Catherine H. Palczewski is a professor of communication studies and women's and gender studies at the University of Northern Iowa, where she also served as the director of debate from 1994 to 2009. Her work focuses on how marginalized groups rhetorically gain access to the dominant public sphere. She directed the AFA/NCA Biennial Conference on Argumentation in 2013 and edited its selected works: *Disturbing Argument* (2014). Her coauthored publications include *Gender in Communication* (2014) and *Rhetoric in Civic Life* (2016).

Angela G. Ray is an associate professor in the Department of Communication Studies at Northwestern University, where she recently held the Charles Deering McCormick Professorship of Teaching Excellence. Her scholarship focuses on rhetorical criticism and history, with an emphasis on popular media, education, and social reform in the nineteenth-century United States. Her 2005 book, *The Lyceum and Public Culture in the Nineteenth-Century United States*, won five major awards, including the Diamond Anniversary Book Award and the Winans-Wichelns Award from the National Communication Association.

Robert C. Rowland is a professor and the director of graduate studies in communication at the University of Kansas. He has published more than one hundred essays in the *Quarterly Journal of Speech, Rhetoric & Public Affairs, Communication Theory, Philosophy and Rhetoric, Communication Monographs,* and other journals. He has also published three books, one of which (*Shared Land/Conflicting Identity*, with David Frank) won the Kohrs-Campbell Prize in rhetorical criticism. Among his scholarly awards is the Douglas W. Ehninger Distinguished Rhetorical Scholar Award from the National Communication Association.

Minhee Son is a postdoctoral research associate at the University of Southern California's Annenberg School of Communication and Journalism. Her work employs mixed-method approaches to identify media and other communication resources that immigrants and ethnic minorities utilize to improve their local conditions. With a keen interest in the role of social context, she has collaborated with community organizations, local media, schools, churches, and other institutions to understand contemporary challenges and opportunities for civic engagement in twenty-first-century urban society.

Sarah Stone Watt is the divisional dean of communication and former director of forensics at Pepperdine University. She earned her Ph.D. at the Pennsylvania State University in rhetoric and women's studies. Her research and teaching focus on the intersections of race, gender, media, and social change in the United States.

Melissa Maxcy Wade is the president of the Glenn Pelham Foundation for Debate Education. She served for forty-three years as the executive director of forensics in the Barkley Forum Center for Debate Education at Emory University, where she was a faculty member in the Division of Educational Studies. She is a principal founder of the Urban Debate League's national education movement. She serves on the Board of Directors of the International Public Policy Debate Forum and has been a political commentator on U.S. presidential debates for various national media since 1976.

David Weeks is the president and cofounder of the National High School Debate league of China (NHSDLC) and the COO of Sunrise International Education. Since he cofounded the NHSDLC, the organization has expanded to running regional and national debate tournaments in thirty-three cities across mainland China, training about fifty thousand students each year. He has been involved in high school Lincoln-Douglas and Public Forum debate since 2002. He graduated from Swarthmore College in 2010 with a B.A. in political science and East Asian studies. He is proficient in Mandarin.

Carly S. Woods received her Ph.D. from the University of Pittsburgh and is now an assistant professor in the Department of Communication at the University of Maryland. Her research and teaching focus on rhetorical history, gender studies, public address, and argumentation. Her essays have been published in *Quarterly Journal of Speech*, *Women's Studies in Communication*, *Argumentation and Advocacy*, *Contemporary Argumentation & Debate*, and *KB Journal*. She is working on a book-length study of women's debating societies in the United States and the United Kingdom.

David Zarefsky is the Owen L. Coon Professor Emeritus of Argumentation and Debate and professor emeritus of communication studies at Northwestern University. His research and teaching are in the areas of rhetorical history and criticism, argumentation and debate, and forensics. He is the author, coauthor, or editor of nine books and the author of more than one hundred articles in professional journals. He is a Distinguished Scholar of the National Communication Association and a Fellow of the Rhetoric Society of America, and served as president of both organizations. He directed Northwestern's intercollegiate debate program from 1970 to 1975.

INDEX

Page numbers in italics refer to illustrations.

AACU. *See* Association of American Colleges and Universities
activation of social norms, and backfire effect, 99
Adler, Mortimer, 177, 178, 181, 182, 185
advocacy-based civic education, 221
affective atmosphere, 151, 152, 154, 157, 158, 161
affective bonds
  as basis of all civic engagement, 211
  Penny Harvest's creation of, 211, 215, 219, 220
African American debate clubs, antebellum popularity of, 28
African American debate clubs in antebellum Charleston. *See also* Clionian Debating Society
  benefits for individual debaters, 26–28, 34
  number of, 26, 290n3
  and value of debate in conditions of oppression, 25, 28, 34–35
African Americans
  and debate participation as project for community empowerment, 161
  decreasing levels of trust in, 164
  women, first to win national debate championship, 166
aidos (respect for communicative partners), in Mendelson's theory of antilogic, 102, 103
Albiniak, Theodore, 238
Algerian liberation movement, 110, 119–20
Allen, Danielle, 164, 166–70, 172
Alliance for Excellent Education, 223
all-purpose arguments, xiii
American Debate Association, and resources for engaging larger public, 134–35
The American Debater (McElligott), 31
American Democracy Project, 239
American Forensic Association, 10

American Political Science Association (APSA), 20–21
American Political Science Review, 269
antilogic theory of Mendelson, 101, 102–4, 106
arbiters, third party, as model of democratic deliberation, xi
Arcecilaus, 102–3
Arendt, Hannah, 167
argumentative dialogue
  and building relationships with others, 180
  developing skills for, 177
  and dialogue as means of relating to others in different moral worlds, 180–81
  as foundation of Western knowledge, 258
  usefulness to debate pedagogy, 180
argument culture, feminist critiques of, 105
argument mapping strategy, and elimination of cognitive biases, 98
arguments, levels of critical thinking about, 182–83
Aristotle, 47, 68, 172, 209
Armstron, Karen, 108
Arneson, Pat, 143
Arnett, Ronald C., 143
Arnot, Madeline, 286n37
Asen, Robert, 252, 256, 264
Association of American Colleges and Universities (AACU)
  and civic education in higher education, 66, 67, 74, 127
  Core Commitments initiative, 67
ataraxia (inner tranquility), 102–3, 107
audience
  debiasing techniques for, 99–101, *100*, 106–7
  and "in-round vision," 183
  problem of, in debate theory, 49
  skills needed for judging impact on, 183
  specific, as focus in technical era, 64, 72
  and transfer challenge, 94–95

audience (*continued*)
  universal: and debate as civic education, 91; as focus in public oratory era, 64, 72; re-inclusion of in modern debate, 76 or Worlds-style debate, 253–54

backfire effects
  psychology of, 99
  rebuttals and, 95, 99–101, *100*, 106
Baird, A. Craig, 69
Baker, George P., 47–50, *48*, 52
Baldwin, Charles Sears, 37, 47
Bartanen, Michael, 81, 108, 152
Beaird, Simeon W., 25–28, 34
Bellen, Joseph, 238
Ben-Gurion, David, 120
Benjamin Franklin Transatlantic Fellows Summer Institute (BFTF), 237–49
  avoidance of U.S.-centric framework, 239
  and coupling of civic engagement and debate training, 237, 240, 245–46, 247–48
  and cross-cultural exchanges, educational value of, 240, 242–43
  focus on individualized education, 240
  instruction in debate and advocacy, 239, 240, 241, 242–44, 245–46
  overview of program, 237, 239
  pedagogical lessons learned in, 247–48
  and promotion of civic engagement, 239–40; 2007–2008 program structure, 241–42, 248; 2011 program structure, 242–45, 248; 2014 program structure, 245–47, 248; experimentation with, 237, 238, 240; success in, 244–45, 247–48; work in community volunteer projects, 239, 241–42, 246
  skills developed in, 237, 248
  study trip, 239
  success of alumni, 249
Bennett, W. Lance, 5
BFTF. *See* Benjamin Franklin Transatlantic Fellows Summer Institute
Biddle, Francis, 154
Bishop, Bill, 96
bizarre arguments, as counterproductive practice, xiii
Bloom, Benjamin S., 182
boomerang effects
  psychology of, 99
  rebuttals and, 99–101, *100*, 106
both-sides debating. *See* switch-sides debating; cultural technology of tournament debate

Bowling Alone (Putnam), 3
Brigance, W. Norwood, 191
Brockriede, Wayne, 180
Broschke, Jon, 238
Brouwer, Daniel, 252
Bsumek, Pete, 128
budgets of colleges and universities, and justifications for forensic education, 77
Burgoon, Michael, 138
Burke, Kenneth, 118, 121
Burns, James M., 153
Byrne, Sahara, 99

Cacioppo, John, 184
Cardozo, Henry, 27, 33
Carneades, 102–3, 107
Castella, Leah, 146
CBYOs. *See* community-based youth organizations
CEDA. *See* Cross Examination Debate Association
CEDA–Miller Center War Powers Debates, 125–35
  and CEDA–Miller Center partnership, benefits of, 130
  civic value of, 132–35
  and civility, 133
  coordination with collegiate debate season, 129
  and curriculum development, 133
  and debaters as civic educators, 132
  and engagement with larger community, 133–35
  format for, 129, 130–31
  large audience for, 131
  media coverage of, 130
  participant selection, 132
  and role of intercollegiate debate in debate of national issues, 126
  topic selection for, 125–26, 131
  venues for, 130, 131
Center for Information and Research on Civic Learning and Engagement (CIRCLE), 4, 5
Chafets, Zev, 115–16
Charleston, antebellum, free black community in, 28–29. *See also* African American debate clubs in antebellum Charleston
Chautauqua movement, progressive revival of, 7
Chen Zhili, 271

INDEX   333

China
   citizenship concept in, 257
   civic apathy in, 274
   fear of exposure to Western ideas, 274
   moral crisis in, 274
   reform as people-based concept in, 270
   valuing of debate skills in, 257, 258
China, and *suzhi jiaoyu* (character education)
   as alternative to traditional testing-based education, 265, 270–71
   as complex concept, 265–66, 269–70
   definition of, 269–70
   as parallel to Western "twenty-first century skills," 266, 272, 274
   role of debate in, 265, 266
   as state-focused education, 271
   vs. *suyang*, 270
China, debate in. *See also* China Debate Education Network (CDEN); National High School Debate League of China (NHSDLC)
   and civic engagement, 257, 258, 266, 275
   cultural preference for indirect statement and, 261
   as exclusively elite practice until early twenty-first century, 266
   and Four Cs of "twenty-first century skills," 272
   as modernizing force in education, 272–73, 275
   as new experience for most students, 272–73
   and one-party state, nature of debate in, 257, 259–60, 265, 274–75
   popularity of, 265, 266, 273
   popularity of English-language debate, 267
   and *suzhi jiaoyu* (character education), 265, 266
   types of debate, 267
   types of topics, 266–67
   typical format for, 266
China, diplomatic relations with, as national topic for 1954-1955
   Cold War political atmosphere and, 152–54
   and conscience of debater, as issue, 69–70
   and relocation of debaters' convictions to debate as democratic technique, 153–57, 298n11
China, education in. *See also* China, and *suzhi jiaoyu* (character education)
   Communist reforms, 268
   and conceptual stretching of terms, 269
   difficulty of reforming, 269, 271
   and Gaokao (National Higher Education Entrance Exam), 268–69
   history of, 267–69
   and Imperial Examination, 267–68
   school schedule as fully absorbing, 273
   traditional testing-based education, 267–69, 270, 275
   and twenty-first century skills, need to acquire, 271–72
China Debate Education Network (CDEN), 256–61
   benefits for Western participants, 260
   and civic education, 250–51, 256, 257, 261
   and civic engagement, 258
   and debate in one-party state, 257, 259–60
   English vs. Mandarin divisions of, 261
   founding of, 256
   structure of program, 256–57
   students' views on, 257–60
   topics debated in, 259–60
   women debaters in, 260–61
Christianity
   and reason, compatibility of, 108–9, 111
   and rhetoric, 117
Christiano, Thomas, 82
Cicero
   and switch-sides debating, 103
   theory of "doctus orator," 179
CIRCLE. *See* Center for Information and Research on Civic Learning and Engagement
circular questioning, and development of *humanitas*, 188–89
citizens
   lack of public knowledge in, 86
   passions of as threat to democracy, Madison on, 84–85, 89
   skills needed by, Madison on, 87–88
citizenship
   Chinese conception of, 257
   definitions of, non-state-based, 252
   definitions of, state-based, 251
   as discursive phenomenon, 252
   and just communication, 178–79
   as male-dominated narrative, 286n37
   as mode of public engagement, 256
   as performed, 250
   rights and responsibilities of: as motive for women's education, 62; speech and debate education and, 2, 8
   as sexed/gendered, 136, 140–42
   universities' role in developing, 250

citizenship (*continued*)
    and women, inclusionary promise vs. exclusionary reality of, 62
    and working out differences with others, 178
citizenship skills, training for development of, 181
civic awareness, debate and, 274
civic education
    academic freedom and, 66, 67
    advocacy-based, 221
    assessment of, as issue, 66–67
    CEDA–Miller Center War Powers Debates and, 132–35
    China Debate Education Network and, 250–51, 256, 257, 261
    as complement to job success, 128
    components of, 67
    definition of, ix–x
    diversity as issue in, 62
    elitist focus of, as issue, 65
    exclusion from modern speech and debate textbooks, 8
    importance to democracy, 87–89, 92, 127
    inclusiveness, strategies for, 62–63
    liberatory forms of, 148
    loss of shared values and, 65
    Madison on necessity of, 87–89, 92
    necessity of, for participation in public life, ix–x
    as Progressive goal, 7
    renewed interest in: with emergence of intercollegiate debate, 37, 45–46, 49–50; and speech and debate programs, 128–29; in twenty-first century, 5–6, 128–29
    role in higher education, debate on, 1–2, 19–20, 65–68, 127
    as sexed/gendered, 136
    as standard for evaluation of debate practices, xii–xiv
    state-based definitions of citizenship and, 251
    in twenty-first century, characteristics of, 127, 128
    Urban Debate Leagues and, 225, 227, 228
    Women's Debate Institute and, 146–48
    Worlds-style debate and, 250–51, 261, 263, 264
civic education, as rationale for debate, ix, x–xi, 1–2, 73–77, 127–29, 190
    as common belief, 81–82, 128
    fraying of relationship, 64
    Madison and, 89–91, 93
    and norms of academic vs. real-world debate, 82, 95, 184–85
    opposition to, 19–20
    in public oratory era, 64
    racist, sexist, and cisist discrimination and, 136, 137, 295n1
    and universalization of liberal cultural norms, 149, 150, 157–61
    value of recognizing, xi, xiv
    vs. winning: and choice of debate topic, 69; greater importance of educational benefit, ix; need to restore balance between, 64, 68; pendulum swings between poles of, 68; strategies for restoring balance between, 75–77; and trained vs. untrained judges, 69, 72–73; twentieth-century shift of balance toward winning, 64, 68–73; Women's Debate Institute and, 146–47
civic empowerment gap, strategies for closing, 6
civic engagement. *See also* Benjamin Franklin Transatlantic Fellows Summer Institute (BFTF); civic education; public deliberation
    affective bonds as basis of, 211
    civic rhetoric as skill needed for, 192
    communities of belonging and, 217
    communities of practice and, 218
    and debate, in China, 257, 258, 266, 275
    decline of traditional forms of, 3–4
    in diverse urban societies, skills needed for, 212–13
    as goal of debate, xi, 248
    literacy as gateway to, 231
    new forms of, 4–5
    in nondemocratic nations, 251
    Penny Harvest and, 206–7, 213–18, 220
    public deliberation and, 192, 203
    as sexed/gendered, 140–42
    universities' importance role in developing, 250
    and upward mobility, 127–28
    Urban Debate Leagues and, 222, 224, 225, 226, 229–30, 232, 233
    use of "live" public policy topics and, 37, 45–46, 49–50, 51
    of women: and men's fear of emasculation, 140–41
        obstacles to, 137; Worlds-style debate and, 251
civic health of U.S.
    declining civic engagement and, 3–4

INDEX   335

speech and debate education as remedy for, 2–3, 5
civic knowledge, public deliberation and, 197–98
civic mission discarded (CMD) model of education, 66, 68
civic mission reclaimed (CMR) model of education, 66, 68
    role of forensics in, 73–77
civic virtue, modern relevance of, as issue, 10
civic voluntarism model, civic skills and, 212
civility
    and CEDA–Miller Center War Powers Debates, 133
    as obstacle to productive debate, 142–45
    performative debate and, 9
    vs. politeness, 143
    speech and debate community as role model for, 76–77
Civil War and Reconstruction, 25, 27, 34, 38
Clark, Frank, 141
classical rhetorical tradition, ethical emphasis of, 6
Clinton, Hillary, 94
Clionian Debating Society, 25–35
    Beaird and, 25, 26
    debate structure in, 30
    and enactment of community involvement, 26–27, 29
    as enclave public, 26–27
    enthusiasm of debates in, 33–34
    as exclusively male, 26
    forced dissolution of, 26
    and free black community in antebellum Charleston, 28–29
    and gratification of intellectual curiosity, 35
    library at, 30, 35
    meetings and activities, 29–30
    members' postwar careers, 27
    and national culture of debate, 28
    questions debated by, 25, 26, 30–33
    slaveholders among, 29, 32
    and slavery, avoidance of topic, 32–33
CMD. *See* civic mission discarded (CMD) model of education
CMM. *See* Coordinated Management of Meaning (CMM) project
CMR. *See* civic mission reclaimed (CMR) model of education
coaches. *See also* Schug, Chayton H.
    early debate on appropriateness of, 284n16
    mentoring by: and circular questions, 188–89; and development of *humanitas*, 186–89; and systemic understanding, cultivation of, 187
    power to influence larger culture, 62–63
    for women, history of, 54
    in Worlds-style debate, 253
Coalescent Argumentation (Gilbert), 101, 104
cocurricular programs, need for, 3
cognitive biases. *See* debiasing techniques; motivated reasoning
cognitive brain science, on passion's influence on decisions, 85–86
Cohen, Herman, 193
Cold War
    and diplomatic relations with China as national topic for 1954-1955, 152–54
    and selection of debate topics, 69-70
    and shift to technical era of debate, 71-72
collaboration
    public deliberation as training in, 201–2, 202–3
    skills needed for, 194
Common Core State Standards, Debate Across the Curriculum program and, 228
communication
    community-building, as index of good society, 178
    heterogeneous norms of, in multicultural urban society, 209–10
    successful, Peters on, 178
communication across different social worlds
    argumentative dialogue and, 180–81
    CMM project on, 179–81
    debate training to develop, 181–85
    strategies for, 179–80
communication curriculum, benefits of including public deliberation in, 191, 192, 194, 203–4
Communication Education, 138
communities of belonging, Penny Harvest program's strengthening of, 207, 208, 213–14, 215–17, 220
communities of practice
    Penny Harvest program and, 207, 208, 214–15, 215–16, 217–18
    Urban Debate Leagues and, 221, 225–26, 227, 228, 229–30, 231, 232–33
community
    and civility vs. productive debate, 142–45
    community-building communication, as index of good society, 178

community (*continued*)
concern for: balancing with argumentative technique, 177, 179–81, 183–85; debate training to develop, 181–85; development of, as goal, 74, 180
debate as means of developing, xiii
as necessity for public deliberation, 211, 213–14
new emphasis on in civic education, 128
Women's Debate Institute and, 146–48
Community Activist debates, 231
community-based youth organizations (CBYOs), as barrier to civic engagement, 212–13
community beyond university
benefits of engaging, 135
speech and debate as means of engaging, 133–35
community of speech and debate participants
and growing levels of distrust in U.S., 164
modern fragmenting of, 10, 73
need to restore civil debate within, 76–77
comparison of arguments
skills needed for, 182–83
value of, in civic debate, 184–85
competitive model of debate. *See also* intercollegiate debate, emergence of; winning
and competition as motivation for learning, x, 68–69, 183–84
and development of concern for community, 183–85
and fragmenting of debate organizations, 10
replacement of with political friendship model, 165, 169–73
Computer Assisted Debate (CAD), 230–31
confined influence backfire effect, *100*
conflict between debaters, and coaches' teaching of *humanitas*, 186–89
convictions of debater
as affective, bodily, and collective, 151–52, 161
as issue in switch-sides debating, 69–70, 114, 149–50, 153
relocation of from issues to debate as democratic technique, 150, 153–57, 161; and ethical distancing of knowledge class, 150, 157
cooperative argumentation strategy
classroom exercises for, 105
vs. competitive strategies, choice in deployment of, 107

and debiasing techniques, 105–6
long table format and, 131
Coordinated Management of Meaning (CMM) project, 179. *See also* Pearce, W. Barnett
application to argumentation studies, 181
on communication across different social worlds, 179–81
and development of *humanitas*, 186–89
and management of differences with others, 177, 180
Coppersmith, Mimi Barash, 61
cost of higher education, and pressure for career-focused education, 66, 67–68
Council of Conservative Citizens, 9
Counterpublics and the State (Asen and Brouwer), 252
counterpublics theory, and citizenship concept, 252
creativity, as skill learned in debate, 185
critical theory-based arguments, counterproductive practices employing, xiii
critical thinking, levels of, 182
critical thinking skills
debate and, 224, 225, 228, 242, 253, 257–58
public deliberation and, 199–200
criticism, as sign of respect, 145
Cronen, Vernon, 181
Cross Examination Debate Association (CEDA). *See also* CEDA–Miller Center War Powers Debates
lack of guidelines on appropriate content, 165
national tournament of 2008, collapse into shouting match, 8
national tournament of 2014, nontraditional debate styles in, 9
and performance debate, 9, 166, 167
and resources for engaging larger public, 134–35
A Crucible Moment (NTFCLDE), 5–6, 127, 132, 177, 192, 194
cultural technology of tournament debate
switch-sides debate as occasion to challenge, 149
embedding of white supremacy in, 150, 158–61, 165, 168–69; necessity of white recognition of, 171
and exclusion of minority participants, 158–61
and removal of ethical claims from lived bodies, 159

social activists' rejection of, 159–62
and universalization of liberal cultural norms, 149, 150, 157–61
curriculum
CEDA–Miller Center War Powers Debates and, 133
Debate Across the Curriculum instructional methods, 228
curriculum on speech and debate
benefits of including public deliberation in, 191, 192, 194, 203–4
as core of liberal arts education, 3
emergence of intercollege debate and, 46–50
increase in, benefits to critical thinking skills, 75, 93
issues in, 3
and mythos, value of including, 111
secular roots of, 108
traditional, alternatives to, 20
turn from oration to critical thinking and argument, 46–50
value of including mythos in, 111

Dalton, Russell, 4
Davis, Michael, 128
Davy, Kate, 143
Day, Dennis, 155–56
debate. *See* speech and debate
Debate Across the Curriculum instructional methods, 228
debate program directors, lack of requisite training, xii
The Debater (Rowton), 31
Debaters of Color Forum, 263
debate societies in nineteenth century. *See also* African American debate clubs in antebellum Charleston; literary/debate societies of nineteenth century
books with suggested debate questions, 31
male privilege and, 25, 26, 28
popularity of, 28
Debating in the Colonial Chartered Colleges (Potter), 38
debiasing techniques
antilogic theory and, 101, 102–4, 106
and *ataraxia* (inner tranquility), 107
for audiences, 99–101, *100*, 106–7
and cooperative argumentation strategy, 105–6
Gilbert's coalescent argumentation theory and, 101, 104, 106
for individuals, 98–99, 101

Lewandowsky strategies for, *100*, 100–101, *102*, 103, 104, 106–7
limited applicability of, 106
and risk of rebiasing, 107
transfer challenge and, 101
deliberative democracy. *See* public deliberation
Delli Carpini, Michael X., 3–4
Dello-Iacovo, Belinda, 271
demagoguery, as danger to free society
switch-sides debating as bulwark against, 153–54, 155–56, 161–62
speech and debate education and, 2, 8, 20
democracy
deliberative, and need to justify decisions, 84–85
importance of civic education in, 87–89, 92, 127
Madison on threats to, 83–85, 89
U.S., basis on deliberative debate, 92
democratic debate
education in, as necessity in democracy, 1–2, 191
exposure to, as benefit of speech and debate, xi
Internet echo chambers and, 5
and irreconcilable differences of opinion, xi
and third party arbiters, xi
Dewey, John, 7, 206, 208–9, 211, 213
Dialogic Civility in a Cynical Age (Arnett and Arneson), 143
Dillard-Knox, Tiffany Y, 300n6
disabled students, and diversity in speech and debate, 9
disagreement
continuing debate despite, 142–45
and democratic deliberation, xi
speech and debate's lessons on, 145
and third party arbiters, xi
dissertation, three-minute, 76
diversity. *See also* minority groups; people of color; performance/identity debate; urban society, diverse; women
awareness of, speech and debate education and, 2
and civic empowerment gap, 6
and empowering of disempowered groups through debate, 161, 221, 222, 227, 228, 231, 238, 263
exposure to, as benefit of speech and debate, xi
impact of increase in, on style and arguments, 261

diversity (*continued*)
    and inclusion as civic ideal, 55, 62–63
    as issue in civic education, 62
    lack of, in speech and debate programs: criticisms of, 8; efforts to remedy, 8–9, 10, 19, 261; Worlds-style debate and, 262–63
    and loss of shared values, 65
    necessity of grappling with, 169
    new pedagogical strategies demanded by, 3, 6
    performance debate and, 164
    teaching toleration and, 286n36
doctoral degrees in speech and debate, introduction of, 7
drone air strikes, as issue, 126, 132–33
Du Bois, W. E. B., 35
Duncan, Arne, 221–22, 273–74
Dwight, Theodore, 30–31

Eastman, Carolyn, 140
Eberly, Rosa, 252
echo chambers
    democratic debate and, 5
    increase in, 94–95
    and motivated reasoning, 96
educational institutions. *See also* curriculum on speech and debate
    civic education as fundamental obligation of, 1–2
    and liberal education, declining support for, 20
    as remedy for declining civic health of U.S., 2–3
education in speech and debate
    civic education as goal of, ix, x–xi, 1–2; Madison's on, 89–91, 93; opposition to, 19–20; value of recognizing, xi, xiv
    comprehensive programs, need for, xiv
    criticisms of as elitist, 8
    debate on best practices in, 238
    development of *humanitas* as goal of, 179, 180
    in early twentieth century, 7, 193
    ethics as necessary component of, 8, 10
    focus on Kahneman's "deliberative thinking" in, 97
    history of, 206
    importance to free democratic society, 1–2, 191
    and improved reasoning power, 2
    as key to civic health, 2–3, 5
    modern, characteristics of, 7–8, 128
    necessary reforms in, 8, 10, 20–21
    nineteenth-century, and male privilege, 25, 26, 28
    portability of skills developed in, 238, 241, 247
    public deliberation in, 193–94
    speech departments, development of, 70–71
    translation into civic engagement, 238
Eisenhower, Jean Hootman, 60
Eliasoph, Nina, 212–13
Ellison, Ralph, 166, 167–68, 170
Emery, Emogene, 61
Emory University, and Urban Debate Leagues, 227, 230, 232
empathy for others
    and political friendship, 170–73
    public deliberation as training in, 201–2
    and recognition of minority sacrifices, 170
engagement, as necessary condition of civility, 142–45
Enlightenment
    and Madison's views on reason, 87
    and origin of U.S. speech and debate programs, 108
    and reason as insufficient defense against prejudice, racism, and anti-Semitism, 112, 120
epoche (suspension of judgment)
    and debiasing, 105, 107
    in Mendelson's theory of antilogic, 102, 103
equal opportunity in higher education, consensus on value of, 65–66
ESL (English as second language) debaters, bias against, 262
ethical reasoning, development of, as goal of speech and debate education, 74–75
ethical reciprocity, and political friendship model of debate, 171
ethics of speech and debate. *See also* convictions of debater
    and civic education, 74
    classical rhetorical tradition's emphasis on, 6
    early concerns about, 51
    exclusion of from modern textbooks, 8
    as necessary part of speech and debate education, 8, 10
    NTFCLDE emphasis on, 6
European Universities Debating Championship, 253–54, 263
expert opinion, Madison on, 88, 289n38

factions, as threat to democracy, Madison on, 83
faculty in argumentation and rhetoric
  power to influence larger society, 62–63
  rise of intercollegiate debate and, 43–44, 51, 284n16
faculty in speech communication, role in debate programs, 53, 284n1
Falwell, Jerry, 115
familiarity backfire effect, 100
The Fear of Freedom (Biddle), 154
The Federalist Papers, 82–84, 86, 88–89
feminists, critiques of argument culture, 105
final summary for general audience, benefits of, 76
Firkins, O. W., 46
First Amendment, and hate speech, 118–19
Foner, Eric, 27
Forensics in America (Bartanen and Littlefield), 108, 152
Frazer, Nancy, 252
free speech
  as democratic technique, debate and, 150, 153–57, 161
  hate speech and, 118–19
  limits of, importance of education on, 2, 8
  as proof of American exceptionalism, 150, 155
Freire, Paulo, 225
Friedman, Ina Rosen, 60

gamification of debate
  and class formation, 156–57, 299n34
  in early twentieth century, 299n34
  necessity of casting off, in liberatory forms of debate, 160–61
  relocation of debaters' convictions to debate as technique and, 150, 158, 161
gender, vs. sex, 295n1
gender identities, marginalized, Women's Debate Institute support of, 146–47, 297n39
gender roles, and outspoken women as disagreeable and unfeminine, 136–38, 140–42, 143, 145, 147
Generation X, civil engagement of, 4
Gilbert, Michael, 101, 104, 106
globalization of debate, calls for, 264
Glover, Renee, 231
Goodnight, G. Thomas, 130
Grandpre, Lawrence, 159, 160–61
Gray, Edward W., 140–41

A Guide to Forming and Conducting Lyceums, Debating Societies, &c. (Morley), 31
Gutmann, Amy, 84, 286n36
Gwynn, Aubrey, 178–79

Habermas, Jürgen, 252
Haidt, Jonathan, 85–86
Hall, Michael, 115–16
Hardy, Aaron, 9
Hart, Phillip, 99
Hart, Sol, 99
Harvard University
  and intercollegiate debate, emergence of, 38, 39–40, 50, 68
  and intercollegiate debate curriculum, 47–50
hate speech, First Amendment and, 118–19
hegemonic social systems, arguments assuming, as counterproductive, xiii
Helping America's Youth Initiative, 231
Herzl, Theodor, 110
higher education, role in civic education, 1–2, 19–20, 65–68, 127
Highsaw, James Leonard, 125
Hines, Darlene Clark, 35
historically black colleges
  and debate as force for social change, 70
  debate programs in, and inclusiveness, 63
  as early adopters of debate, 70
  and Worlds-Style debate, 63
Holocaust, and reason without moral restraint, 120
honor societies, 70
  and balance of civic and competitive conceptions of debate, 70, 71
Hooker, Juliet, 169, 170, 172
hooks, bell, 143
Huber, Joan, 59
humanitas
  balancing with argumentative technique, 179–81
  debate training to develop, 181, 185–89
  development of, as goal in debate pedagogy, 179, 180
humanities, erosion of support for, 20
humility about correctness of opinions
  as benefit of speech and debate, xi
  exposure to cultural differences and, xi
Hyames, Isadore A., 27

identity debate. *See* performance/identity debate

imitation, in antilogic tradition, 103–4
individual perspectives, individual's blindness to cultural forces shaping, 171
informed logic tradition, 289n36
Intercollege Debates (Nichols), 37–38
intercollegiate debate, emergence of, 36–52
  and audience, focus on, 49
  and college debate curriculum, 46–50
  and decline in student participation, 51
  as distinct from history of oratorical instruction, 36
  documentation on, 37–38
  evolution into intellectual sport, concerns about, 48, 51, 52
  factors in popularity of, 40–41
  Harvard-Yale debates of 1892: explosion of interest following, 38, 39–40, 50, 68; minor intercollegiate debates prior to, 38, 39, 283–84n13, 283n9
  and hiring of speech and debate faculty, 43–44, 51, 284n16
  and hope for mutual support of state and college, 46
  institutions active in, 46
  large audiences for, 41, 42, 45, 46, 51
  in last decade of nineteenth century, 37
  limited research on, 36
  national tournament competitions and, 71, 72
  and new focus on persuasive argument vs. elocution, 37, 40, 42, 46–50
  and old collegiate debate societies, withering of, 41–44
  and renewed engagement with political issues, 37
  research project on, 37, 38–39, 52
  student publications as source on, 39
  use of "live" public policy issues as topics, 44; detailed research required by, 44–45, 51; and turn from focus on individual talent to civic engagement, 37, 45–46, 49–50, 51
intercollegiate debate, role in debate of national issues, 126
Internet
  and civic engagement, evolving forms of, 5
  and growth of Worlds-style debate, 254
  and opinion echo chambers, 5
Interstate Oratory Contest, 71
Iraq War, and public debate, 82
Islam, reason-based argument in, 110, 111
Isocrates, 178–79

Jenkins, Earnestine, 35
job success, civic education as complement to, 128
Johnson, Korey, 9, 166–67
Johnson, Steven, 258
Johnstone, Henry, 180, 185, 189–90
Judaism, and reason, 111
judges
  community members as, 41, 43
  and ideological commitments as obstacle to objectivity, 70, 91
  as models of citizen audience, xi
  mutually preferred judging and, 173, 302n52
  trained vs. untrained, 69, 72–73
  in Worlds-style debate, 253
judging
  in political friendship model of debate, 171, 172–73
  revisions to emphasis civic responsibility, 75
  revisions to rebalance rhetorical canons, 76
just communication, rhetorical training and, 178–79

Kahan, Daniel, 96
Kahneman, Daniel, 85, 87, 88, 96–97, 97, 106
Kaine, Tim, 130, 133–34
Keith, William M., 53, 128, 299n34
Kennedy, George, 116–17
Keyes, Corey, 66–67
Kim, Heejung, 210
Kipnis, Andrew, 271
Knauff, Harriet Morgan, 57
knowledge about arguments, levels of, 182–83
Koch, Christian, 252
Koger, Larry, 29
Kozol, Jonathan, 223–24, 229

Lave, Jean, 225
LBS. *See* Leaders of a Beautiful Struggle
leaders, unenlightened, Madison on, 83–84
leadership, debate training as preparation for, 27–28
Leaders of a Beautiful Struggle (LBS), 233
learning, participation and, 225
Lee, Edward, 222, 223, 224, 226–27, 230, 232
Levinson, Meira, 6
Lewandowsky, Stephan, 100, 100–101, *102*, 103, 104, 106–7
Liang Qichao, 270
liberal education, erosion of support for, 20

INDEX 341

liberalism, simultaneous negrophobia and negrophilia of antiblackness in, 159, 160–61
Liberty University, 112
Liberty University debate team
  and complementary relationship of mythos and logos, 115–17, 119, 121
  success of, 115
lifestyle politics, 5
literary/debate societies of nineteenth century. See also Clionian Debating Society
  absorption into intercollegiate debate system, 41–44, 51
  abstract, general topics debated in, 44
  postbellum decline in popularity, 38, 40, 41, 42, 50–51, 68
Littlefield, Robert, 81, 108, 152
Littlejohn, Stephen W., 179–80, 185
Little Rock, Arkansas, civil rights struggle in, 167–68
lived experience, as evidence in debate, 163, 168–69
Llano, Steve, 255
logos
  as complement to mythos, 108; at Liberty University, 115–17, 119, 121; in public debate, 120–21; at University of Oregon, 117–19; at Whitefield Academy, 113–14, 117, 119, 120
  definition of, 108
  importance of testing by argument, 109
  mythos undergirding, 112
long table format, 131
Ludeke, Conrad D., 27
Lu Xun, 268

Madison, James
  criticisms of antidemocratic impulse in, 84
  on debate pedagogy, 89–91, 93
  on elected representatives, manipulation of public opinion by, 88
  on expert opinion, 88, 289n38
  faith in reason, 85, 289nn40–41
  as founding father of U.S. democracy, 82
  modern relevance of arguments, 88–89, 92
  on necessity of civic education in democracy, 87–89, 92
  on need to justify decisions in deliberative democracy, 84–85
  on power of knowledge, 127
  on public debate: and choice of topics for debate events, 89–90, 92–93; as key to rational decision making, 83, 86–89, 92; and universal audience focus, value of, 91; and value of "switch-sides" debate, 90–91
  as realist on pitfalls of democracy, 82–83, 84, 86, 87
  romantic faith in democracy, 86
  on skillset needed by citizens, 87–88
  on threats to democracy, 83–84, 89
  on tyranny of the majority, 83
  views on public reason, 87
"Madman's Diary" (Lu), 268
maieutic learning, Adler on, 181
Makau, Josina, 101, 102, 105, 180
Malcolm X, 94, 226
male privilege, and nineteenth-century debate societies, 25, 26, 28
Marty, Debian, 101, 102, 105, 180
Mathews, David, 1–2, 20
Matthews, Richard, 82, 85, 289nn40–41
Maynes, Jeffrey, 95, 98–99, 106
McBath, James, 185
McCarthyism
  as danger to civil liberties, 154–55
  and diplomatic relations with China as national topic for 1954-1955, 152–54
  and relocation of debaters' convictions to debate as democratic technique, 153–57
McElligott, James N., 31
McKinsey Global Institute, 271
Mendelson, Michael, antilogic theory of, 101, 102–4, 106
Mendenhall, Beth, 147
Merton, Thomas, 64, 68
metacognitive skills, and removal of cognitive biases, 95
  in individuals, 98–99, 106
Michelson, G. G. Rosen, 58, 59
millennial generation, civil engagement of, 4
Miller, Rosalind Schnitzer, 58
Miller Center. See also CEDA-Miller Center War Powers Debates
  mission and programs of, 129–30
  and publicity for CEDA-Miller Center War Powers Debates, 134
minority groups. See also diversity; people of color; performance/identity debate; entries under African American
  decreasing levels of trust in, 164
  invisibility of, and performance debate, 166–69, 168

342   INDEX

minority groups (*continued*)
  sacrifices of: failure to recognize, and invisibility, 167–68; focus on, in performance/identity debate, 166–67, 167–68; recognition of, as path to political friendship, 170–73
Mitchell, Gordon, 129
Moon, Dreama, 143
Moral Conflict (Pearce and Littlejohn), 179–80
Morley, Charles, 31
Morris, Charles, 137–38
Morrow, Edward R., 153
motivated reasoning. *See also* debiasing techniques
  and cognitive bias, 95–98, 106
  and Kahneman's intuitive thinking, 96–98, 106
  research on, 96
Muir, Star, 90
Mullen, Shirley, 65
mutually preferred judging, 173, 302n52
mythos
  as complement to logos, 108; at Liberty University, 115–17, 121; mythos underlying logos, 112; in public debate, 120–21; at University of Oregon, 117–19; at Whitefield Academy, 113–14, 117, 119, 120
  definition of, 108
  importance of testing by argument, 109
  value of including in speech and debate curriculum, 111

NAATPS. *See* National Association of Academic Teachers of Public Speaking
National Association for Urban Debate Leagues, 227, 273–74
National Association of Academic Teachers of Public Speaking (NAATPS), 7, 46
National Commission on Excellence in Education, 272
National Communication Association, 203, 284n1
National Debate Tournament (NDT)
  lack of guidelines on appropriate content, 165
  and performance debate, 166
  and resources for engaging larger public, 134–35
National Developmental Debate Conference (2009), 238
National High School Debate League of China (NHSDLC)
  as biggest English-language debate league in China, 265
  outreach by, 273
National Individual Events Tournament, women's success gap in, 138–39
National Intercollegiate Commission on Debate and Discussion, 152–53
National Speech and Debate Association, 75, 228
National Task Force on Civic Learning and Democratic Engagement (NTFCLDE), 5–6, 127, 177, 192
National War Powers Commission, 129, 134
A Nation at Risk (National Commission on Excellence in Education), 272
A Nation of Speechifiers (Eastman), 140
NDT. *See* National Debate Tournament
Nehru, Jawaharlal, 110, 120
networking, and Penny Harvest program, 215, 219
network pragmatics
  and building of affective bonds, 211
  emphasis on deliberative processes, 208
  Penny Harvest program and, 207–8, 211, 215–16, 219, 220
network theory, and creation of affective bonds in diverse urban societies, 211
new rhetorics, and complementary relationship of mythos and logos, 121
NHSDLC. *See* National High School Debate League of China
Nichols, Egbert Ray, 37–38
Nisbet, Erik, 99
Nixon, Richard M., 94
noncompetitive debate, twenty-first century increase in, 128
nondebatable identity claims, as counterproductive practice, xii
non-traditional debate practices, Penn State women's debate team in 1930s-40s and, 60
North American Women's Debating Championships, 261
NTFCLDE. *See* National Task Force on Civic Learning and Democratic Engagement
Nyhan, Brendan, 99

Obama, Barack, 1, 3, 5, 8, 125
O'Donnel, Timothy, 128
O'Donnell, Brett, 115, 116
Olbrechts-Tyteca, Lucie, 64, 72, 91, 121
open-minded dialogue
  characteristics of, 189–90
  public deliberation as training in, 201–2

Open Society Foundations (Open Society Institute), 227, 256
Opportunity Nation, 127–28
orator, cultured, as ideal, 179
"Oratory and Debating" (Baker), 47
overkill backfire effect, 100, *100*, 104, 105

Pacifica Forum, 118–19
The Paideia Proposal (Adler), 177, 178, 181, 182
Paradox of Liberation (Walzer), 110
parliamentary debate. *See* Worlds-style debate and Pi Kappa Delta
partisanship, x, 76–77, 96, 202, 221
Partlow-Lefèvre, Sarah, 128
passion of citizens
 influence on decisions, modern research on, 85–86
 as threat to democracy, Madison on, 84–85, 89
Pearce, Kimberly, 180
Pearce, W. Barnett
 on better world of compassion and love, 180
 on bifurcation points for intervention in conflict, 186
 and CMM project, 179
 on communication across different social worlds, 179–80, 187
 as National Debate Tournament champion, 189
 on open-minded dialogue, 189–90
 on questions, three types of, 188
 on transcendent eloquence, 185
Peitho (Greek goddess), 138
Penn State
 debate program, xiv
 interwar growth in women's enrollment, 55
Penn State women's debate team in 1930s-40s, 53–63. *See also* Schug, Clayton H.
 and civic education, 54–55, 57–58, 61–62
 civic ideal of inclusion and, 55
 and debaters' careers, 57, 58, 60
 and debaters' self-confidence, 56–57, 60, 61
 demographics of debaters, 55
 and development of feminist consciousness, 57, 58–59, 60–61, 62
 and gendered assumptions about women, 54–55, 55–56, 59
 impact on debaters' later lives, 56–58, 60–61, 62
 popularity of debates, 55
 postwar continuation of sex-segregated teams, 61

Penny Harvest, 205–20
 and affective bonds, creation of, 211, 215, 219, 220
 and building of self-worth, 211, 213
 communicative training by, 212
 and communities of belonging, strengthening of, 207, 208, 213–14, 215–17, 220
 and communities of practice, links to, 207, 208, 214–15, 215–16, 217–18
 and community as necessity for public deliberation, 211, 213–14, 215, 220
 goals of, 214, 215
 leadership conferences, 219–20
 in Los Angeles, 207, 208, 214, 219
 and networking, benefits of, 215, 219
 and network pragmatics, 207–8, 211, 215–16, 219, 220
 overview of program, 207, 211, 216, 218–19
 training in civic engagement by, 206–7, 213–18, 220
 training in public deliberation by, 206–7, 208, 212, 213–14, 215, 219, 220
people of color. *See also* diversity; minority groups; performance/identity debate
 female, and pressure for silence, 137
 lack of in speech and debate programs, efforts to remedy, 8–9
 and nontraditional debate styles, criticism of, 9
 and traditional debate competition, lack of success in, 8–9
 and traditional forms of debate, barriers to participation in, 11
Perelman, Chaïm, 64, 72, 91, 121
performance/identity debate, 163–73
 changes to policy debate style and substance, 163
 controversy created by, 164, 166–67, 168–69
 critics of, 9
 debate community's resistance to, 164, 168
 distinction between performance and identity debates, 300–301n10
 focus on sacrifices of minority groups, 166–67, 167–68
 and greater diversity within policy debate, 164
 and identity questions, 163
 and increase in "clash of civilizations" debates, 168–69
 invisibility of minority groups and, 166–69
 lack of communication with traditional debaters, 168–69

performance/identity debate (*continued*)
  likely longevity of, 164
  lived experience as evidence in, 163, 168–69
  need for recognition of, 158, 169
  and nondebatable identity claims, as counterproductive, xii
  and norms of civility, 9
  origin in Black discourse practices and values, 300n6
  and political friendship model of debate, 170–73
  as profoundly personal, 166
  radical critique of hierarchies of power in, 165, 168–69, 171
  as reflection of larger cultural polarization, 164
  rejection of social unity or common goals in, 166
  as social activism, 163
  success of, 166–67
  types of arguments used by, 163–64, 165
Perry, Michael, 111, 120
Peters, John Durham, 178, 180, 185
Petty, Richard, 184
Pew Research Center, 86
phronesis (practical wisdom), and debiasing, 107
Pi Kappa Delta, 70
  and fragmenting of debate organizations, 10
  National Convention, 71, 72
policy debate. *See also* switch-sides debating; CEDA–Miller Center War Powers Debates; China, diplomatic relations with, as national topic for 1954–1955; Cross-Examination Debate Association (CEDA); National Debate Tournament (NDT); political friendship model of debate; white privilege, debate structure as encoding of; *other specific topics*
  activists' rejection of cultural technology of, 159–62
  and civic engagement, 126, 128, 135
  criticisms of as elitist, 8
  fragmenting of organizations in, 10
  and sacrifices of minority groups, need for recognition of, 170
  traditional: characteristics of, 163; demands for change in, 164, 166; lack of communication with performance/identity debaters, 168–69
politeness
  vs. civility, 143
  and women's gender roles, 143

political discourse, modern, vernacular style of, 1
political friendship
  Allen on, 164, 172
  and surrender of unearned privilege and power, 171
political friendship model of debate
  and ethical reciprocity, 171
  judging of arguments in, 171, 172–73
  as replacement for competitive model, 165, 169–73
political solidarity
  necessity of cultivating, 169
  and political friendship model of debate, 169–73
postmodernism, on expert opinion, 88
Potter, David, 38
pragma-dialectic theory, 95, 99, 289n36
presentation standards in speech and debate
  encoding of white privilege in, 150, 158–61, 165, 168–69; necessity of white recognition of, 171
  social activists' rejection of, 159–62
presidential war powers. *See* CEDA-Miller Center War Powers Debates
Progressive Era
  civic education as goal in, 7
  and rise of competitive debates, 68
  speech and debate tradition in, as model, 6–7, 20
propaganda, as danger to free society
  exclusion from modern textbooks, 8
  speech and debate education and, 2, 8, 20
Protagoras, 102
psychology literature, argumentation debiasing theory and, 101, *102*, 106
public deliberation, 191–204
  advantages over debate, 193
  BFTF training in, 245–46
  and civic knowledge, 197–98
  community as necessity for, 211, 213–14
  and community engagement, 192, 203
  complex problems addressed by, 192
  connection to everyday life, benefits of, 193
  and critical thinking skills, 199–200
  definition of, 191
  and empathy for others, 201–2
  emphasis on cooperation and collaboration in, 202
  history of in U.S., 193–94
  importance to free democratic society, 191
  incorporating into communications curricula, benefits of, 191, 192, 194, 203–4
  and open-mindedness, 201–2

Penny Harvest training in, 206–7, 208, 212, 213–14, 215, 219, 220
and pragmatic optimism, 203
as preparation for collective action, 202–3
projects in: assessment of, 197; and benefits of hands-on learning, 200; lessons learned in, 196–97, 197–203; at South Dakota State University, 194, 195, 198, 199–203; at Wabash College, 194, 195–96, 197–203
resources on, 203
revival of interest in, 194
stages of, 191–92
as training for rhetorical citizenship, 192
as Western norm, 210
Public Forum debate
in China, 193, 267
at University of Oregon, 118–19
public oratory era
characteristics of, 64
civic education as rationale for debate training in, 64
forensics as public good in, 64, 69, 72
and rebalancing of modern rhetorical canons, 76
replacement by technical era, 68–73
and universal audience, focus on, 64, 72
public sphere theory, and citizenship, 252
Putnam, Robert, 3, 212

Quarterly Journal of Public Speaking, 7, 53, 68–69
Quarterly Journal of Speech, 193, 264

racial segregation in debates, history of, 70
rational thought
improved power of, through education in speech and debate, 2
Madison on public debate as key to, 83, 86–89, 92
modern relevance of, as issue, 10
Rawls, John, 85
reactance, and backfire effect, 99
real-world application of debate training. *See* transfer challenge
real-world argumentation
vs. academic norms, 82, 95, 184–85
and backfire effect, 99–101, *100*, 106
and motivated reasoning, 95–98
value of objective analysis in, 184–85
reason. *See also* logos
as insufficient defense against prejudice, racism, and anti-Semitism, 112
religion as check on excesses of, 112, 120

rebuttals, and backfire effects, 95, 99–101, *100*, 106
Rehg, William, 94, 245
Reid-Brinkley, Shanara Rose, 158–59, 313n36
Reifler, Jason, 99
religion. *See also* mythos
as check on amoral rationality, 112, 120
exclusion of from American speech and debate, 108
normative humility and pluralism of, 112
and reason, compatibility of, 108–9, 111, 120–21
and scripture, interpretations of, as contested, 111–12
secular students' lack of familiarity with, 120; as handicap in real-world interactions, 109–10, 119–20, 121
religious extremists, as unrepresentative minority, 110, 112
religious fundamentalists, lack of familiarity with logical argument, as handicap in real-world interactions, 109–11, 119, 121
religious schools, graduates' high rate of loss of faith, 110–11, 113
residential colleges, emergence of, and popularity of debate, 68
resolutions, social activists' challenging of, 159–62
respect for views of others
as benefit of speech and debate, xi
vs. civility, 142–45
and development of political solidarity, 169
as goal of forensics education, 74
Mendelson's theory of antilogic and, 102, 103
and political friendship model of debate, 169–73
reward system. *See* judging
rhetoric
history of, and exclusion and sexualization of women, 137–38
training in, and just communication, 178–79
rhetorical citizenship, public deliberation as training for, 192
rivalries between colleges, as source of intercollegiate debate popularity, 40–41
Robbins, E. C., 81
Roosevelt, Theodore, 69
Roseneil, Sasha, 62
Rowton, Frederic, 31
Rudick, Kyle, 143
Ruffin, Ameena, 9, 166–67
Rumsfeld, Donald, 82

sacrifices of minority groups
    failure to recognize, and invisibility, 167–68
    focus on, in performance/identity debate, 166–67, 167–68
    recognition of, as path to political friendship, 170–73
Sartori, Giovanni, 269
Schlesinger, Arthur, Jr., 154–55
Schneider, Carol Geary, 66, 77
Schnurer, Maxwell, 238
Schofield, Martha, 25
schools
    black graduation rates, 223
    educational apartheid in, 223–24
    Hispanic graduation rates, 223
    as sites of civic education, 211, 213, 219
    and social costs of dropouts, 223
    urban, and training in public deliberation, 206
    and Urban Debate Leagues as pedagogical tool, 228
schools of debate practice, vitriolic argument between
    as counterproductive, xiii
    and fragmenting of debate community, 10, 73
Schraw, Gregory, 98
Schug, Clayton H. *See also* Penn State women's debate team in 1930s-40s
    on benefits of women's debate, 57–58
    career at Penn State, 56
    and cost of working in women's program, 59
    debaters' self-confidence and, 56–57, 60
    growth of Penn State's women's team under, 55
    hard work demanded by, 57, 60
    and inclusiveness, 62
    influence on students, 58
    papers of, at Penn State, 56
    and promotion of feminism, 59, 60–61
    and promotion of women's debate, 55, 56
Schweninger, Loren, 29
SDSU. *See* South Dakota State University
season, benefits of shortening, 75
Selby, James, 113, 114, 120
selective attention and perception, and backfire effect, 99
September 11th terrorist attacks, and civic engagement, 3
sex, vs. gender, 295n1
sexism. *See also* speech and debate as sexed/gendered

    and citizenship as sexed/gendered, 136, 140–42
    and civic education as sexed/gendered, 136
    and civic engagement as sexed/gendered, 140–42
Sheehan, Colleen, 83
Sheldon, Henry, 50
Sherman, David, 210
Shuster, Kate, 147
simulations of topical debates, at University of Oregon, 117–18
Skocpol, Theda, 5
Sloane, Geoffrey, 154
Smith, Elijah, 166
Snider, Alfred, 238
Snowden, Edward, 126
social activism. *See also* performance/identity debate
    and personal experience as conviction-cum-ethical demand, 160
    and rejection of cultural technology of tournament debate, 159–62
    Urban Debate Leagues and, 222, 224, 228, 229, 231, 232, 233
social justice allies, 62, 286n39
social media, and civic engagement, evolving forms of, 5
Souls of Black Folks (Du Bois), 35
South Dakota State University (SDSU), public deliberation projects at, 194, 195, 198, 199–203
Southern Poverty Law Center (SPLC), 118, 119
Southern Speech Journal, 61
special interest groups
    control of politics by, 5
    Progressive Era concerns about, 7
speech and debate. *See also* curriculum on speech and debate; education in speech and debate; *other specific topics*
    American tradition of, 68
    and balance of civic good vs. personal growth, 68
    citizenship as constituted by, 252–53
    and civic awareness, 274
    and civic education, 73–77
    counterproductive practices, xii–xiv
    in early-twentieth-century assimilation efforts, 211
    as epistemic, 73
    as force for social change, 70
    and Four Cs of "twenty-first century skills," 221–22, 272, 273–74

as historically affluent white male activity, 224, 260–61
history of, 206
and learning not available in classroom setting, 181, 183–84, 185–86
liberatory forms of, and discarding of liberal values, 157, 160–61
life skills learned in, ix
limitations of, in multicultural urban society, 206, 208, 210–11
new forms of, dominance of forensic model in, 206
norms of, in academic vs. real-world debate, 82, 95, 184–85
postwar boom of, 61
as site of activism, 222
substantive, demise of, 1
as tool of empowerment, 161, 221, 222, 227, 228, 231, 238, 263
white male hegemony as dominant paradigm in, 54
speech and debate as sexed/gendered, 26–28, 34, 136, 145
exclusion and sexualization of women, 137–40
and outspoken women as disagreeable and unfeminine, 140–42, 143, 145, 147
Women's Debate Institute and, 146–48
women's low levels of participation, 138, 295n1
women's success gap, 138–39
Speech Association of America, 152–53
Spivak, Gayatri, 297n39
SPLC. *See* Southern Poverty Law Center
Squires, Catherine R., 26, 27
Stables, Gordon, 129, 134
strategic essentialism, 297n39
strategy evaluation matrix, *100*
and removal of cognitive biases, 98–99, 101, 106
style and delivery, focus on in public oratory era, 47, 64, 76
surprise, as tactic, xiii
survey research, and multicultural urban society, 209–10
switch-side debating.
alternatives to, 297n5
as bulwark against demagoguery, 153–54, 155–56, 161–62
as civic education, 49, 90–91
in classical rhetoric, 103
debate on: from 1954 to 1966, 149; arguments for and against, 69; in early twentieth century, 299n34; as occasion to challenge cultural technology of tournament debate, 149
and debater's convictions, as issue, 69–70, 114, 149–50, 153
and elimination of cognitive biases, 98, 115–16
and empathy toward minority views, 150
and universalization of liberal cultural norms, 149, 150, 157–61
systemic understanding, and development of *humanitas*, 187

Tacitus, 138
technical era
characteristics of, 64
forensics as private good in, 64, 72
fragmenting of debate community in, 73
national debate competitions and, 71, 72
replacement of public oratory era, 68–73
and specific audience, focus on, 64, 72
technologies, new, issues in deployment of, 6, 10
Thinking, Fast and Slow (Kahneman), 85, 87, 88, 96–97, 97, 106
thinking, intuitive
vs. deliberative, 85, 96–97, 97
and motivated reasoning, 96–98
Thomashow, Mitchell, 81
Thompson, Dennis, 84
Tocqueville, Alexis de, 193, 212
topics for debate
debate on rationale for debating and, 69–70
debate societies and selection of, 30–
and engagement with larger community, 134
selection of: for citizenship training, 89–90, 91, 92; in nineteenth-century debating societies, 30–33; in early tournament debates, 43–45, 69–70, 71
topoi of public life
definition of, x
knowledge of, as benefit of speech and debate, x–xi, xii–xiii
in U.S., as constitutive tensions, x–xi
Toulmin, Stephen, 88
tournament format, development of, and shift toward competitive model of debate, 71, 72
"Toward Robust Public Engagement" (Waisanen), 143
Tracy, David, 120

transfer challenge
    audience and, 94–95
    debiasing strategies and, 101
    defined, 94
    metacognitive skills and, 95
transwomen, and pressure for silence, 137-138
Trapp, Robert, 257
trust between citizens, decreasing levels of, 164
truth, as goal of debate, restoring focus on, as goal, 10
"twenty-first century skills"
    Chinese desire to acquire, 271–72
    and Chinese *suzhi jiaoyu* (character education), 266, 272, 274
    Four Cs of, and debate, 221–22, 272, 273–74
    Western discourse on, 272
tyranny of the majority, Madison on, 83

UDLs. *See* Urban Debate Leagues
uncertainty, learning to manage, as benefit of speech and debate, xi
United States
    debate as remedy for polarization in, 275
    as democracy at risk, 20–21
United States Universities Debating Championship (USUDC), 254, 263
University of Chicago, and immigrants of 1920s, education of, 205
University of Nebraska–Lincoln, women debaters at, 54
University of Oregon
    as secular institution, 112
    speech and debate at, and relationship of mythos and logos, 117–19
University of Southern California (USC), and Penny Harvest, 207, 214, 219
Urban Debate Leagues (UDLs), 221–33
    and activism, 222, 224, 229, 231, 232, 233
    and broadening of debate topics to include activist agendas, 228, 232
    and challenging of affluent white male dominance, 224–25, 228, 232
    and civic education, 225, 227, 228
    and civic engagement, 222, 224, 225, 226, 229–30, 232, 233
    and communities of practice, 221, 225–26, 227, 228, 229–30, 231, 232–33
    community support for, 229
    and Computer Assisted Debate, 230–31
    and debate across socioeconomic divides, 221, 222, 224, 227, 232, 233
    and debate as antidote to traditional education in deference to authority, 225
    and diversity of debate, 9
    and empowerment of students, 221, 222, 227, 228, 231
    expansion to middle and elementary schools, 227
    and Four Cs of twenty-first century skills, 221–22, 273–74
    history and growth of, 227, 232–33
    impact on privileged students' views, 229
    and inclusiveness, 63
    multigenerational participation in, 221, 222, 228, 229, 231
    number of participants in, 227
    as pedagogical tool, 228
    and resistance to educational apartheid, 224
    and respect, engaging students with, 231, 232
    skills developed by, 221–22, 224, 225
    and student academic performance, 227, 228, 231
    student tasks in, 225–26
    teacher-student collaboration in, 225, 228, 232
urban society, diverse
    and affective bonds, creation of, 211, 219
    and assimilation efforts of early twentieth century, 205, 208–9, 211
    and CBYOs as barrier to civic engagement, 212–13
    as challenge to civil society models, 205–6
    and civic engagement: civic skills needed for, 212–13; Penny Harvest Program and, 213–18, 220
    and heterogeneity of communication norms, 209–10
    and limitations of forensics models, 206, 208, 210–11
    and proliferation of civil society groups, 206
    as resource, 209
    and school training in public deliberation, 206
USC. *See* University of Southern California
USUDC. *See* United States Universities Debating Championship

values analysis strategy
    and elimination of cognitive biases, 98
    and skills needed for civic engagement, 194
van Eemeren, Frans, 289n36
"Varsity Debaters (Did They Ever Look Like This, Boys?)," 56

Vats, Anjali, 128
Verba, Sidney, 212
Villadsen, Lisa, 252
Vital Center (Schlesinger), 154–55
voter turnout, U.S., decline in, 3

Wabash College
  Democracy Fellows program, 196
  public deliberation projects at, 194, 195–96, 197–203
Wagner, Sara Bailey, 58
Waisanen, Don, 142, 143
Wallace, Karl, 152–53
Walzer, Michael, 110
Warner, Ede, Jr., 158, 160, 238
Warner, Michael, 252
War Powers Resolution of 1973, 129, 133–34
Wash, Ryan, 166
Watson, Carly W., 147
WDI. *See* Women's Debate Institute
Weber, Mark, 118–19
Wenger, Etienne, 225
Weston, William O., 27
Whitefield Academy, and complementary relationship of mythos and logos, 110, 112, 113–14, 117, 119, 120
Whitehead, James, 240
white privilege, debate structure as encoding of, 150, 158–61, 165, 168–69
  necessity of white recognition of, 171
Who's Afraid of the Big Bad Dragon? (Yong), 269, 275
Willamette University, and China Debate Education Network, 256
Willingham, Daniel, 242
winning
  vs. civic education, as rationale for debate: and choice of debate topic, 69; greater importance of educational benefit, ix; pendulum swings between poles of, 68; restoring balance between, 64, 68, 75–77; shift of balance toward winning, 64, 68–73; and trained vs. untrained judges, 69, 72–73; Women's Debate Institute and, 146–47
  discarding focus on, in liberatory forms of debate, 160–61
  learning of perspective on, ix
  as motivator for students, xii, 68–69, 183–84
  overemphasis on: as counterproductive, xii; undermining of larger social goals by, 74–75
  schools' embrace of, 70

Withey, Elsie Douhett, 58, 59
Wittig, John, 189
women. *See also* sexism; speech and debate as sexed/gendered
  civic engagement of: and men's fear of emasculation, 140–41; obstacles to, 137
  in early Republic, relative freedom to speak, 140
  education of, responsibilities of citizenship and, 62
  gender roles for, and outspoken women as disagreeable and unfeminine, 136–38, 140–42, 143, 145, 147
  and voting rights, 140, 141
women and debate participation. *See also* Penn State women's debate team in 1930s–40s
  barriers to, 11
  in China Debate Education Network, 260–61
  in Clionian Debating Society, 30
  criticisms of lack of, 9
  and debate as force for social change, 70
  development of women's teams, 54
  dress expectations and, 145
  early history of, 54, 285n6
  efforts to increase, 9
  first African American winners of national championship, 166
  increases in, 261
  low levels of, 54
  media coverage of, in 1930s–40s, 55–56
  and sexist discrimination, 137
  in twentieth century, variation in level of, 54, 61
  and Urban Debate Leagues, 227
  and Worlds-style debate, 263
women of color, and pressure for silence, 137
Women's Debate Institute (WDI)
  and debate as civic education, 146–48
  and inclusiveness, 63
  and marginalized gender identities, support of, 146–47
  and women's participation in debate, 9
Woods, Carly, 128
Worlds-style debate, 250–64. *See also* China Debate Education Network (CDEN)
  audiences for, 253–54
  average person as target audience for, 253–54
  in China, 267
  and citizenship in global context, 250, 253, 262

Worlds-style debate (*continued*)
   and civic education, 250–51, 261, 263, 264
   and civic engagement, 251
   and coaches, constrained role of, 253
   crafting of arguments in, 253, 254
   cultural biases in, 262
   and debaters of color, sensitivity to offense, 263
   and disempowered groups, efforts to include, 262–63
   diversity of participants, 254
   dominance of deductive, claims-oriented argumentation in, 261
   and ESL debaters, bias against, 262
   format for, 253
   growth of, 253, 254
   international perspective of, 254, 255–56
   judging in, 253
   language-based divisions of, 261
   lessons learned in, 250
   number of participants, 254
   recent locations of championships, 253
   rules in, 255
   skills learned in, 312n12
   types of topics debated in, 254–55, 255–56, 262–63
   women and, 263
World Universities Debating Championship (WUDC), 253–54
worldview backfire effect, *100*, 100–101, 104
World War II, 55
   and shift to technical era of debate, 71–72
   and women increased participation in debate, 54
WUDC. *See* World Universities Debating Championship

Yale University, and intercollegiate debate, emergence of, 38, 39–40, 50, 68
Yan Fu, 270
Yong Zhao, 269, 275
Young, Iris Marion, 90–91, 158, 299n45
Young, Kelly, 125–26
young people, and civic engagement, 3–5

Zboray, Mary Saracino, 31
Zboray, Ronald J., 31
Zhou Ji, 271
Zuckerman, Phil, 108, 120

RHETORIC AND DEMOCRATIC DELIBERATION

Other books in the series:

Karen Tracy, *Challenges of Ordinary Democracy: A Case Study in Deliberation and Dissent* / Volume 1

Samuel McCormick, *Letters to Power: Public Advocacy Without Public Intellectuals* / Volume 2

Christian Kock and Lisa S. Villadsen, eds., *Rhetorical Citizenship and Public Deliberation* / Volume 3

Jay P. Childers, *The Evolving Citizen: American Youth and the Changing Norms of Democratic Engagement* / Volume 4

Dave Tell, *Confessional Crises and Cultural Politics in Twentieth-Century America* / Volume 5

David Boromisza-Habashi, *Speaking Hatefully: Culture, Public Communication, and Political Action in Hungary* / Volume 6

Arabella Lyon, *Deliberative Acts: Democracy, Rhetoric, and Rights* / Volume 7

Lyn Carson, John Gastil, Janette Hartz-Karp, and Ron Lubensky, eds., *The Australian Citizens' Parliament and the Future of Deliberative Democracy* / Volume 8

Christa J. Olson, *Constitutive Visions: Indigeneity and Commonplaces of National Identity in Republican Ecuador* / Volume 9

Damien Smith Pfister, *Networked Media, Networked Rhetorics: Attention and Deliberation in the Early Blogosphere* / Volume 10

Katherine Elizabeth Mack, *From Apartheid to Democracy: Deliberating Truth and Reconciliation in South Africa* / Volume 11

Mary E. Stuckey, *Voting Deliberatively: FDR and the 1936 Presidential Campaign* / Volume 12

Robert Asen, *Democracy, Deliberation, and Education* / Volume 13

Shawn J. Parry-Giles and David S. Kaufer, *Memories of Lincoln and the Splintering of American Political Thought* / Volume 14